'In this commentary Rabbi Jonathan Wittenberg has captured the wisdom of the ages for all men and women of faith or of none.'

Sir Terry Waite, KCMG CBE

'What Rabbi Jonathan Wittenberg has given us here is nothing less than an old-new *midrash* for the 21st century. He has read deeply in the full range of Jewish sources, including the mystical tradition. But he has also taken into view much of modern literature, science and theology. Week after week, his *midrash* brings them all together, always highlighted by his inquiring mind, his commitment to great moral decency, and his ongoing sense of wonder at the natural world. This is a contemporary Jewish classic.'

Art Green, Founding dean Hebrew College rabbinical school

'Rabbi Jonathan Wittenberg has offered these rich reflections on the Torah to his own Jewish community, but also as a gift to Christians whose discipleship cannot but be enlarged by the wisdom that he shares. The "companionship of the Torah" to Jewish people which Jonathan describes speaks in turn of the companionship of Jewish people and the Jewish tradition to all Christians for which we are indebted, and I receive here, again, with care and gratitude.'

The Most Revd and Rt Hon. Justin Welby

'In an age of partisan rage, endless stress and the temptation of despair, we all need a teacher who is resolute, reliable, gentle and wise. In Rabbi Jonathan Wittenberg, we have such a guide and companion. As he unveils deep wisdom in the passages of Torah, familiar and less known, we can feel the light warming the hidden crevices of our soul, making it possible once again to think, to hope and to breathe.'

Rabbi Dr Bradley Shavit Artson, Roslyn and Abner Goldstine Dean's Chair, Ziegler School of Rabbinic Studies, American Jewish University

'In this engaging and memorable cycle of reflections on the weekly portions of Torah readings, Rabbi Jonathan Wittenberg makes the riches of generations of Jewish scholarship, wisdom and lived experience accessible to a wide audience, Jews and non-Jews. Christians in particular will find themselves repeatedly enlightened and challenged by the insights which the rabbi draws from, a part of their scriptures which are both familiar and strange to them.'

The Rt Revd Dr Michael Ipgrave, Chair of the Council of Christians and Jews

Also by Jonathan Wittenberg

The Silence of Dark Water: An Inner Journey
Walking with the Light: From Frankfurt to Finchley
My Dear Ones: One Family and the Final Solution
Things My Dog Has Taught Me: About Being a Better Human

LISTENING FOR GOD IN TORAH AND CREATION

A weekly encounter with conscience and soul

Jonathan Wittenberg

HODDER &
STOUGHTON

First published in Great Britain in 2023 by Hodder & Stoughton
An Hachette UK Company

1

A CIP catalogue record for this title is available from the British Library

Hardback ISBN 978 1 529 39583 9
Trade Paperback ISBN 978 1 529 39587 7
ebook ISBN 978 1 529 39584 6

Typeset in Bembo MT by Hewer Text UK Ltd, Edinburgh
Printed and bound in Great Britain by Clays Ltd, Elcograf S.p.A.

Hodder & Stoughton policy is to use papers that are natural, renewable and recyclable products and made from wood grown in sustainable forests. The logging and manufacturing processes are expected to conform to the environmental regulations of the country of origin.

Hodder & Stoughton Ltd
Carmelite House
50 Victoria Embankment
London EC4Y 0DZ

www.hodderfaith.com

To my family, especially
to my wife Nicky and our children Amos, Libbi and Kadya;
to my brother Raphael, his wife Lena, their children
Gideon and Danny, and the grandchildren;
and to my spiritual family,
the community of
The New North London Synagogue.

נְצֹר בְּנִי מִצְוַת אָבֶיךָ וְאַל־תִּטֹּשׁ תּוֹרַת אִמֶּךָ
קָשְׁרֵם עַל־לִבְּךָ תָמֶיד עָנְדֵם עַל־גַּרְגְּרֹתֶךָ
בְּהִתְהַלֶּכְךָ תַּנְחֶה אֹתָךְ
בְּשָׁכְבְּךָ תִּשְׁמֹר עָלֶיךָ וַהֲקִיצֹותָ הֵיא תְשִׂיחֶךָ:

Keep, my child, the commandment of your father,
Don't forsake the Torah of your mother.
Bind them against your heart at all times,
Hang them like a jewel around your neck.
Wherever you go they will guide you:
When you lie down, they will protect you,
And when you awake, they will give you speech.
(Proverbs 6:20–2)

CONTENTS

LEVITICUS

NUMBERS

DEUTERONOMY

CONTENTS

FOREWORD

BY JONATHAN FREEDLAND

It's always described as the most widely published book in history, the book found in every hotel room in the world – but how many of us have really read the Bible, and how deeply have we absorbed it? Plenty of secular-minded readers will not be too troubled by that question. They will make three assumptions. First, that they already know the basic stories and themes. Second, that most of those stories consist of pretty childish fare. And third, that they could only have relevance or resonance to a believer. In this remarkable book, Rabbi Jonathan Wittenberg demolishes each one of those assumptions.

For one thing, he opens up the Torah, the first five books of the Hebrew Bible, in such a way that all but the most learned scholars – and even some of them – will find something new on every page. Of course, there are the apparently familiar characters – Adam and Eve, Abraham, Isaac and Jacob, Moses – but there are also the likes of Pinchas, Betsalel and one Zelophehad. Even those stories we think we know, Wittenberg swiftly reminds us, we don't. So we learn that 'the first human being is androgynous' according to the Talmud, containing both male and female. Those two sides were like conjoined twins that had to be separated, so that man and woman could 'relate to each other face to face'. There is no male primacy, still less supremacy. Eve was not second to Adam: instead, 'man and woman are co-created'.

Second, through Wittenberg's commentary, we soon see that these tales are anything but suitable solely for younger readers. The pain of sisters Rachel and Leah, their competition for the love of the same man, is a wholly adult drama. The same is true of Abraham's binding of Isaac, centred on a father's willingness to sacrifice his son and the son's wounded incomprehension, a trauma that he will never shake. It's all here: betrayal, envy, lust, childlessness, vanity, heartbreak.

Third, none of this requires belief in a supernatural deity. Wittenberg addresses the question from the outset, giving his own account of the authorship of the Torah, one that is compatible with, but not dependent on, a traditional conception of God. Even if one cannot accept his approach, with its suggestion of the Torah as a joint enterprise of the divine and the human, it hardly invalidates the material within.

On the contrary, Wittenberg demonstrates the value of these texts – for Jews and non-Jews alike – simply by engaging with them. We soon realise they yield compelling lessons for twenty-first-century life, whether via a meditation on idolatry – with a rumination on the current worship of the self that takes us from the story of the golden calf to the smartphone selfie – or through insights on everything from leadership (and its frustrations) to disability. Just as every Shakespeare play is contemporary, so we see that the Torah is timely because it is timeless.

It helps that Wittenberg is a scholar whose expertise is hardly confined to his own patch. He quotes Jewish sages Rashi and Maimonides, but also Shelley, Milton, Blake and Goethe. His references range from second-century rabbinic commentary to Eisenhower and Gandhi. Like a Talmudist of old, he can drill into the meaning of individual letters in a single word, but he can also unpack the lyrics of Leonard Cohen. What's more, he is an unusually gifted writer: he describes ancient enmities, passed down the generations and exploited by eager demagogues, as 'heirloom grudges'.

The result is a book that is not only relevant for today, but which will last. It is full of lessons for life, about how human beings relate to the natural world – warning us that, if anything, the suffering felt by animals is worse than our own – and how we relate to each other, including advice not to see 'people as they appear to us now without appreciating, or troubling to find out, who they once were'. A man with dementia in a wheelchair might be a D-Day veteran. A woman seen only as a generic 'asylum seeker' might, in fact, be a doctor or IT specialist.

Listening for God in Torah and Creation is, as promised, full of conscience and soul. But it also brims with moral resolve, empathy and the deepest possible wisdom. It is proof that the Torah is a living, breathing thing – and that Jonathan Wittenberg deserves his place among the rabbis who, for millennia, have served to reveal its truth and its beauty.

ACKNOWLEDGEMENTS

Every day for decades I've recited the blessing thanking God for the privilege of engaging with the words of Torah. Rarely has this meant so much to me as during the challenging period of lockdowns, when I would get out of bed, feed the birds, the guinea pigs and the dog, and settle down to work at what eventually became this book. Although I began to write years earlier, during those bewildering times this work became my discipline, my banister to hold on to, and, on those mornings when the words magically seemed to flow, my source of joy. I am grateful to life and the God of life for allowing me these many hours of creative grace.

I love old Jewish books, especially those volumes of Torah and Talmud in which one can feel the indent of the letters on the paper. Voices speak in them, the spirits of the generations of students of Torah who loved and devoted themselves to those words through the ages. These are my ancestors in faith, guides to the heart and soul, to the conscience and the knowledge of what constitutes just and compassionate conduct. I am thankful to them for their voices and their wisdom.

My community, the New North London Masorti Synagogue, has been my spiritual home for over forty years. Its leaders encouraged me in the uncertain days when I was seeking my path, and bravely appointed me rabbi before I was really fit for the job. But the task formed me, disciplining, inspiring and humbling me with its privileges and challenges. It afforded me countless opportunities to listen to people as they speak from the heart at the most stirring moments of their lives, in joy and, all too often, in grief. Its members have been my teachers in conversations at synagogue, in my home, and in hospital and hospice corridors. My congregation is the context in which I have studied, taught, learnt, debated and agreed and disagreed about the meanings and values of Torah, and how we should live by them in today's world. My community has been my school, my debating chamber and my prayer space. It has made me who I am.

I am thankful for my teachers. It is hard to single out anyone but I am especially grateful to Dr Joanna Weinberg for her thoughtful and rigorous instruction during my studies for the rabbinate at Leo Baeck College, and for her friendship then and since. In addition, ever since he gave me his personal semichah, conferring the status of rabbi and teacher, I have tried not to be unworthy of my teacher Rabbi Dr Aryeh Strikovsky, may his memory be for a blessing. Immersed in Torah and versed in its every field, he was conscious of the demands of the modern world yet totally unworldly, humble and generous with his knowledge.

I appreciate my colleagues in Masorti Judaism, my wider Jewish home. My teacher par excellence, Rabbi Dr Louis Jacobs, set the whole tone and tenor of my approach to Torah. I also want to express my special appreciation for my colleague Rabbi Chaim Weiner; for thirty years we have worked together in a spirit of warm mutual respect, our very differences strengthening our companionship. I want to acknowledge too my affectionate respect for Ronnie Cohen, my friend of forty years, a leader and inspiration in my community. He has taught me the meaning of faithfulness to one's friends, one's people and one's God. I want to thank Claire Mandel who, as executive director of my community for over fifteen years, has combined a love and knowledge of Judaism with unending attention to practical detail and compassionate care for our congregation. I am grateful, too, to many Christian friends and colleagues, and especially to Professor Nicholas Sagovsky, for their inspiration and encouragement over many years.

My family have been extraordinarily generous and forbearing. 'I can do this,' Nicky observed, when she said 'yes' and agreed to become a rabbi's wife. She has always loved and respected our shared Jewish practice, supported me in all my work and in the values at its core, and given me space, sometimes by engaging and sometimes by wisely refraining from engaging. Our children Amos, Libbi and Kadya each in their own way live out those values, often with greater commitment and sensitivity than I do. I love my wife and I love our children; I'm proud of them and grateful to them. Living in the goldfish bowl of a rabbinic household is not always easy. They've handled a range of intrusions and assumptions with largely good-humoured resilience and a generous understanding of why community is so important. Our dogs Safi, Mitzpah and lately Nessie have often sat beneath my desk, waiting for me to give them due attention.

My brother Raphael and I are deeply conscious of our family's rabbinic heritage. Our grandfather Dr Georg Salzberger served as rabbi in Frankfurt-am-Main until the Nazis forced him and his family to flee. His eldest daughter Lore, our mother, whom we lost very young, said that she too would have wanted to be a rabbi if the vocation had been open to women at the time. Her youngest sister Isca, who became our second mother, still at the age of hundred speaks to us warmly of her childhood in a rabbi's family. Her work as a psychotherapist has had an immeasurable influence on my own appreciation of people. Although he's been gone for almost fifteen years, my brother and I hear our father Adi's voice in all the melodies of the Jewish year. Our father's grandfather was head of the rabbinic court of Berlin when he died suddenly at the age of seventy in 1937, a mercy, since it spared him the fate of many of his descendants in the Holocaust. This family history has formed us both and I owe to it the core of who I am.

This book would never have seen publication without the positivity of my agent Jonny Geller, and the steady encouragement of Andy Lyon at Hodder Faith. Andy has given me the warmest support with my writing for over a decade, through three entirely different book projects from *Things My Dog Has Taught Me* to things I've been taught by Torah. I am very grateful to him and the whole team at Hodder. Jessica Lacey has maintained a perfect balance between kindness, understanding and urgency in seeing the writing through its editorial stages. Nicki Copeland has been insightful and thorough, as well as breathtakingly efficient, in scrutinising the manuscript, helping me to clarify important issues, locate references and make the work accessible to Christian as well as Jewish readers. But any mistakes, and I'm sure I've made them, remain my own.

I am grateful to life for all these privileges and blessings.

INTRODUCTION

'She's got a question for you,' said our Sabbath guest, looking encouragingly at her five-year-old daughter. After a pause to overcome her shyness, the little girl asked: 'Who made God?'

I've no idea how I responded at the time, or how I would answer now. But this book is the result of such moments, a product of forty years of living in community, facing questions great and small and trying not to be unworthy of the depth of Jewish tradition and the history of my people.

I'm grateful to my congregation for supporting, and for challenging, me. Sermons may seem like monologues, but in truth they're a heartfelt attempt to respond to listening to people of all ages in all kinds of life situations: How do I manage my grief? Can there be a God in this cruel world? Are there any Jewish prayers for my sick dog? How do I love my neighbour if I struggle to love myself? How do I live a values-driven life in a materialistic world? How do I remain sensitive to the fragile wonder of creation? How do I reconcile my multiple identities and loyalties?

Behind these personal questions are the wider issues that torment our societies: injustice, suffering, abuse, racism, war, the fear of climate collapse. This book is about my struggles with these challenges. I often don't have answers; faith isn't chiefly about certainties, but how we try to live in a generous, compassionate and committed way in the face of uncertainties.

My central resource is three thousand years of Jewish literature, rooted in the Torah, the five opening books of the Hebrew Bible. It is a culture of ceaseless, unsparing exploration of the relationships between God, humanity and creation, society and the individual, and the ideals versus the realities of spiritual and ethical life. I'm equally inspired by the kindness, courage, imagination, integrity and devotion of countless people of all faiths and none, which I witness almost daily.

I haven't written this book for Jews only, but also for fellow seekers of all creeds and none, especially Christian colleagues and companions because we share so much of our textual heritage. I'm mindful of Abraham Joshua Heschel's pithy definition in his 1963 speech 'Religion and Race': 'What is an idol? Any god *who is mine but not yours*, any god concerned with me but not with you . . .'[1] I've never thought of God as God of the Jews, but always as the God of us all, encompassing and transcending all differences and divisions. God speaks in all life; God is present in the birdsong and the meditations of the trees as much as, to quote Wordsworth, in 'the still sad music of humanity'.[2] I believe our religions are different paths to the same goal of service. What matters most are not our divergences in ritual and dogma, important as they are, but the kinds of people we become as we try to follow the path of faith and care for each other and all living beings.

This book is structured according to the Torah readings, which, alongside the festivals, define the flow of the Jewish year. Every *Shabbat* morning one, and occasionally two, of the fifty-four weekly portions into which the Torah is subdivided is read in public in the synagogue. The cycle commences with 'In the beginning' on the autumn festival of *Simchat Torah*, 'The Joy of Torah', and concludes one year later with the closing words of Deuteronomy, before it starts all over again after a gap of about five minutes.

In an age that prizes novelty, it may sound dull to read the same stories in identical instalments year by year. But the older I get, the more I realise how far this is from the truth. I remember meeting my father's Uncle Ernst on one of his visits to London. He'd been an army doctor in the First World War, was interned by the Nazis in Buchenwald, escaped to America and was now in his late nineties. He smiled at me with that look of wizened kindness one sometimes sees in the very elderly and, indicating the volume on the table before him, said: 'I like to study the Torah with a different commentary every year. In that way I always see it with fresh eyes.'

The narratives and laws of the Torah become our frame of reference; we grow with them, and they grow in us. Torah is the organising narrative of Jewish experience. It becomes entwined with the story of our own lives, forming an inextricable part of our self-understanding and discourse. Over time, the meanings we perceive in the Torah alter and deepen. What we once passed over as irrelevant may suddenly become important, and vice versa. A passage may long have been familiar, but never resonated so deeply in us before. Like Jacob waking from his dream of a ladder from earth to heaven, we may find ourselves saying of a story, a verse or even a single word, 'God is in this place, and I did not know' (Gen. 28:16). Why, asks the great mediaeval commentator Rashi (1040–1115), does the Torah say, 'On this day the Children of Israel arrived at Sinai,' and not, 'On that day'? Because, he answers, the Torah should be new to us every day.[3] We are no longer the same person as we were yesterday, so our Torah cannot remain the same either.

The companionship of the Torah is, and always has been, the one constant throughout the existence of the Jewish People, the secret of its strength in times of suffering and the source of its joy in periods of reprieve.

Forced by waves of persecution to flee from one land of exile to another, time and again the Torah's laws, rites and appointed seasons served communities as the blueprint for the recreation of a vibrant spiritual, educational and social life. In Chagall's picture *Solitude*, an elderly Jew clasps the Torah while in the background smoke rises as his former home town burns. Next to him, a calf with a gentle face plays the violin, as if to say, 'I have my instrument of music and you have yours.' My grandfather used to quote the verse from Psalms, 'Your statutes are my songs in the lands of my earthly sojourn' (Ps. 119:54).

What do we mean by Torah?

Strictly speaking, 'Torah' refers to the text itself, known as the *Chumash*, the Pentateuch or band of five, the first section of the *Tenakh*, the three-part Hebrew Bible which, as well as the Torah, includes the Prophets and the Writings. But from the beginning of rabbinic culture, it was understood that Moses received not one but two Torahs on Mount Sinai, the *Torah Shebichetav*, the Written Torah, and the *Torah Shebe'al Peh*, the Oral Torah, the debates, interpretations, rules, customs and traditions that make the Torah, at any time and in any place, always an entire way of life. Hence the rabbinic saying that even the answers to the questions disciples were destined to ask in the distant future were revealed at Sinai. Some take this literally; to most, it means that the insights of future generations, so long as they are deeply rooted in Torah, are Torah too.

Just as growth rings accrue around the heartwood of a tree, so layers of rabbinic discourse encircle the words of Torah and become an intrinsic part of their vitality. This can be seen in the very layout of the classic editions not only of the *Chumash*, but also of all seminal Jewish works. In the centre of the page is the text itself, surrounded by commentaries and super-commentaries, which refer not only to the passage under debate but also to each other in a long, immensely varied yet organically connected intergenerational debate.

Torah becomes richer with every community and context in which Jews live, as ancient texts and venerated practices are brought to life in new geographical, social and cultural environments. 'There are seventy faces to Torah' is a byword of rabbinic exegesis. *Halakhah*, Jewish law and practice, is largely established, though always subject to further debate (Midrash Bemidbar Rabbah 13:15–16). But the scope for homiletic interpretation, for fresh literary and spiritual insights into how the Torah can be understood, is infinite. The aptness of one explanation never implies the inadequacy of any other, for, as the rabbis said of the disputes between Hillel and Shammai and their followers, it's not a question of deciding who's right and who's wrong, but rather of appreciating that 'These and these are the words of the living God' (Talmud Eruvin 13b).

Therefore, despite the centrality of the Pentateuch, Judaism is not the religion of the Bible but rather the religion of Torah, not the religion just of the text but also of how rabbis and communities have lived by and have interpreted and continue to interpret it. Once the Torah was given by God to Moses, authority was passed to the learned to expound its meanings according to their understandings and sensitivities. The Torah itself empowered the leaders and teachers of future generation to apply its laws and values according to their best insights. This leadership was never inclusive, but a meritocracy of the scholars. Until modern times, it excluded the voices of all but very few women, an irreparable impoverishment of rabbinic sources. But its debates did at least take place in the down-to-earth context of community life with its everyday practical social and economic challenges, and the rabbis regarded no subject as too mundane on the one hand, or too abstruse on the other, for their consideration.

They venerated every word of the Torah; they never regarded a single sentence, syllable or letter as redundant, including even what might look to the untrained eye like repetitions or, dare it be said, boring verses. They argued passionately over every detail. They made unlikely connections between seemingly unrelated passages, bridged only by as minimal a link as the use of the same word or phrase. They saw apparent discrepancies or gaps in the narrative as fertile opportunities for imaginative explorations, often for entire homilies and stories. 'Never underestimate them,' my teacher, Rabbi Professor Magonet, would say. 'There's always an astute perception behind what may look at first glance like mere rabbinic fancy.' The rabbis were frequently playful with language, never seeing this as contradicting their reverence for Scripture. While maintaining that the Torah never lost its plain meaning, they were anything but literalists. They mined, refined and sometimes radically redefined what they understood the Torah to say. Their interpretations were not rarely dictated by what they knew the Torah had to mean in the context of the issues they were facing. It's a chastening but also an exhilarating thought that we are part of that same ongoing engagement in examination and debate, however small our contribution may be.

It is through these processes that Judaism as we know it was, and continues to be, created. As the contemporary philosopher of Judaism Moshe Halbertal noted in *People of the Book*,[4] once a canon of sacred writings is sealed and no further texts are admitted, as was the Hebrew Bible by the second century CE at the latest, new realities can only be addressed through the exposition of the works already included. This means that they have to be interpreted with generosity and imagination, because all future challenges have to be met with reference to this same core of Scripture.

Different ways of reading the Torah

Rabbi Ishmael, a close colleague of the first- to second-century Rabbi Akiva, formulated thirteen methods by which the Torah should be expounded.[5] The number connects these measures to the traditional enumeration of the thirteen attributes of God's mercy. The obvious inference is that just as God is understood to be merciful, so God's word should be explained with mercy and compassion, in accord with justice and truth. I believe this to be the fundamental direction of travel of rabbinic interpretation.

It is probably from the thirteenth century onwards that the Hebrew term *pardes*, 'paradise', a Persian loan word, became understood as an acronym for four different kinds of scriptural signification: *peshat*, 'plain', the text's so-called simple meaning; *remez*, 'hint', its allegorical dimension; *derash*, 'search' or 'exposition', its homiletical potential; and *sod*, 'secret', its mystical resonance. To study Torah is thus to enter the paradise of the sacred word, with its source in the divine revelation and its infinite possibilities of meaning.

Peshat is not as simple as 'plain' suggests. Rashi describes his particular purpose as 'coming only [to explain] *peshuto shel Mikra*, the basic meaning of Scripture'. He defines this as 'settling each word according to its manner', a challenge that involves engaging with the semantic meaning, syntax, word order and often the pre-established rabbinic understanding of every verse, a far from 'simple' endeavour.[6]

Remez refers to the metaphorical and allegorical potential of the text, as Michael Fishbane wrote in *Sacred Attunement*: 'The exegetical mystery of *remez* lies in its assumption that truth lies beyond appearances, and that meaning is more than meets the eye.'[7]

Derash, or *midrash*, involves creative imagination, investigating potential relationships between seemingly unconnected passages and ideas, and exploring the unstated. It often takes as its starting point a seemingly unremarkable detail in the text, which it exploits to pursue a deeper question, a moral or theological 'why?'

Yet it is *sod*, the 'secret' layer of meanings, that relies on the most radical understanding of Torah as revelation. We read the Torah as narratives and laws, but to the mystics this is only a concession to the limitations of the human mind and language. To them, the Torah is holy communication; it is white fire on black fire, aflame, like the burning bush, with the divine presence, transcending comprehension. *Sod*, as Melila Hellner-Eshed has noted:

> . . . invites the readers . . . to enhance their visionary capacity and to look deeply into reality and into the narratives of the Torah to discover the divine light concealed within. This intensification of vision allows the viewers to see hidden lights and causes them to shine with a great radiance.[8]

Engaging with these rich and diverse modes of interpretation, the contemporary student of Torah has the privilege, and responsibility, of sitting at the far end of the same table as Rabbi Akiva and his generation of the first and second centuries CE, as Rashi and Rashi's commentators, and as the Kabbalists and Hasidic masters. We are simultaneously students and participants in the same ongoing, vital discourse.

Traditional versus historical-critical approaches

Prior to the Enlightenment, the traditional Jewish approach was to regard the Written Torah as God's eternal sacred word, leading to profound reverence for the text and faithful compliance with its commandments. This is the foundation of Orthodox Judaism and can be pithily expressed as: God spoke the words, the rabbis interpreted them and we must obey.

But, despite its grandeur and simplicity, for many this understanding has become increasingly difficult to uphold since the development of the text-critical approach, or 'higher criticism', as advocated by Julius Wellhausen (1844–1918) and the many scholars, Christian and Jewish, who have since followed in his wake. In the words of my own teacher, Louis Jacobs (1920–2006):

> Thanks to the massive researches of a host of scholars in various disciplines during the past 150 years, [and by now rather more,] a

consensus has emerged about how the Torah came about ... It has come to be seen that the tremendous entity we call the Torah, comprising the Pentateuch, the rest of the Bible, the Mishnah, the Talmud – and the elaborations on all of these in Jewish thought – is not static but dynamic, the constant interaction of the divine with the human. That the Torah contains a divine element no religious supernaturalist will wish to deny. But the human element, too, is quite obviously present.[9]

The disciplines he refers to include archaeology, history, comparative literature and linguistic and literary analysis. In his poignantly titled work, *Sacred Fragments*, Neil Gillman (1933–2017) notes that the conclusions derived from these investigation are 'fatal to the dogma of Mosaic composition' because they show beyond reasonable doubt that the Pentateuch is a 'composite of a number of documents, each of which circulated independently, first orally and later in writing'; and because many of the traditions of the Bible are paralleled in the literature of other Near Eastern religions.[10]

The consequences are far-reaching. According to Jacobs:

Instead of the notion of a static transmission of a corpus of revealed truth, one now sees human beings reaching out to God, engaged in a process of trial and error, and influenced by the civilisations in which they live ...

In summary, he argued that the Torah needs to be understood as revelation *through*, and not just as revelation *to*, human beings.[11]

It's easy to understand why some would see this view as undermining the clear and direct authority of the Torah. An orthodox colleague once whispered to me that he rejected the text-critical approach not because he thought its conclusions were wrong, but because it took away the basis for obeying the *mitzvot*, or commandments. Against this important critique, I would argue that the authority of the *mitzvot* does not lie in their being literally dictated by God. For the Jewish People have not merely passively understood them as God's will, but have also shaped and refined them in accord with their deepest understanding of what that will is and has to be. Generations of Jews have reached out to God by both following and interpreting the Torah's commandments; they have listened to God through them, devoted their lives to obeying them, and have in so doing both sanctified and been sanctified by them. Across millennia, Jews have been guided, humbled, inspired and purified by the Torah's laws and the struggle to understand and keep faith with them. They have dedicated themselves to them with all their 'heart, soul and might', and have not rarely been called upon to give up those lives because, and for the sake, of their faith (Deut. 6:5).

I don't believe that the results of empirical research can, or should, be ignored or dismissed. God, as Louis Jacobs noted, quoting the Talmud, is truthful and loves truth; truths, including sacred truths, cannot and should not be repressed (Yoma 69b). To do so risks embarking on a dangerous path of intellectual control, potentially leading to a regressive religious authoritarianism. I consider it essential to read the Torah, and all sacred writings, in a critical light, following the axiom that there is no text without context. The Hebrew Bible, Gospels and Quran all contain ethically difficult passages. The Torah has disturbing things to say about war, gender relationships and those it regards as idolaters. From the earliest times the rabbis found ways of disarming such texts by reinterpreting them or declaring them no longer relevant. But the dangers of literalist, non-contextualised readings remain. Considering such passages from a historical perspective allows them to be seen in their social, economic and political context, not as the unchanging will of God, but as how that will was understood at the time of composition. Furthermore, not only difficult passages benefit by being studied in this manner. Knowledge of the legal and social context of its laws and narratives can shed light on the moral and spiritual meanings of the Torah through comparison with what preceded them. Judaism should be seen as dynamic not just from the Torah onwards, but from within the Torah itself.

Yet despite my conviction, I set these words down with a degree of trepidation. Just as we need to know when to put our critical spectacles on, we equally have to understand when to take them off. Torah requires us to give ourselves to it. If we constantly hang back and examine it critically it won't stir our conscience or waken our soul. The Talmud praises the Children of Israel for their response at Sinai because they said, 'We will do,' before 'We will hear' (Exod. 24:7). 'Rash nation,' observes the Talmud, carefully placing this criticism in the mouth of a heretic (Shabbat 88a). As every lawyer warns, one should never sign a contract without first reading the fine print. Yet the Jewish People accepted the Torah before they knew what it contained. The point is that we cannot appreciate the meaning of the Torah and its commandments without following them and experiencing their impact on our lives. If we want them to guide us, we cannot only subject them to our scrutiny; we must also allow our lives to be subjected to theirs.

A touching story tells of two seekers who meet at a crossroads between Vilna, the home of the hugely influential Talmudist and scholar, the Gaon Elijah ben Solomon Zalman (1720–97), and Mezerich, where the Hasidic leader Dov Baer (d. 1772) held court.

'I'm going to Vilna to learn to master Torah,' said the first.

'And I'm going to Mezerich to learn to let the Torah master me,' replied the second.

The daily prayers make no mention of 'mastering' Torah. But they do speak of *limmud Torah* and *ahavat Torah*, the study and love of Torah and its way of life. We ask God to 'open our hearts to understand, listen to, study, teach, keep and carry out all the words of the Torah's teachings with love'. Learning and love are surely ways of being mastered by Torah, without any forfeit of mind, heart or conscience. The etiquette when one carries a Torah scroll is to hold it against one's right shoulder. I find this counterintuitive; I always want to place it over my left shoulder, so that it rests against my heart.

I have set out these background thoughts simply to say that the following pages are my own offerings of love of Torah within the great tradition of Judaism. They are inspired by the writings of generations of commentators and mystics, the insights of poets and thinkers of different faiths and philosophies, discussions with fellow seekers, challenging questions, humbling interactions in hospital corridors, the goodness and courage I have so often been privileged to witness, and the sheer beauty of nature. I have set down my reflections as a tiny but deeply felt contribution, with reverence for the unfathomable depths of Torah culture and with respect for the knowledge, wisdom and devotion of the rabbis and teachers across the centuries, through many exiles and numerous tribulations.

I believe in a Judaism that has as its core the teachings of the Torah, the Prophets of Israel and the Hebrew Bible as they been pondered, prayed and argued over word by word through the extraordinary works of the Mishnah, Talmud, Midrash, Responsa and the entire two and a part millennia of rabbinic culture. This is a Judaism forged in the crucibles of exile, persecution, marginalisation and martyrdom, but also challenged and enriched by other faiths, by the arts and sciences and by the political cultures of enlightened humanism and universalism. It is a Judaism that has, throughout and despite these trials of history, preserved and deepened the search for God and for the sacred in every human being and every living thing. It is a Judaism that fights for justice against tyranny, compassion against cruelty, and human dignity against all forms of bigotry and contempt. It is a Judaism that, while contributing to and learning from the rest of the world, has maintained its spiritual, legal-halakhic, ethical and communal disciplines, cultures and integrity. Above all, it is a Judaism filled with appreciation and concern for life, as the daily prayer says, repeating the word 'life' for emphasis, 'You have given us a Torah of life and the love of kindness, righteousness and blessing, compassion, life and peace.'

The challenge is to study, interpret and endeavour to live day after day by this Torah of respect and love of all life. I am grateful to everyone who may join me on this journey into Torah. It can be followed according to the cycle of the Jewish year, by reading the relevant sections on each *parashah*, or weekly portion. But key themes have also been referenced in a short index for the reader who wishes to trace the treatment of specific topics.

I hope these thoughts may touch the heart, eliciting reflection and debate and inspiring different insights in people I might yet have the privilege to meet. I am grateful to my family, my community, my numerous teachers and the God of life for enabling me to set down these words.

NOTE TO READERS

This brief guide is intended as an aid to readers who may not be familiar with the core compositions of the Jewish canon and some of the key rabbis most closely associated with them.[1]

Judaism's most central text is the Hebrew Bible, often referred to by the acronym *TeNaKh*, where 'T', *tav*, stands for *Torah*, the most sacred and significant section, 'N', *nun*, for *Nevi'im* or Prophets, and 'Kh', *caph*, for *Ketubim*, Writings, of which the Psalms are the most often cited in what follows.*

Not quite the first, but the most significant early rabbinic text is the Mishnah, organised according to subject, composed of six orders and subdivided into tractates on every facet of Jewish life from the festivals and temple-related rituals to matrimonial, agricultural and civil law. Rabbis of the Mishnaic period, which stretches from the first century BCE to the close of the second century CE, generally carry the title 'Rabbi' and include such figures as Hillel (first century BCE), and Rabbi Akiva (first and second century CE), who, together with several of his colleagues, was martyred by the Romans during the period of the Hadrianic persecutions (117–138 CE) and the Bar Kochba revolt (132–135 CE). The name 'Mishnah' is derived from the verb *shoneh*, meaning to repeat, probably because the material was repeated until committed to memory and recalled mentally for analysis and debate. Rabbi Judah the Prince (*c.*135–*c.*217) is credited with editing the Mishnah in the north of Israel around 200 CE. A distinctive tractate of the Mishnah is Avot, generally known as *The Chapters of the Fathers*, to which I often refer, and which, rather than rules, includes the favourite wisdom sayings of the key teachers across the generations of the Mishnaic period.

The Mishnah forms the basis of the Talmud, in which each individual teaching is followed by the detailed debates of the rabbis, known as *Gemara*, encompassing matters of *Halakhah*, law, and *Aggadah*, lore and

---

* Through this work my English translation is eclectic, often according to my own preference, but based largely on the Authorised and Revised Authorised versions, as well as on the Hertz Chumash, 2nd edition (London: Soncino Press, 1960) and the Jewish Publication Society Bible (1986). Jewish and Christian verse numbering occasionally differs. Where this is the case, the traditional Jewish verse reference is given first, followed in brackets by the Christian numbering.

homily. The process by which the Talmud was edited towards the close of the fifth century CE remains the subject of research and speculation. There are two Talmuds, the more significant being the Babylonian Talmud, since it was there that the most important centres of Jewish learning were situated during the Talmudic period and afterwards, while the Jerusalem Talmud was edited in the Land of Israel. Teachers of the Talmudic period carry the title 'Rav'. Learning Talmud remains the most significant, and most challenging, discipline of Jewish study. The Mishnah and Talmud together form the core of the Oral Law, which, according to tradition, was studied from memory and, unlike the Written Torah, not committed to writing.

Between the late Middle Ages and the Renaissance, a number of key codes of Jewish law were composed, of which the most important are the *Mishneh Torah*, by Maimonides (Spain and Egypt, 1138–1204), and the *Shulchan Aruch* by Joseph Caro (Spain, Turkey, the Land of Israel, 1488–1575). They, and the voluminous commentaries on them, remain, alongside the Mishnah and Talmud, the essential touchstones for any debate on matters of Jewish law to this day.

During the Middle Ages, other forms of Jewish literature also flourished. Most important for this book is the genre of Midrash, especially the great compendia of midrashim on the books of the Torah: *Bereshit, Shemot, Vayikra, Bemidbar* and *Devarim Rabbah*. It is hard to be precise about the dates when each of these and other collections of Midrashim were redacted. As noted in the Introduction, the root meaning of 'midrash' is 'searching' or 'investigation'; this varied genre includes everything from brief insights to more extensive explorations. Midrash probes the gaps in the narrative left by Scripture, notes and analyses intertextual relationships between sometimes seemingly unrelated verses across the canon, and raises, often just by implication, wider moral, social and theological issues. One midrashic interpretation does not negate another; frequently parallel midrashim are set side by side, offering a multitude of possible ways of thinking about the text at the centre of which is always a word, a verse or a story from the Torah or the rest of the *Tenakh*.

No less important is the genre of verse-by-verse or section-by-section Torah commentary. In the eleventh century, Rabbi Shlomo ben Yitzhak, known by his acronym 'Rashi' (France, 1040–1105) wrote his classic commentary on the Torah and *Tenakh*. I refer to it regularly, together with the key commentaries of Abraham ibn Ezra (Spain, *c.*1090–*c.*1165) and Moses ben Nachman, Nachmanides, known by his acronym as the Ramban (Catalonia and the land of Israel, 1194–1270). A more recent author to whom I also often refer is Samson Raphael Hirsch (Germany, 1808–88). The genre of verse-by-verse Torah commentary is vast and ongoing.

A further significant mode of Jewish literature is Kabbalah, literally 'receiving', the lore and writings of the mystical tradition. A key text is the Zohar, the Book of Splendour, which, though piously attributed to the second-century Rabbi Shimeon bar Yochai, is now known to have been written substantially by Rabbi Moses de Leon (1240–1305) and his circle in Spain in the thirteenth century. The Kabbalah had a further seminal period of flourishing in the Land of Israel in the sixteenth century. Key kabbalistic ideas underlie much Hasidic thinking, the pietist and some-times populist spiritual revival which began with Rabbi Israel ben Eliezer, known as the Ba'al Shem Tov (c.1700–60) in Ukraine, and spread across Eastern Europe until the Nazi Holocaust. Hasidic leaders are generally referred to by the title 'Rebbe'. I am greatly indebted to the *Chumash Peninei Hahasidut*, a rich compendium of Hasidic insights on virtually every verse of the Torah, to which I frequently refer.[2] A particularly signif-icant and more recent Hasidic leader is Rebbe Kalonymus Kalman Shapira (Poland, 1889–1943), to whom I often turn. He was martyred in the Holocaust and became known subsequently as the Rebbe of the Warsaw Ghetto.

Among twentieth- and twenty-first-century theologians, three rabbis hold special importance for me: Louis Jacobs (England, 1920–2006), my rabbi and mentor, for his deeply traditional yet text-critical approach to Torah; Abraham Joshua Heschel (Poland, Germany, North America, 1907–72) for his deep Hasidic piety combined with his fearless commit-ment to social justice; and my friend and teacher Arthur Green (North America and Israel), for his profoundly personal yet universalist spirituality, rooted in a comprehensive knowledge of Jewish mysticism.

Finally, a word on the Jewish day, week and year. Every weekday contains three services: *shacharit* in the morning, *minchah* in the afternoon and *ma'ariv* in the evening. The morning and evening prayers have at their heart the recital of the *Shema*, the meditation, taken from the Torah, on God's oneness and the love of God, and the *Amidah*, or 'standing prayer', consisting of a fixed sequence of praise and petition. Sabbath prayers include *mussaf*, an 'additional' service, and the weekly Torah portion is read in full. It is a basic principle of Judaism that Jews are obligated to study and meditate on the Torah every day and every night.

The Jewish year is rich in traditional festivals. It is hard to be exact about dates since Judaism follows a lunar calendar, which, however, is closely tied to the solar cycle, allowing a variation of approximately one month in the civil dates on which these festivals fall. *Rosh Hashanah*, the New Year, comes in September or early October, followed on the tenth day by *Yom Kippur*, the Day of Atonement. Five days later comes *Sukkot*, Tabernacles, concluding with *Simchat Torah*, the Joy of Torah, the date on which the annual cycle of Torah readings is both completed and recommenced. *Chanukkah*, widely referred to today as the Festival of Lights, falls in December or early January; *Tu Bishevat*, the New Year for Trees, in January or early February; and *Purim*, the celebration on which the Scroll of Esther is read, in February or March. *Pesach*, Passover, may begin in late March, but more often comes during April. *Shavuot*, the Feast of Weeks, or Pentecost, falls in May or early June.

THE BOOK OF GENESIS
בְּרֵאשִׁית

··

In the beginning

'*Bereshit bara*, in the beginning God created the heavens and the earth' (Gen. 1:1). Every time I read these opening words I'm gripped by awe. The world unfolds, light and dark, land and sea, birds and animals, the whole wondrous evolution of life. The words emerge, simple and beautiful, flowing with the articulation of this rhythm of day and night, aeon and epoch. Was what follows ever meant as a factual account, or was it intended instead to express a different truth, a song of praise to the glory of creation, telling us that nothing is merely thing but always precious and unique, because the life force that flows through all beings belongs to the same sacred energy? That is how I read this magnificent first chapter of the Hebrew Bible.

Bereshit bara: the words come as from nowhere onto the parchment scroll of the Torah. What mystery lies in the blank margins above and before them: what is there prior to utterance or even conception, before God's name is first spoken? The classic Jewish answer is that we cannot know or comprehend. There is God. That God is one, the Creator who has no creator, the Unmoved Mover, the first cause which has no prior cause. I will never have an answer for the child who asked me who made God. 'Do not ask what is before or after,' the Mishnah warns (Hagigah 2:1).

But God, as the Jewish mystical tradition makes especially clear, is only a name, a word in human language for that which transcends all names and all language: the ineffable, unfathomable source of all. God, the one and only deity, is unknowable, yet brought, by the very fact of being named, within the confines of our imagination and speech. We must therefore be constantly aware that whatever we say about God is always an imposition. It does not and cannot describe God as God truly is because our account is ineluctably coloured by the limitations and presumptions of our understanding. The ultimate reality lies always beyond, in the realms of the indescribable.

Richard Dawkins' assertion in *The God Delusion* that the God of the Bible is 'the most unpleasant character in all fiction' is exaggerated and one-sided, and based ultimately on a misconception of who or what God is.[1] But he has a point that God as portrayed by humanity does sometimes behave in ways that are vengeful, misogynistic, homophobic or racist, as well as compassionate, just and loving. However, the responsibility for this does not lie with God. Rather, once 'God' has become a noun in human language and the ineffable has been introduced, and reduced, to the terms of human discourse, that 'God' is inevitably made the bearer of the hopes and ideals, but also of the assumptions, prejudices and ulterior motives of every tradition and culture within which he or she is portrayed.

Talking about God is therefore a dangerous affair. God does not necessarily 'do' what the sacred, but inevitably human, record of Scripture ascribes to him or her. We cannot hear or see or know God as God is, precisely because the very capture of a concept in human thought renders that concept human, often all too human. Therefore, as the twelfth-century philosopher Maimonides admonishes throughout the first section of *The Guide for the Perplexed*, in which he explains as figurative all the anthropomorphic qualities that Scripture ascribes to the Deity, God is neither 'jealous' nor 'angry' nor even necessarily full of loving kindness. God is.

Transcending any and all further descriptions lies the unnameable reality to which this three-letter noun is no more than a pointer, a single syllable in the English language. Images of God, so strongly condemned in the Bible, can be constructed not only with stone but also with words. We must never forget that, beyond our own conception, our need to label and describe or, more unscrupulously, to co-opt and manipulate 'God', resides that which is outside the reach of the imagination and beyond the taint of the numerous motives ascribed to it across different religions and throughout history.

The Kabbalists, students of the Jewish mystical tradition, have circumlocutions for that which lies outside language, preceding all discourse and all thought: *Ein Sof*, The One Without End; *Havayah*, Being; or even, as I once found mentioned, *Sod Ha'ephshar*, The Secret of the Possible.

The Zohar, the core text of Kabbalah, probes the indescribable through the imagery of cosmic myth:

Within the most hidden recesses a flame of darkness issued, from the mysterious *Ein Sof*, a mist within formlessness . . . From deep within the flame there flowed a spring . . . It was not knowable at all until, by force of its breaking through, one hidden sublime point gave forth light. Beyond that point nothing is known. Therefore, it is called 'Beginning' – the first utterance of all.[2]

That is the closest that language can reach to communicating what cannot be told. This unnameable essence, from which all being emerges and into which it subsequently returns, is what we call 'God'. We give this being a name and ascribe to it actions and attributes because we need a point of reference, because, since we are only human, we cannot dispense with language or overcome our limitations, and because, from the first, we have found it essential to pray to, invoke, yearn for and speak about the transcendent.

Perhaps the most we can know of God is that God is the source of all vitality and the quintessence of all being. As Rabbi Judah Hehasid, the twelfth-century author of *Shir Hakavod*, the *Hymn of Glory*, wrote:

> I shall sing and weave you melodies; it is for you that my soul
>   yearns . . .
> I shall tell of your glory although I have not seen you;
> I shall imagine you and call you by affectionate names
> Though I do not, and cannot, know you.

'And God said, "Let there be . . ."': Where God speaks

> I have fallen through time and found the enchanted world.
> Where all is beginning.
>   Nan Shepherd[3]

'I'm sorry to offend you, but I don't believe in God.' I was at the local hospice, by the bedside of a Catholic lady whom I had never previously met. 'I've survived the cancer twice,' she continued, 'but this time I know it's the end. I'm not religious. I'm a down-to-earth sort of person, and here's what I believe. The sea is full of fishes; some die, others are born. It's the same with the birds and the animals, and with us humans too. Some of us die, others are born, but life itself goes on. That's my faith. I've no time for a God in heaven who rules the world. Sorry if I've offended you, but that's what I think.'

Far from upset, I was moved by this woman's frank respect for life with its basic rhythms of birth and death. What she described as unbelief I took as awareness of a world full of vitality, alive with the presence of God intuited in the midst of existence, in the red and black feathers of a wood-pecker and the unfurling leaves of the spring. I don't believe in a hands-on interventionist God somewhere up in the skies either, who exercises direct control over life on earth.

The Talmud explains that the world was created in 'Ten Utterances', the ten occurrences of the words 'And God said' in the opening chapter of Genesis, the ode to wonder with which the Bible begins. With typical exactitude, the Talmud notes that the phrase occurs only *nine* times, before resolving the discrepancy by counting 'In the beginning' as the first of the ten. These Ten Utterances constitute a parallel mode of revelation to the Ten Commandments. They are the sacred speech by means of which all things come into being and are endowed with their particular vitality.

To the mystics, God's word is not a one-off command that summoned forth life out of chaos long ago. God's voice in nature is endless and enduring; it is the invisible resonance that ceaselessly imparts life to all existence, the rhythm at the core of all consciousness. By its virtue all creation lives. 'And God said' is therefore a mistranslation; the correct rendition is 'And God says'. For if that sacred speech were to stop, nothing would survive.

According to the tractate *Perek Shirah*, The Chapter of Song, all existence sings.* The elements themselves, the sky, earth, sea and rivers, as well as the plants and animals, all have their special song based on their unique verse in the Bible. The heavens say, 'The skies declare the glory of God,' and the earth responds, 'From the ends of the land we have heard songs.'[4] Wheat sways to the words, 'From the depths have I called to you, Eternal,'[5] while the swallows cry, 'So that the soul may sing of your glory and not be silent, God.'[6]

To the unknown authors of this tractate, God's speech is not an idea but an experience, the consciousness of an affinity, the awareness of kinship with an infinitely greater whole. Such an understanding of the world is not solely the province of mystics. There is a growing awareness that animals and indeed plants perceive and respond to life in sophisticated ways, communicating in modes to which the assumed superiority of human reason has made us blind. Students of the natural world, of octopuses and whales, forests and fungi, are making us aware of symbioses and sensitivities, ways of conceiving and relating, to which we have paid little heed. The poet Adam Kirsch quotes natural history writer Charles Foster: 'Evolutionary biology is a numinous statement of the interconnectedness of things,' and adds that this preaching translates easily into religious terms.[7]

---

* *Perek Shirah*, once considered to be a tractate of the Mishnah, is in fact first mentioned in the work of Salmon ben Yerohim in the tenth century: 'Pereq Shirah: a litany of verses spoken by the creatures & works of Creation (after the arrangement of Natan Slifkin)', The Open Siddur Project, opensiddur.org/readings-and-sourcetexts/mekorot/non-canonical/esoteric/hekhalot-writings/perek-shira-chapter-of-song (accessed 6 June 2023).

Often, when I think of the ignorance, contempt and cruelty with which we treat the rest of nature I feel ashamed of being a human.

The issue, therefore, may not be whether creation sings, but whether we are capable of being sensitive to its music. Are we willing to hear and respect the uniqueness and sanctity of all life, or do we only listen to the ricocheting echoes of our own stridency?

The psalmist captures the challenge perfectly:

Day utters speech to day, night transmits knowledge to night.
There is no speech, there are no words, their voice is not heard at all.

(Ps. 19:3–4)

At first sight these verses appear to contradict each other. On the one hand, every moment is vibrant and vital; the earth is alive with a speech apprehended by the heart even if the physical ear is unable to detect it. On the other hand, there is nothing worth listening to, nothing out there to be heard. Beyond the immediate cacophony of sounds lies only endless emptiness; there is nothing deeper, nothing sacred, with which we can connect.

Yet, because the Hebrew is ambiguous, the psalm can be understood very differently, yielding an alternative reading in which the two verses don't contract but rather affirm each other:

Day utters speech to day, night transmits knowledge to night.
There is no speech, there are no words, *in which* their voice is not
heard.

I read the psalm both ways. I long to become more attuned to creation, hearing within life's countless differentiations a great oneness, a sacred vitality flowing through all things, to which devotees of all faiths have given the name God. I'm happiest in such moments of attentiveness because the world is full of wonder and life sings, restoring the soul, just as hidden sources of underground water replenish deep wells.

But at other times I hear only the noise of humanity's constant preoc- cupation with itself, at every level and on every scale, individual, societal and national. The notion that all existence sings, that there is a God in this cruel world present even in secret, even hidden far within the material realities and daily perturbations of life, seems like a wilful avoidance of truth. The very idea of faith feels less like reaching after a deeper reality and more like clasping on to an entrenched falsehood.

7

Yet, despite everything, I am convinced that life calls out in its tenderness and exhilaration, in its suffering and anguish, in modes often inaccessible to the ear but audible to the spirit. The sound may often be a lament or an elegy, the cry of a child whose home has been swept away by floods, of an animal being slaughtered. But it is also the music of the endless, irrepressible energy of existence, the unbounded exhilaration of life, the joy of the birds at dawn. God, if one may so name the sacred energy that flows through all things, does sing within creation.

Humans – and the rest of creation

The Rebbe of Lubavitch reputedly chided his son for mindlessly tearing leaves off a tree and crushing them in his fingers. 'How do you know that your "I" is more precious to God than the "I" of that tree?' he asked him. 'True, you belong to the domain of the human, and it to the domain of vegetation. But both are filled with God's Holy Spirit.'[8]

The Torah opens with the bare elements. The sacred text begins by invoking reverence for the earth and for nature; through them God's spirit first moves. Creation unfolds in a vast developmental chronology; days become aeons as life evolves from plant and bush to bird and fish, mammal and human. Every dawn and every night, every flower and every animal is good. But only the whole work in its complementarity and interdependence is *very* good. Only then does God rest and bless the Sabbath, the day that calls all things home to the original dream of a harmonious and peaceful world, whatever else may subsequently unfold in the distracting interactions of time.

This magnificent work of God is now entrusted to the unproven care of human beings, giving them a unique role within the ecology of creation: 'Rule over the fish of the sea, the birds of the sky, the animals, all the earth and every moving creature which crawls upon it' (Gen. 1:26). The key Hebrew word is *veyiredu*: the Hebrew-Aramaic Lexicon translates it as 'have dominion, rule, dominate'.[9] God, it seems, wants humans to have mastery over everything. But the great eleventh-century commentator Rashi offers a chastening qualification: everything will depend on how they conduct themselves:

This verb contains both the word *ridu'i*, rule, and *yeridah*, descent: if humans prove worthy, they will rule over the wild and domestic animals; if they prove unworthy, they will fall beneath them, and the wild animals will rule over them.[10]

Siftei Chachamim, a super-commentary to Rashi by Shabbetai ben Joseph Bass (1641–1718), suggests that God issues this warning to reassure the angels who object to the making of humans because, having free will, they are bound to do wrong and put the whole of creation at risk.

But there's no hint of caution when God blesses the first human beings and endorses their right to power in almost identical words: 'Fill the earth and subdue it; rule over the fish of the sea, the birds of the skies and all the animals which move upon the face of the earth' (Gen. 1:28). It's hardly surprising, therefore, that the Bible has been widely understood as granting humankind a God-given licence to treat the rest of creation as little more than a means to its own ends. This so-called 'Judeo-Christian heritage' is held responsible for our anthropocentric and colonialist attitude to the natural world in which all other beings have value only in so far as they serve the needs of humans, who are entitled by divine sanction to subjugate them all.

Environmental engineer and researcher Dr Malcom Ferdinand makes a disturbing link between colonising other peoples and colonising nature: they have in common:

> . . . a certain way of inhabiting the earth, some believing themselves entitled to appropriate the earth for the benefit of a few . . . This 'colonial habitation' . . . is a violent way of inhabiting the earth, subjugating lands, humans, and non-humans to the desires of the coloniser.[11]

This is, perhaps, the implicit assumption behind what Canadian writer and activist Naomi Klein describes as unbridled 'deregulated capitalism', the right to utilise and monetise anything and everything with little regard for the cost to other people, nature and the earth itself.[12]

But this is patently not the relationship between God, humanity and the world that the Hebrew Bible intends. On the contrary, 'The earth and its fullness belong to God' (Ps. 24:1). Human beings are entrusted by God to be not exploiters but caretakers of creation, responsible in God's name for the welfare of all life, as expressed in the warning that the rabbis put into God's mouth: 'Do not destroy my world because there is no one who can come after you and put it right' (Midrash Ecc. Rabbah, 7:13). The Bible stands in categorical opposition to that utilitarian devaluation of everything which Thomas Berry so painfully decries when he laments how today:

> . . . nothing is holy, nothing is sacred. We no longer have a world of inherent value, no world of wonder, no untouched, unspoiled, unused world. We have *used* everything. By 'developing' the planet, we have been reducing Earth to a new type of barrenness.[13]

A truer insight into how the Hebrew Bible understands humankind's role in creation is based on God's instructions to Adam and Eve when he places them in the Garden of Eden 'to work it and keep it' (Gen. 2:15). The Garden represents the world; we're permitted to make a living from the earth, but we remain responsible for protecting and caring for it. Our usage of the world's agricultural and mineral resources must therefore be governed by the requirements of sustainability and biodiversity, as well as the demands of social justice. But a careful reading of the verse shows that what is called for goes deeper, as Ellen Davis suggests:

> *Avad*, 'work', generally denotes not just work itself, but *working for* and *serving*, as in its frequent usage to indicate the service of God. Hence humanity's task should be viewed as '*working for* the garden, serving its needs'. Even the connotation of worship (cautiously implied) may inform our understanding.[14]

While *avad* can refer to everyday work, as in the Ten Commandments' 'Six days shall you labour' (Exod. 20:9), it is also frequently used to indicate the service of God. Hence, as used in reference to the Garden, it implies not merely work, but an attitude of reverence and respect towards the object of that work, in this case the earth itself. Davis continues: '*Shamar*, "keep", indicates not only preserving but also observing and obeying, as in the fourth commandment: "*Shamor* – Keep the Sabbath day and make it holy" (Deuteronomy 5:12).'[15]

Our relationship to the earth must not merely be utilitarian but also spiritual; the world both inspires and requires our reverence and wonder. This is the true attitude of the Hebrew Bible toward creation, as well stated by Llewellyn Vaughan-Lee: 'Our guardianship of the planet means taking responsibility for its physical *and* its sacred nature, and their interrelationship.'[16]

To the mystics, the entire Bible is based on precisely this understanding that everything on earth is a manifestation of sacred energy, as stated in the

Zohar: 'There is no space empty of the divine presence.'[17] The very structure of the opening chapter of Genesis sets human beings not apart from but within creation, integrated into the flow of unfolding relationships between water and land, grasses, trees and all the animals. Cruelty towards other forms of life is abhorrent; God's mercy 'extends over all God's works' (Ps. 145:9).

We live at the fateful juncture where the choice between exploitative domination and responsible trusteeship is a matter of life and death for many of the species on our planet. Albert Einstein foresaw the need for a fundamental change in outlook, now more urgent than ever:

> A human being is part of the whole called by us 'the universe,' a part limited in time and space. We experience ourselves, our thoughts and feelings, as something separate from the rest – a kind of optical illusion of our consciousness. This delusion is a kind of prison for us . . . Our task must be to free ourselves from this prison by widening our circle of understanding and compassion to embrace all living creatures and the whole of Nature in its beauty.[18]

Ellen Davis quotes a remarkable prayer by the fourth-century Christian scholar Basil the Great; his words could not be more relevant today:

> O God, enlarge within us the sense of fellowship
> With all living things, our brothers the animals
> To whom thou gavest the earth as their home in common with us.
>
> We remember with shame that in the past
> We have exercised the high dominion of [humankind] with ruthless
>   cruelty
> So that the voice of the earth, which should have gone up to thee in
>   song,
> Has been a groan of travail.
>
> May we realize that they live not for us alone
> But for themselves and for thee,
> And that they love the sweetness of life.[19]

With whom did God consult?

God says to every human being: 'Let us make a human being – you and I together.'

Rebbe Avraham Mordechai of Ger[20]

God, the rabbis understood, was a risk-taker. This made the angels unhappy: they wanted God to play safe.

The cue in the text on which the rabbis based this presumed disagreement is simple. On every other day of creation God says, 'Let there be . . .' But halfway through the sixth day, referring specifically to the creation of humans, God says instead, 'Let us make . . .' With whom, though, is God speaking when there isn't anyone else there in heaven? The rabbis had several suggestions. The least exciting option is that God is employing the royal 'we'. But why, then, doesn't God do so earlier? More engaging is the idea that God does in fact have company: the angels. Midrash imagines them in fierce debate:

> Rabbi Simon said: When God came to create the first human beings the angels were divided into different camps: some said, 'Don't let them be created.' Others said, 'Do.' Scripture states: 'Lovingkindness and truth have met; righteousness and peace have kissed.' Lovingkindness said, 'Let them be created, because they'll do acts of kindness.' Truth said, 'Let them not be created because they're full of lies.' Righteousness said, 'Let them be created because they'll do justice.' Peace said, 'Let them not be created because they're full of arguments.' . . . Rav Huna Rabba of Tsipori said, 'While the angels were busy debating, God got on with making them, then turned to the angels and said, "What's the point of arguing? Humans have already been created."'
>
> (Midrash Bereshit Rabbah 8:5)

Perhaps the 'angels' represent an internal doubt in God: is it worth the risk of creating independent beings with a will of their own, who are bound sooner or later to behave in ways that threaten the very enterprise for which they were made? It's an ancient version of the Frankenstein dilemma: might such a creature, with needs of its own, defy the will and hopes of its creator, and both destroy and, ultimately, self-destruct? It could be said that today humankind faces somewhat similar issues in relation to artificial intelligence.

Whatever the case, God decides it's a chance worth taking, for it's with precisely such a free being that God wants to be in relationship. Thus creation culminates in an act of relinquishment: in the words of the poet Cecil Day-Lewis, for God, too, 'love is proved in the letting go'.[21]

In the same midrash, Rabbi Simon notes that the Hebrew word for 'very' is composed of the same letters as *adam*, 'humankind'. At the close of each preceding day of creation, God sees that the work is 'good', but on the sixth day God observes that 'it is *very* good'. That 'very', Rabbi Simon suggests, refers to humans who, alone in creation, possess free will and the capacity to disobey. The latter derives from their *yetzer hara*, their evil inclination, which the rabbis considered to be part of the human psyche from birth. It is not in fact truly 'evil', but, like the id, represents the drive and passion without which no one would be motivated to do anything. It becomes dangerous only if ungoverned by the *yetzer hatov*, 'the good inclination', the knowledge and willpower to do what is right. It's precisely this internal tension and their capacity for choice that makes God create humans. Angels are safe, but boring. God raises the stakes, leaving the entire adventure of history dependent on that 'very', on what human beings will do with their free will.

In 'The Concept of God After Auschwitz', Hans Jonas describes a deity who withdraws from creation, renouncing omnipotence in order to allow evolution to take its course unimpeded by divine intervention. So long as life forms remain simple, the universe develops steadily: 'before the advent of knowledge God's cause cannot go wrong'. But then:

> [God] trembles as the thrust of evolution, carried by its own momentum, passes the threshold where innocence ceases and an entirely new criterion of success and failure takes hold of the divine stake. The advent of man means the advent of knowledge and freedom . . . To the promise and risk of this agency the divine cause, revealed at last, henceforth finds itself committed, and its issue trembles in the balance.[22]

Within what Jonas calls his 'myth', one can detect the Kabbalistic concept of *tsimtsum*, the voluntary contraction by God to make space for life to unfold. Embracing the science of evolution, Jonas posits a God who is no longer, willingly or unwillingly, omnipotent.

The story of the Garden of Eden suggests that, despite endowing them with free will, God remains ambivalent about wanting humans to exercise it fully. By forbidding them to eat from the tree of knowledge, God renders this the most interesting thing for Adam and Eve to do. God both wants and doesn't want them to take their destiny, and with it the fate of all existence, into their own hands. God warns them that they will have to bear the responsibility for the consequences of their conduct. Yet in that very outcome, God is complicit; disobedience is necessary and inevitable. As social psychologist Erich Fromm (1900–80) writes, eating from the Tree of Knowledge may be a sin from the point of view of religious authority:

> From the standpoint of man, however, this is the beginning of human freedom. Acting against God's orders means freeing himself from coercion, emerging from the unconscious existence of pre-human life to the level of man. Acting against the command of authority, committing a sin, is in its positive human aspect the first act of freedom, that is, the first *human* act . . . The act of disobedience as an act of freedom is the beginning of reason.[23]

As he observes elsewhere, freedom and the capacity to disobey are inseparable.

The Talmud notes that each day of creation ends with the words 'day three', or 'four' or 'five'. Only at the conclusion of the sixth day is there a definite article: 'It was evening, it was morning, *the* sixth day' (Gen. 1:31). It takes this as a hint at another, future sixth day, the sixth of Sivan, when Moses will receive the Torah: 'This teaches that God made a pact with the works of creation, telling them: "If Israel accepts the Torah you will survive. If not, I'll turn you back to chaos"' (Shabbat 88a). I understand this universally to mean that if humankind accepts being bound by a moral law, nature will survive; if not, disaster will ensue.

God wants to engage with beings endowed with genuine agency. Yet God depends on them to use that freedom to follow the divine will and do what they're taught is just and good. Against the advice of the angels, God has entered into a relationship of mutuality and dependence. The destiny of all creation is at stake.

In God's image

I found myself driving along the motorway late at night, hoping to reach South Manchester then get back home to London in time for at least an hour's sleep before work. I'd asked a friend: 'Am I crazy?'

'No,' he'd replied. 'Sometimes there are things one simply has to do.'

The previous day, a mural of Marcus Rashford, the black England football star who had campaigned courageously for free school meals for children from impoverished homes, had been defaced by racists. The three black footballers who had missed their penalties in the European Cup Final shoot-out had faced a bombardment of racist insults. I simply had to go to Manchester, stand next to the mural on a wall near where Rashford grew up, and show my respect.

I told my community from my car, 'I'm doing this on behalf of us all. It's because my grandfather was in Dachau; it's because of what we as a people have been through and must not let others suffer. It's what being Jewish means.'

They understood immediately: 'Go,' they said. 'Go in all our names.'

The first thing the Bible tells us about human beings is that we are all created in the divine image, with no exceptions: 'God created the human being in God's image, in the image of God, God made him; male and female God created them' (Gen. 1:27).

Since in Jewish belief God has no image or likeness, the obvious question is: what does this actually mean? Rashi explains, sparingly, that humans were created 'with understanding and intelligence'.[24] Maimonides, who devotes much of the first part of his *Guide for the Perplexed* to arguing that God neither has nor can have shape or form, understands the divine image as the capacity for knowledge:

> For the intellect that God made overflow unto man, and which is the latter's ultimate perfection, was that which Adam was provided with before he disobeyed. It was because of this that it was said that he was created 'in the image of God and in God's likeness'.[25]

The Catalonian Halakhist, mystic and commentator Nachmanides (1194–1270) explains likeness as similarity in form and deed, without attributing any specific 'form' to God:

> The human being is like the lower and the higher beings in form and beauty, as it is written, 'God crowned him with glory and majesty.' This is his purpose, that by virtue of wisdom, knowledge, ability and aspiration, though his body is like dust, his soul should be like the higher beings.[26]

Samson Raphael Hirsch (1808–88) explains any likeness between humans and God in terms of our potential role, rather than as any intrinsic quality.

He relates the word *adam*, 'humankind', to *hadom*, 'footstool'; human beings are God's footstool on earth: 'Without the intervention of human beings ... God would have to accomplish alone all the truth, mercy, justice and love which God wants to bring about on earth.'[27]

Others argue that the divine image is the capacity for speech, moral awareness or conscience. Dorothy Sayers strikingly observes that, since all we so far know about God is that God creates, the divine image must refer to the capacity for creativity.

But irrespective of exactly what it means, the Torah is making an essential point: this image is possessed by every human being, without exception. At the beginning of human history there is neither black nor white, Jew or non-Jew, believer or unbeliever, free person or slave. Nobody is not created in God's image; no one is devoid of it. It is the birthright of every human being. This amounts in biblical terms to what the 1948 Universal Declaration of Human Rights states in its opening article: 'All human beings are born free and equal in dignity and rights. They are endowed with reason and conscience and should act towards one another in a spirit of brotherhood.'

The Declaration endeavours, not always successfully, to use gender-neutral language. But the Bible, it is argued, refers only to the creation of man; the first woman is fashioned later, from his 'spare rib'. This reading, which permeates western culture and is used both to justify and to attack the notion of male supremacy, is challenged by the Talmud. It notes that the first human being is androgynous; God makes them both 'male and female' (Gen. 1:27). Arguing that the key term *tsela*, mistakenly translated as 'rib', really means 'side', it explains that God separated the male side of the first human from the female side, like the parting of Siamese twins joined back to back. God wants man and woman to be able to relate to each other face to face, as the Torah says, 'I shall make him a helpmeet, *kenegdo*' (Gen. 2:18), that is, opposite and facing him. Man and woman are thus co-created (Berachot 61a).

Describing the procedure by which witnesses are warned prior to giving testimony in potentially capital cases, the Mishnah asserts the fundamental equality of every individual, irrespective of gender or race:

> It was for this reason that the human being was created *yechidi*, single and unique: to teach you that anyone who destroys a single life is considered by Scripture to have destroyed an entire world, while anyone who saves a single life is as if they saved an entire world. And to promote peace, so that no one can say, 'My ancestors are greater

than yours.' . . . And to proclaim the greatness of The Holy Blessed One: for if a person strikes many coins with the same stamp, they are all alike. But the King of the king of kings, the Holy Blessed One, strikes every person with the stamp of the first human being yet no one is exactly like anyone else. Hence every person must say: 'For my sake the world was created.'

(Sanhedrin 4:5)

The Mishnah offers two complementary understandings of the word *yechidi*: 'individual' and 'unique', emphasising both the equality and the individuality of every person. Everyone brings into the world their particular perceptions and gifts, their irreplicable portion of God's image. No one else will experience the world in exactly their way. Therefore, every birth is an inimitable gift and every death an irreplaceable loss. It is up to us to fulfil our unique potential, which we alone can realise. Abraham Joshua Heschel (1907–72) puts this in strikingly challenging terms:

> It is precisely because God *has* an image that idols are forbidden. *You* are the image of God. Every human being is God's image . . . You can't *make* God's image; you can only *be* God's image.[28]

These are the principles that drove me up the motorway that night. They must be affirmed not just in theology textbooks but also, urgently and repeatedly, in the public square.

God's questions

'And you?'

I remember with shame how, as we watched a programme about the remarkable work of Médecins sans Frontières, Doctors without Borders, my father looked at me and said quietly, 'And what about you? What will you do with your life?' My father died many years ago, but I still hear that 'What about you?'

When Rabbi Shneur Zalman of Liadi (1745–1812), the founder of Lubavitch Hasidism with its focus on intellect as well as soul, was imprisoned in St Petersburg, his gaoler, realising that the 'criminal' he was tasked with guarding was a man of deep faith, questioned him: 'Why did God ask Adam, "Where are you?" (Gen. 3:9) when God knew perfectly well where he was?' The rabbi answered:

God asks everyone 'Where are you? Where are you in the world? Where are you in your life?' To each person a specific number of days and years are allotted in which to do good to others before God. Therefore consider: Where are *you* in *your* world? How many years of your life have already gone by? What have you achieved in them?[29]

The rabbis were scathing about those who missed the point of God's questions: 'There are four on whose barrel God knocked and found it full of foul water: Adam, Cain, Balaam and Hezekiah' (Midrash Bereshit Rabbah 19:4). Winemakers can tell the quality of the contents by striking the side of the cask and listening to how it resonates. The four characters mentioned in this Midrash fail that test. They presume they're being asked for information, as if the all-knowing God lacks a few key facts. In missing the true import of the question, they betray their lack of awareness. God wants to know from Balaam why he's keeping company with men intent on hiring him to curse the Children of Israel. 'Who are these people with you?' is not a request for details, as Balaam assumes when he blithely answers, 'The King of Moav sent to me; go curse this people' (Num. 22:9–11).

Hezekiah makes a similar mistake when God asks him why he's showing off the Temple treasures to the ambassadors from Babylon, who are bound to mark it down as the perfect target for a future raid, as events subsequently prove (Isa. 39:1–7).

But neither of their failings is as grievous as Cain's when, in response to God's pointed inquiry, 'Where is Abel your brother?' he notoriously responds, 'Am I my brother's keeper?' (Gen. 4:9), creating the precedent of all precedents for the denial of responsibility.

But is the Midrash fair to Adam, who does, after all, give an honest reply? God's question to him consists of just one Hebrew word, '*Ayekhah?* Where are you?' (Gen. 3:9). Rashi explains it as 'an attempt to draw him into conversation':[30] maybe he'll admit that he's eaten the forbidden fruit. Adam's answer falls short of full disclosure but isn't an evasion or excuse. Later he will place the blame on 'that woman you gave me' (Gen. 3:12), but for now he's remarkably honest: 'I heard your voice in the garden and was afraid because I'm naked, so I hid (Gen. 3:10). Adam tries to conceal himself among the trees, literally '*inside* the tree of the garden' (Gen. 3:8).

Many of us spend much of our lives hiding in the thickets of our habits and routines, evading the 'Where are you?' which, whether or not we believe it comes from God, life aims ever more unerringly at us as we grow older. We try not to hear the question, and struggle to know how to answer. It's not surprising that Adam's instinct is to hide; it's our intuitive response to the awareness that we're naked, vulnerable and mortal.

It's brave of Adam to acknowledge that he's afraid; many of us lack the courage to admit it. When God calls, Adam doesn't pretend he hasn't heard; he doesn't retreat further into the depths of the garden in the hope of finding a better hiding place. He comes forward and answers.

The rabbis speculate about what species the tree of knowledge was; in Jewish tradition it wasn't an apple. Was it perhaps an etrog, the fragrant citrus fruit taken in thanksgiving alongside the palm-branch, myrtle and willow on Tabernacles?* Or some giant form of grain, since wheat proverbially brings knowledge? They conclude that it must have been the very fig tree from which Adam subsequently plucked leaves to conceal his nakedness: who else would offer refuge to a sinner when God was on the case, except the tree that shared the guilt?

The truth behind this seemingly trivial concern with nomenclature is that it's often precisely behind what we think will give us knowledge and power that we hide ourselves from our intrinsic nakedness. We answer the question 'Where are you?' by talking about our possessions and achievements, about whom and what we know. But sooner or later the question strikes home: 'Where are you in your life?'

Maybe we're unexpectedly diagnosed with a serious illness, a friend is killed in an accident or a parent dies whose protective presence we took for granted, imagining it would last for ever. We find ourselves on the front line, summoned from our hiding place, afraid of God, of destiny, of our very awareness that we are naked: 'Where are you in your life?' . . . 'What about you?'

That's how I now hear that question from my father. It was challenging at the time; at twenty-two years old I was uncertain what to do with my life, full of anxiety and prevarication. 'Come on,' my father was saying, 'come out of hiding, face yourself and the world; make a contribution.' But now his challenge resonates even more deeply. You've eaten from the tree of knowledge; you know you're naked and mortal. So where and who are you? Are you kind? Unkind? Truthful? Self-deceiving? Aware? Unaware?

Don't spend your life hiding from yourself among the trees in the garden.

---

* The rabbis understood the Torah's phrase 'Fruit of the goodly tree' (Lev. 23:40) to refer to the etrog, a tender citrus fruit looking a bit like a lemon but with subtler colouring and a tapering end. It has a wonderful fragrance. Great store is set by finding a beautiful specimen.

Cain and Abel

In the whole of world literature there are few responses more notorious than Cain's rejoinder: 'I don't know. Am I my brother's keeper?' He can't possibly not know where his brother is. The very ground he's standing on is at that very moment absorbing the blood that he himself has just shed. 'Where is Abel your brother?' ought not to be too difficult a question to answer.

But it's not just Cain who fails to provide an adequate response. Attention almost invariably focuses on the second half of his excuse, 'Am I my brother's keeper?' Of course he is! Yet the Midrash tries to explain his denial, crediting him with exactly the kind of inventive exculpations with which so many of us attempt to justify ourselves: 'You're blaming me! You made him, so it's your job to look after him!' 'I', that is the same 'I' who declared 'I am the Lord your God', is the One who's responsible for my brother, not me. And that 'I', God, is you (based on Midrash Tanhuma, Genesis 9:4)!

Wrapped into Cain's excuse is not only, 'God, it's your fault for not stopping me,' but also, 'You shouldn't have provoked me in the first place.' In this respect Cain deserves a modicum of understanding: God has displayed considerable bias. God's preference for Abel's gifts may be under-standable since he offered 'the firstborn of his flocks and their fats', although Cain preceded him in bringing a sacrifice (Gen. 4:3–4). But that doesn't explain why God prefers not only Abel's lambs, but also Abel himself, 'paying no regard' not only to Cain's produce but also to Cain as a person (Gen. 4:5). It's no wonder he feels aggrieved. Perhaps God does bear a portion of the responsibility.

But that can't account for the fact that it was Cain who did the deed. His denial makes him the prototype of all the liars who proclaim with blood-stained hands that they know nothing about the murder: 'Me? I saw nothing. I did nothing!'

This leads back to the first part of Cain's answer: '*Lo yadati*, I don't know,' or better, 'How should I know?' or maybe even, 'Why should I care?' The connection between the two halves of his response is crucial; all too often the denial of knowledge and the abdication of responsibility go together.

Allowances may have to be made. Perhaps it really is possible to have such a degree of moral and cognitive dissociation that one fails to recog-nise what one is doing even in the very thick of the action. In an extraor-dinary act of defiance at the Birkenau death camp on 23 October 1943, a Jewish prisoner seized a gun from the guards at the entrance to the gas chamber and fatally wounded Unterscharfuehrer Josef Schillinger. The latter's last words reputedly were, 'O God, what have I done to deserve such suffering?' History suggests that such extraordinary failures to understand our own actions are less infrequent than we would like to think.[31]

It seems obvious that the great antidote to dissociation is its opposite: connection. We should learn from Cain that the less we say 'I don't know', the more unlikely we are to deny responsibility. If ignorance is the prelude to contempt and murder, it should follow that the more people truly know and interact with each other the safer they ought to feel. Pluralism, encouraging people of different backgrounds to mix together, is partly based on this assumption. Rabbi Hugo Gryn, an Auschwitz survivor famous for his struggles against racism, reflected on the town of Berehovo where he grew up:

> While Jews and non-Jews depended on each other for many of the essentials in life, and we lived in the same society, we were not really part of the same community. There was hardly any visiting, sharing, or gossiping. I realize now that of Berehovo's three big and beautiful churches, I had never been inside any of them, and the chances are that none of the Christians ever set foot in any of our synagogues. And when the chips were down, I do not know of a single instance of a Jew [from Berehovo] being saved or hidden by a non-Jew.[32]

Though it's not the most positive reason for promoting cross-cultural cooperation, his conclusion that 'you can only be safe in a society that practises tolerance, cherishes harmony and can celebrate difference'[33] makes every sense.

But is it true? Cain did know Abel; throughout history many of those who turned on their fellow citizens knew them well. One has only to think of the massacres in Rwanda, or of how, under Nazism, though neighbours did sometimes help neighbours, it was frequently the people next door who gave Jews away. 'Knowing' is a fragile state. Under fire from hatred it easily collapses, as those who cynically incite racism understand all too well.

Mladen Vuksanović recorded how in his town of Pale, during the Bosnian war, Serbs and Croats, Christians and Muslims, who had lived together, sharing businesses and intermarrying for centuries, were driven apart in a mere matter of weeks:

Friday 3 July 1992

At dawn Dado and his family leave. I don't know whether I'll ever see him again. We've spent together our entire childhood, our youth and our adult lives. Now a sinister, criminal hand that knows no mercy severs us like wood for kindling. I learn that the Serb authorities have taken a decision that all Muslims must leave Pale and the surrounding villages by 5 July.

A convoy of buses stands for hours on the main road. Same scenes as yesterday. More people come to ask: 'Are there any Muslim houses around here?' My wife says to one fellow, raising her voice: 'No, there aren't! Neither Muslim nor Croat ones! There were only *human* houses here.'[34]

No doubt those who took possession of 'empty' houses found themselves almost instantly ignorant about their previous occupiers. Those few Jews who returned to their home towns after the Nazi Holocaust, in the usually vain hope of finding family members, almost always encountered hostility, while the people who had taken possession of their homes displayed a feigned ignorance that their owners had ever existed, betrayed only by the hatred they vented on the survivors for having failed to die and go away forever.

Cain both knows and doesn't know. The knowledge he hasn't attained lies in the deeper meaning of the word 'know' as used elsewhere in the Bible, such as when the Children of Israel cry out from their bondage and God 'knows' (Exod. 2:25). God's 'knowing' does not consist in the recognition of anything tangible, like a fact or an object, but in compassionate solidarity. In that regard, Cain's answer is correct; this kind of knowledge he does not possess.

NOACH (6:9–11:32)

Destruction

We humans are sleepwalking towards desolation. The impoverishment of the Earth's life is accelerating to such a pitch that in this very century,

within the lifetime of children now being born, unchecked population growth, destruction of tropical forests and the effects of climate
change on all wild habitats could send up to one half of all species now
living into extinction. It is . . . a crime for which our descendants will
hardly be able to forgive us.

Eleanor O'Hanlon[35]

In 1968 two important leaders made reference to the final scene in Moses'
life. On 3 April, Martin Luther King gave his last, prophetic speech in
Memphis, Tennessee: 'I just want to do God's will. And he's allowed me
to go up to the mountain. And I've looked over. And I've seen the
Promised Land. I may not get there with you. But . . . we, as a people, will
get to the promised land!'[36] The next day he was assassinated.

Later that same year, the environmentalist Wendell Berry wrote in very
different terms about that same scene:

I have been unable to escape the sense that I have been to the top of
the mountain, and that I have looked over and seen, not the promised
land vouchsafed to a chosen people, but a land of violence and sterility
prepared and set aside for the damned.[37]

The Bible offers a precedent for our own age of climate challenge and
threatening catastrophe: the story of Noah. As the clocks in Times Square
and other cities tick away the hours remaining for us to muster the collective will to act decisively to prevent environmental collapse, we can learn
much from the sins of Noah's generation. Though typically sparing with
words, the Torah provides sufficient indications of the nature of their
misdeeds, expanded in the imaginative world of Midrash, for uncomfortable comparisons.

Although separated by the span of ten generations, the narrative of the
flood is followed swiftly by the story of Babel. The 'generation of division', as rabbinic Judaism refers to the tower-builders, was set on making
a structure so tall that its top would reach heaven. Even now, thousands of
years later, the remains of the ancient ziggurats at Ur dominate the semi-
desert, nullifying the stature of everything else around them, exactly as the
architects of Babel intended. But in the process of creating this testament
to their might and skill, they forfeited their humanity. A midrash describes
how the architects wept whenever anyone dropped a brick but cared nothing when mere people fell to their deaths. Sadly, this is not a society we are
unable to recognise.

The generation of Babel feels like a repeat of the epoch of Noah when the world was 'filled with lawless violence . . . and all flesh had corrupted its ways on earth' (Gen. 6:11–12). This sparse indictment provides further opportunity for midrashic elaboration. People stole, but only amounts so insignificant they fell below the minimum threshold of what constituted a crime. Since they couldn't be prosecuted for theft and were seen to act with impunity, their behaviour became normalised: everyone did it. This was the 'unfair trade' of the ancient world, with its cutting of corners, meanness of spirit and ethos of exploitation. It can be seen as a precursor of today's multinational economy in which we take from the land but don't replenish its resources; buy produce in mass at the lowest achievable cost; pay farmers, pickers and transporters as little as possible and resell at as high a profit as the market will bear. As a result, the Midrash notes, 'all flesh had corrupted its *darco*, its *way*, upon the earth,' the ancient equivalent of a corrosive environmental footprint, a destructive and unsustainable relationship with the earth.

The flood is thus presented in the Bible not as a gratuitous act by an impetuous deity, as in its ancient near-eastern antecedents in which people are so noisy that the gods can't bear them and determine to wipe them out. The waters that 'blot out all existence' (Gen. 6:7) drown a civilisation already engaged in the process of self-destruction.

In the Torah, Noah silently follows God's commands without demur. But in the world of Midrash, he remonstrates with his unheeding contemporaries throughout the one hundred and twenty years it takes him to build the ark. They respond with mocking disbelief:

Noah the righteous rebuked them with sayings hot as burning torches. They reacted with contempt. They said to him:

'Old man, what's the point of that ark?'

He replied, 'God will bring upon you a great flood.'

They said, 'A flood of what? If it's a flood of fire, we have this thing called an *alita*; if it's a flood of water and comes up from the ground, we've got iron plates to cover it over. If it comes from the sky, we've a product called *ekev*. (Others say it was called *ekesh*.)

Noah told them: 'God will bring the flood from between your feet.'
(Talmud Sanhedrin 108b)

It matters little what exactly *alita*, *ekev* and *ekesh* are. Noah's contemporaries place their faith in their genius for technological innovation; they can't imagine that anything might exist beyond their power to control. Focusing on their own brilliance at problem-solving, they fail to consider how their lifestyles might be contributing to those troubles in the first place. Noah's warnings move them not to humility but to further pride. Their reaction is disturbingly familiar. Scientific innovation must be a significant part of the response to our current ecological challenge. But, as in the generations of Noah, the crisis in which we find ourselves is not just technological but also social, moral and spiritual.

The instruction to Noah to take two of every species into the ark may be understood as a reminder that humankind is not superior to and independent of, but interdependent with the rest of creation and able to survive only in respectful relationship with it. The ark represents a biome, a biosphere in miniature, albeit able to endure only briefly in its enclosed and isolated state. Noah's endless tasks on board, which Midrash describes as utterly exhausting from dawn till dusk, represent our ultimate responsibility for the wellbeing of all creation, not just ourselves. For the loss of even one single species is an irreparable disaster which God, even the seemingly punitive God who brings the flood, cannot bear to countenance.

A time to speak

Noah is not just a man of few words; for more than six hundred years he's a man of none at all. Until the flood has come and gone, its waters risen and abated, until the earth has become habitable once again and he's planted a vineyard and got drunk, he utters not one single syllable. When he does eventually open his mouth, what emerges is a curse.

Noah is, however, a doer. God orders him to build an ark; he does as God demands. God instructs him to take two of every unclean species of animal and seven of every clean; he does as God requires. When, after the waters have risen higher than the tallest mountains and blotted out the whole of creation, the ark finally lands and God tells him to open its doors, he does so without comment, exactly as commanded.

But is it always right to obey without question, to contemplate disaster without remonstration, when the lives of countless others are at stake?

Noah, according to the biblical account, never reasons why; unlike Abraham in Genesis 18, he never protests God's decree. 'Is every single human being really wicked?' he might have challenged. Is the entire human race at fault? If people have done wrong, do the birds and mammals also deserve to die? God, how can you turn so impetuously against your own creation, which you so recently described, day after day, as 'good'? Noah raises no such questions. The Torah does not indicate that he experiences so much as a single moment of hesitation. He does, without demur.

Jewish tradition blames him for this silence. He may indeed be a *tzaddik*, a righteous man, as the text acknowledges. But he is a *tzaddik im pelz*, 'a righteous man in furs', as the caustic Yiddish compliment pithily puts it. He may be good at heart, but if he wraps up his goodness in his own thick coat and keeps himself warm in snug isolation, of what value is his virtue? Such insulated sainthood is of little use to society; its impact on others is nil. 'Noah was a righteous, perfect man in his generations,' the Torah states (Gen. 6:9), explaining why he found favour with God. The Talmud takes up the issue: 'in *his* generations he was righteous, but in better times he'd have been nothing special'. Or is it the other way round: in such evil times it's an outstanding achievement to be righteous at all (Talmud Sanhedrin 108). What Noah is not, by either account, is committed to his contemporaries. 'The impact of Noah's silent acquiescence in the destruction of the world is devastating,' says Avivah Gottlieb Zornberg in her book of reflections on Genesis, *The Beginning of Desire*.[38] It represents, in French philosopher André Neher's damning phrase, 'unqualified apathy'.[39]

Yet, though Noah never speaks either before or during his year in the ark, there is a silent eloquence to one of his last actions before he opens its doors to reveal a devastated world. He's already released the raven, who doesn't return but overflies the earth until the floodwaters have abated. Now he takes the dove, a bird known for its faithfulness, and 'sends it away *from himself*' (Gen. 8:8). The verb is in the emphatic, causative form: '*vayeshalach* – he sent away'. Why, then, does the Torah add that Noah did so *mei'eilav*, 'from himself', when this has already been made clear? The inclusion of this apparently redundant word invites us to picture a man reluctant to part with the creature: we envisage him holding the dove in his hands, hesitating before releasing it over the still swirling water, then pushing his cupped hands out in front of him and carefully opening his fingers to feel its wings extend as the bird rises in flight.

When the dove returns in the evening, Noah 'sends forth his hand and takes her and brings her to himself into the ark' (Gen. 8:9). The text again adds the seemingly unnecessary words 'brings her to himself'. Noah, they suggest, cares tenderly about this bird. He is no longer a person indifferent to the rest of creation. Or was he perhaps always at heart a man who cared? Maybe it was rash to judge him so harshly beforehand? Maybe, rather than wasting his breath in futile remonstrance, he set about preserving whatever he could, two of every species, the entire gene pool of creation, saving his energy for action.

According to the Zohar, the thirteenth-century core body of Jewish mystical texts, when Noah finally opens the doors of the ark and sees the desolate landscape all about him, he weeps. God chides him, saying: 'Why didn't you weep earlier, before it was too late?'[40] The rebuke seems both hypocritical and cruel, since it was God, not Noah, who brought the flood in the first place. Or perhaps God is only projecting on to Noah the regret God also feels. For the same grounds God gave earlier for destroying all life, that 'the inclination of the human heart is evil from youth', are now presented as the very reason why God is determined never to do this again: 'I shall not persist in cursing the earth on account of humankind, since the inclination of the human heart is evil from its youth' (Gen. 6:5; 8:21). Has God, too, discovered a new tenderness towards creation?

As for Noah, the feelings that make him weep pursue him for the rest of the almost 350 years he's destined to survive after the flood. The Talmud notes that four people saw a new world. Among them is Job, whom God rewards following the destruction of his entire family and possessions with a new wife and children and even greater wealth than he had had before (Job 42:10–16), as if that could compensate him for the trauma brought down on him from heaven. Noah has it even harder. Although his family survives, where a mere year earlier there were forests, farmlands and villages, nothing presumably now remains except a desolation of mud, the uprooted carcasses of trees, the decomposing bodies of animals and the half-rotted wings of dead birds, the lucent glory gone from their broken feathers. He becomes 'a man of the land' (Gen. 9:20); maybe he wants to make peace with the earth which he, like God, has realised is not just good, but too good to be destroyed. Among his horticultural successes is his vineyard. It's not surprising that he gets drunk; perhaps he can't help but see in his nightmares the people, animals and landscapes as they once were, the dead still walking across the fields, the slivers of land he's laboured so hard to bring back into fragile cultivation. Maybe this is the only way to escape from the haunting questions: is there something I could and should have done? Is there something I failed to say or do?

Perhaps the Zohar is correct: Noah should have wept earlier. Or perhaps it's only after everything is over that he can allow himself to give way to tears. Maybe he cries now because his year in the ark has brought home to him how precious life is; he's learnt to love if not all, at least some, of the creatures for which he was delegated to care, which he had to feed, keep clean and, by day and by night, console in the unfamiliar ambience of a rolling ship. So, when faced with the departure of the gentlest of birds, he is anxious and hesitant, unwilling to entrust to the uncertainties of a new and unknown earth this creature he's come to love. When it returns, he reaches out and draws it in, holding it, perhaps, for a moment against his heart. If this is indeed so, he won't be the only human who learns to love rather late, who is left with the remorse of 'if only' as he stretches out his hands towards lives that are no longer there to entrust themselves to his care.

LECH LECHA – GO! (12:1–17:27)

Walking . . .

'Go', says God to Abram, '*Lech lecha*; get you gone from your land, your mother country and your father's house to the land which I will show you' (Gen. 12:1). With these words, the spiritual journey of every individual and the collective journey of the Jewish people, perhaps of every people, commences. They're heard at life's beginning, when, according to the Kabbalists, the soul parts reluctantly from God and descends into the body. They sing in the wind that carries us ineluctably over life's ocean like the skiff in the 'Skye Boat Song': 'Onward, the sailors cry.' Those who love us will say them quietly after we die: 'He's gone.' They're the unspoken hope that somehow life's journey continues, in realms unknowable from earth. That's why *Lech lecha* resonates so deeply, why I tremble when we read these words in the Torah.

I used to be drawn to the mystics who, with typical licence, read *lecha* not simply as an emphatic particle, 'Get *thee* gone', but as '*to* you': go *to yourself*; make life a journey of ever deeper self-discovery until you reach the wellspring of your spirit. As Rebbe David of Lilov (1745–1814) taught: 'You must travel until you arrive at the roots of your own soul, of – *you*.'[41] His reading is supported by the final words in the verse which, translated literally, mean not 'the land which I will show you' but 'the land where I will show you *you*'. Rabbi Shneur Zalman of Liadi expresses this most clearly: 'Go . . . to the land which I will show *you*, to the place where I'll reveal to you your own true self'.[42]

It's a journey that never takes less than a lifetime and, though we may

28

walk countless miles, it invariably leads us to the one thing we cannot leave behind however far we go: our innermost self. It's the story of the Jew from the hamlet in Eastern Europe who dreams of a treasure buried beneath the Karlov Bridge in Prague. After walking for many days, he arrives and furtively starts to dig in the darkness. But the watchman sees him and demands to know what he's doing. When the Jew tells him, the man bursts out laughing and retorts, 'I too had a ridiculous dream – that underneath the stove in the hovel of a miserable Jew in some God-forsaken village there was buried a heap of gold.'

Why, then, do so many of us go so far to seek what is so near? It's not just the fantasy that the grass is always greener on the other side of the fence. It's because certain kinds of truth have no meaning unless we discover them for ourselves. Love, wonder, wisdom, heartache: other people's words can never enable us to know them. Only our own journey can bring us to the doors of our inner selves; only life itself can instruct our heart. The journey both takes us and makes us into who we are.

However, as I grow older, I'm increasingly compelled by a more basic explanation. It too is a play on words, though not one I've encountered in the classic commentaries. *Lech lecha* instructs us to 'go to you', to *the you*, to the other person we encounter in every interaction. Life is a voyage not just towards our own inner self but also to other people: who we are is what we mean to them, and they to us. We are not fulfilled solely by and for ourselves, as Rebbe Elimelech of Grodzisk (1823–92) insisted in a very different interpretation from his Hasidic colleagues: 'Distance yourself from your own self; your purpose in life should not be yourself.'[43]

Life's goal is not self-fulfilment, but service. When the Torah teaches us to 'serve the Lord your God with all your heart' (Deut. 11:13), it means not simply devotion in prayer, but a life engaged with community and dedicated to justice and kindness. I cannot give an account of myself before God without reference to how I treat my parents, siblings, partner, children, friends, neighbours, the poor, refugees and those who are ill – as in the first century BCE sage Hillel's much-quoted maxim, 'If I am not for myself, who am I? But if I am only for myself, what am I?' It is not I, but others, who will give the true account of my life.[44] Our life's journey is summed up in *lecha*, 'to you', in what we contribute for good or bad to each and every 'you' we encounter, from the cashier at the till and the homeless person in the street to our closest friends and family.

I've been to cemeteries too often over the years. I look across the field of graves and the questions rise from the very earth: 'To what does it all add up? What's the point?'

'Go to you,' is the best answer I know. What remains of us on earth after we die, apart from our decaying bodies, is what we leave in other people's hearts and minds. I'll always remember the words I once heard a grieving wife say at the stone-setting for her husband: 'Your place was in my arms; now it's in my heart.' Our true homes, the lands we reach on our journey, lie in each other's hearts.

But how far does that 'go to' reach? I once received a letter asking me to write a commentary about an accompanying photograph; it was a picture of an elderly doctor carefully examining a refugee – caring for someone whom our society often ignores. 'Go – to the *you* of others who need you,' is God's most urgent command. There are countless voices in the world crying out, 'Is anyone there? Will you go – to me?'

Yet the interpretations of Rebbes David of Lilov and Elimelech of Grodzisk are not wrong; we do and must seek self-realisation and fulfilment. But we won't attain it by making it our chief goal. The secret of happiness is not to pursue it as if it were an end in itself, but to serve and care for others, be they people, nature, God or all of them together. In finding the 'you' towards whom we travel, we also find our best and deepest 'me'. Our journey inwards and our journey outwards may ultimately be the same.

How Abraham hears God

Why, of all possible people in the ten generations that separate him from Noah, is it Abraham to whom God chooses to speak? The Torah offers no reason. It doesn't inform us at the outset, as it did with Noah, that Abraham was righteous or walked with God. At this juncture the text ascribes no virtues to him whatsoever. We are not told how he is in any way different from his ancestors or contemporaries.

Rebbe Yehudah Aryeh Leib Alter of Ger (1847–1905) suggests the simplest of reasons: God didn't speak only to Abraham; God speaks to everyone. The difference is that Abraham listened. He heard God's voice and faithfully followed it to an unknown destiny in an unfamiliar land. Rebbe Yehudah Aryeh Leib explains God's instruction to the entire people in a similar way: the Torah says '*im* shemo'a tishme'u *el mitzvotai*, if you listen, really listen, to my commandments' (Deut. 11:13). The verb is doubled in the emphatic form known as the infinitive absolute, but he interprets each half of it separately: 'If you listen, you shall surely hear.' God speaks all the time; the problem is that humanity is insufficiently attentive. God calls out to all of us in that 'voice of fine silence' which Elijah intuited on God's mountain (1 Kgs 19:12). Abraham heard and followed.

What enabled him to hear? The rabbis exploit the Torah's silence, filling the gaps in the narrative with legends. According to one of the most popular, Abraham's father Terach was a manufacturer of idols. One day when his father was out and Abraham was left to serve the customers, he smashed all the idols, leaving the hammer in the hands of the largest. When his father returned, he furiously demanded to know what had happened. 'A fight broke out among them,' Abraham explained. 'They attacked and destroyed each other until only the biggest was left.'

'They're just lumps of clay,' his father retorted.

'Can't your ears hear what your own mouth has just said?' Abraham replied.

Twelfth-century philosopher Maimonides offers a more refined version, yet based on a similar logic. From the age of three, Abraham began to ask questions about the true cause of all phenomena. His mind gradually travelled from one possible answer to another, ascending from smaller causes to greater, until it became clear to him that there must exist an ultimate cause, which caused all other causes without itself requiring any prior cause: an unmoved mover, God.[45]

A contrasting legend describes Abraham's discovery of God in more intuitive terms, imagining him on a journey, perhaps from Ur to Haran:

> It's like a man travelling from place to place who saw a building on fire. He said: 'Should it be concluded that this building has no owner?' The owner glanced down at him and said, 'I am the owner of this building'. Similarly, Abraham asked himself: 'Do you suppose the world has no owner?' God glanced down at him and said, 'I am the owner of the world.'
>
> (Midrash Bereshit Rabbah 39:1)

'Glanced' suggests a moment of revelation. The same Hebrew word *hetzitz* appears in the Song of Songs to describe the deer that 'stands behind our wall, looks in through the window, *glances* through the lattice', before running swiftly back to the safety of the hills (Song 2:9). It suggests something momentary and fleeting. The Talmud uses the word to refer to the elusive perception of God, the brief, half-seeing, half-not-seeing awareness of God's presence. In the parable, Abraham has a sudden, intense experience of the living God.

But why is God inside the burning building? Why doesn't God escape? If it was a person, one would shout at them to get out. What's the use of remaining inside, calling to random passers-by that the burning structure belongs to you, especially when you're God and can presumably pass unharmed through the hottest of flames?

Yet maybe that's the point. Abraham sees a world on fire with violence and brutality. The God he encounters is not distant and apart, remote and indifferent in the safety of the heavenly heights. The God he hears is a God in need, a God calling out for help.

Over the centuries, the Midrash accrued commentaries and commentaries to commentaries. One such super-commentary, pseud-epigraphically attributed to Rashi, explains:

> Abraham saw the heavens and the earth, the sun shining by day and the moon and stars by night. He said, 'Is it possible that there should be something as great as this without a ruler?' The Holy Blessed One looked out at him and said: 'I am the master of the world.'

It's hard to avoid the conclusion that the author of this comment, which reads like a simplified version of the argument from design, has missed the point. The building is not in a state of architectural perfection, but on fire, at imminent risk of destruction.

The brief observation by Rabbi David Luria (1798–1855) seems more pertinent: 'The wicked devour the world by fire. When Abraham saw this, he pondered in his heart, thinking: "Maybe there is no ruler."'[46] It's a sharp rejoinder to naive believers, blind to the cruel realities of this world.

Rabbi Ze'ev Einhorn (d. 1862) offers a subtler explanation. The world in its glory testifies to God. But seeing it consumed by the fires of human wickedness, Abraham is confused and wonders if God has abandoned it to its fate. God therefore 'glances out' and tells him that the destruction is intentional. God punishes evil, yet still desires the worship of the righteous.

What I sense in the parable is a God who calls out in anguish from the midst of creation, who cares passionately, yet who is vulnerable, caught in the thick of the flames, in need of help. Others simply pass by unheeding, or they notice the burning building but fail to hear the voice crying out. Abraham hears and heeds.

The God of Abraham calls out to us still, in millions of human beings sick or starving with no help at hand, in the birds and animals on the edge of extinction. This God is not an all-powerful, infinitely benevolent wonderworker, ready and able to intervene with unlimited capacity in the affairs of humankind. This is a God who says: 'The world that is on fire is both my world and yours. I am present in every person, I live in every living being, and I desperately need your help.'

Be a blessing

A boy sets out to find his path through life but doesn't know in which direction to go. After a while, he meets an old man and there is something about his presence that fills the boy with trust.

'I've come from your home,' the old man tells him.

The boy looks at him in surprise. 'You know my house?'

The old man nods. 'I know your parents, and your parents' parents too.'

They look at each other in silence for a long time, until eventually the boy recognises him. 'You are Abraham,' he says eagerly. Then his questions begin: 'So how did you find your path?'

The old man smiles but doesn't answer.

'Was it the promise of the land?'

The old man shakes his head.

'Was it the promise of children as many as the stars in the sky?'

Again the old man shakes his head.

The boy is perplexed. 'So how did you find your way?'

'It wasn't the land or the children. It was because I was told, "Through you all the families of the earth will be blessed." I understood then that a great responsibility had been placed on my shoulders. That was what helped me find my way.

'Through *you*,' the old man says again, and disappears.

This is the essence of a short story written by Lore, my mother. She called it 'The Pathfinder'. One of my few memories of her is how she sat by my bed once when I was ill, correcting the proofs of the slim book of tales that was published, sadly, posthumously. I was five when she died, but she left us her stories. 'Through *you*, the old man said again, looking at the boy, and disappeared.'

This is her legacy, and the legacy of Abraham to the Jewish People and the world: what directs our path through life is the responsibility of trying to be a blessing.

'I will bless you and make your name great; and you shall be a blessing,' says the Torah (Gen. 12:2). Why, asks Rabbi Berachiah, when God has already said, 'I shall bless you,' does the text need to add, 'And be a blessing'?

> God said to Abram: 'Until now it was up to me to bless my world. From now on blessings are in your hands. Bless whoever you see fit to be blessed.'
>
> (Midrash Bereshit Rabbah 39:11)

It's important to receive blessing, but even more important to be a blessing. The former is a privilege; the latter a task that can determine the course of our life. Or maybe they are connected: our capacity to bless depends on our ability to experience and transform what we receive from life into blessings.

There are many kinds of blessing. The Torah includes lists of practical, tangible blessings: 'Blessed be the fruit of your womb and the fruit of the land. Blessed be your oven and your kneading bowl. Blessed be your going out and your coming home' (Deut. 28:4–6).

But blessing another person is different. It may include material gifts, but that is not its essence. Blessing someone is about noticing and fostering the goodness they already have within them, even if they aren't aware of it themselves. In the moving words of Rachel Remen, a doctor working with patients close to the end of their lives and with those caring for them:

> When we recognise the spark of God in others, we blow on it with our attention and strengthen it, no matter how deeply it has been buried or for how long. When we bless someone, we touch the unborn goodness in them and wish it well. Everything unborn in us and in the world needs blessing.[47]

That's why parents and teachers have so much power to bless; good teachers perceive a child's gifts, their eagerness and creativity. They understand how to put their hands around that flame and nurture it, just as the sunlight warms the earth so that the seeds in its soil can grow.

Blessings often touch us at the most ordinary moments. A greeting in the street, a kind word in a queue, and we are drawn from dull impatience into our better selves. Anyone can bless, and we do it sometimes without even knowing it. Nothing is needed except our humanity, and the awareness of the humanity of others. Remen continues:

> When we bless others, we offer them refuge from an indifferent world. The capacity to bless life is in everybody. The power of our blessing is

not diminished by illness or age. On the contrary, our blessings become even more powerful as we grow older. They have survived the buffeting of our experience.[48]

Maybe that's why we almost always picture the older blessing the younger, as in Rembrandt's painting of Jacob blessing Joseph's children, where the light in the darkened room falls across the patriarch's face, over his white garments, down to his hands and onto the two young boys. I remember vividly the blessings of my elders, my grandfather, my father and my teachers. They still bless me in my memory; I feel their hands on my head. I carry their blessings in my heart, mostly as encouragement yet sometimes as reprimand: be the person I blessed you to be.

But the young also bless their elders. Children make us see the world anew; they rejuvenate our jaded 'I've seen all that before'. 'Look,' they say, running with outstretched arms. 'Look! This flower! That tree!' Wonder is itself a form of blessing that expands the soul, and children restore it to us. They can't bring back our childhood, but they can resurrect our inner child; middle age and old age have few greater blessings than that.

'I will bless those who bless you,' says God to Abraham, indicating the mutuality of blessing. Perhaps it's wrong to think of blessings as one person's gift to another, old to young or young to old. Blessings connect us, enabling us to strengthen the best within each other. As Rachel Remen reminds us:

Blessing life moves us closer to each other and closer to our authentic selves. When people are blessed, they discover that their lives matter, that there is something in them worthy of blessing. And when you bless others, you may discover this same thing is true about yourself.[49]

VAYERA - AND HE APPEARED (18:1-22:24)

The sin of Sodom

The divine, as exile, is in each human other who faces us, defenceless and vulnerable, asking to be received into our midst . . . My hospitable relationship with the stranger, in sum, gives meaning to my relations with all strangers, proximate or distant, human or divine.

Richard Kearney[50]

From the very first mention of the place, the Torah tells us that the people of Sodom are 'great sinners before God'. But it doesn't explain what their sin is (Gen. 13:13). The rabbis, reading the Bible intertextually, turned to a verse from Ezekiel: 'Behold, this was the iniquity of Sodom your sister: she and her daughters had the pride of plentiful bread, peace and tranquility, but she didn't strengthen the hand of the poor and needy' (Ezek. 16:49). They understood Job, too, to be referring to Sodom when he spoke of 'a land out of which comes bread . . . a place whose stones are sapphires, and which has dust of gold' (Job 28:5–6).

From these verses, the Talmud creates a backstory behind God's decision to 'go down and see' if the people of Sodom and Gomorrah 'have done like the cry coming up to me from *her*' (Gen. 18:20–21). The pronoun clearly refers to Sodom, since most cities are feminine in the Bible, but the Talmud understands it differently:

> There was a young woman who used to take bread to the poor in a pitcher [so that the citizens of Sodom wouldn't notice]. This came to the attention [of the city's judges, who had passed a law refusing entry to outsiders and forbidding anyone to offer assistance to strangers on pain of death]. They smeared the girl with honey and left her on the city wall, where hornets ate her alive.
>
> (Talmud Sanhedrin 107b)

The Talmud identifies the girl as Plotit, a daughter of Abraham's nephew, Lot. It is 'her' cry to which it understands God to be referring.

The Talmud elaborates further on the cruel laws of the city:

> When a poor person came to Sodom, everyone would give them a dinar with their name written on it. But they wouldn't sell them any bread. When they died of hunger, they would all come and take back their coins.
>
> (Talmud Sanhedrin 107b)

There's evidently nothing new about cities replete with wealth in which the hungry sleep in the streets. Nor is there anything novel about rich countries trying to prevent the poor from entering their borders or threatening with sanctions anyone who might assist them. According to the Talmud, the judges of Sodom decreed that anyone crossing into their territory by ferry had to pay four dinars, while anybody who swam the river had to give double:

Once a certain launderer arrived there. The people of Sodom told him to pay four dinars for the ferry. He said: 'I swam across.' 'Then it's eight dinars.' He refused to pay, so they beat him black and blue. When he came before the judge to seek compensation, he said: 'Pay your assailants a fee, as they treated you with bloodletting, as well as the eight dinars for swimming across the river.'

(Talmud Sanhedrin 107b)

'Fortress Europe' is not a new phenomenon, and frontiers like the Rio Grande have been patrolled for many decades. Some years ago, I stood on the Greek island of Lesbos, looking across the sea to Turkey, from where thousands of refugees were daring to undertake the perilous crossing in fragile dinghies. It was an unusually quiet day, with scarcely any boats arriving, so I wandered down to the beach where I picked up an orange life jacket. A woman from one of the many charities rescuing people from the water took it and tore open the lining: 'Look! This material is absorbent. It'll fill up with water in no time. It's not a life jacket but a death jacket!'

The story of Sodom contrasts sharply with the welcome Abraham and Sarah offer to strangers:

He looked up and saw: there were three men standing before him. He ran towards them from the entrance of his tent, bowed down to the ground and said: 'Please, if I have found favour in your eyes, do not pass your servant by.'

(Gen. 18:2–3)

To this day, Abraham and Sarah are regarded as the model of *hachnasat orchim*, the mitzvah of welcoming wayfarers and guests, and their tent is taken as the prototype of every open and generous home.

In a disturbing analysis of the theology of welcome, Richard Kearney notes that host and hostile, guest and enemy, both derive from the same Latin word, *hostis*. The implication is that we have a choice: we can see strangers as enemies or we can welcome them as guests. Hebrew, too, offers an intriguing duality: *nachri*, 'foreign', and *hakir*, 'recognise', come from the same root letters *nun*, *chaph*, *reish*. The latter, *hakir*, indicates acknowledgement of the humanity of the other, as when Ruth the Moabite, an outsider in the land of Israel, thanks Boaz for 'recognising' her and allowing her to glean in his fields despite her being a 'foreigner' (Ruth 2:10).

37

Is the 'other' we encounter enemy or guest? Twentieth-century French philosopher Emmanuel Levinas suggests that how we make the choice is the essence of religion: 'to follow the Most High is to know, also, that nothing is of greater importance than the approach made towards one's neighbour . . . My very uniqueness lies in my responsibility for the other.'[51]

The Mishnah notes that people have one of four attitudes to money. The wicked person says, 'What's mine is mine and what's yours is also mine.' The righteous person says, 'What's yours is yours and what's mine is yours too.' The person who says, 'What's yours is mine and what's mine is yours,' is considered a fool. But most interesting is the Mishnah's definition of the average person, who says, 'What's mine is mine and what's yours is yours.' At first hearing this sounds reasonable enough; society depends on respecting other people's possessions. But the Mishnah adds a rider: 'Some say this is the way of Sodom.'[52] A city in which we refuse to share, where the rich consider themselves entitled to their wealth while the poor deserve what they get and where there's no commitment to social responsibility and generosity, is devoid of conscience, merciless and cruel. It lacks moral imagination and is truly wicked.

Challenging God

'I don't like the word "bystander",' a Holocaust scholar told me. 'The fact is we're all bystanders; we can't help it. The question is: are we passive or active standers-by?'

Abraham is definitely an active bystander. He refuses to stay silent when he learns of God's plans to destroy Sodom, even though he's well aware of its evil reputation. He challenges God in the name of the very justice God purportedly upholds: '*Chalila lecha*, this profanes you' he accuses God. 'Shall the judge of all the earth not do justice?' (Gen. 18:25). *Chalal* means 'void'; if you behave like that, God, it'll void your reputation of meaning.

So he bargains: 'If there are fifty righteous people in the city, will you still destroy it and not spare the place for the sake of the fifty righteous people within it? (Gen. 18:24). Under pressure, God concedes, and continues to yield as Abraham progressively argues the numbers down from fifty to ten. Yet Abraham and God retain something in common: they both stress how these few good people must be 'within the city'. Since it's perfectly clear that they live in Sodom, the words must indicate something more than mere geography. Abraham ibn Ezra explains:

'"*Within the city*" means that they show their fear of Heaven openly.'[53] Israeli Bible scholar Nehama Leibowitz develops his point:

> The few can turn the scales and save the place if the righteous individuals are 'within the city', playing a prominent part in public life and exerting their influence in its many fields of activity. But if they merely exist, living in retirement and never venturing forth but pursuing their pious conduct unseen and unknown, they will, perhaps, save themselves, but will certainly not possess the spiritual merit capable of protecting the city.[54]

Yiddish has a phrase for good people who refuse to get involved, like Noah in his silence: *tzaddik im pelz*, a righteous person in a fur coat. Such individuals keep themselves to themselves and do little for anyone else. Society is not changed by types like that. It would be unfair to call them indifferent; in the safety of their homes they no doubt condemn the ills of the world and even try to avoid participating in them. But they don't speak out; in public they remain silent. They fail to live up to Abraham Joshua Heschel's definition of a religious person, one who is:

> . . . maladjusted; attuned to the agony of others; aware of God's presence and of God's needs; a religious person is never satisfied, but always questioning, striving for something deeper, and always refusing to accept inequalities, the status quo, the cruelty and suffering of others.[55]

Heschel lived by his creed: he stood shoulder to shoulder with Martin Luther King in the Civil Rights movement though the 1960s and spoke out with him against the Vietnam War. Describing what changed him from a contemplative scholar into an impassioned activist, he wrote:

> Indifference to evil is worse than evil itself. Even the high worth of reflection in the cultivation of inner truth cannot justify remaining calm in the face of cruelties that make the hope of effectiveness of pure intellectual endeavours seem grotesque.[56]

Abraham's intervention in the fate of Sodom proved to be in vain. Unable to find even ten righteous individuals within it, God destroyed the city. The following morning Abraham watched the smoke rise from its ruins.

Yet Abraham didn't entirely fail. At the end of their argument, the

Torah notes, strangely, that 'God went away' but Abraham 'returned to his place'. It's as if God is forced out of the ring while Abraham goes back victorious to his corner. He can't save Sodom, but he does his best to hold God to account. According to rabbinic tradition, this is exactly what God wants from him, and needs from us. God instructs Abraham not just to 'walk *with* me' but to 'walk *before* me' (Gen. 17:1). I made him my delegate in the world, a midrash has God say, precisely so that I should do nothing without his consent, suggesting that his role was to command not just 'his family and household' but even God 'to practise righteousness and justice' (Gen. 18:19; Bereshit Rabbah 39:2). Abraham, a further midrash explains, is like a servant whom, whenever they enter a dark alley, the king orders to walk in front and light the way.

In the ensuing centuries, whole communities and their rabbis and poets frequently called upon heaven to bring down judgement upon the heads of corrupt and cruel powers, including at times their own leaders. They understood that the responsibility for engaging, even when the smoke was rising from the ruins, lay not just with God but also with us here on earth.

Abraham is *Avinu*, our father, the father of the Jewish People, not just because of genealogy, but also because he had the courage to speak out, even on behalf of a city he had little reason to favour. He is *Avram ha'Ivri*, Abram the *Hebrew*, literally 'the one on the other side', the one who is prepared to take issue, even when 'all the world is on this side and he on the other' (Bereshit Rabbah 42:8).

As the Torah subsequently commands, none of us is at liberty to stand idly by the blood of our neighbour (Lev. 19:16). We are required to involve ourselves in the concerns of our society; God's reputation as just and compassionate depends on how we behave in God's name. Even if we believed in an omnipotent God ready to intercede in human affairs, we would still be obligated to take action. But if, as in the account of the argument with Abraham over Sodom, God 'goes away' and does not, to all appearances, engage directly in the affairs of this world, then everything depends on us. Therefore, it is all the more imperative that we do as Timothy Snyder, writing about times of dangerously spreading populism and bigotry, insists:

> Take responsibility for the face of the world: Life is political, not because the world cares about how you feel, but because the world reacts to what you do . . . In the politics of the everyday, our words and gestures, or their absence, count very much.
>
> Stand out. Someone has to.[57]

The binding of Isaac

The short, terse narrative of the *Akedah*, the binding of Isaac (Gen. 22), has a long and painful history in Judaism.

The story is hauntingly troubling. We watch Abraham take his servants, the wood for the sacrifice and his son. Later we learn that he has also brought the knife. Three days pass in silence, then a short dialogue interrupts the narrative, punctuated by the repeated words 'my father' and 'my son', before Abraham 'sees the place from far off' (Gen. 22:4). He builds the altar, lays the kindling, binds his son, lies him on top of the wood, 'sends forth his hand, and takes the knife to slaughter his child' (Gen. 22:10). Only then does heaven speak. There is no indication that without this intervention Abraham would of his own accord have refused to do the deed.

It's possible there was an ancient story, long lost, in the literature of the cities of Akkad or Ugarit in which the hero proceeded to kill his son at his god's command. The biblical narrative could then be understood as delivering precisely the opposite message: contrary to what listeners familiar with similar legends might anticipate, this god, the God of creation and life, detests human sacrifice, especially the slaughter of children. This abhorrence is repeatedly made explicit later in the Bible. Abraham doesn't say no to God when God commands him to offer up his child, so that God can say 'No!' to Abraham and to all humankind ever after.

That may indeed be the purpose of the narrative. But it doesn't account for its impact in the history of Judaism. Century after century, under one power after another and in many countries of exile, Jews were killed because of their faith, and heaven did not intervene. Perhaps that is why the story became known as *Akedat Yitzhak*, the binding of *Isaac*, although the Torah uses no such phrase but presents the episode as the trial of Abraham. The victim lies bound upon the altar, helpless before the might of Rome, the Crusaders, the Inquisition, the Cossacks and the Nazis. The power of the *Akedah*, 'the binding', lies not in its being a factual record of what transpired between the forefathers, which may or may not have been the case, but in that it was, and remains, meta-history. The *Akedah* frames, articulates and gives meaning to generation after generation of tragic Jewish experience.

It was almost certainly Roman oppression in the first and second centuries that brought the *Akedah* to the heart of the liturgy of Rosh Hashanah, the New Year. The destruction of Jerusalem in 70 CE was followed by the Hadrianic persecutions with their ban, on pain of torture and death, on the public teaching and practice of Judaism, leading to the Bar Kochba revolt which was ruthlessly crushed in 135 CE.

The connection between the *Akedah* and the Rosh Hashanah service is threefold. First, it forms the Torah reading on the festival. Second, the New Year is described as 'a day of blowing the horn' (Num. 29:1), which rabbinic tradition understands to refer to the shofar, the hollowed-out horn of an animal. The Talmud specifies that this should be a ram's horn 'in memory of the binding of Isaac', when Abraham replaced his son with a ram (Rosh Hashanah 16a). The shofar's raw cry, piercing the silence in which the entire community listens, reverberates across the history of sacrifice. Third, when at the centre of the liturgy we affirm the covenant between God and the Jewish People, we ask God 'to recall in mercy the binding of Isaac' and remember how Abraham 'overcame his feelings for his child in order to perform Your will with a perfect heart'. It's as if we're saying to God: 'Consider what the Jewish People have gone through for your sake and, in return, keep faith with us.'

But it was during the Crusades, especially the First Crusade in 1096, that the *Akedah* became the reference point for recording the terrors the Jews of the Rhineland were forced to face. En route to Jerusalem to drive out the so-called infidels, the Crusaders encountered the thriving Jewish congregations of Worms, Speyer, Mainz and Cologne. By the end of the eleventh century these were well-established centres of Jewish life and teaching. The communities, which received little warning of the disaster about to engulf them and at best generally ineffective protection from the crown or local bishop, were besieged, offered the brutal choice between violent death or forced conversion, and slaughtered anyway.

The literature from these years, recorded in *Sefer Hadema'ot*, The Book of Tears, in frank prose and vivid, terrifying poetry, reads like accounts of the Einsatzgruppen from the Eastern Front in 1941. Faced by violence and enforced apostasy, parents chose to die alongside their children, preparing the knife for the sacrifice, blessing God's name and slaughtering their sons and daughters before killing themselves for the sanctification of the name of heaven. An anonymous fragment reads of how:

> In afore times, when Abraham was ready and willing to bind up his
> son,
> A voice came from heaven: 'Withhold your hand from slaughter!'
> But now, how many sons and daughters are slaughtered in Judah
> And no one hastens to save those slain by the sword or burnt on the
> pyre.[58]

Mainz was an influential capital of rabbinic learning. In a play on its Hebrew name, *Magenza*, it was known as *Magen veTsinah*, Shield and Shelter of Jewish life. Its Jewish community was utterly destroyed in the First Crusade. Its new synagogue, consecrated in 2010, captures in its architecture the pain of its history. On the walls and above the ark, sentences from the Song of Songs, understood as an allegorical love poem between God and Israel, are interspersed with lines from the meditation attributed to Rabbi Amnon who, according to legend, composed it under torture in the same city: 'Who shall live, and who shall die? Who by fire . . . and who by the sword?'

A century later, in 1190, the Jews of York suffered a similar fate to the Rhineland congregations. Besieged in Clifford's Tower, all those who had not killed themselves were slaughtered as they emerged.

In one of his final compositions, 'You Want It Darker', Leonard Cohen takes as his refrain Abraham's reply to God, *'Hinenni'*, and trans-lates it into a response not just to Jewish history, but to the whole of human destiny. He opens with the words of the Kaddish, the meditation recited by individual mourners after a bereavement, as well as by the whole community in times of collected grief: 'Magnified and sanctified be your great name'. But instead of continuing, like the Kaddish, with God's praises, he sees a desecrated God, tortured and destroyed by human treachery. Innumerable candles burn like souls crying out in vain for help. Yet instead of nurturing these flames of life and hope, we put them out. And yet we say to God *'Hinenni'*: here I am. But for what is it that we are ready? The helplessness of human fate? The hopelessness of trying to do what's right? The recognition that we have no other option but to walk willingly toward a destiny which we can neither chose nor have the capacity to avoid?

Hinneni – I am here

For whom are we present? And for whom, just when they may need us most, are we absent? A friend recently described her late father as the embodiment of *hinneni*, 'here am I'; he had always been there for her and for many more besides. He'd personified responsibility to others, especially his nearest and dearest; they owed it to his memory to live with as much presence and sensitivity as they could. That's the kind of human being most of us would probably like to be, but our relationships are often more ambiguous than that.

Abraham says *hinneni* three times in the narrative of the *Akedah*. But are they all equally sincere? The first is the most famous: 'It came to pass after these matters that God tested Abraham; God said to him, "Abraham," and he said, "Here am I"' (Gen. 22:1).

Abraham obeys God's command to offer up his son without demur. Leonard Cohen's translation of his one-word response is apt: 'I'm ready, Lord.' He rises early and, despite an entire entourage of servants, saddles his own donkey, which Rashi interprets as an act of special dedication.

Hinneni expresses our immediate personal response to life's call. It's a concatenation of two basic words, *hinneh*, generally translated as 'behold', and *ani*, 'I'. One might have imagined that they would add up to something like, 'Look, this is me,' a biblical version of, 'I do things my way and couldn't care less what other people think.' But the opposite is the case. As Rashi explains, *hinneni* is 'an expression of humility and readiness'.[59] It means, 'I'm there for you,' whether that 'you' is God, one's partner, one's child or life itself.

Ani, 'I', has been reduced to a suffix, a '*ni*' at the end of *hinneh*, embodying in language how the 'I' of the ego has become the 'I' of awareness and service: I'm present, alert to life's *hinneh*, its call to attention, its 'open your heart and be here'. It's the *hinneni* of the birdwatcher: quiet, alert, not wanting to frighten away the tiny, feathered maker of that music. It's the *hinneni* of the carer, watching the pained movements and pre-empting the needs of her companion. It's a word I write about with a disturbing consciousness of inadequacy. I know I've failed as much or more than I've succeeded in my own life's *hinneni*. I've been there for others, that's true. But I've also often not been there, at least not fully, and at times not at all. Sometimes I've deserved the classic rebuke, 'Where were you when I needed you?' Sometimes I've said the right thing but my mind was elsewhere.

There's no doubt about the sincerity of Abraham's response when God calls him; he takes Isaac exactly as instructed and walks with him to the place for the sacrifice. There's nothing ambiguous, either, about his reaction when, knife in hand, at the critical moment he hears the angel cry out, 'Abraham! Abraham!' commanding him to stay his hand. *Hinneni*, he says, and does as instructed (Gen. 22:11).

It's the *hinneni* in between that is troubling: 'Isaac said to Abraham his father: he said, "My father," and he said, "*Hinneni*, here am I, my son"' (Gen. 22:7). 'Father' comes twice and 'son' once in this simple verse, although we know perfectly well who Abraham and Isaac are to each other. The words poignantly frame the relationship between parent and child, which, with its inherent imbalance of power, demands more than any other that we honour the trust implicit within it. How, then, can Abraham have spoken that impossible *hinneni*? Was he merely mouthing the syllables as he walked beside his son, his head and heart elsewhere with his God? More likely he was half present, caught by the pull of conflicting allegiances, torn between his child and his faith. He no doubt meant to be fully present for his son; probably he thought he even was.

But what must that *hinneni* have felt like to Isaac, at the time and in retrospect? 'You told me you were here for me, but you weren't. You were there for something else.' The rest of his life is shadowed by the experience. It's not surprising that when, decades later, his eyes 'dim from seeing', he hears his own son say that same word 'father' and responds with the same *hinneni*, he mistakes whom he's really with (Gen. 27:18).

Maybe this is the true meaning of the binding of Isaac. Abraham didn't actually kill his son. But he did sacrifice him in a different, subtler way, by putting his relationship with God first.

After the episode on Mount Moriah, father and son never meet again. The text, which twice stresses how 'they walked the two of them together', uses the words 'walked' and 'together' for a third time, when Abraham and his servants go back to Beersheva (Gen. 22:6, 8, 19). But there's no mention here of 'the two of them': Isaac isn't there; he doesn't come down the mountain with his father. The Torah fails to mention him at the end of this chapter at all.

It's easy to blame Abraham. He's not the only person whose professed *hinneni* is open to question. I hear many people say with the self-blame of retrospect, 'If only I'd been there with him! If only I'd listened!' How honest is our own *hinneni*, and to whom? For how much of our lives have we imagined we were there, but were at best merely present in absentia? Leonard Cohen sung of a 'broken hallelujah';[60] sometimes an equally broken *hinneni* is the best we can manage.

CHAYYEI SARAH – THE LIFE OF SARAH (23:1–25:18)

A life within the tent

Soon after they were married, Rabbi Aryeh Levin, famous for his kindness, took his wife to the surgery: Doctor, he said, 'My wife's foot is hurting us.'[61]

That's not how Abraham behaves towards his wife. They come from the same family; in Jewish tradition Sarah is his niece, his brother Haran's daughter, and she accompanies him on his wanderings from the first. She's very beautiful, as Abraham acknowledges, and she's faithful. Twice Abraham passes her off as his sister, a dissembling half-truth excusable only, as he admits, in order to save his life (Gen. 12:11–13; 20:2). But these are not the only occasions when he doesn't treat her well.

There's the matter of Hagar. At Sarah's suggestion, Abraham takes a second woman: 'God has prevented me from childbearing; sleep with my handmaiden, maybe I can be built from her' (Gen. 16:2). Hagar instantly falls pregnant and assumes a superior manner towards her infertile mistress, prompting Sarah to turn on Abraham in her anguish, accusing him of failing to protect her: 'I gave you my handmaiden to bed; now that she sees she's pregnant, she mocks me. God judge between you and me' (Gen. 16:5). A midrash puts it bluntly: 'You stand there listening to me being humiliated and say nothing' (Bereshit Rabba 45:5).

Perhaps Sarah is less than completely fair: maybe Hagar reserves her glow of superiority for when she and her mistress are alone together, while giving no outward indication to Abraham that his wife is being mistreated. Yet he shouldn't have needed prompting to understand that Hagar's pregnancy would inevitably be painful for his Sarah. Instead of comforting her, 'Abraham offered little more than a shrug', suggests Carolyn Custis James in *Lost Women of the Bible*.[62] 'Do what you like with [Hagar],' Abraham replies to Sarah (Gen. 16:6), showing as little sympathy for his future child and its mother as he does for his wife of many years. Sarah, with her husband's connivance, proceeds to take out her anger on Hagar, humiliating her in turn until she flees, pregnant and alone, into the desolation of the wilderness.

There's a further reason for Sarah's anger. God has just spoken to her husband in a vision and promised him a great reward. His response is to ask: 'God, what will you give *me*, since *I* go childless ... since *to me* you have not given children' (Gen. 15:2–3). An astute midrash has Sarah over-hear this tryst between her husband and his God. His 'I' and 'me' strike at her heart:

It's like two men who go to borrow seed for sowing from the king. The first said, 'Lend me some seed' and [the king's servants] gave it to him. His companion said to him, 'God judge you for what you've done to me. Had you said, "Lend *us*," I would have been given some just like you.' Here too, had you, Abraham, said, 'You haven't given *us* children,' God would have given me [a child] just as God has given one to you. But since you said, 'You haven't given *me* any children' God has given [a child] to you but not to me.

(Bereshit Rabbah 45:5)

Plenty of people know all too well what it's like to be a mere auxiliary in someone else's life. More than once in their story it seems as if God and Abraham have stitched up destiny between them, leaving Sarah as merely a minor, albeit essential, member of the supporting cast. Her role, like that of many women since, is simply to produce the successor.

Her place when the three angels come to inform her and her husband that they will at long last have a child (Gen. 18:1–15) can be seen as symbolising her life. When they arrive, she's sent to the kitchen to bake. She's hidden behind the tent flap, listening in, just as with the dialogue between Abraham and God in that night vision. When the angels call for her, she's out of sight. Perhaps it's unease at the inequality between the couple that makes Rashi comment:

The angels knew perfectly well where Sarah our mother was. Rather, they asked the question in order to teach us that when people receive hospitality, they should ask the husband about the wife's wellbeing and the wife about the wellbeing of her husband.[63]

Rashi adds, uncomfortably, that the angels wanted to highlight Sarah's modesty 'to make her attractive to her husband'.

At least on this occasion, Sarah has a voice, albeit from behind a tent-flap. It's not until Isaac is born that she finally rejoices openly: this is her moment, her sole moment, of triumph. 'God has brought me laughter, whoever hears will laugh with me. Who would have said of Abraham that Sarah would nurse his child? Yet I've born him a son for his old age' (Gen: 21:6–7).

When, some years later, Abraham sets out for the mountain to sacrifice that son, he fails to tell the boy's mother. As if in collusion, the text repeatedly refers to Isaac as 'your [singular] son' and 'his son', but never as 'your [plural] son', let alone 'their son'. In striking contrast, the prophetic reading the rabbis chose to accompany this story in the annual cycle of readings focuses almost entirely on the Shunamite woman and her relationship to her beloved only child, who, like Isaac, is saved from death at the last moment (2 Kgs 4:1–37).

After what could be as much as a century of marriage, Abraham's life partner dies at the age of 127. But he's not there. Had he been with her, the text wouldn't have had to tell us that 'he *came* to mourn and weep for Sarah' (Gen. 23:2). Rashi references the midrash that she collapsed and died on hearing what her husband had almost done to their beloved boy.[64]

Yet Jewish tradition has not regarded Sarah merely as an oppressed and sidelined woman. It empowers her in those brief spaces the text accords her. She has her own relationship with God. She doesn't say to Abraham, 'I can't get pregnant,' or, 'You're not able to make me pregnant,' but, '*God* has prevented me from having children' (Gen. 16:2). When Isaac is born, she doesn't say, 'I'm so happy,' but, '*God* has brought me laughter' (Gen. 21:6). She has her own space, her own tent, a room of her own, as is made clear when, after her death, Isaac leads his bride Rebecca 'to the tent of his mother Sarah' (Gen. 24:67). This is her temple, sanctified by the commandments attributed in rabbinic tradition to women, blessing the baking of bread, lighting the *Shabbat* candles and observing the rules of marital purity. Like the Tent of Meeting which travels with the Children of Israel through the wilderness, it is enveloped as a reward by the cloud of God's protective presence.

This can be taken as little more than valorising the patronising view that a woman's proper place is in the tent. But Sarah's role can be understood in deeper ways, as writer Penina Adelman suggests:

According to Midrash, Sarah's tent foreshadowed the *ohel mo'ed* (the Tent of Meeting) with its accompanying fire, sacrifices, and the cloud of the *Shekhinah* [God's presence]. Sarah and Rebecca were precursors of the priesthood; they were the holy women of their sacred tents.[65]

Adelman's approach in imagining a greater role for Sarah within the text's curt references epitomises a hard-won struggle to reclaim a profound spiritual place for women in the almost always unequal and sometimes cruel spaces left to them in a sacred canon defined by men, a rabbinic tradition developed by men and communities governed by men.

Yet, when those communities fell within the power of rulers who confined them within the oppressive bounds of ghettoes and Jew-streets from which they were often expelled and, in their exile, persecuted and sometimes killed, time and again it was the women who saved their families and turned the few square cubits left to them into sanctuaries.

Be'er Lachai Ro'i – the well of the living God who sees me

Where does one go when one is lonely and bewildered? At what inner refuge can the broken-hearted find restoration?

Isaac 'came from coming from the well of the living God who sees me' (Gen. 24:62). To understand why he went there and the nature of the place requires returning to the story of Hagar, who gave it its beautiful and resonant name. She found it in her aloneness and wretchedness, in the wilderness. Given to Abraham as a concubine by his childless wife Sarah in a 'rent-a-womb' arrangement (such affairs are well documented in ancient legal literature), she immediately fell pregnant, leaving it painfully clear which of the couple was responsible for their infertility. Unwisely, Hagar triumphed in Sarah's humiliation, who in turn made Hagar's life miserable, causing her to flee in desperation into the desert. There the angel of God found her, 'by the spring in the wilderness, by the well on the road to Shur' (Gen. 16:7). Four times the angel tries to console her; three times the Torah repeats the identical words, 'And the angel of God said to her,' while Hagar remains silent. Only the promise that she will bear a son and found a powerful dynasty finally brings her comfort.

After the angel's departure, Hagar acknowledges that she has experienced the presence of God, whom she names, saying, 'You are a God who sees me', adding in explanation, 'Have I not seen further, after I saw?' (Gen. 16:13–14). A midrash suggests that although she has previously seen angels in Abraham's household, now she has encountered God directly. But this doesn't account for the puzzling ambiguity of her words: *acharei ro'i* can mean either 'after I saw' or 'after the one *who saw me*', as if to say,

'I saw deeper after I knew myself seen.' Rashi comments simply, 'For you, God, behold the misery of the oppressed.'[66]

A well in a dry climate is always a meeting place. It's where Abraham's servant finds Rebecca; where, at Aram Naharayim, Jacob sees Rachel for the first time and falls instantly in love; and where, in the desert of Midian, Moses rescues Jethro's seven daughters, one of whom he later marries. Wells are social spaces. But Hagar's 'well of the living God who sees' is a well set apart, a space not of communal but of spiritual encounter.

The Torah locates it between Kadesh and Bared, somewhere in the Negev. But it's also one of those special places in the Bible that is both nowhere and anywhere. *Kadesh* means holy and *bared* is hail; the well mediates between the raining-down of life's onslaughts and the safety of sanctuary. It has no specific coordinates; only the spirit can guide us there. But we recognise the place when we find it, for here the whirling kaleidoscope of thoughts and emotions slows down. The waters from 'the well of the living God who sees' restore us; we no longer feel abandoned before life's blows.

The Zohar, the core text of the Jewish mystics, refers to a deep well on high; it represents *binah*, understanding, and is the mother and womb of creation.[67] It gives form to the sacred spark of divine wisdom; from it, life streams down into the complex channels of this material world. It is a place of *teshuvah*, retreat and re-creation; here, the heart finds healing and the febrile mind rediscovers calm. Wounds are cleansed and cauterised and the exhausted spirit receives a transfusion of new life.

The Zohar describes *binah* as a well 'on high' because wisdom flows secretly into it from the mysterious source that nourishes all existence. But height and depth are often interchangeable metaphors. Hence this secret well is also a gathering place of subterranean currents, deep enough for the hidden waters that lie beneath even the fiercest desert to seep through and replenish those internal pools from which the soul yearns to drink as urgently as 'the deer longs for pools of water' (Ps. 42:1). If for any length of time we cannot find this well and access its waters, we don't die; we just live on, exhausted, vexed and fractious.

The well lies deep below life's noisy landscape of conflict, aggression and injury. It's not a place of simplification; it doesn't offer solutions. Injustice is still injustice and unmerited suffering remains unfair. Rather, life's cruelties and impossibilities are somehow made less unbearable, without necessarily being explained. The living waters wash the weariness out of the mind and heart. The soul is reinvigorated; resilience is restored.

Hagar goes back to Sarah and gives birth to her son. But when she's driven out for a second time, it is to here that she returns. Once more an angel addresses her and again God opens her eyes to reveal 'a well of water' (Gen. 21:19). It is here, years later, that Isaac finds her when, according to Midrash, he comes to collect her so that she can marry Abraham after Sarah's death. He too is evidently familiar with the place. The Torah doesn't disclose where he goes after his father unbinds him from the altar. The text tells us nothing about his whereabouts; there's no mention of him even at his mother's funeral. It's only with the arrival of his wife-to-be, Rebecca, that the Torah explains: 'Isaac came from coming to the well of the living God who sees' (Gen. 24:62).

Perhaps he, too, goes there for relief and restoration, to settle his heart after the unimaginable anguish through which God and his father have made him pass. Perhaps, like other victims, he comes here again and again, spending the rest of his life trying to recover from an insuperable trauma. Noting the unusual construction, 'he came from coming', Nachmanides suggests that Isaac returns regularly to the well to pray.[68] Later, he devotes years to digging and re-digging other wells because the Philistines keep filling them in (Gen. 26:15–18). There may be a deeper reason too: his life is a prolonged search for a healing which he can never fully find.

Yet it's not Isaac but Hagar who names the well after 'the God who sees'. In his Torah commentary *Be'er Mayyim Chaim*, the *Well of Living Waters*, Rebbe Chaim of Tchernowitz (1760–1817) explains:

> She named it as true and enduring testament that the Holy Blessed One sees the pain of the oppressed and watches with mercy over the lowly and rejected. This well is a sign for all generations that there is none like God who hears the prayers of every mouth and sees the sorrows of every creature. This is the meaning of 'the well of the living One who sees', that is to say, this well is a sign that the living God sees me, that the Eternal God sees all my troubles and redeems me.

Yet in the subsequent verse, the subject is masculine: '*He* called the place . . .' (Gen. 16:14). Perhaps, then, it's not just Hagar but also Isaac who names the well, since they both have a similar experience there. Maybe it awaits us all when we discover the location where the living waters cleanse our thoughts and set free our tears.

This is the place I inwardly mean when I greet mourners with the traditional words of consolation: *Hamakom Yenachem. Makom* is a rabbinical name for God, hence the conventional translation, 'May the All-Present One comfort you.' But the literal meaning of *makom* is simply 'place'. The words therefore have an added significance: May you find the place within you where the living waters flow. May life console you there and bring you restoration.

TOLDOT - THESE ARE THE GENERATIONS (25:19-28:9)

Rebecca

Rebecca is that nice girl who comes running up to Abraham's servant at the well and not only gives him the drink he has asked for but also draws up gallon after gallon of water to slake the thirst of his ten desert-weary camels. She's the obedient young woman who conforms to God's plans, says 'yes' when her family ask her if she will go with Abraham's servant and rides bravely off with her handmaidens to become the wife of Isaac and the second of the matriarchs (Gen. 24).

But what is her life actually like? Pious literature has her pick up exactly where her predecessor leaves off. Isaac brings her 'into the tent of Sarah his mother' (Gen. 24:67) and, like many men since, expects, or is understood to expect, her to replicate his mother in all her ways. That Sarah actually was the woman the Midrash describes is itself a pious fiction based on a traditional view of the ideal Jewish wife, for which the Torah provides no evidence whatsoever:

> While Sarah lived, the cloud of God's presence was attached to the entrance of the tent. When she died it went away, but when Rebecca came it returned. All the days of Sarah's life the doors of the tent were open wide [for guests]. When she died that ended, but when Rebecca came the tent was open once again. All the days of Sarah's life her bread was blessed. When she died that ceased, but when Rebecca came it returned. All the days of Sarah's life, a candle burned from Sabbath eve to Sabbath end. When she died that stopped, but when Rebecca came the flame was restored.
>
> (Bereshit Rabbah 60:16)

In a moving poem about the four matriarchs, Polish-American poet Kadya Molodowsky describes the lonely sorrows each of them had to endure. She focuses on Rebecca and Isaac's difficulty in conceiving and paints a tender and compassionate, but also romanticised, picture:

For high-born brides now poor,
Who blush to bring patched underclothes
Before their mothers-in-law,
Mother Rebecca leads camels
Laden with white linen.[69]

But who is Rebecca, and what is life with Isaac actually like? It soon emerges that she is no mere follower without a mind of her own. Just as Isaac prefers one of his children, Esau, so does she: Jacob. It is she who instigates the plot to trick her visually impaired husband into blessing Jacob, her favourite, instead of the son Isaac prefers:

I heard your father tell your brother, 'Bring me hunted meat . . . and I will bless you' . . . Now listen, my son, to what I say . . . Go to the flock . . . Bring two nice young goats for me to cook tastily . . . Take them to your father so that he blesses *you*.

(Gen. 27:6–10)

When Jacob objects that his father will feel his skin and find him out, earning him curses instead of blessings, she bluntly overrules his objections: 'Upon me be your curse, my son. Just listen to me and go' (Gen. 27:8–13).

What has happened in the intervening years to turn this obedient young girl into a woman who has no qualms in deceiving her husband? What has life been like for her, taken far from the land of her birth to provide heirs for this family embroiled in God's plans? An astute contemporary poem by Dr Tamar Meir offers a moving insight:

After your mother's death you brought me into the tent:
'Here are the candles,' you said, 'And here are the dishes.'
. . . But you didn't explain
What to do with that cloud hovering
Over your heart,
Or how to restore blessing
To that childhood which turned sour,
Or how, from Shabbat eve to Shabbat eve, to light up
Love in the eyes.[70]

Her poem is a midrash on a midrash. The cloud, which later in the Torah and in classic rabbinic literature represents the protective presence of God, has become a brooding heaviness of heart. It's no longer dough that sours as it rises to become bread, but her husband's life which turned bitter when he was bound on the altar. Unlike the *Shabbat* lamps, the light in his traumatised eyes refuses to be rekindled. How could Rebecca have known in advance that she would walk into the aftermath of so much trouble? Which of us knows beforehand, or even after many years, what truly lies in the depths of our partner's psyche, with which we too must now live? Such occluded places exist in all our souls, larger or smaller. If we don't accept them and, when we can, attend to them with compassion, they will keep even the most faithful of partners – at least some of the time – apart.

Rebecca's lack of respect for her husband's disability doesn't reflect an insensitive personality. Rather, it feels like the outcome of long years of frustration living alongside a man whose heart has been made inaccessible through trauma. Tamar Meir's poem speaks to more recent terrors, the silence of the inarticulable that haunts the marriages of Holocaust survivors and refugees, each partner alone at night with their nightmares while by day they live on in peripheral proximity. But the verse also reflects the experience of a woman married to someone whose previous history she was never told and which, despite the initial love with which he draws her into his mother's tent, involuntarily causes him to withhold the core of himself, leaving her to live day after day alongside the impenetrable heaviness of a man whose soul she can never truly access. It's no wonder her affections turn to her home-loving younger son.

The Torah tells us nothing about Rebecca after Jacob has left home. 'Listen to what I'm counselling you,' she says to him once again, advising him to flee to her brother's family in Haran and stay there until Esau has calmed down and 'forgotten what you did to him' (Gen. 27:43–5). She never acknowledges that it was she who instigated the plan that left the older of her twin sons hurt and angry.

Jacob leaves home after receiving his father's blessing, this time openly and honestly. Rebecca never sees her favourite child again. When he comes back with his wives, children and numberless flocks, there's no mention of his mother: he returns 'to Isaac his father' (Gen. 35:27). The Torah doesn't even inform us of Rebecca's death. We learn later that she was buried in the cave of Machpelah (Gen. 49:31), where her long-lived husband eventually joined her, to continue the silence between them.

Isaac's eyes

The Torah doesn't say that Isaac is blind, only that he can't see truly. In this limitation he is far from alone: which of us perceives clearly what others around us sometimes readily observe? As with Isaac, the cause often lies in the wounds and fears that occlude our clarity of vision.

A careful examination of the Hebrew shows that, although it was impaired, Isaac didn't entirely lose his sight. Rather, 'his eyes became *dim from seeing*' (Gen. 27:1). The critical word is *mei're'ot*, 'from seeing', specifically the prefix *mei*, 'from'. As ever, rabbinic literature offers alternative interpretations.

One explanation is that it's his bias towards Esau, his favourite whom he loves for the meat he hunts, that makes Isaac unable to see what's going on right under his nose. For, as the Torah says, 'bribes blind the eyes of the insightful and pervert the words of the wise' (Deut. 16:19).

Isaac's predilection is puzzling. Smells are deeply evocative: perhaps the savour of roasting meat reminds him of the horror of being bound on the altar and the inexpressible relief that it wasn't him but a hapless animal that was burnt in the end. No doubt we all carry memories, often awoken by associations of which we aren't even aware, which risk making us prefer one child, one person, over another for no apparent cause and which can lead us to reopen old wounds and generate fresh conflicts.

In contrast, Rabbi Elazar ben Azariah, a leading rabbi of the first to second centuries CE, regards Isaac's impaired vision as a blessing. God afflicts him with this disability so that he's unable to go out and overhear people in the marketplace gossiping about his older son. Esau, described as a hunter in the Torah, is infamous in rabbinic tradition because of his cruelty as a killer. The Torah identifies him with Edom (Gen. 25:30), which the rabbis interpreted as a cypher for Rome. Esau is thus the ancestor of the violent armies under the domination of which Rabbi Elazar ben Azariah lived. In his view, God mercifully makes the elderly Isaac housebound to save him from the shame of seeing people point at him and whisper, 'That's the father of the scoundrel Esau.' This captures the anxiety relatives of wrongdoers may feel, that wherever they go there will be barbs, silences or sympathetic glances, behind which lies the insinuation that they too must be responsible, or negligent, otherwise their child wouldn't have committed such crimes. God protects Isaac from such humiliation by making his eyesight fail.

But, in perhaps the most compelling interpretation of Isaac's blindness, the word 'from' is understood differently: Isaac's 'eyes have grown dim *as a result of* seeing'. Something he once experienced has had such an impact on him that it has permanently distorted his capacity to see. It's easy to surmise what that might be. Rashi states:

> At the very moment when Isaac lay bound on the altar with his father intent on slaughtering him, the gates of heaven opened: the ministering angels saw the scene and wept. Their tears fell from their eyes straight down into his. As a result, his eyes grew dim.[71]

Seventeenth-century poet John Milton employs a similar image to describe his own blindness: 'So thick a drop serene hath quenched their orbs.'[72] In case his explanation should seem too fanciful, Rashi offers a simpler alternative: God made Isaac blind so that Jacob would take the blessings. God did what was necessary to ensure that destiny would follow its intended course.[73]

But it's the first of Rashi's interpretations that is the more compelling. It describes what we would now call post-traumatic stress disorder. Isaac's sudden reprieve notwithstanding, his world is irrevocably transformed by the experience of being tied down on the altar by his father and watching him pick up the knife. Afterwards, nothing ever looks or feels the same; everything is refracted through the lens of this trauma. He can't escape the intervention of its shadow to focus even on what's happening before his very eyes. Invisible as the finest contact lenses, it reconfigures his world. It's a reality familiar to many who have had to live through war, violence, torture, persecution and the shock of accidents and disasters.

After the binding, Isaac and his father never meet again until the latter's funeral. Instead, Isaac goes to *Be'er Lacha Ro'i*, 'the well of the living God who sees'. Drinking from it for a long time, he comes to see what others cannot, but fails to notice what others clearly can. He doesn't realise that Jacob is not Esau, but he does perceive the complex path of destiny that will lead his grandchildren down to Egypt. The longest-lived of the three patriarchs, Isaac is still alive when his deceiver child is in turn deceived. He watches and weeps as Jacob cries out in grief when his sons bring him the blood-soaked remains of Joseph's many-coloured coat, saying, 'This we have found' (Gen. 37:32). God, a midrash explains, has revealed to Isaac that Joseph is not dead, but alive and well in Egypt. But this is a secret that the divine will forbid him to disclose. Instead, he weeps; he cries for his son, for his grandson, and maybe also for all those in the generations to come who find themselves victims of overpowering destiny. For he himself has lain beneath the knife and absorbed the tears of heaven.

VAYETSE - AND HE WENT OUT (28:10-32:3)

'There's God in this place'

I inherited from my mother's parents a small ark, made by my father out of oak. Its red curtain is embroidered with the words '*Da lifnei mi attah omed*: Know before whom you stand'. A gift for my grandfather on his ninetieth birthday, it contained an equally small Torah scroll, sadly no longer usable. I imagine this might have been the scroll he took with him, when, a recently ordained rabbi, he served as an army chaplain in the First World War. He would have needed a portable Torah to carry in his rabbinic kit bag for services at the front.

'Know before who you stand' is frequently chosen as a quotation above the synagogue ark. But what does 'know' mean in this context? Jacob's famous dream casts an otherworldly light over the question:

Behold a ladder placed towards the earth, its top reaching towards heaven; and behold, angels of God ascending and descending on it. And behold, God standing on it, saying: 'I am the God of your father Abraham and your father Isaac . . . And behold I am with you.'

(Gen. 28:12–13, 15)

Four times the word *hinneh*, 'behold', draws Jacob ever deeper into the core of his vision, God's promise to protect him. No dream could be more comforting to a penniless young man overtaken by darkness in the middle of nowhere, the safety of his childhood home far behind him and an uncertain future ahead. But it is not at this, or at the ladder connecting earth and heaven, that Jacob marvels when he wakes up. Rather, he exclaims, 'There's God in this place, and I did not know.' English cannot capture the starkness of the Hebrew: *Yesh Adonai* – there's Godness here, and I didn't realise.' Rashi, in his brief comment, inhabits Jacob's voice: 'Had I known, I wouldn't have gone to sleep.'[74] According to rabbinic legend, throughout his previous twenty-two years of Torah studying at the (imagined) college of Shem and Ever, Jacob never once slept.

Sleep is a frequent metaphor for lack of awareness, the dimming of consciousness. Rebbe Moshe Chaim Ephraim of Sudlikov (1748–1800) expanded on Rashi's comment: 'The exile of the spirit is like sleep. When one wakes up, one is amazed at oneself: Had I known such luminous truth existed, I would never have gone to sleep.'[75]

If sleep is spiritual exile, *da'at*, 'knowledge', is spiritual wakefulness. 'Knowledge' in the Hebrew Bible rarely refers to the mere awareness of a thing or fact. It indicates relationship. This may be the physical intimacy of man and woman, as when 'Adam knew Eve his wife' (Gen. 4:1); it may be close emotional connection or spiritual at-oneness. When the Children of Israel cry out from their slavery in Egypt, their anguish ascends before God, who hears and knows. There, the normally transitive verb 'know' carries no object; the text simply says, 'God knew' (Exod. 2:25). God's knowing and knowing God have in common that they refer not to the accumulation of facts or the assent to propositions, but to a realisation that fills the mind and touches the heart.

To the kabbalists and mystics, *da'at*, 'knowledge', is the *sefirah*, or 'domain', of awareness in which flashes of intuition become steady consciousness, centring our thoughts and guiding our speech and actions. For Rebbe Menachem Nachum of Chernobyl (1730–89), the whole purpose of creation is so that:

> . . . we become aware and know of God's existence. Even though God's true nature lies beyond our grasp, once we recognize that God exists, we will do everything for God's sake, fulfilling 'know Him in all your ways' [Prov. 3:6] and becoming united with Him.[76]

This knowledge is rooted in the soul. Just as awareness of self permeates all our thoughts so that we can't help but think of how our every interaction affects us, the knowledge of God can become so deeply integrated into our consciousness that we regularly ask ourselves, in the words of Rabbi Kalonymus Kalman Shapira (1889–1943):

> What am I doing in God's presence and how can I be in this state when I'm standing before God exalted and most high . . . until such thoughts become bound in our very consciousness no less than our awareness of our own self.[77]

Most of us attain only infrequent flashes of such knowledge. We may rarely 'know God' in this deepest sense. But what we may come to know is that such knowing exists, and this itself can be life changing. Occasional moments of realisation are sufficient to guide our soul and conscience, just as one doesn't have to know every constellation but only to recognise a few key stars in order to navigate life's ocean.

Often, preoccupied with daily tasks, we forget that it's even possible to know. The mundane takes over. But sometimes, in places special to us, or on which, like Jacob, we unexpectedly stumble, a sound may alert us or the stillness stir us, bringing, like the angels in his dream, wonder down to earth. Afterwards, when we try to account for the experience, we too might say, 'God is in this place, and I did not know.'

Rachel, Leah and the naming of the children

There can be much pain in an 'also': 'Jacob *also* slept with Rachel, and *also* loved Rachel more than Leah' (Gen. 29:30). The tense relationship between the sisters is as much the fault of their father as of their husband. Jacob falls instantly in love with Rachel. It's for her that he labours for seven years; it's her and only her he ever intends to marry. But he, the deceiver, is deceived by his father-in-law and fails to recognise that the woman with whom his great love is consummated is not Rachel but Leah. The two women are caught between the sins and the weaknesses of the men who make the decisions that determine the course of their lives. Yet it's they who pay the price in long, tense years of anguish.

A popular midrash makes out that the relationship between the sisters remains close, at least initially. Realising her father's intentions, Rachel shares with Jacob secret signs by which he can know whether or not it's really her who has been delivered to him in the pitch dark of the nuptial tent. But then, taking pity on her sister for the humiliation to which she would be exposed, she selflessly shares these signals with Leah. She can't, of course, forewarn Jacob, who ends up the victim of their conspiratorial secret.

Yet, while never suggesting that they hate each other, the narrative, the longest section in the entire Torah devoted to the thoughts and feelings of women, shows how the best years of Rachel and Leah's lives are spent fighting for their husband's affections and their own self-esteem.

The Torah doesn't relate what Jacob said to Leah the morning after; it records only his angry exchange with his father-in-law Laban. All we know is that a mere half dozen verses later Leah is referred to as 'hated' (Gen. 29:31). The commentary *Da'at Zekenim* from the twelfth and thirteenth centuries shrewdly fills in the gaps:

He said to her: 'Deceiver, daughter of a deceiver, During the night I called you *Rachel* and you answered. Now I'm calling you *Leah*, and

still you answer!' She said: 'Is there anyone who has no disciples? Your
father called you Esau and you answered,' meaning, I learnt the arts of
deception from you!

It's allegedly because of words like these that Jacob began to hate her. Few
of us love those who point out our faults. But there's a simpler explanation
for Leah's feelings. To know oneself unloved in marriage, to witness each
day how much one's sister and fellow wife is adored, to have done nothing
to bring about this state of affairs, to be powerless either to remedy or to
escape from it, to see the years stretch hopelessly ahead: all this adds up to
feeling rejected, despised and hated.

God intervenes, paying Leah back for her suffering by enabling her to
conceive and bear children, while Rachel remains infertile. But the hurt
remains, as the names of her sons make clear, with the possible exception
of Judah (which means 'praise'). They all testify to her pain, and to her
longing for her husband's affection:

> She called him *Reuben* ('see, a son') for she said: 'God has seen my
> affliction and now my husband will love me.' She . . . said: 'God has
> heard how I am hated and given me this [child] *also*, and she called
> him *Shimeon* ([God] has heard my misery).
>
> (Gen. 29:32–3)

But one 'also' cannot compensate for another. The names of her children
continue to express her loneliness and longing: 'She conceived again and
gave birth to a son and said: this time my husband will *yilavei*, keep
company, with me, for I have born him three sons.' Intriguingly, the gender
of the pronoun now unexpectedly changes; '*He* called him *Levi* (my
companion)' (Gen. 29:34), as if, perhaps, Jacob assented to her proposition
that it was worth his while spending time with her in bed.

By now romance has given way to motherhood as the currency of the
competition between the sisters. Their offspring are marked by their
mothers' sufferings and struggles, as so many children are. Destiny will
exact from them the price for the rivalry into which they are born.

When Rachel 'sees' that she has borne Jacob no children she becomes
jealous in turn: 'She said to Jacob: "Give me children or I die"' (Gen. 30:1).
A painful Talmudic comment likens four kinds of persons to the dead:
people with blindness, people with leprosy, people who have no children
and the destitute (Nedarim 64b). Society is still struggling to learn how to
respond with sensitivity to the suffering of each of these groups.

Jacob shows no mercy: '[He] was angry with Rachel and said, "Am I in God's place, who's withheld *from you* the fruit of the womb?"' (Gen. 30:2). Rachel isn't expecting miracles; all she wants is her husband's sympathy and prayers, just as Isaac prayed with Rebecca. But, according to Rashi, who puts the emphasis on Jacob's '*from you*', what she gets is the very opposite: 'You're telling me to do like my father. But my situation isn't the same as his. My father had no children. I have. God has withheld children *from you*, but not from me.'[78] The rabbis blame Jacob for his response: 'Is that how you answer someone in pain? In the future *your* sons will bow down before *hers*' (Bereshit Rabbah 71:7).

When, years later, Reuben brings home mandrakes, a traditional aid to fertility, for his mother, Rachel, still childless, begs her sister to share them, provoking Leah into giving vent to feelings harboured inside her for years: 'Is taking away my husband such a small thing that now you *also* need to take my son's mandrakes?' (Gen. 30:15).

The little word 'also' is like a scorecard of the sisters' respective hurts. This entire scene is played out in front of the children.

When Rachel eventually becomes pregnant, her consolation is only partial; she names her son after both her suffering and her hope: 'She said, "God has gathered in my shame," and she called him Yosef, saying, "May God add [*yossef*] me another child"' (Gen. 30:23–4). Joseph will be burdened all his life by the impact both of his mother's early favoured status and of her sense of inferiority, which even his arrival cannot alleviate. She dies giving birth to his brother, whom she names with her final breath *Ben Oni*, son of my sorrow. She probably has more than her death pains in mind (Gen. 35:18). Jacob immediately changes the name to Binyamin, 'son of my right hand' or possibly, as Rashi explains, 'son of days' since he was born in Jacob's old age.

Rachel dies first. Centuries later, Jeremiah envisages her weeping as her descendants pass her burial place on their long journey into exile, carried off by their Babylonian captors. The last thing she would have seen as her eyes closed in death was her baby being carried away. The Torah never records how Leah dies.

Kadya Molodowsky composed moving epitaphs for each of the sisters:

For those whose eyes are tired
From watching neighbourhood children . . .
Mother Rachel brings healing leaves
Discovered on distant mountains,
And comforts them with a quiet word:

At any hour, God may open the sealed womb.[79]

Her tribute to Leah is even more poignant:

> To those who cry at night in solitary beds,
> And have no one to share their sorrow,
> Who talk to themselves with parched lips,
> To them comes Mother Leah, quietly,
> Shielding both eyes with her pale hands.[80]

VAYISHLACH – AND HE SENT (32:4–36:43)

Wresting blessings

'I will not send you away before you bless me' (Gen. 32:26). With these words Jacob refuses to let go of a difficult encounter.

He's reached the Yabok River; it marks not just the geographical but also an emotional boundary between the country of his childhood to which he's returning and the land of his sojourn with his father-in-law Laban. When he crossed this border on his way out, fleeing his brother's wrath after taking his blessing, he had his great dream of a ladder reaching from earth to heaven. At its top was God, promising him protection wherever he went and a safe return home. It would be hard to imagine more comforting tidings for a penniless young man with only the stones for his pillow and the stars for a blanket. Immediately afterwards he met Rachel and fell instantly in love.

Now, twenty years later, a successful shepherd with two wives, two concubines, eleven sons, one daughter and another child on the way, as well as huge flocks of camels, donkeys, goats, sheep and cattle, he's on his route home when he has another encounter with God. Once more he finds himself alone in the liminal night-space between the dusk of his past life and the new light of his future. These are the restless, dream-broken hours when, according to Keats, conscience 'still lords / Its strength for darkness'.[81] Fearing his brother, who he's been told is approaching with four hundred men, he divides his family to ensure that at least one part will survive Esau's attack. Jacob leads them across the Yabok River, then, according to Rashi, goes back to fetch some jars he's left behind,[82] when 'a man struggled with him until the dawn arose' (Gen. 32:25(24)).

Who is it with whom he wrestles in the bleak pre-daylight hours? The text omits to tell us his name or from where he's suddenly appeared. Afterwards, Jacob 'calls the place *Peniel*, saying, "I have seen God face to face"' (Gen. 32:31(30)). But that needn't mean that the strange figure is God, as if, like in Greek and Roman myths, God could assume mortal form. Hosea describes the assailant as an angel, locating the encounter at Bet El, the very place where Jacob had his great dream (Hos. 12:5(4)).

Midrash identifies him as Esau's guardian angel, with whom Jacob has to fight spiritually before their anticipated physical battle. It's the third round of their protracted conflict. In the first, Jacob acquires Esau's birthright, if not by downright dishonesty, at least by cunning, taking advantage of his brother's urgent, heedless hunger. In the second, he gains his father's first and best blessing by impersonating his older twin. Now, in the third, he confronts his brother's guardian angel. Perhaps it should be understood not as a celestial other, but as his brother calling out to him from inside his own head. It's precisely in those long night hours, dislocated from space and time, that the *dramatis personae* of our unsettled past reify as spirits and haunt and taunt our battling consciousness. Jacob has Esau on his mind. He's prayed to God to save him from his brother; he's sent servant after servant with propitiatory gifts. But these practical precautions cannot protect him from the Esau who assails him from within, who is as much his own self as his twin. His brother's pain hits him now with sudden force. Did he catch, as he hurriedly threw his borrowed garments back to his mother, Esau's 'great cry' of hurt: 'Is one blessing all you've got? Bless me too, my father!' (Gen. 27:38)? Does he hear those words louder now?

Another voice joins the fray, Laban's accusatory excuse for giving him the wrong sister: 'It's not done like that in *our* place; we don't put the younger before the older' (Gen. 29:26). And he himself, how could he have done it? How could he have mistaken any other woman in the whole wide world for his beautiful, seven-years-longed-for Rachel?

In the morning, when the light grew bright,
The truth in all its fullness was revealed:
The mighty lover couldn't tell the difference
Between the sweetness of Rachel and the affections of Leah.
Sad is Laban's deception,
But sadder by far is Jacob:
Laban deceived Jacob,
Jacob deceived himself.[83]

Be'eri Tsimmerman

Maybe, then, it's with himself that Jacob wrestles until dawn. The Torah describes his assailant as 'a man' (Gen. 32:24). The older man he's meanwhile become fights with his younger self who first crossed this river twenty years before. Returning after a long absence to a previously known place often brings forgotten sights back to mind: one suddenly remembers what's round the corner; voices heard decades ago speak again in one's head. Jacob meets Jacob: the boy he was and the man he now is struggle all night long.

Weary in the pre-dawn shadows, Jacob, exhausted, should surely feel relief at his attacker's plea to be released: 'Let me go, for the dawn has arisen.'

But he refuses: 'I shall not send you away until you bless me' (Gen. 32:27(26)). That line should be the motto of everyone who battles with life's adversities.

Perhaps it's because of this that Jacob is associated with the quality of truth. He can scarcely be regarded as truthful by nature. On the contrary, he deceives, is deceived and will be deceived again, until by the end of his life he's a man more lied against than lying. Rather, it's his unwillingness to let go, his determination to fight, not with others but with himself, his insistence on making blessings even out of his faults, that earns him his new name Israel: 'you have struggled with God and overcome' (Gen. 32:29(28)). He hasn't vanquished for ever; this isn't his final conflict. What he's victorious over is the temptation to abandon the effort. His legacy to his descendants, the people of Israel, is that he, and they, will wrestle with themselves, with their destiny and with God, and will not give up until they wrest blessings from them all.

What becomes of hurts?

Unhealed hurts are not necessarily cured by the passage of time. Generations inherit their ancestors' pain. Like Abraham, who puts the wood for the sacrifice on Isaac's back, we too often place burdens on our children from which they are bound to suffer.

Sometimes the anguish is unspoken; silence is part of the sorrow. The suffering lies in the untold stories, the holes in the narrative, the sudden references to places, people, relatives with an unexplained familiarity that makes their appearance strange and disconcerting, like the naming of ghosts. The second generation, even the third, feels compelled to probe the disjunctions, the hiding places where lie the griefs and angers that ambushed their childhood.

At a book-signing for my book *My Dear Ones: One Family and the Final Solution*,[84] several people bent over me and said, almost inaudibly, things like, 'My uncle was Jewish, came from Vienna in 1938; no one talks about that.' 'We're Irish Catholics, but my grandmother was Jewish, escaped Germany, hid it until her deathbed, which means so am I. Family secret; don't tell.'

Sometimes anger is passed down from generation to generation like the insignia of a legion. Enmity is loyalty; you prove who you are by showing you hate the people your ancestors hated. The only thing you know about your enemy, the sole salient fact, is that you're against them, and they, by mere dint of being who they are, must be against you. The world is full of these heirloom grudges lying latent in musty corners of the memory until, in an opportune moment of fresh discontent, some demagogue arrives with a genius for mobilising these spectres to take up arms and be avenged. Scabs are picked off old wounds, rusty hatreds polished up for battle. Sometimes it happens within a single lifetime; sometimes resentments sleep for generations.

Jacob's fears about his forthcoming encounter with Esau are well founded. The messengers he sent to deliver his propitiatory offerings return to report the failure of their mission: Esau is approaching with four hundred men (Gen. 32:7). Jacob divides his camp, keeping his favourites Rachel and Joseph in the safety of the rear. Next, he prays. Then he fights with the unnamed figure rabbinic tradition identifies as his brother's guardian angel, whom he vanquishes not by force, but by saying, 'I won't let you go until you bless me.' The history of the world would be different if every conflict were resolved in this manner.

When he finally meets Esau, Jacob's worst fears are not realised. On the contrary, 'Esau ran to him and embraced him; he fell upon his neck and kissed him (Gen. 33:4). But did Esau really mean it? Rabbinic tradition is sceptical. His kiss wasn't wholehearted, comments Rashi, before qualifying this cynical view by citing the second-century Rabbi Shimon bar Yochai: 'It's common knowledge that Esau hates Jacob. But at that moment love welled up in him and he kissed him with all his heart.'[85]

But the doubts have a long history. The word *vayishakehu* – 'and he kissed him'– is written in the Torah with dots above it, a trope understood as casting doubt on whether the word truly means what it says. According to some opinions the letter *shin* is free of dots, leaving *vayikacho*: 'and he took him'. But as well as being the name of a letter, *shin* means 'tooth'. The subtext, then, is that, while appearing to kiss him, Esau takes Jacob in his teeth, an ambiguity that captures perfectly the suspicion that, however charming old enemies seem, they must never be trusted. And distrust restores the enmity.

Even if the encounter is sincere, it lasts a mere moment. There's a pointed tone to Esau's suggestion that Jacob take back his propitiatory gifts: 'My brother, let what's yours be yours' (Gen. 33:9) and to Jacob's curt rejection of his brother's offer of protection: you go your way, I'll go mine (Gen. 33:14).

Rabbinic tradition has its reasons for not trusting Esau. He loves the cruel sport of hunting; the only other hunter in the Torah is the tyrant Nimrod. Esau doesn't merely part with his birthright for a bowl of hot soup; he 'eats, drinks, gets up, goes and despises' (Gen. 25:34) – a sequence of five consecutive verbs found nowhere else in the Torah, indicating contempt. Deeper grounds lie in Esau's lineage as the rabbis understood it. No sooner is he named than we're told that 'Esau is Edom' (Gen. 25:30), and Edom, to the rabbis, meant Rome, the empire that sacked Jerusalem and sent the Jewish People into two thousand years of exile. When Rome became Christian under Constantine, Edom became their oblique way of referring to Christendom. Isaac's bewildered observation that 'the voice is the voice of Jacob, but the hands are the hands of Esau' (Gen. 27:22) came to signify the outcry of generations of Jews, persecuted and killed by Christian hands.

But rabbinic literature also reveals a degree of understanding for Esau. His injuries go deep, and wrongs will out. Midrash posits a close relationship between him and his grandson Amalek:

Esau said to Amalek, 'How I have striven to kill Jacob, without success! Be sure to avenge me!'

Amalek said: 'How can I hope to prevail against him?'
Esau replied: 'The moment his descendants commit a sin, jump on them.'

(Yalkut Chukkat 764)

Amalek feels his grandfather's wrongs deeply; they define his identity. When, centuries later, Haman decrees death to every Jew throughout the Persian Empire, and Mordechai 'cries a great and bitter cry' (Esther 4:1), the rabbis hear an echo of Esau's 'great and bitter cry' on learning that his brother has stolen his blessing (Gen. 27:34). Though Shushan, where the drama between Haman and Mordechai is played out, is a thousand years and hundreds of miles from the world of the patriarchs, the connection is clear: Haman is a scion of the royal line of Amalek, Esau's grandson.

Mordechai is a descendant of Benjamin, the younger son of Rachel, Jacob's favourite wife.

Unaddressed hurts travel down the generations until the hour of payback comes. Few really want to inherit their ancestor's wounds, but even fewer have the skill to heal them.

VAYESHEV - AND HE DWELT (37:1-40:23); AND MIKKETZ - AT THE END (41:1-44:17)

Garments of many colours – Joseph's story

My grandfather loved the story of Joseph. He saw in Joseph a person who develops from an insufferable teenager into a true servant of God with the magnanimity to forgive his brothers and the wisdom to see God's hand in everything that happened: 'Don't upset yourselves and don't be angry that you sold me down [to Egypt], because God sent me ahead of you to save our lives . . . It was not you, but God, who sent me here' (Gen. 45:5, 8). I'm less sure. I wonder who this Joseph really is. Does he himself know? Or is he like a manikin, dressed up by others and never his own person?

Joseph's life is a tale of three garments, possibly four. The first is the infamous coat of many colours. The Torah tells us nothing about its origins, but in his novel *Joseph and his Brothers*, Thomas Mann creates a fascinating backstory. The garment is sewn from the cloth Laban gave to Jacob to make a wedding gown for Rachel. A generation later, he fashions it into a coat for his son, telling him all about it:

> 'Rachel received the garment and was a splendour incomparable as we sat at the wedding feast and I kissed the image of Ishtar. But when I handed the bride the flower and lifted her veil that I might see her with my seeing hands, lo, it was Leah, whom the devil had craftily brought into the bedchamber . . .'

> 'And did Mami too wear the wrap in her time?'

> 'It is no wrap. It is a sumptuousness, a piece of material to be used as one will . . .'[86]

Given by one deceiver, Laban, to another, Jacob, treachery and rivalry are woven into the garment's very fabric. But this is not how Jacob sees it. His favourite wife, his only true love, died in childbirth. Her firstborn looks exactly like her; just as she was 'beautiful in figure and feature' so Joseph is 'handsome in figure and feature' (Gen. 29:17; 39:6). No parent should prefer one child over another, say the rabbis. Yet who can entirely blame Jacob? The coat represents the transference of his first love to her firstborn child, who dons it with the same lack of awareness shown by Jacob in giving it to him in the first place. Jacob will soon be deceived by it a second time, when his other sons hand it to him dipped in goat's blood and he cries out in misplaced recognition, 'My son's coat; a wild beast has devoured him' (Gen. 37:33).

As for Joseph, he struts about in the sunshine of his father's bias. Yet he, too, is put upon; he didn't choose to be burdened with such favour. Nevertheless, he's also culpable; he ought to have some inkling of his own part in how his brothers treat him, a responsibility of which it's unclear if he ever becomes aware. When a stranger, identified by the rabbis as the angel Gabriel, finds him lost in a field, Joseph tells him that he's looking for his brothers. But whether he ever truly finds them, not just physically when they 'see him coming from afar off' (Gen. 37:18), but also emotionally and fraternally, is hard to know.

The second item of clothing to determine Joseph's destiny is the garment his master Potiphar's wife strips off him as she attempts to seduce him and pull him into bed. It symbolises his rejection of her illicit approaches and his refusal to betray her husband's trust. But she cunningly uses it to dismiss him, adding a touch of racism as she displays her prize to her household while falsely relating to them the exact opposite of what actually happened: 'Look, he [my husband] brought us in this Hebrew fellow to make a mockery of us' (Gen. 39:14). It's not surprising that when his wife tells him all about it, Potiphar throws Joseph into jail. Strikingly, the Hebrew word for garment, used repeatedly in these verses, is *beged*, from the same root as *begidah*, 'betrayal'.

None other than Pharaoh himself gives Joseph his third set of apparel, dressing him in silks and placing a gold chain round his neck (Gen. 41:42). These robes and the status they represent define his life no less than the many-coloured tunic which led to such disaster. Years later, when famine has the entire region in its grip, they too distance him from his brothers. But this time it is to the brothers' disadvantage; it is Joseph who catches them in his trap. He recognises them, but they don't recognise him. In the meantime, he subtly puts together his plot to test whether they are ready to take responsibility for his one full brother, Benjamin, 'the son of his mother' (Gen. 43:29), as they refused to do for him.

But when the moment of encounter comes, and Judah movingly reveals a deep and generous understanding of their father's special bond with his youngest child, does Joseph, even as he reveals his true identity to them, finally find his brothers? Or is he still acting out a part, albeit one assigned to him by the very highest:

> Not you but God sent me here and made me like a father to Pharaoh, master of his house and ruler of all Egypt. Hurry and bring up my father. Tell him: 'So says your son Joseph, God has made me master of all Egypt, come down to me, don't delay.'
>
> (Gen. 45:8–9)

This sounds like the Joseph we know from his childhood, displaying the same superiority, only, given both his sufferings and his current position, with considerably greater justification.

Joseph has found his brothers physically; he embraces them, introduces several of them to Pharaoh and ensures they are well provided for on the best land Egypt has to offer. When Jacob dies and the brothers bow down once more before Joseph and beg him for forgiveness, he behaves with magnanimity (Gen. 50:15–21). But he doesn't live alongside them; he retains his authority over them just as much as over the rest of Egypt. So who is he now, not just to his brothers, but also to himself?

We're offered glimpses of the inner Joseph. He rejects the advances of Potiphar's wife, refusing to 'commit such a sin before God' (Gen. 39:9). Rashi comments that in the moment of temptation the image of his father flashes before his eyes. Joseph remembers his home and family, as shown in the names he gives his sons: 'Menashe, for God has caused me to forget all my troubles and my father's house'; and 'Ephraim, for God has made me fruitful in the land of my misery' (Gen. 41:51–2). An inner world of decades of suffering and longing are revealed. Joseph weeps, repeatedly and profusely, when he first sees his brothers, again when he makes himself known to them, and possibly yet again when he and his father meet. Finally, on his deathbed, he insists that his bones be taken back to Canaan when God eventually redeems the Children of Israel (Gen. 50:25). In those last moments, one senses that all his power and glory has been for him a great adventure in what is ultimately the wrong direction, and that underneath it all he is still the 'Hebrew boy' (Gen. 41:12) who longs for home.

As for us, do we, too, go through life wearing the garments others have dressed us in or, if we are fortunate, we ourselves have chosen, in order to protect our raw centre which still longs for our father or mother? Yet do we at the same time remain, somewhere within ourselves, the unheard child crying out from the pit of our soul? Every year on the Day of Atonement we confess, '*Bagadnu*, we have betrayed'. Endowed with the capacity for love and trust, we garb ourselves and each other in expectations and disappointments that cling to us as intimately as our skin. Perhaps we, like Joseph, struggle to find and to be found by our brothers and sisters, partners and children, and, in the midst of life's turmoil, sometimes lose not only them but also our true selves.

Lies lived and truths untold – Jacob's story

Each member of Jacob's family lived with the truth of his own story, but it was those very stories that prevented them from sharing them with each other. So together they lived a lie. They were all caught up in it, not least Jacob himself. When his brothers sent him Joseph's many-coloured garment dipped in goat's blood, 'he recognised it and said, "My son's coat; a wild beast has devoured him," and mourned for his son many days' (Gen. 37:33).

But what exactly did he recognise? The ravaged item held out for his inspection clearly belonged to Joseph; it was the coat he had given him with such blind love. But the rest was conjecture; he couldn't have known what exactly had happened to his favourite child. His 'recognition' is therefore painfully incomplete. Correct about the coat, he is mistaken about how it came to be in its bloody state. Goat's blood, notes Rashi, looks very like human blood; that's why the brothers chose it in which to douse the coat.[87] Jumping too swiftly to conclusions, Jacob is overcome by grief: 'All his sons and daughters rose up to comfort him but he refused to be consoled, saying "I will go down to my son in mourning to the grave"' (Gen. 37:35)

The rabbis saw grief as an unavoidable part of life. They followed Ecclesiastes' counsel that there is 'a time to mourn' (Eccles. 3:4), but also the implied corollary, that there's a time to cease from mourning because the death of our loved ones must ultimately be accepted. Why, then, does Jacob persist in his grief? Midrash notes that the Torah tells us that, 'Judah was comforted' for the loss of his wife, yet Jacob, the father of them all, 'refused to be consoled' (Bereshit Rabbah 84:21). This is because 'it is decreed that the dead are forgotten from the heart', comments the Talmud bluntly, but surely not accurately (Massechet Sofrim 21). Perhaps this is the ancient way of saying that life must go on. But it's very different if one believes that one's loved one is still alive:

> Even though our father Jacob said, 'A wild beast has devoured him,' he meant it only as conjecture. He hadn't lost hope of finding him. He therefore refused to be comforted so that Joseph's memory would remain in his heart and he would never give up looking for him.[88]

The death of a child is unlike the passing of other relatives. To bereaved parents, the passage of the years brings not consolation but further loss, the sharp awareness that their son's or daughter's contemporaries are starting a new school, going on dates, having children of their own. Meanwhile, treasured memories gradually fade: he had that way of looking at things; she wore a scarf in just those colours on our last holiday. Holding on to recollected details exacts its cost in pain, but so does the loss of them. Love, memory and heartache cling to each other. In his searing exploration of parental grief, David Grossman writes how:

> I'd like to learn to separate
> memory from the pain . . .
> You see, that way I can remember more of you:
> I will not fear the scalding of memory.[89]

Yet perhaps it isn't in order not to forget that Jacob clings to his grief. Maybe in his heart of hearts he really does believe that Joseph is still alive; it's the not knowing that makes him unable to let go. It's hard enough to believe that someone one loves is dead and gone forever when one has watched them die and witnessed the body being laid in the grave. It's harder by far if one wasn't present and saw nothing. I know this from experience: I was considered too young to visit my mother when she was dying in hospital, let alone to attend the funeral. Forty years later I was still having dreams that maybe it was all untrue, that she was alive somewhere in some home or asylum where they'd placed her for reasons I would never be told. For Jacob, such speculations can only have been encouraged by the constant sense that he was surrounded by pretence and that something essential was being concealed from him.

Feelings of self-doubt and guilt may also be wrapped up in Jacob's response: 'It was all caused by the coat that I, his father, went and gave him. Why did I do it? Why did I send him to his brothers when I could see how much they hated him? Am I even more blind than my father Isaac?' Maybe in Jacob's unconscious he himself is the 'wild beast' who devoured his beloved Joseph. If he were indeed to 'go down in mourning to his son' and meet him in the nether world, how would he explain himself, and what would Joseph say in return?

It's little wonder Jacob remains trapped in this frozen state of sorrow for twenty years. One can imagine him repeating day after day, year after year, the same lines about going down in grief to the grave, long after the rest of the family have become sick of hearing it. Only their bad conscience holds them back from telling him to shut up. Eventually their guilt, like their patience, wears thin. The problem is no longer what they did to Joseph back then, but their father's unbearable behaviour. They avoid him as much as they can, minding their sheep.

Or do they? They live with their lie, but their lie also lives within them. 'We found this,' they tell their father. (Which of them actually said the words, or was it a chorus? Did they speak with half-hidden glee, or had the dawning appreciation of the impact this would have on the old man rubbed the shine off their triumph?) 'We found this,' they say. 'Recognise: is it your son's coat?' (Gen. 37:32). They don't say, 'It's our brother's.' That would require a depth of acknowledgement on their part which it will take them years to reach. Their fake attempt at consolation offers no true comfort. Just as 'words that come from the heart reach the heart',[90] so words that don't come from the heart fail to move it. Hence they are bound to endless re-enactment of the same charade, a wearying, frustrating and dishonest cycle in which they remain trapped for two desultory decades. Only the famine will release them.

But do their memories remain static? Maybe their conscience slowly reshapes the scene, adding back into it details they failed to acknowledge before: the sight of Joseph in the pit, his desperate cries, the impact on the rest of them of Judah's warning, Reuben's distress. The more they think about it, the less they feel able to share, not just with their father but also with each other. Perhaps their responses are no longer the same? Reuben, Judah, where are their thoughts now? It's a subject they dare not address. Their commitment to non-communication has, gradually but irreversibly, become unbreakable.

The Torah nowhere records that they ever tell their father what they actually did. After Jacob's death, they plead with Joseph for forgiveness, claiming, 'Your father commanded before he died, saying, "Thus shall you say to Joseph: Please forgive your brothers' sin because they dealt badly with you"' (Gen. 50:16–17). Rabbinic tradition reads this not as evidence that Jacob was eventually informed of what truly happened long ago in Shechem. Rather, their assumption is that the brothers put these words in their dead father's mouth to strengthen their appeal to Joseph's magnanimity. Jewish law takes this as proof that it's permitted to tell white lies for the sake of peace.

There is one further participant in the miserable family drama: Isaac, the longest-lived of the patriarchs. After the brothers have handed over Joseph's bloodied garment, the Torah notes that 'his father wept for him'. It would seem obvious that the father referred to is Jacob. But Rashi takes it differently: '[The father is] Isaac [who] wept for the anguish of his son Jacob but did not himself mourn because he knew that Joseph was still alive.'[91]

Midrash elaborates:

Isaac wept when he was with Jacob, but when he left his presence he would wash, anoint himself with oil and eat and drink. Why, then, didn't he tell his son? He said to himself: 'God didn't reveal this to Jacob, so how can I?'

(Bereshit Rabbah 84:21)

Perhaps he felt, unconsciously, that this time it was his son's turn to be the one who failed to see. Or maybe he had come to realise through his own challenging experiences that we are left with no other choice than to submit before a destiny we can neither control nor understand.

So, for the rest of their lives, each member of the growing clan nurses their uneasy consciousness, trapped, but also protected, within the collective culture of untruth. They are hardly the only family to carry on for decades in this dysfunctional manner.

Twenty years later – the brothers' story

The way we understand our actions decades later is rarely the same as how we think of them at the time. Voices to which we gave scant attention may ring very differently with the passing of the years. Something unclear in our thoughts, some inchoate intuition, draws us back to them, a discomfiting recognition that we missed or dismissed some matter of importance. Slowly, we begin to listen, until words we never heeded become the most compelling voice in our conscience.

A surreal midrash tells of how Titus swallowed a flea which grew and grew inside his head until it killed him. His skull was opened and an insect the size of a small bird was found flapping frantically against its bony cage. It's the rabbinic way of saying that his guilt for the destruction of the Jerusalem Temple swelled until it occupied his every thought and devoured his mind (Midrash Tanhuma, Korach).

It's hardly surprising that Joseph's brothers can't stand him. He uses his preferential status as his father's favourite to snitch on them; he has not only imperious dreams of how he's going to lord it over them, but also the vanity to tell them all about it.

'Look,' they say to each other as they spot him in the distance on his mission to 'see how they are faring and report back', 'that dreamer of dreams is coming' (Gen. 37:14, 19). They have the perfect opportunity for revenge: who would ever know if they were to kill him, throw his body into a pit and tell their father that some wild animal had got him on his thoughtless jaunt? They act with a heartless connivance which often characterises group behaviour; had they each taken a moment alone to reflect, they might have got the better of their cruel first intentions.

Reuben persuades them not to kill Joseph outright. Feeling guilty after sleeping with his father's concubine Bilhah, he's acutely aware of the cost to the conscience of wrongdoing (Gen. 35:22). His words have an urgency that makes the brothers stop short of doing the worst, and instead they throw Joseph alive into a pit. If he cries out, if he pleads with his brothers to save his life, the text passes over it in silence. We learn only that 'the pit was empty, there was no water in it' (Gen. 37:24), which the Talmud takes to mean that it was full of snakes and scorpions (Shabbat 22a). With callous indifference, the brothers 'sit down to eat bread'. They take out their packed lunches, probably brought to them by the very same Joseph whom they have just dumped in a hole in the ground, and pass round the pitta. Maybe, in a gesture of contemptuous mercy, they throw him the crusts.

More than twenty years pass before we learn anything more about what they felt on that fateful day. Plenty happens in the meantime, especially to Joseph. He becomes Potiphar's steward, is falsely accused by the latter's wife and put in jail, interprets Pharaoh's butler's and baker's dreams, is hurried up from prison to explain Pharaoh's nightmares and promptly made viceroy of Egypt to preside over seven years of plenty before a universal famine grips the entire Middle East. We know, too, the essential details of Judah's life: he takes a wife, has three sons, marries two of them off but God dislikes and kills them, before, himself widowed, he sleeps unawares with his daughter-in-law Tamar and makes her pregnant with twins (Gen. 38).

But in the household of Jacob, time stands still. Just as when they first break the news that they have 'found' Joseph's blood-stained coat and 'all his sons and daughters rose up to console him but he refused to be comforted' (Gen. 37:35), so, twenty years later, the same scenario prevails. Jacob continues to mourn his best-loved son while the rest of the family presumably maintain the same dishonest silence about what actually happened.

Or maybe it's more complicated than that. Maybe the situation is far from static: perhaps there are times when nobody mentions anything at all and the occasional thought passes through the brothers with relief, as they shepherd their goats, that bygones are finally bygones. But then that very notion produces a counter-reaction; an uneasy conscience, an unsettling premonition, leads one of them to whisper to the brother he trusts most: 'Do you ever feel bad about what we did?' A third brother, intuiting what they're saying in their huddle, turns on them: 'Leave it alone.'

'Leave what alone?'

'You know perfectly well.'

They surely all do, because they can't help hearing, in solitary hours and in dreams the sparse text doesn't relate, the long-ago cry from the pit, and they understand that, in some unforeseeable manner, it speaks their destiny.

The famine in Egypt forces them to face it. Standing before the very brother whose claim on their mercy they ignored two decades earlier and whom they still don't recognise, they sense themselves in the hands of a controlling force whose power they feel in their bones but which they cannot fathom. Maybe it's the man's assurance that he fears God which prompts their whispered confession: 'We're surely guilty about our brother, when we saw his mortal anguish as he pleaded with us, but we wouldn't hear. That's why these troubles have come upon us' (Gen. 42:18, 21). The scene stands before them more vividly now than when it actually took place. Reuben reminds them sharply: 'Didn't I tell you, "Don't sin by the boy," but you wouldn't listen? Now, his blood, too, is required' (Gen. 42:22). This 'too', explains Rashi, refers to the blood of their father whose misery they've witnessed all these slow years.[92]

Their confession, which, unbeknown to them, Joseph overhears, comes suddenly and unsought, as if it had long been waiting on the tip of their conscience. When, on the journey home, the first of the brothers to open his sack of grain calls out to the others that his money has been returned, they whisper to each other in terror: 'What's God doing to us?' (Gen. 42:28). Filled with trepidation, they tell their father what's happened to them, explaining that unless they bring their youngest sibling with them 'that man, the lord of the land' will never again sell them grain or release the brother he's holding hostage (Gen. 42:30, 33–4). They flatly refuse to return to Egypt unless Benjamin accompanies them; their anguished father equally flatly refuses to let him go.

Only the threat of starvation and the adept intervention of Judah persuades the old man to yield (Gen. 43:8–9). This time, all eleven brothers sit down, unbeknown to them, with Joseph to eat. When he catches them in his cunningly planned trap to test if they will behave towards Benjamin with a solidarity they refused to show him twenty-two years earlier, they don't plead ignorance. They say neither, 'We didn't do it; someone must have planted that goblet in Benjamin's sack', nor, 'It's Benjamin's fault, so he can take the blame.' Instead, Judah speaks on behalf of them all: 'What can we say? How can we justify ourselves? God has found out the sin of your servants' (Gen. 44:16). He doesn't specify what sin; their whole lives have come up for judgement.

Joseph's brothers are not alone in pushing voices they don't want to hear down into the pit of forgetfulness and covering them over with denials. We retell our stories, reframe the narrative and let events fall from our minds into that reservoir of unconscious memory where, inconveniently, nothing is entirely lost. Maybe destiny will never call us to account; maybe life will never bring us to that impasse from which honesty is the only way out. Or maybe, in some manner we cannot exactly anticipate but long have feared, the truth will suddenly confront us.

Taking responsibility – Judah's story

Two matters turn the family fortunes round. The first is the famine; the text tells the facts in a mere three Hebrew words, a blunt brevity English cannot match: 'The famine was severe in the land' (Gen. 43:1). Jacob and his sons may argue, but there's no gainsaying the simple reality. If they can't reach a decision on whether or not Benjamin will accompany them to Egypt, hunger will have the last word. 'Why did you have to tell that man in Egypt that I had a further child?!' Jacob laments, without agreeing to let the lad go (Gen. 43:6). They've rehearsed this fruitless exchange time and again, ending in the same entrenched stalemate. It's a version of those refrains so many families know only too well, when, despite their differences, they're held together by inertia, the contempt engendered by familiarity, or mutual guilt, rather than by trust and affection.

Meanwhile, the storehouse is almost empty. It's Judah who finally breaks the deadlock. 'Send the boy with me,' he insists. 'I'll stand pledge for him; from my hand shall you seek him' (Gen. 43:8–9). There's something about his words that makes Jacob yield; amid the prevailing falsity, Judah strikes a note of integrity. Perhaps it's because he inadvertently reminds Jacob of what he himself said long ago on his flight back to Canaan, when Laban accused him of stealing the household gods. After watching in silent fury as his father-in-law fruitlessly searches his wives' tents, he gives vent to his anger:

> What have you found of anything that's yours? Put it right here, in front of our eyes . . . Your ewes and goats did not miscarry; I never ate the rams of your flock. I brought you no torn animal; it was I who made good the loss. *From my hand did you seek it*, whatever was stolen from me by day or stolen by night.
>
> (Gen. 31:37–9)

Now, decades later, his son Judah unwittingly echoes those very words: 'from my hand shall you seek him'. Something shifts in Jacob's heart; he lets the boy go.

Why is it Judah who finds the right words? One view is that the Bible needs him to be a hero. David, the ancestor of the Messiah, is born from his lineage. After the conquest by Sennacherib of the ten 'lost' tribes of Israel in the eighth century BCE, only the Kingdom of Judah survives. Therefore, the original Judah, the patriarch, has to be allotted a redemptive role from the start.

While this may be the case, the Torah provides a more immediate reason. It interrupts the account of Joseph's fortunes to make place for a secondary story which has seemingly little bearing on the primary plot. The key events are succinctly related: Judah marries off his eldest son to Tamar. When he dies because he's 'bad in God's sight', Judah gives her to his second child, Onan, who refuses to have intercourse with her and meets the same fate. Unwilling to chance his third son, Shelah, with this femme fatale, he sends her back to her father's house despite knowing that custom requires him to give her his youngest son so that she can bear a child and heir (Gen. 38:6–11).

Realising that her father-in-law has no intention of honouring this obligation, Tamar, now a tied woman unfree to marry anyone else, takes her destiny into her own hands. Hearing that Judah has been widowed, she dresses as a sacred prostitute. Judah falls for her charms and, failing to recognise who she is, has sex with her. In lieu of payment he leaves behind his staff, signet ring and purse in pledge, items he's unable to redeem since Tamar promptly changes back into her widow's clothes and seemingly disappears. When Judah is informed that Tamar is with child, he orders her to be burnt. She, however, returns his ring and staff with the message, 'It's by the man to whom these belong that I'm pregnant' (Gen. 38:25). 'Recognise!' she demands, employing the very words Jacob's sons had used when presenting their father with Joseph's blood-soaked coat. Judah acknowledges not just that they are his, but that he's responsible for what she's done: 'She's more just than I,' he concedes, 'because I never gave her to my son Shelah' (Gen. 38:26). The honesty of this scene contrasts sharply with the deceit that has settled over the rest of Jacob's household.

Perhaps, then, what changes Jacob's mind is that he senses Judah knows the meaning of integrity. He took responsibility when called to account before and will, if necessary, do so again. No doubt still anxious and sore at heart, Jacob consents to letting Benjamin go and, a mere two verses later, all eleven of Jacob's sons stand within Joseph's power.

When Joseph entraps them, it's once again Judah who finds the right words. Joseph has had his silver goblet planted in Benjamin's sack. He orders his servant to pursue the brothers and accuse them of theft. In disbelief, they declare that 'the man in whose sack the goblet is found shall die' (Gen. 44:9). When it's duly discovered, they troop back to Joseph in dismay to offer themselves as slaves. Not so, he insists: 'The man in whose hand the goblet was found shall be my slave; as for you, go back in peace to your father' (Gen. 44:17). His words are cunning and ironic: what 'peace' can they possibly have? Will these so-called brothers prove sufficiently heartless to abandon Benjamin, just as they forsook Joseph himself in that pit? What fate awaits them if they don't?

This is the cue for Judah to intercede, whereupon he describes with deep understanding Benjamin's special place in his father's heart as the sole remaining child of his best-loved wife: they are bound together 'soul to soul' (Gen. 44:30). Let him, Judah, therefore remain behind in Egypt, 'a servant to my master', while Benjamin goes back home.

It's at this moment that Joseph can contain himself no longer: his 'brothers', the sons of Leah, have taken responsibility for his full 'brother', the only other child of Rachel. They haven't forsaken Benjamin as they did him. For just one moment, before he sends everyone else out of the room, Joseph the man, the brother, the child, emerges, despite his royal Egyptian robes. He weeps (Gen. 45:1–2). Judah's integrity has brought Joseph, too, to reveal his truth.

VAYIGGASH – AND HE DREW NEAR (44:18–47:27)

....

Who cries?

This feather stirs; she lives! If it be so
It is a chance which doth redeem all sorrows
That ever I have felt.

William Shakespeare[93]

What actually happens when father and child finally meet after more than twenty years? Their love has remained intact: the old man still mourns for his son, presumed dead; his son, though viceroy of Egypt, still aches to know how his father fares. Joseph's first words after revealing himself to his brothers are, 'Is my father still alive?' (Gen. 45:3). Jacob's heart misses a beat when he is informed that 'Joseph yet lives' (Gen. 45:26). He simply can't believe it, until they repeat his exact words and show him the carriages he's sent. Only then do his spirits revive. 'God's presence, which had departed from him, returns to rest upon him,' explains Rashi.[94] His soul is restored. 'Enough,' he says, 'Let me go and see him before I die' (Gen. 45:27–8).

God comes to him in a night vision at Bet El one last time. Three times God says to him, *anochi*, 'I', and promises three times to abide with him and his descendants in their exile: 'I will go down with you and I will surely bring you back up' (Gen. 46:4). With this assurance, recalled with pained hope by his distant descendants in many bitter flights, he continues down to Egypt to see his beloved child.

The Torah describes their encounter with characteristic brevity:

> Joseph harnessed his chariot and went up to Goshen to meet Israel his father; he appeared to him; and he fell upon his neck, and he wept profusely. And Israel said to Joseph, 'Let me die now after seeing your face, since you're still alive.'
>
> (Gen. 46:29–30)

The text is ambiguous. Who does what? Which of them, father or son, is the subject of the verbs 'appear', 'fell upon' and 'weep'? Rashi explains:

79

'He harnessed his chariot': Joseph harnessed the horses himself in his eagerness to see his father.

'He appeared to him': Joseph appeared to his father.

'He wept profusely': He [Joseph] wept unusually much, but Jacob did not fall on Joseph's neck, nor did he kiss him.[95]

For Rashi, then, the subject of each of the verbs is Joseph: the son rushes up to his father, hugs him and weeps profusely. All the anguish of his orphan years bursts forth in those tears. Meanwhile, the old man keeps his composure as if transfixed by some vision.

Nachmanides disagrees:

It seems to me that the correct reading is that Jacob's eyes were already somewhat heavy with age, so that when Joseph arrived in Egypt's second chariot of state with the mitre over his face in the manner of Egyptian royalty, and was therefore unrecognisable to his father – and his brothers hadn't recognised him either – the text relates how, after he appeared to him and he'd looked closely and recognised him, he fell upon his neck and wept just as he had wept for him throughout the time he hadn't seen him until that very day. After that [Jacob] said: 'Let me die now after seeing your face.' It's common knowledge which of the two it is who weeps, the elderly father who finds his son alive following grief and despair, or the young man in his royal estate.[96]

Nachmanides' words come from the heart. He himself was forced into exile following a public disputation in Barcelona in 1264 with Pablo Christiani who accused the Talmud of defaming Jesus. Writing from Jerusalem in 1267, he describes the sorry state of the tiny Jewish community there and how he finds consolation in weeping at the Western Wall of the Temple. Then he adds:

Oh I am the man who saw affliction. I am banished from my table, far removed from friend and kinsman, and too long is the distance to meet again . . . I left my family, forsook my house. There with the sweet and beloved children, whom I brought up on my knees, I left also my soul. With them, my heart and my eyes will dwell forever.[97]

Only a person who has known how it feels to long to behold an adored face, to hear once more a beloved voice, can appreciate Jacob's meeting with his son. I think of the parents who sent their children to the safe haven of Britain on the trains of the Kindertransport in 1938 and 1939. I imagine them returning to silent homes, opening the doors to their children's rooms, reassembling the items strewn across the floor in the haste of packing because they'd suddenly heard there was an extra place in a group leaving that very night. I see them sitting on the bed, exhausted, overwhelmed by the weeping they'd fought so hard to contain at the parting, each subsequent day defined by the shedding or the holding back of tears.

Rashi has an altogether different understanding of Jacob's state of mind: 'He did not fall on Joseph's neck or kiss him; our rabbis say that he was reciting the *Shema*, meditating on the oneness of God.'[98] How strange that this is what he should be doing in the moment he sets eyes on his long-lost child! Is he unable to express his emotions, self-absorbed or simply heartless?

Surely not; the father who weeps every day for his son is not without a heart. Rather, time has stopped for Jacob; time has been transcended. This moment now, that day years back when he and Joseph parted, his night-time encounter with the angel, Rachel's dying words, that hour by the well when he first met and kissed her, have all elided in his mind and one light flows through them all. This coming together, the unification of these moments, their simultaneous brevity and eternity, the falling away of the years in between, has him in its grip. He can't embrace Joseph because he's embraced already in a great oneness, a coming together of his life, his children and his destiny, which includes and transcends this encounter. Rebbe Yisrael of Tshortkov observes: 'The meeting of Jacob and Joseph is in itself the recital of the *Shema*.[99]

I remember the first time I revisited as an adult the house where I was born, the home from which, when I was five years old, my grandfather took me for a walk so that I wouldn't see the ambulance carry my mother away to the Glasgow Royal Infirmary, from where she never returned. I wept most of the hundred miles until we arrived at that small street off the Milngavie Road, while in my mind those long-ago years drew side by side with now, as I drove with my soon-to-be wife, my life in between a strange bewilderment.

Famine in the land

In biblical and Mishnaic times, famines were frequent across the Middle East. Abram went down to Egypt because of a famine in Canaan. God instructed Isaac not to do likewise when the country was afflicted a second time. The harshest famine came in Jacob's old age; the entire Middle East was affected, with Egypt, normally one of the fertile breadbaskets of the region, hit worst of all. It is against this background of natural disaster that the destiny of Jacob's family is brought to a head.

The famine proves to be Joseph's making. Even as he interprets Pharaoh's dreams, he senses his opportunity: 'Let Pharaoh find a wise and perspicacious man and appoint him over the land of Egypt' (Gen. 41:33). Pharaoh's reaction is presumably exactly what Joseph intended: 'Since God has made all this known to you, there can be no one more perspicacious or wise than yourself' (Gen. 41:39). Pharaoh acts in haste but not necessarily in folly: famines are never good news for rulers. To have a clever and ambitious young man at hand at such a time, a foreigner at that, whom it'll be easy to blame if matters go wrong, presents a perfect way forward. Scarcely a few hours after learning of Joseph's existence he puts the ring of royal authority on his finger.

Jewish tradition, critical of Joseph for his early behaviour towards his brothers, largely praises his conduct as vizier. What, though, is its legacy?

He sets to work at once, travelling the length and breadth of the land. As the Eco Bible observes, he gives:

> . . . immediate attention to the natural world – sun, rain, wind, and insects – and long term attention to the coming drought and famine . . .
> In contrast, many of today's corporations buy agricultural land from indigenous people, then leave the local population without sufficient means to feed themselves.[100]

He arranges for grain to be stored locally, preventing future problems of distribution and ensuring that the entire country, not just its wealthiest regions, will be provided for in the tough years ahead. He 'embodies foresight, self-discipline, and concern for the larger community'.[101] One contemporary rabbi goes so far as to suggest that he uses the seven years of plenty to teach the Egyptians to set limits to their immediate consumption in order to save for the future.[102]

But, as the famine persists and the situation becomes ever harder, the decisions Joseph has to make become even more challenging. When they can no longer pay for grain with money or animals, the Egyptian populace plead with him for their very lives:

> All we've got left are our bodies and our land. Why should we perish before your eyes, we and our land? Buy us and our land in return for

bread. We and our land will become enslaved to Pharaoh. Give us seed so that we can live and not die, so that the country doesn't become a wasteland.

(Gen. 47:18–19)

Nachmanides comments that Joseph listens in part, but not in full. He does acquire the Egyptians' land for Pharaoh. For although, as the biblical historian Nahum Sarna notes, nationalisation must have come about during the reigns of several Pharaohs, 'It is attributed to Joseph to acknowledge his genius and highlight the ingratitude of the [later] Pharaohs who "did not know him".'[103] But, Nachmanides continues, Joseph does not acquire the Egyptians' persons for Pharaoh. He refuses to turn them into slaves; instead, they become tenant farmers. Normally, he observes, share-croppers would expect to give eighty per cent of their yield to the crown. But Joseph reverses the proportions: only twenty per cent of the grain goes to Pharaoh while the rest is kept by the farmers to eat and sow.

Yet there are undertones. The first time the phrase 'slaves to Pharaoh' occurs in the Torah is here. The words echo uncomfortably; we know what they will mean in a few generations' time. Joseph transfers the people into towns. It's a widespread phenomenon to this day that in times of famine rural populations migrate to the cities in search of work, only to find themselves homeless and hungry. So why does Joseph encourage this movement? To remind the people that they no longer own the land, suggests Rashi, adding that it's for the same reason that he also shifts the population of one city into another.[104] This also serves to protect his brothers against the charge that they're mere foreigners and itinerants, since no one is a true native anymore. Rashi's grandson Rashbam, Samuel ben Meir (c.1085–1158), laconically likens Joseph's actions to those of the Assyrian emperor Sennacherib who forcibly transferred the populations of the territories he conquered 'to a land like their own' so that they [the victims of this policy] could claim no ancestral rights.[105]

Such a comparison with the tyrant who laid most of Israel waste in the eighth century BCE is hardly complimentary. Perhaps, though, Rashbam's point is that this is simply what every monarch did in ancient, and not so ancient, times.

At any event, the Egyptian people are profoundly grateful, hailing Joseph as their saviour: 'You've saved our lives! May we find favour in your eyes, our master! We shall be slaves to Pharaoh' (Gen. 47:25). Pharaoh, too, must have been deeply thankful; as an unnamed commentary points out, the famine was a disaster for Egypt yet a blessing for him because all the country's wealth was transferred into his coffers.

But memory is fickle; the past is always subject to reconstruction as times change and power falls into new hands. Prosperity brings forgetfulness, as Moses later warns the Children of Israel in his dying address (Deut. 32:15). It's far from impossible to imagine that, within a few years, the word begins to spread among the Egyptian populace that it was Joseph, that Hebrew, who took all our money, stole our land and turned us into slaves. The famine wasn't really that bad; we didn't actually have to sell our farms. We were lied to; they lined their own pockets by pretending the situation was worse than was actually the case.

Perhaps the Pharaoh of the Exodus, who 'knew not Joseph' (Exod. 1:8), was all too aware of what his people had to say about him. Maybe he had his ear to the ground and sensed that the time was ripe to listen to the popular mood: measures against the descendants of that foreign upstart would be well received; those people had to be put back in their place in order to make Egypt great once again. Everyone was waiting for it; those Hebrews had been eating the fat of the land for far too long.

An unsettled present often stores up trouble for an uneasy future.

VAYEHI - AND HE LIVED (47:28-50:26)

....

'And Jacob lived seventeen years' – time in Jacob's life

Time is regular only in clocks; it flows unevenly through the human heart. It's a revealing exercise to conduct an audit of our lives to assess when time has moved quickly, when slowly, when it's stopped altogether and when it's seemed to go backward, before leaping forward once again.

I would often go straight from secondary school to my grandparents' house. I'd always known that my grandfather was a rabbi, but I realised only in my late teens just what this meant and I did not want to squander my opportunity to ask him questions. 'How come,' I asked him one evening, 'Jacob is supposed to be such a good person when he cheated his brother so shamelessly?'

My grandfather made no attempt to justify the patriarch. 'The rabbis blame him severely for his conduct,' he replied. 'But the Torah also says that the seven years he served Laban for the hand of Rachel passed so quickly that they seemed to him like just a few days. Someone who loves like that can't be all bad.'

Fifty years later I still think about that answer. My grandfather met my grandmother at a celebration of the carnival-like festival of Purim in 1912; she was very beautiful and he fell instantly in love. The following year they were engaged, but then came the First World War; he enlisted as a chaplain and was sent to Verdun on the Western Front. He and his fiancée wrote to each other every single day. When it became clear that the war would be over neither by the close of 1914 nor by the Christmas of 1915, or even 1916, as the Kaiser kept promising, my grandfather took a month's furlough and married my grandmother in the late spring of 1917. They kept their love letters as their greatest treasure. In 1938 the Nazis stole them; those were the only possessions about the loss of which I ever heard my grandparents complain, though they had to leave everything behind when they fled Germany. So my grandfather well understood what it meant to be in love and have to wait for year after year.

When Jacob saw Rachel for the first time, 'he kissed her and lifted up his voice and wept' (Gen. 29:11). According to Midrash, he cried not only because he had fallen helplessly in love, but also because 'he saw by the Holy Spirit that they would not lie together in the grave' (Bereshit Rabbah 70:12). In the wonder of love, time as measured by clock and calendar dissolves; Jacob sees only himself, his beloved and eternity. Maybe this, too, was an experience my grandfather understood, since I once heard him say, without offering any further explanation, 'In truth, there's no such thing as time.'

Thus the hours flow unevenly through Jacob's life. Seven long years of service to his uncle contract into a mere few days. 'Give me my bride,' he says to Laban, 'My days are fulfilled' (Gen. 29:21). The Torah doesn't tell us how swiftly his first nuptial night passes in non-recognition, or how heavily the minutes weigh as Jacob absorbs the reality of his deception. Maybe time not only stops but also springs backwards when Laban tosses him the rebuttal: 'It isn't done in *our* place to put the younger before the older' (Gen. 29:26). There he is, back in his parents' tent, advancing with that dish of goat's meat towards his father whose hands travel slowly over his arms and face but fail to feel their way to the truth.

Afterwards come the years of domesticity and thrift, the quarrels between his wives and concubines and the birth of his eleven sons and single daughter. Those are the decades in which age imperceptibly catches up on us, slipping into the limbs and features, whispering, but not so silently that one can consistently avoid hearing, 'You're young no longer.'

'Touch thirty and you're forty before you know it,' a wise woman once told me. 'And maybe fifty too.' Slowly the toll of work-laden weeks and sleep-deprived nights adds up: 'These twenty years I've been in your household . . . I bore the devouring heat by day, the icy cold by night' (Gen. 31:41, 40), Jacob shouts at Laban when he overtakes him on his flight back home and rummages through his possessions to find out who has stolen his household gods. Perhaps Jacob is remonstrating not just with his father-in-law but with life itself: this is how I've spent the best part of my life and now it's gone forever.

Rachel's death in childbirth is the turning point, the beginning of Jacob's decades of mourning and trouble. From now on the initiative lies with his children: Reuben's misconduct with Bilhah, Shechem's seduction of Dinah, Shimon and Levi's violent revenge, the long saga of Joseph. 'Shall we really come, I, your mother and your brothers, and bow down before you?' Jacob chides when his favourite son unwisely shares his dreams (Gen. 37:10). For so long children follow their parents; after that, parents follow their children. Jacob is no longer the chief protagonist in his own life's story.

The Torah tells us that Joseph looks just like his mother, using identical words to describe them both (Gen. 29:17; 39:6). The past relinquishes the present only on condition that it haunts it. Concluding too quickly that Joseph has been devoured by an evil beast, Jacob must have felt that what happened to his best-loved wife was happening all over again. For in his final hours, he calls Benjamin a devouring wolf (Gen. 49:27), a so-called blessing explained perhaps by an unconscious conviction that the first thing his youngest son did was kill his own mother in childbirth. Now, once again, all he has left is blood-soaked garments.

Twenty years pass in stasis as his sons and daughters rise to console him and he refuses to be comforted, saying only, 'I shall go down to the grave to my son' (Gen. 37:35). This same scene is re-enacted over and again, an endless charade to the falsity of which none of them dares confess. Time has stopped for Jacob; only the deceit and distrust continue to grow, their grip more implacable year by year. Perhaps, the falsehood aside, that's how it is for parents with the death of a child. Maybe, just as in the homes of many bereaved parents, Joseph's tent has remained untouched, his things just as they were on the fateful day when he walked off to see his brothers. Only part of the mourner moves onwards in time; the rest of the heart remains behind, keeping vigil with the dead. Ask anyone stricken by grief how long it is since their loved one died and they will likely say, 'A moment ago and forever.'

When Jacob finally allows himself to be parted from Benjamin, his only other child who reminds him of Rachel, time begins to move once again. When he learns that Joseph is alive after all, his spirits soar: 'Let me go and see him before I die' (Gen. 45:28). Midrash suggests that when they meet after twenty-two years, Jacob is absorbed in reciting the *Shema*: to this timeless moment only the timelessness of God can bear witness.

When Joseph brings his aged father to see him, Pharaoh is struck by his venerable appearance and asks point blank, 'How many are the days of the years of your life?' Jacob, perhaps overcome by sudden exhaustion at the strange inexplicability of everything, replies grimly, 'Few and bad have been the days of the years of my life; they haven't attained to the days of the years of the lives of my fathers' (Gen. 47:8–9). It's a saddening answer from someone whose life has been so rich in adventure.

There's no suggestion that Jacob becomes the reigning patriarch once again, honoured and celebrated by his family. Joseph supports him through the seventeen remaining years of his life, and no doubt still loves him, but he lives in exile, not just from his homeland in Canaan but also from ownership of his own life. Only at the end is his power restored, the angel who redeemed him, and from whom he refused to be parted without being blessed, granting him one last opportunity to confer blessings upon his sons and grandsons (Gen. 48:15–16, 20; 49:1–28).

His final wish is to be buried alongside his ancestors, to join them in that world unafflicted by the depredations of time (Gen. 49:29).

Identity

My great-grandfather Jacob Freimann died suddenly of a stroke in December 1937, soon after his seventieth birthday. It was a mercy; he was spared the torments that tore his widow and all six of his children from their homes and left her and two of them and their families dead, murdered in the gas chambers. The horrors of Nazism passed over him as he lay at peace in the old Jewish cemetery of Holesov, the small town in Moravia where he'd served as rabbi for twenty years before being called to Posen and, in the last years of his life, to Berlin, where he became head of the rabbinical court.

He was a true scholar of Torah, a man of piety and integrity, committed to orthodox Judaism while facing the challenges of his swiftly changing world. Sometimes I imagine meeting him. What would he say to me? Would he be ashamed of me, his inadequate descendant, lacking his deep

Talmudic knowledge, grasp of detail in Jewish law and clear, unwavering belief? Would he ask me in that world of truth, as the rabbis refer to the beyond, 'Are you, after all these generations, faithful?' According to rabbinic tradition, that's the question Jacob asked his children on his death-bed. Here in this foreign land, a tiny minority, have you remained true to your heritage and to your God? This challenge of multiple and competing identities has, from the first, troubled Jews throughout the ages.

With failing strength, the last of the patriarchs gathers his sons around him. His final request, which he has already made Joseph swear to fulfil, is to be buried in the Cave of Machpelah in the Land of Canaan (Gen. 49:29–32). This is where he belongs, alongside his ancestors. Joseph will express a similar wish despite his prestige in Egypt: take my bones with you when you leave (Gen. 50:25). Their demands are not surprising; to this day many who sideline their Judaism for much of their lives neverthe-less regard it as the core of their identity. They may not have lived as Jews, but they wish to die as Jews and be buried alongside their fellow Jews in a Jewish cemetery.

A striking midrash explores what it is that Jacob wants from his children:

> When he lay dying, Jacob summoned his children and questioned them one by one. [He said to them,] 'Listen to the God of Israel, your father in heaven: are you harbouring any issues with God in your hearts?' They said to him: 'Hear, O Israel our father; just as you harbour no quarrels with God in your heart, so we have no quarrels with God. Rather, "The Lord our God, the Lord is one."'
>
> (Sifrei Devarim Va'Etchanan 31)

The midrash attributes to Jacob's children the words subsequently recorded by Moses and destined to become known simply as the *Shema*, the core creed of Judaism. The midrash suggests that, throughout his life, Jacob was worried in case any of his children should prove unfaithful to the family heritage. Their responses came as a gratifying relief:

> [When he heard them,] Jacob replied and said, 'Blessed be God's name, the glory of whose kingdom is for ever and ever.' Then the Holy Blessed One said to him: 'This is what you've wanted all your life, that your children should recite the *Shema* when they rise up and when they lie down.'
>
> (Sifrei Devarim Va'Etchanan 31)

I vividly remember how my own father came into my room late one night when I was sixteen and asked me if I still said the *Shema* before going to sleep. He'd taught me the words phrase by phrase in the weeks after our mother died, coming up quietly to my brother's and my bedroom to comfort us and saying, 'If you're good, I'll tell you the next verse tomorrow.' I can't recall how I answered him then, because in my teens I'd neglected to say it; but every night since, unless overtaken suddenly by sleep, I've made sure to recite the *Shema*.

When Jacob dies, Joseph collapses over his body and weeps. Swiftly regaining his composure, he orders 'his servants the doctors' to embalm his father, before requesting Pharaoh's permission to follow his wishes and bury him in Canaan (Gen. 50:1–5). Pharaoh's entire entourage, 'the elders of his household and all the elders of Egypt . . . even chariots and horsemen' go up with Joseph and his brothers to accompany Jacob's body. When the huge procession halts near the Jordan, the Egyptian presence is so great that the locals are drawn to comment that 'a great mourning has befallen Egypt' (Gen. 50:7–11).

Yet even here, despite the remarkable respect accorded the last of the patriarchs by the Egyptian hierarchy, the Torah's words carry a warning. 'Horsemen' and 'chariots' will soon appear in the Torah again, as the cavalry units with which the subsequent Pharaoh who 'knew not Joseph' will trap Jacob's terrified descendants in the desert. Evidently, politics were as fickle then as they are now. One day the host nation honours you; the next, you find yourself its victim. My mother's father served in the German army for the duration of the First World War; in 1939 he was forced to flee the very country for which he'd risked his life. However much he saw himself as German, this was not how Germany now saw him. He was a Jew.

Joseph's prestigious position in Egypt presumably remains intact for the rest of his life. Yet he, too, doesn't want to be buried in its sands, whatever honours Pharaoh himself would undoubtedly have accorded him. This is not where he ultimately belongs; he is still at heart a *naar ivri*, as the chief butler long ago described him, 'a Hebrew lad' (Gen. 41:12).

So where do we who are part of religious or ethnic minorities actually belong? Do we present ourselves as 'more English than the English', trying to convince ourselves that this is not just who we are but also how we are regarded? Do we keep our 'other' identity as private as possible, following Rabbi Jonathan Sacks' witty rephrasing of Descartes, following Sydney Morganbesser: *Incognito ergo sum*?[106] Or do we embrace our multiple identities, even in the face of rising nationalism and populism?

LISTENING FOR GOD IN TORAH AND CREATION

In whatever way we choose to live, in whichever country and with whatever security, insecurity or status, many of us harbour Jacob's wish to be interred *el avotai*. Though it's tempting to translate his words as 'with my ancestors', the preposition *el* really means 'to': what Jacob actually asks is to be taken for burial '*to* my ancestors'. However multiple his identities may have been in this temporal life, he wants his identity in eternity to be unambiguous: he must be laid to rest among his people.

'In a coffin in Egypt'

The book that opens with expansion closes in contraction. The beginning is all creation, as God's spirit hovers over the inchoate waters before the divine vitality radiates outwards to fashion all existence. The mystics teach that this process commences neither with the initial chapter of the Bible, nor with its first verse, nor with its opening words '*Bereishit barah*, in the beginning of the creating,' nor even with the letter *bet* with which the Torah starts, but with the tiny dot within it invisible in the scroll of the Torah. Like matter from the big bang, the sacred energy that animates all being expands outwards from a single unknowable point to form all that is. Fifty chapters later, this magnificent work ends in a box: 'Joseph died, one hundred and ten years old. They embalmed him and he was put in a coffin in Egypt' (Gen. 50:26).

It's an abrupt and bewildering conclusion: how can the work that has taken the universe as its circumference and God as its spirit cease in the narrow confines of a coffin, leaving the reader, like Joseph, somehow within it? The very notion is frightening; I've heard several people express terror at the thought of waking up trapped as a result of some appalling mistake in a chest-high, shoulder-wide prison to hammer and scream in futile panic until the oxygen is used up. The end of Genesis always leaves me anxious and dismayed. Its final word is *beMitzrayim*, 'in Egypt', the name of the country where the Children of Israel will shortly begin to suffer. But, derived from the root *tsar*, it also carries the meaning of narrowness and constriction. This is where *Bereshit*, the Book of Creation, leaves us, confined in a coffin in an alien land. Maybe this is how it's meant to be, the text in its very structure embodying the spirit's journey from the wonder of birth and growth to the narrow closure of physical death.

The Book of Exodus, in Hebrew *Sefer Shemot*, literally 'the Book of Names', opens by telling us simply that 'Joseph died, and all his brothers and all that generation' (Exod. 1:6), before embarking on its narrative of enslavement and redemption. Meanwhile, Joseph's remains lie abandoned for generations, and with them the stories of the ancestors, their struggles, their failures and the blessings entrusted to them, seemingly lost in a foreign land.

But, in truth, Joseph's bones are not entirely forgotten. They will come back to life, though not in physical form. They will be restored in a different dimension, as Joseph himself foresaw on his deathbed when he looked into the future: 'God will surely remember you, and you will carry my bones up with you out of this [place]' (Gen. 50:25). Not just his bones, but also his dreams will be borne onwards for generations in story and song.

The Torah records how Moses fulfils his ancestor's last wish. In the aftermath of the tenth plague, despite all his responsibilities, he remembers to take Joseph's remains with him (Exod. 13:19). A striking midrash explains how, amid all the chaos, he manages to locate them:

Serach, daughter of Asher, was still alive from that generation. Moses went and asked her, 'Where are Joseph's bones?' She told him, 'The Egyptians made him a coffin out of metal and put it in the Nile to bring blessing to its waters.' Moses stood on the banks of the Nile and called out, 'Joseph, Joseph, the hour has come for the fulfilment of God's promise to redeem Israel, and of the oath you made the Children of Israel swear. Hear now, because they're waiting for you. Reveal yourself. If you do not do so, we shall be accounted innocent of the vow.' Immediately Joseph's coffin rose to the surface.

Mechilta deRabbi Shimeon bar Yochai

This fanciful account is a remarkable metaphor for how we carry our ancestors with us. Their 'bones' may take the form of undated pictures in an album discovered in the bottom of a drawer. They may be just names, or we may only know that they once had names, that they came from somewhere we haven't heard of and died in places we never visited. They may be no more than a mention in a letter we almost threw away but which suddenly caught our eye; they may be a footnote in a biography. But, somehow, they call out to us, provoking more than casual curiosity: this person was one of us, holds part of our story. We write to relatives, scrutinise family trees with a persistence that takes us by surprise. We summon forgotten ancestors back into our conscious knowledge. We locate someone, somewhere, who still remembers something, who can put a name to the unlabelled photo or add one more paragraph to the story. We stand like Moses on the riverbank and call out: where are you? Who were you? What troubles did you pass through?

In this manner, not always but not rarely, the dead rise back to the surface and become articulate once again. We don't know their words exactly as they might have spoken them, but we have the bones of their biographies and an inner compulsion that makes us listen. We carry them with us, winding our own stories around theirs and theirs into ours. They travel with us on our unfinished journey to the land of our destiny. They become our poetry and songs as in Osip Mandelstam's poem:

> Mounds of human heads are wandering into the distance.
> I dwindle among them. Nobody sees me. But in books
> much loved, and in children's games I shall rise
> from the dead to say the sun is shining.[107]

Thus, Joseph's skeleton, placed in a coffin, an *aron*, in Egypt, accompanies the Children of Israel on the unending road to God's Promised Land, through countless travails and generations of stories. But 'coffin' doesn't only signify 'coffin'. In the Book of Exodus, *aron* no longer means a casket for the dead but refers instead to the Ark of the Covenant, the *Aron Habrit*, inside which are not bones but the tablets of stone engraved with God's commandments, the essence of God's revelation. This double meaning may be a mere semantic coincidence, yet it suggests a deeper connection. These two *aronot*, Joseph's coffin and the Ark with God's word, carried by the Children of Israel on their long pilgrimage through the desert, travel with us to this day. They could scarcely be more different, yet they belong closely together. We listen out for God through the stories of our ancestors, and God's voice leads us back to our ancestors' stories. Their origins are even connected: creation unfolds when God's spirit hovers over the void, and our narratives develop when our ancestors' spirits rest upon us, helping us to distinguish between the light and the dark, the dry land and the dangerous waters, across and between which we have to pass.

Meanwhile, we must bide our time. Joseph lies dead in Egypt, submerged beneath the waters of the Nile beside which his descendants serve out their time as slaves. Destiny is delayed; there is much in the meantime to be endured.

THE BOOK OF EXODUS

שְׁמוֹת

SHEMOT (1:1–6:1)

I don't know

'There arose a new king who did not know Joseph' (Exod. 1:8). The Talmud puts the question: could the ruler of Egypt really have been so unaware of the history of his own country as to be ignorant of the identity of the man who had saved its entire population from starvation? Or was this merely pretence, a deliberate political decision not to recognise his indebtedness to the forebear of those foreigners who were now multiplying at such an alarming rate throughout his land (Sotah 11a)?

Not knowing, the refusal to admit or acknowledge, has a history in the Torah; Cain does 'not know' the whereabouts of the brother he has murdered (Gen. 4:9). The ruler of Egypt is neither the first nor the last to deny all knowledge.

I thought of that Pharaoh on a grey autumn day when I stood opposite the Lorelei, the forbidding tower of rock around which the Rhine River is forced to bend sharply, creating deadly currents. According to legend, a siren sits on its wind-blown top, luring hapless mariners with her seductive songs to their deaths far below. The German-Jewish poet Heinrich Heine wrote a ballad on the subject, which, set to an inveigling melody, became such an ineradicable part of popular folklore that even Hitler could not prevent it from being sung. But since, under Nazism, any Jewish contribution to German culture had to be denied, the authorship of the poem was altered to 'anonymous'. My grandparents often spoke about this deception, a prelude to more brutal lies of fatal consequence.

Persecutors often begin by 'not knowing' their victims. They make themselves ignorant of their individual identities and stories and treat them only as a group to be sneered at. Their role in society is forgotten, written out of the fake history promulgated by popularists and demagogues. They cease to merit consideration as human beings and equals. Under Nazism, Jews first became *Untermenschen*, sub-humans, then vermin; Tutsis in Rwanda were labelled mere insects, cockroaches.

Obstinate and foolish as Pharaoh may appear in his later confrontations with Moses, at the start of his career he is cunning and adept. 'Come, let us deal wisely,' he admonishes his nation (Exod. 1:10). The verb, *nitchakhmah* a cohortative form built from the reflexive of *chakham*, 'wise', is an invitation to collusion: we know what we need to do together, don't we, you and I? Throughout the ages, racists have employed the same means of appeal, carefully manipulating prejudices and fears – 'there are too many of them over here' – to their own ends. The Egyptian people will pay a terrible price for this policy into which they are co-opted, willingly or not, just as other countries have done since.

Pharaoh develops his plan in careful stages. First he places a levy on the Children of Israel, then he imposes a regime of harsh labour. Only when these means fail to prevent them from 'breeding' and 'swarming' does he command first covert, then open, killing. The thirteenth-century commentator Nachmanides offers a revealing analysis of the reasoning behind these subtly orchestrated measures; he evidently knew all too well how such pernicious regimes function:

> Pharaoh and his shrewd advisors did not see fit to smite [the Children of Israel] by the sword because this would constitute a major act of betrayal, killing for no reason a people who had entered the land by command of a former king . . . Rather, he instructed them to act subtly, so that the Children of Israel would not realise that he was treating them with hostility. For this reason, he imposed a levy on them, it being common practice for resident aliens to pay a special tax to the king . . . Afterwards he secretly ordered the midwives to kill the boy babies on the birthstool, so that even the mothers would not be aware of their actions.[1]

Only after these policies have failed does Pharaoh take more open measures. Even then, he proceeds with cunning:

> After that, he commanded all his people: 'All boy babies born, throw them into the river' – that is, you do it [but not me]. He didn't want to order his ministers to kill them by the royal sword or throw them [personally] in the river. Rather, he told the people that whenever any of them found a Jewish child they themselves should throw it into the river. Should the boy's father cry out to the king or ministers [for justice] they would say, 'Bring witnesses and we'll punish [the guilty party]'.[2]

There were, of course, never any witnesses ready to come forward. Should they have done so, one can imagine the kind of justice they would have encountered.

Nachmanides' comments remind me of my father's reaction when we watched a television series about the early years of Nazi Germany. The crassness of the portrayal annoyed him: 'The Nazis did everything with so-called scrupulous legality, according to the letter of the law, which they malignantly twisted. At least at first, before they turned to open violence.'

Nachmanides' most disturbing observation focuses not just on Pharaoh but on human nature in general:

> Once the reins of the king's authority were loosened, the Egyptians would search in the [Israelites'] houses, entering at night under false pretences and taking the children away. That is why Scripture says [of Moses' mother], 'She could hide him no longer.'[3]

If everything is permitted, some people will stop short of nothing. That's why the rule of law is so important: just law, justly applied, protects us not only from what others might do to us, but also from what we might do to others. Once law becomes a mere parody of justice, effectively an inducement to commit crimes with impunity because no one calls us to account, there may be no limit to the wrongs we might prove capable of perpetrating. It could be argued that Pharaoh's worst crime is not even what he inflicts upon the Children of Israel, but what he brings down upon his own nation. Some of them he turns into killers; others he abandons to their deaths.

'Don't you know that Egypt's ruined?!' Pharaoh's advisors finally impress on him after seven deadly plagues have devastated the land (Exod. 10:7). Once again, he fails to face the facts. In 'not knowing' the humanity of others, Pharaoh and his followers end up not knowing, and betraying, their own people.

At the heart of this blindness lies a further, no less fundamental, not knowing. When Moses first appeals to Pharaoh to let the people go to serve their God, he answers: 'I don't know this God, and I won't let the Children of Israel go' (Exod. 5:2).

The point of his retort is not that he's an atheist; presumably he does recognise the Egyptian gods, of whom he's chief. It's that he considers himself answerable to no one, least of all to this God of the Hebrews. He can do as he pleases; there's no one to whom he needs to render account.

Whether or not this is true he will presently find out. But, as with so many tyrants since, in the meantime, innumerable people suffer and die.

How slavery works

The Pharaohs of history know exactly how to tighten the screws. The subtle cruelties of their systems are strikingly contemporary; they've changed little across the ages.

Nachmanides explains the sequence of events. At first Pharaoh appoints ministers to seize Israelite men and force them to do shift work on royal construction projects. But when this fails to slow down the Hebrews' birth-rate:

> Any Egyptians who needed workers were authorised to take Israelite men and make them perform whatever jobs they needed. They then further decreed that the slaves would have to work at making the bricks and mortar as well. For at first the [Egyptian] overseers would supply the bricks and the slave-gangs would construct the buildings. But now they made them do this task too, commanding them to bring earth and form it into bricks with their hands and feet. Only the straw was provided for them by the palace.[4]

Soon the slaves have to find even that for themselves.

The cruelty of the system lies not only in the backbreaking work but also in the structures of enforcement. Pharaoh has both 'overseers' and 'officers' at his command:

> The overseers were Egyptians and the officers Israelites. Each overseer had authority over a number of officers and the officers were appointed to make the workers fulfil their tasks.[5]

The slaves are not ordered about directly by their Egyptian masters but by their fellow Israelites, who presumably have little choice but are forced or induced to become officers. It is they who have to face the fury of their overlords when their squads fail to meet the daily quotas, as quickly becomes the case when they are no longer supplied with the straw needed to make their bricks:

> The Israelite officers whom Pharaoh's overseers had appointed over [the slaves] were beaten and told, 'Why yesterday and today have you failed to fulfil the quota of bricks required of you previously?'
>
> (Exod. 5:14)

Caught between their Egyptian persecutors and the slave-teams for whose impossible tasks they've been bullied into taking responsibility, the officers cry out to an oblivious Pharaoh before turning on Moses and Aaron for making things worse by interfering: 'You've made us stink in the sight of Pharaoh and his servants; putting a sword in their hands to kill us' (Exod. 5:21).

Moses goes back to the desert in despair and complains to God. Meanwhile, Pharaoh and his minions continue to benefit from the clever workings of the system in which the frustrations of the victims are vented on their own leaders.

The Torah says nothing about the feelings of the Israelite officers. With whom do they identify most? Their protest indicates that they feel a deep solidarity with the very people they find themselves forced to berate. But with what inducements might their overseers have bribed them to become officers in the first place? Might some of them have abused their positions in return for favours or concessions? The text is silent.

Pharaoh's system is all too familiar. From the early days of the concentration camps, the Nazi authorities appointed Kapos from among the prisoners. They became an essential part of the structure of oppression, key, as Himmler told his generals, to 'holding down sub-humans'. Their role allowed 'a small gang of SS men to dominate large camps', as well as being an effective way of 'driving a wedge between prisoners'.[6] Kapos held power and privileges; this placed them even more firmly in the grip of their Nazi masters, whose commands they had to carry out and between whom and the inmates under their authority they had to mediate. They were in the end 'auxiliaries of terror'.[7] Yet some managed to use their position with quiet humanity, earning a reputation among the prisoners for principled decency. Others 'became the scourges of prisoners' lives',[8] as the accounts of survivors frequently testify.

The system proved so successful that the Nazis extended it to the ghettos in which they gathered their victims across occupied Europe before deporting the survivors of the overcrowding, starvation and misery to death camps. They appointed a *Judenrat*, a council of Jewish leaders, led by a *Judenaelteste*, an Elder of the Jews. These were tasked with carrying out the brutal commands of the SS, with whom they were constantly forced to negotiate on totally unequal terms. Adam Czerniaków, the *Aelteste* in the Warsaw Ghetto, took his own life on 23 July 1942, after his pleas to spare the children in the orphanage run by Janusz Korczak were ignored. In a note to his wife, he wrote: 'They demand me to kill children of my nation with my own hands. I have nothing to do but to die.'[9]

The pressures on the Hebrew officers in Egypt may have been less absolute, but they must nevertheless have been brutal, caught as these officials were between the oppressors and their victims. It's not surprising that it is they who waylay Moses on his exit from the palace, begging him to leave them alone and blaming him for making matters even worse. Frustrated in every direction, mocked by Pharaoh, distrusted and undermined by his own people, Moses complains to God: 'Why have you treated this people so badly? Why did you send me?' (Exod. 5:22).

It's unlikely that he found God's answer, just wait and see, either convincing or helpful. From where was salvation to come?

The women

The first acts of resistance are carried out by women.

For generations, Pharaoh and his minions dominate. The Children of Israel suffer and endure. Bowed in slavery, the men make bricks and toil; they have no time for planning for the future. Even hope and imagination are in bondage. *Sagar aleihem hamidbar*, 'the desert closed them in' (Exod. 14:3), taught Rebbe Shalom Noach Berezovsky, rereading the last word not as *midbar*, 'wilderness', but as *medaber*, 'speaking': their *speech* is closed off, no one speaks up for them, they have no voice.[10] No one even has a name; they're presented as a mere 'them', they're just slaves.

The first people to be singled out are women, the midwives Shifrah and Puah, who fear God more than they fear Pharaoh and refuse to obey his command to kill the Hebrew boy babies. They are extraordinarily brave; throughout history many have died for lesser acts of defiance. Next is the as yet unnamed mother who places her baby in a basket on the Nile, and the older sister who's not afraid to intervene with Pharaoh's own daughter who, in turn, courageously adopts the Hebrew baby and calls him Moses.

Throughout history it is often the women who have been the mainstay of resilience. The Torah focuses on slave labour, the bullying and whipping when the daily quota of bricks is not met. But there's another way of destroying a people's morale: by attacking their homes and family life. Maybe it's because the hearth is at the centre of every culture, and because it's by the women that most families are held together that it's so frequently among them that resistance begins. The ancient rabbinic commentary *Sifrei* notes:

'God saw our affliction': this refers to separation from the way of all
the earth, as it says, 'God saw the Children of Israel, and God knew.'[11]

'The way of all the earth' is a euphemism for intimacy and domesticity.
The authors of this midrash were no doubt familiar with the practices of
contemporary tyrants; they knew all too well that the deliberate destruction of family life was, cruelly, also 'the way of all the earth'. Heart-rending
testimony from every corner of the world bears this out. The worst of all
the terrifying punishments God warns the Israelites that their conquerors
will inflict on them if they forsake the commandments is the loss of their
children: 'You will bear sons and daughters, but they won't be yours
because they'll go into captivity . . . Your eyes will yearn for them all day
long' (Deut. 28:41, 32).

Too many people today understand exactly what these terrible words
mean. In a leaked document published by the *Washington Post*, Chinese
state media set out their regime's plans for the persecuted Uyghur people:
'Break their lineage, break their roots, break their connections, break their
origins.'[12]

Uyghur women are subject to forcible separation from their husbands
and to sterilisation, fates horrifyingly familiar to women through the ages:

> Black women have watched, from the time they were dragged in chains
> to America's shores, their loved ones, their community, their collective,
> systematically picked off, hunted, and killed with impunity.[13]

Therefore, while the Torah focuses mainly on the slave labour of the men,
the Midrash creates a parallel narrative about the women, drawing on the
un- and under-stated in the text. As in many accounts of resilience, much
of the evidence emerges only afterwards. When, months after liberation
and deep in the desert, Moses asks the people to bring materials for the
construction of the tabernacle, the women offer their mirrors. Rashi
explains: 'The daughters of Israel had mirrors into which they looked
when putting on their jewellery; these too they did not hesitate to donate
to the tabernacle.'[14]

But, he adds, Moses rejects their offering. This negative reaction, as his
Midrashic source explains, is because the women have used them to
provoke desire:

> Pharaoh decreed that the men were not allowed to sleep at home, so
> that they couldn't have intercourse with their wives. Rabbi Shimeon

ben Halafta said: What did the Israelite women do? They went down to draw water. God put little fishes in their buckets; some they cooked and some they sold to buy wine. Then they went to the fields, taking food to their husbands . . . Once they'd eaten and drunk, the women would take out their mirrors and look at themselves together with their husbands. The wives would say, 'I'm better looking than you,' to which the men would respond, 'No, I'm the more handsome.' In this manner they would arouse their desire.

(Midrash Tanhuma to Pekudei, 9)

The Torah provides no direct evidence for any of this, but in typical fashion the Midrash finds indications in the text. Despite Pharaoh's measures the birth rate among the Hebrews continues to rise: 'The more [the Egyptians] oppressed them, the more their number grew' (Exod. 1:12).

The women must therefore have had ways of circumventing Pharaoh's decrees. A further hint is that, years later, amid the hardships of life in the desert, the people nostalgically recall 'the fish we ate for free in Egypt' (Num. 11:5). But what the Midrash creates around these sparse clues is the story of an entire subculture in which, as so often among persecuted peoples, it's the women who have the resourcefulness to carry on.

It's easy to dismiss mirrors as mere accoutrements of vanity. But they're also a means of restoring pride and self-respect, precisely the feelings oppressors want to destroy because they're the source of inner strength. In holding up their mirrors, the Hebrew women are not only trying to make their men feel like men once again so that they can get pregnant. They are saying something more: 'I'm showing you God's image in your own face; remember what you're worth.'

Moses is angry when these mirrors are offered as gifts for the tabernacle, but God takes a different view:

You treat these items with contempt? It's those very mirrors which gave birth to all those hosts in Egypt. Take them and use them for the base and basin of the bronze laver for the priests to wash and sanctify themselves.

(Midrash Tanhuma 9)

Far from being rejected as artefacts of indulgence, they must be fashioned into instruments of purity and holiness.

The Midrash's carefully constructed story testifies to the widespread truth that it's often the women who save their families and people. I need only think of my grandmother who, when my grandfather was imprisoned in Dachau concentration camp, turned away the young Nazi who banged on the door holding out a ten-mark note, shouting, 'Heil Hitler! I'm buying this house.'

'You'll have to speak to my husband,' my grandmother calmly replied. 'It belongs to him.'

'When will he be back?' the Nazi asked.

'You ought to know,' she retorted. 'It's your people who took him away.'

She was one of thousands of women, who, when their husbands were arrested across Germany and Austria after Kristallnacht in November 1938, found the courage to keep their families alive.

'My brother'?

The decisive moment in Moses' life is not when he turns aside to gaze at the burning bush. It comes earlier, at the close of his childhood, when: 'He grew up and went out to his brothers and saw into their burdens, and watched an Egyptian man smite a Hebrew man of his brothers' (Exod. 2:11).

'Brothers' occurs twice in the sentence. But who are they? Whose 'brother' does Moses understand himself to be?

At no point does the Torah indicate that anyone has told Moses that he is not Pharoah's daughter's son but an adopted child of uncertain origin, most likely plucked from among the dead and dying babies cast up along the banks of the Nile. Did his mother, whom, unknowingly, Pharoah's daughter hired as wet nurse, quietly instruct her child, before sorrowfully returning him to the palace, that he was in truth a Hebrew: 'Never let on! And never forget!'? Or did Pharoah's daughter tell him herself: 'Actually, I adopted you'? Or did some servile minister, resentful of the precocious young man, whisper to him just loudly enough for everyone else to hear, 'You're not one of us. You don't belong here; you're just a slave'? Perhaps that's the meaning of 'Moses grew up'; he embraced the reality of who he really was. As Rashi notes, the Torah has already told us that Moses has grown up.[15] The repetition indicates that he grew in stature, meaning, maybe, that he discovered his true identity.

A simple reading of the verse suggests that the 'brothers' to whom he goes out must be Hebrews. This is made clear at its close, since the man whom he sees the Egyptian taskmaster hit is 'a Hebrew, of [Moses'] brothers'. There's no ambiguity here. Perhaps this is the reason Moses 'goes out' in the first place, leaving behind the privileged world of the palace: he wants to see at first hand the cruel reality on which its power is founded, the slavery of those he knows to be his true blood-brothers.

If so, Moses shows an integrity most people lack. For centuries, the well-to-do of rich nations have chosen not to look too closely into the harsh existence of those whose cheap labour produces the wealth that makes their lives easy: the slave trade, colonialism, the plunder and exploitation of human and natural resources.

But the twelfth-century commentator and grammarian Abraham ibn Ezra understands Moses'brothers to be 'the Egyptians'.[16] 'Incomprehensible', observes the classic super-commentary to his famously terse notes. 'Egyptians' must be a misprint! Assuming, though, that ibn Ezra wrote exactly what he meant, and that this is no mere copyist's error, his explanation is, in its own way, compelling. Moses leaves the palace believing he's Egyptian. Perhaps it is even *their* burdens he wants to see: if Nazi guards often found their duties irksome and exhausting, why shouldn't the same have been the case for other, earlier persecutors?

What he witnesses changes Moses, profoundly and irrevocably. Perhaps some inner doubt about who he truly is surfaces in his consciousness. Or perhaps what happens is not about identity but identification, about moral rather than genetic personhood. He watches, noting the suffering and injustice. The Torah doesn't say that he merely saw the burdensome work of the slaves but that 'he saw *into* their sufferings'; as Rashi explains, he saw 'the heavy burdens on the weak, the light loads on the strong'.[17] Moses feels for them; perhaps for the first time, he identifies with the victims of the system of which he has until now been a beneficiary: 'He saw himself in their labours; he empathised and grieved with them.'[18]

He doesn't want to be counted among the persecutors; his true brothers are the persecuted. By the time he returns to the palace he knows who he is and has to be. He will remain there for just one more night; he has truly 'gone out' from there forever. He won't return for forty years, and then only as Pharaoh's apotheosis.

Maybe, therefore, the ambiguity of 'brother' is precisely the point. This is the decisive encounter on which Moses' entire future is founded. If the Egyptians are his brothers at the start of the sentence, that is no longer who they are by its end. What he sees that day transforms his life and determines his identity for ever.

But how can that be, when it's God's revelation at the burning bush decades later that sets the course of Moses' life? An astute midrash links the two experiences. Observing how the bush 'burns but is not consumed',

Moses determines to go closer and investigate this great marvel (Exod. 3:2, 3). God watches his movements, noting how 'he turned aside *to see*' (Exod. 3:4). The meaning is surely obvious: Moses turns away from the familiar shepherd's track to look more closely at the bush. But the midrash understands matters differently. What God has observed is not Moses' current decision to approach the burning shrub, but something he did much earlier, when he turned aside from his Egyptian entourage '*to see* into the suffering' of those whom he subsequently understood as his true brothers. That was the actual moment of revelation; the burning bush is only God's follow-up (Midrash Shemot Rabbah 1:27). Or maybe Moses is himself that burning bush, his conscience the place where pain and outrage have long been smouldering until they finally burst into open flame, casting light on the steep, ineluctable path of responsibility ahead, forcing him to come to terms with God's voice inside him with its inescapable call: 'Go to Pharaoh. Tell him: "Let my people go".'

There is at least one further way of understanding the word 'brothers' in the critical verse. Perhaps it refers neither to Hebrews nor to Egyptians, but to both. Moses, sensitised to such complexities because he himself carries a multiple identity, part as a child of Israelites, part as an adoptee into the Egyptian royal household, understands that all people are ultimately brothers and sisters. The Egyptian who smites the Hebrew is as much his brother as the Hebrew who is smitten. He realises, like Nelson Mandela contemplating the task that lies before him on his release from Robben Island, that ultimately 'the oppressor must be liberated as surely as the oppressed', because 'the oppressed and the oppressor alike are robbed of their humanity'.[19] Ultimately, even they, too, are brothers.

VA'ERAH (6:2–9:35)

God in history

'What's happened to God since then?'

Everyone turns towards the speaker. It's Passover night, the night of the story, and we're sitting at the table reading the Haggadah, the compendium of blessings, narratives, questions and songs recited, debated and argued over at the *Seder*, the ritual Passover gathering and meal, about a God who delivers the Children of Israel from the burdens of slavery with a mighty hand and an outstretched arm. Around the table are Holocaust survivors and refugees from Apartheid South Africa and Iran.

'What's God been doing since bringing us out of Egypt?'

Where now is the God of the Bible whom the prayerbook describes as 'eternally powerful' and 'strong to save'? The question troubles us all.

The Haggadah emphasises God's agency and God's unmediated involvement in history. God alone directs events and delivers the children of Israel from Egypt. Salvation comes:

> . . . not by means of an angel, nor a seraph, nor an emissary, but from God the Holy and Mighty, as it says in the Torah: 'I shall pass through the Land of Egypt on that night . . . and enact judgments against all the gods of Egypt,' I, and no other.[20]

Human agency, including even the role of Moses, is set aside. At the core of the action is God alone, performing signs and wonders, more powerful even than Pharaoh and the mightiest of tyrants.

It's a scenario which, the Haggadah insists, has happened not just once but time and again through history: 'In every generation they rise up against us, but the Holy Blessed One saves us from their hands.'[21]

God redeems the oppressed with indefatigable power.

The speaker at our Seder develops his question: 'Has God changed since then? Are we no longer worthy? Or what?'

The challenge echoes back down Jewish and global history, from the cry of despair at the close of Lamentations, 'For you have utterly abandoned us' (Lam. 5:22), through the psalmist's misery, 'They mock us, saying "Where is your God?"' (Ps. 42:10), to the expulsions and persecutions of the Middle Ages, the slaughters of the Crusades, the slave trade, concentration camps, mass killings by the *Einsatzgruppen*, gas chambers, death marches, the persecution of the Uyghurs, and all the forms of torture and murder with which the powerful have massacred the innocent. And God has remained silent.

Has God changed since then? Is it a different God?

No; at least, I do not believe so. I can't construe how that could make sense. What has altered, though, is how we see God, and that is all we have: not an account, were such a thing possible, of God as actually God is but only as we humans have tried to understand God. Even the Torah cannot portray God, but only God as God is seen by humans to be. Between ourselves and ultimate truth, our own preconceptions, cultural conditioning and limitations are always interposed.

So how can the question be answered? Perhaps our ancestors, some three thousand years ago, inheriting the tradition of the great liberation, understood that God was, had to be, couldn't not be involved in it; that life, creation and all the forces of nature must be on the side of freedom, that tyranny cannot sustain itself, that it is destined to self-destruct, albeit after imposing unquantifiable misery on countless victims. For dictators set themselves up against the God of life, whose presence is the sacred energy that flows through all things. Therefore, nature must inevitably turn against them. Perhaps certain tyrants secretly know this and resist even more fiercely the insistent, 'Let go, let go,' which God puts into the mouth of Moses, but which they hear also from within and which they know will ultimately cause them to crumble and fail. Perhaps, finally, as these truths are formulated over generations into the written narrative of the Torah, it is ever more deeply understood by those who transmit and edit the story that only God's spirit possesses the strength capable of defeating earthly might, that only God can be the ultimate mover, the power greater than all powers, to whom human nature and nature itself must bow.

Nevertheless, the rabbis choose to emphasise not just God's power but also God's compassion. Why, they ask, did God select a mere bush from which to address Moses when a mountaintop might have been more fitting, and why specifically a thornbush? Because, explained Rabbi Yannai, God is like our twin, and 'just as with twins, if one of them has a headache the other feels it too' (Midrash Rabbah 2:5). God appears caught in thorns out of empathy with a people caught up and trapped in pain.

This God who suffers with us calls out not just to Moses in the desert of Midian, but to all humanity throughout history. God not only 'suffers in all [our] suffering' (Isa. 63:9), but also pleads with us to do something about it. 'Moses Moses,' God calls, repeating his name without leaving a pause in between (Exod. 3:4). The appeal is urgent, commanding. For Moses there will never be a return to pasturing sheep in the wilderness, just as he could never sleep easily in Pharaoh's palace after he understood who his brothers truly were. Once we hear God's voice within suffering, of any kind and anywhere, we can never in good conscience return to our life as it was before.

'God does not cause our misfortunes,' wrote Harold Kushner in his classic *When Bad Things Happen to Good People*. We turn to God in our suffering 'precisely because we can tell ourselves that God is as outraged by it as we are'.[22] God suffers with us and, in so doing, helps us find the endurance to bear our tribulations and, hopefully, emerge from them in the end. God gives us the determination to challenge cruelty and injustice because God cries out from its midst.

I find such a God easier to relate to than a deity who once had the power to intervene in human affairs but has either lost that capacity or decided not to use it. A God 'who hates suffering but cannot eliminate it'[23] and who therefore commands us to act for justice and mercy's sake is more comprehensible to me than an all-powerful deity who once intervened in history with plagues and storms but has since refused to do so.

But is this a lesser, diminished God? God may ultimately be invulnerable because God is present in all life across eternity. But God is not invulnerable in the here and now, for God is dependent on and subjected to whatever we do with that tiny part of God that resides within us and others. Thus Hugo Gryn, who was deported from his hometown of Berehovo to Auschwitz in the summer of 1944, recorded his belief that God was present in that unimaginably terrible place and that God was crying too:

> I would like you to understand that in that builder's yard on that Day of Atonement, I found God. But not the God I had childishly clung to until those jet streams dissolved over Auschwitz. People sometimes ask me 'Where was God at Auschwitz?' I believed God was there Himself – violated and blasphemed. The real question is 'Where was man in Auschwitz?'[24]

The issue, then, may not be, 'Is God here?' but, 'Are we here? Are we listening to God's cry?' As Hans Jonas wrote in his remarkable lecture, *The Concept of God after Auschwitz*:

> For reasons decisively prompted by contemporary experience, I entertain the idea of God who . . . responds to the impact on his being by worldly events, not 'with a mighty hand and an outstretched arm', as we Jews on every Passover recite in remembering the Exodus from Egypt, but with the mutely insistent appeal of his unfulfilled goal.[25]

Life for the ordinary Egyptian?

Acquaintances of my grandfather told of their last encounter at the railway station when they were finally able to flee Nazi Germany. As they walked anxiously along the platform, a porter whispered to them, 'At least you're able to get out. We can't.' He was an 'ordinary' German, safe from the persecution to which Jews, socialists, communists, homosexuals and others were subject. He had no immediate cause to escape from what his own country was doing, supposedly in the interests of citizens like himself. But he understood where it would all end. He was one of millions destined to be a victim of his own nation's leadership.

The Torah doesn't tell us what life was like for the average Egyptian under the Pharaoh who, like so many tyrants at the outset of their rule, calls on his people to join him 'in dealing wisely' with those Hebrew foreigners (Exod. 1:10). But there are glimpses and, as ever, Midrash fills in many gaps.

The first to feel the pressure are the midwives, whom Pharaoh instructs to kill all Israelite boy babies on the birthstool. Although many commentators take these women, Shifrah and Puah, to be Hebrews, an equally strong tradition understands them to be Egyptian. Why otherwise would Pharaoh turn to them to carry out his orders? Also, they are described as 'fearing God', a form of words used in the Torah to indicate a basic moral code respected by non-Hebrew peoples. Experiencing a deep sense of moral injury at what they are commanded to do, the midwives defy their leader. They are followed in this choice by Pharaoh's own daughter, who takes pity on the baby boy whom her handmaidens rescue from the Nile. The scene at the water's edge suggests this is not the first time she has witnessed the grim results of her father's policies and been moved to intervene.

There must have been other Egyptian people who chose to have no part in the persecution of their fellow human beings, despite the temptation to turn a blind eye and enjoy the benefits of a Hebrew underclass of slave labourers whose lives were at the disposal of anyone who wished to exploit them. Like millions since, they must have felt morally compromised every day, yet powerless before the outrages committed by their own populace, while knowing that there would be a terrible price to pay for policies in which they had no desire to be part. They would have had no choice but to dig around the Nile alongside everyone else in search of drinkable water when their river was turned to blood, and to join in clearing away the piles of stinking dead frogs, maybe whispering to someone they thought they could trust, 'Look what that Pharaoh's done for us.'

As the impact of the plagues grew, bringing misery to everyone, more of the Egyptians may have considered with some justification that they were the ones who were really suffering, or at least that 'we were victims too'. Those lazy Hebrews were to blame, Moses and that infernal God of theirs, as well as that failure of a Pharaoh. Perhaps some Egyptians who felt that way nevertheless did their best for the slaves; or maybe, as was the case for Pharaoh himself, the outrageous behaviour of the God of the Hebrews hardened their hearts.

Yet they couldn't escape Moses' growing reputation or the realisation that whatever he threatened to do invariably came to pass. When they heard his warning about the forthcoming hailstorm, 'those of Pharaoh's entourage who feared God's word hurried their servants and cattle indoors, while those who paid no attention to God's word abandoned their servants and cattle in the field' (Exod. 9:20–21).

Rabbinic commentary isn't generous towards these Egyptians. The text doesn't say that 'they feared God', but only that 'they feared God's word'. They were afraid merely of the consequences; their concern was solely for their property.

But by the eighth plague, even Pharaoh's closest advisors were prepared to speak out, not out of any love for Moses, but because the results of their leader's obstinacy were staring them in the face: 'How much longer will this man be a snare to us? Send the people away and let them worship the Lord their God. Haven't you yet realised that Egypt is ruined?' (Exod. 10:7).

If this was how their ministers felt, what about the average citizen? Noting the Torah's puzzling observation that 'God granted the people favour in the eyes of the Egyptians' (Exod. 11:3), Nachmanides commented:

> [This shows] the Egyptians didn't hate [the Hebrews] because of the plagues. Rather, their sympathy for them grew and they found favour in their eyes to the extent that they said, 'We're the ones in the wrong, robbing and violently mistreating you. It's only right that God should favour you.' Moses, too, who brought the plagues down on them, was regarded as a great leader throughout Egypt.[26]

He attributes remarkable forbearance to a population who, by this point in time, had suffered terribly, albeit because of their own leader. Since then, other peoples have often taken the easier route, blaming the victims rather than their own government's policies.

Rashi took a more sanguine view. By the time the plagues were over the Egyptians had only one desire: to get the Hebrews out of their country. When, on God's instruction, the Children of Israel asked them for gold and silver, they thrust it into their hands and urged them to leave: 'Even what they didn't ask for the [Egyptians] gave them: 'You're saying "just one"; take two and be gone.'[27]

How did the Egyptians face the news of the final, most terrible plague? A striking midrash takes us into the minds of those who knew they were going to die:

> All the firstborn Egyptians gathered and said to their fathers, 'Everything Moses has said, he's done. Don't you want us to live? Send the Hebrews away for our sakes because, if you don't, we're going to die.' Their fathers replied, 'Even if every single Egyptian dies, the Hebrews aren't going anywhere.' What did the firstborn do then? They went together to Pharaoh and cried out, 'We beg you, send this people away. It's because of them that this evil is going to overtake us.' He told his servants to whip them across their legs. What did they do in return? They took their swords and killed their fathers.
>
> (Midrash Tanhuma: Bo 18)

The Egyptian firstborn are not the only children to fall victim to their elders' hard-hearted folly.

On my return from my first visit to Germany, friends asked me what I had experienced most, fear or anger. But in truth I had felt something entirely different, partly because the people I was with had either been young children or not yet born during the Third Reich. What possessed me on the journey home was gratitude that I hadn't had to live under a government that turned the law into an instrument of evil and forced me, at the risk of my life, to become complicit in actions that were irrefutably wrong. Had that happened, would I have had the courage to resist? I couldn't know. But, mercifully, I'd been spared the test.

BO (10:1–13:16)

....

'I have hardened Pharaoh's heart'

I often think of Shakespeare's King Lear, driven to distraction, unable to comprehend his daughter's lack of compassion:

> Then let them anatomize Regan; see what breeds
> About her heart. Is there any cause in nature
> That makes these hard hearts?[28]

The words remind me of Moses' seemingly impossible mission to Pharaoh. Almost everyone translates God's instruction as, 'Go to Pharaoh,' but the words '*Bo el Par'oh*' really mean 'Come to Pharaoh' (Exod. 10:1). Whereas 'go' suggests confrontation, 'come' sounds like an invitation. But telling Moses to 'come' to someone by whom his message has repeatedly been rejected seems like a futile command, especially since it's none other than God who has calculatedly hardened Pharaoh's heart.

Generations of commentators have struggled with the notion of a God who hardens hearts. Is that what God really does, and if so what kind of god is God? How can all the suffering caused by Pharaoh's intractability be justified, especially if the true mover is in fact God? And does God really predetermine and control our responses?

From the Torah onwards, God is understood to want open, not closed hearts. Moses beautifully describes how God will 'open your hearts and the hearts of your children, to love the Lord your God with all your heart and all your soul, so that you may live' (Deut. 30:6).

One isn't fully alive if one's heart is closed. The Talmud puts the matter simply: 'the Merciful One desires the heart' (Talmud, Sanhedrin 106b). The daily prayer, which begins with asking God to open our lips, ends with the hope that God will open our hearts. Judaism's daily meditation, the *Shema*, calls on us to love God 'with all [our] heart'. The heart is always in danger of closing; if we don't work at keeping it open it is liable to contract and forfeit its sensitivity. One of the first sins to which we confess on the Day of Atonement is the coarsening of the heart.

For Pharaoh, his very position makes the challenge harder. As is the case throughout history, 'power tends to corrupt, and absolute power corrupts absolutely'.[29] It turns kings into tyrants and rulers into despots. As Nachmanides notes, initially it is Pharaoh himself who repeatedly closes his heart (Exod. 7:13, 22; 8:15, 19, 32; 9:7). Only later does God do the hardening (Exod. 9:12). The great twelfth-century legalist and philosopher Moses Maimonides understands this in itself to be part of Pharaoh's punishment:

It is possible that a man should commit either one grievous iniquity or a multitude of sins so that the Judge of Truth will decree against him that, whereas this sinner committed those sins of his own free will and consciously, repentance should be withheld from him altogether, and grant him no leave to repent . . . It is therefore written in the Torah: 'And I will harden Pharaoh's heart' (Exod. 14:4), because at the beginning he sinned of his own free will, and meted out evil to Israel who sojourned in his land, even as it is said: 'Come, let us deal wisely with them' (Exod. 1:10).[30]

Maimonides' analysis is based on the Talmudic observation that when a person repeats a wrong it becomes habituated. Our responses become so deeply engrained, especially when others endorse our decisions, as the yes-men around tyrants invariably do, that it's almost impossible for us to change our ways and re-educate our conscience.

According to Maimonides, then, God only hardens Pharaoh's heart once he himself has done so beyond redemption. But is this true, since at the very outset God says to Moses, 'I will harden Pharaoh's heart' (Exod. 4:21), suggesting that Pharaoh may never have had full freedom of choice but was predestined to be the paradigmatic opponent of God's will, so that God's power could be demonstrated for all time?

I struggle to believe in such a God. Therefore here, as elsewhere, I prefer a less literal, more literary reading. The Torah cannot tell us about God or God's actions as they truly are but only as the author-editors choose to see them. The aim of the Exodus story is not just to record the Children of Israel's slavery in Egypt, but also to show that there is a force in history greater than the mightiest rulers. Tyrants and their minions must in the end self-destruct; they are bound to become the victims of their own corrupt policies. As Archbishop Desmond Tutu reputedly said when asked what would become of the rulers of Apartheid South Africa: like Pharaoh, they will bite the dust. The Torah ascribes this ultimate agency to God; God is the force that causes their power to crumble. But Pharaoh, like his fellow despots through the ages, remains responsible for choosing his own path.

After seven plagues it seems clear that he's unable to change his disastrous course. What point is there, then, in God asking Moses to 'come' to him when's repeatedly proved inflexible? Two Hasidic interpretations offer contrasting explanations. According to Rebbe Meir of Apt (1767–1831), God commands Moses to 'come' to Pharaoh precisely because he has hardened his heart. But he understands 'hardened' differently, and explains it according to its post-biblical, rabbinic usage in which the same word, *kabed*, can mean to sweep or clean out. God invites Moses to 'come' to Pharaoh because God has cleaned his heart out. There's nothing left to fear; it's become a mere cavity, an emotionless void.

Levi Yitzkah of Berditschev (1740–1809) also focuses on the word 'hard' but offers a more optimistic interpretation. Noting that, as well as hardness, *kavod* can mean heaviness in the sense of weight or dignity, he understands 'I have hardened his heart' to mean not that God has once again made Pharaoh immune to mercy, but the very opposite, that God has restored his *kavod*, or dignity, rendering him susceptible to feeling once again. That's why God now invites Moses to 'come' to him in his new-found openness. It's as if God were saying: 'I never give up on the human heart.'

Perhaps the underlying question is whether there is such a thing as irredeemable evil, an utterly impenetrable heart. My grandfather told me several times how angry he was when he learnt that Hitler had taken his own life: 'He should have been forced to face what he'd done; he should have been made to repent.' I remember wondering whether Hitler would have been capable of such a thing, and what might have led my grandfather to believe that he was.

The plague of darkness

Rebbe Nachman of Breslav, the great storyteller to whose grave in Uman thousands make the pilgrimage every New Year, used to say: '*Asur Lehitya'esh*, It is forbidden to despair.' To this was added, by him or by subsequent folklore, the rhyme: '*Rak Lismoach Yesh*, Only ever be happy.' It's no surprise to learn that he suffered periodically from severe mental anxiety.

The Sabbath on which the ninth of the Ten Plagues is read was chosen by the UK Jewish community as *Mental Health Awareness Shabbat* because, understood metaphorically, darkness was felt by some to have a particular resonance with mental illness.

The Torah describes this bleak plague as *choshekh afelah*, a darkness so thick that, like the London smog of 1952 which finally led to the Clean Air Act, 'nobody could see his brother or get up from his place for three days' (Exod. 10:23). This indicates not just physical but also social and psychological darkness. The Torah's exact words are *lo kamu ish mitachtav*. 'no one could rise up from their low place'. On an emotional level, that place signifies those deep confines of our personal Egypt (the Hebrew for Egypt, *Mitsrayim*, literally means 'narrow spaces'), where, at the lowest moments in our lives, we may feel ourselves helplessly and irredeemably trapped. If we've been spared visiting those bleak inner realms, we've been fortunate.

One feels oneself go down and down to where one's terrors become one's dominant reality; down to the basement of the soul, where the sign above the entrance reads like the portal to Dante's hell: 'Abandon hope all you who enter here.' There one sits, mentally locked in, staring at the grey-brown walls, seeing no means of escape, taunted and tempted in the bleakest hours by the thought that maybe there's only one way out. One feels utterly, unreachably alone. 'No one could see his brother': even if those who love us and whom we love are right there with us, we do not truly see them and cannot properly hear the words with which they try to touch us.

The nineteenth-century Rebbe Yehudah Aryeh-Leib of Ger understands this inability to see or be seen as both the cause and essence of the plague:

> Since 'no one could see his brother' or realise what those around them needed, since no one could be bothered about other people's needs, the result was that 'no one could move from their place'. People remained stuck in the same low state and couldn't get themselves out of it.[31]

He interprets the darkness morally, as the plague of a society in which an ethos of selfishness is so thoroughly imbued that no one even thinks to care about others. He is doubtless correct that what brings light and hope to any community is the capacity to notice and respond to each other's troubles and needs. But considered from inside mental pain and depression, his words may come across, paradoxically, as cruel. The people one loves may be doing their utmost to help. But some impenetrable membrane separates them off. They belong to another universe. They could be one's parents, partner or children; one knows their concern is genuine. But they and their love travel along coordinates that have no point of intersection with one's own state of mind. And that augments the torment, the thought that even at this very moment one may be failing terribly those whom one loves the most, because one is unable to escape the elsewhere in which one is trapped and to love them back as they deserve.

When someone takes their own life, relatives may say: 'I was there. I kept telling him I loved him. Wasn't my love good enough?' The issue is probably not the insufficiency of this love but that, in the cruellest hours, it cannot breach those invisible walls, that impermeable internal membrane.

The Torah continues: 'But the Children of Israel had light in *their* dwellings' (Exod. 10:23). The basic meaning is that only the Egyptians were left in the dark, together with those among the Children of Israel who ignored or defied God's instructions. But the plague didn't affect those Israelites who had faith in God; *their* houses were not invaded by the surrounding darkness. However, Rabbi Chaim ibn Attar (1696–1743) takes 'their' to refer not to the homes of the Israelites but to those of the Egyptians. Whenever an Israelite entered the house of an Egyptian, they brought light with them into their neighbour's benighted dwelling, highlighting the difference between the two nations.[32] He presumably didn't mean it that way, but it may have seemed to those Egyptians as if they were being deliberately taunted.

If one identifies with such an experience for a moment, it must have felt close to what people struggling with painful difficulties sometimes say: everyone else is just fine; they don't appear to have troubles; their children are doing brilliantly; they haven't lost their jobs; their marriages aren't in trouble; their nights aren't tormented with worry; they suffer no mental tortures.

It's trite, and usually pointless, simply to explain that this isn't true, that many of us have miserable days, that very few people aren't beset by troubles and anxieties of their own. In the world of emotional darkness, it can feel as if everyone else is in the sunlight, capped with their self-satisfied halo.

Yet that is no reason to keep one's distance and forsake one's friends when they are down. The art, though, as we may well know from being low ourselves, is not to imagine that one is bringing in the sunshine, but rather to step down towards the darkness and encourage our companions to rediscover their own inner light.

At the close of the *shivah*, the seven days of mourning, one says to the bereaved: '*Kumu, kumu*, rise up, rise up,' and offers a hand to help them out of their traditional low chairs. Similarly, we have to hope that the hands stretched out to us in our worst hours, and the hands we in turn hold out to others, will make contact and that we'll manage to help each other face the world once again. We never fully fathom the inner reality of other people's lives, or even the depths of our own. Yet we can and must endeavour to recognise each other even in the darkness, acknowledging the pain its long hours bring. If the doors of our hearts and communities are open, if there is thoughtfulness and kindness, maybe the light will slowly filter back in. Hopefully, we will be able to turn back from our dark places and into the daylight with relief.

The Torah opens with God hovering over the void where 'darkness covers the deep' and calling out, 'Let there be light' (Gen. 1:1, 3). It's an eternal metaphor for the spirit of God inside us, appealing to us to rediscover the wonder of light.

The night of the story

The Exodus is both story and meta-story, for once and for always. Even as the action unfolds, before Moses has informed the people about the final devastating plague, he addresses future generations, instructing them how these events should be commemorated until the end of time. The Exodus is to be retold and relived until the dawn of redemption:

> This day shall be for you a memorial; you shall celebrate it as a festival to God throughout your generations . . . When your children say, 'What does this service mean to you?' you will tell them, 'It is the Passover sacrifice to God, who passed over the houses of the Children of Israel in Egypt when smiting the Egyptians, but saved our homes.'
>
> (Exod. 12:14, 26–7)

A literary-historical explanation for this emphasis on telling the story might be that the account was written long after the dramas it describes. It looks back to them in order to explain the origins of long familiar rites and commemorations. Its purpose is not simply to set down what occurred; it neither could be nor is meant to be an objective account. Rather, based on inherited folk memory and myth, it tells the story of the Exodus to impress upon the people their indebtedness to God's power and their consequent obligation to obey God's commandments. This does not imply that the Exodus never happened in any shape or form, but only that, consciously and unconsciously, it was retold by generation after generation until it was finally set down in the Torah in more or less precisely the form that we have it today, thousands of years later.

The insistence that future communities must tell, teach and study it is a defining feature of the Exodus narrative. The night when the Children of Israel finally leave Egypt is to be remembered forever, its key events re-enacted in every generation 'staff in hand and shoes on feet' (Exod. 12:11). The bitterness of slavery must be tasted, the dry bread chewed, the roasted meat of the paschal lamb carved up before midnight.

Almost no other *mitzvah*, commandment, has been as well observed as this injunction to retell the story of the departure from Egypt. The Passover Haggadah – the name literally means *Telling* because this is *the* story par excellence – is the most frequently reprinted book in the entire library of Judaism. It closely follows the instructions in the Torah as expanded in the

Mishnah: 'Now you pour the first cup; now the child asks; now you answer, saying, "We were slaves in Egypt"' (Mishnah Pesachim 10). These rituals are further explained in the Talmud and elaborated and interpreted throughout the generations up to the present day, resulting in hundreds of different editions of the Haggadah, each with its own commentary and illustrations. For the Haggadah is the story of then, now and all time, the meta-story that encapsulates the essence of all Jewish, perhaps all human, history: the ever-repeated, ever-unfinished journey from slavery to freedom.

The Haggadah combines memory and imagination; every family threads into it their own experiences. It becomes a fourfold story, four narratives intertwined. The first is the Torah's account of what happened back then in Egypt. The second is how the rabbis interpreted it, set down largely while they were subject to the tyranny of Rome. The third is our own family history, how our grandparents survived the pogroms of Poland and the Pale or suffered the terrors of Nazi Europe – or other persecutions in different lands. The fourth, expressed symbolically, is our internal story, our battle with those inner Pharaohs who hold us prisoner from the selves we truly could be, were we able to break free and reach the promised land of our vision and potential. Maybe that is why we recite the Haggadah over four cups of wine, framed by four questions, in response to the challenges of four different children, four facets of our own self.

For simply telling the story isn't sufficient; it must be prompted and provoked by the recreation of occasion: the unleavened bread, the bitter herbs, the long wait before the meal. Hence the name *Seder*, meaning 'order': Passover night is carefully constructed to elicit debate. Questioning and curiosity are at its heart. The *Seder* must not be a monologue but a colloquy, a gathering of stories, an experience.

Four times the Torah insists: 'When your children ask you, saying, "What's this?" you tell them . . .' (Exod. 12:26; 13:8, 14, Deut. 6:20). The rabbis famously interpret these four references as representing four different 'sons' or character traits: the wise, the wicked, the dull or uninspired, and the person too unfamiliar or too reticent to ask. Their aim was probably not to categorise different types of personality, but rather to ensure that every kind of discourse was included. There must be encouragement to engage, room for challenge and time for detail.

There are subtle differences between the two ancient sources on which the rabbis here drew. According to the second-century *Mechilta*, the so-called 'simple' child who blandly asks, 'What's this?' should be given an equally simple answer, while the 'wise' child is to be informed about all the laws of Passover down to the very last particular. But in the Jerusalem Talmud these responses are reversed. The scholarly consensus is that this Talmudic text is probably corrupt; it makes no sense to swap the answers round in this manner. Why would one tell a knowledgeable child the barest basics? It makes no sense. The Haggadah follows the *Mechilta*; this is the version illustrated and analysed in hundreds of editions through the ages.

Yet the Jerusalem Talmud may be making an important point. The 'wise' child mustn't be allowed to get away with being so clever that he misses the essential message amid all the details. Why do we tell the story of our slavery in Egypt? Why does the Torah remind us over and again to remember? Why do we refer to the Exodus in the prayers every morning and evening without exception, and in the *Kiddush*, the blessing said over wine, with which every *Shabbat* and festival is sanctified? Why is it *the* story, the meta-story, of Judaism? The question deserves a clear and simple answer: once we were slaves; now we are free, and from that experience of slavery we learn the values that give this freedom meaning. From being the victims of systemic injustice, we understand the significance of justice. From suffering cruelty, we appreciate the supreme importance of compassion. From being deprived of all respect, we realise the meaning of dignity. These basic yet all-encompassing truths must never be forgotten; they must not be suppressed by dictators, taken for granted out of indifference, obfuscated by sophistry or trampled down by bullies because everyone else fails to speak out. They are the heart and conscience of Judaism.

That is why the most basic question must be asked and asked again, not only about the Exodus, but also about the Torah and faith itself: 'What's this? What's it all for?' That's why the Torah insists, even as the events unfold, that the story which takes us 'from slavery to freedom' must be told and retold, bound on our arms, set between our eyes and placed upon our hearts.

BESHALLACH (13:17–17:16)

The Song at the Sea

In the dark times, will there also be singing?
Yes, there will be singing.
About the dark times.

(Bertolt Brecht)[33]

It's the way in which spirituals create a world moved by compassion, redemption and justice while in reality enslaved people inhabit a world of inequality and deep cruelty. At least while singing, they are transported to this better place.

(Simon Lichman)[34]

My father found refuge from Nazi Germany in Jerusalem. Here he and his family endured the long years of the Second World War, the uncertainty and violence as the British Mandate came to an end, Israel's War of Independence, the siege of Jerusalem and the uneasy times that followed. 'Were it not for the music,' my father would say, 'we couldn't have made it through.'

I often puzzle over the phrase near the beginning of the Song at the Sea, 'Ozzi vezimrat Yah, God is my strength and my song' (Exod. 15:2). What connection can there be between song and strength? Then I remember my father's words.

In the summer of 1942, on the very date Hitler had set to celebrate Leningrad's fall, Dmitri Shostakovich's *Symphony No. 7*, since known as the *Leningrad Symphony*, was played in the war-ravaged city for the first time. Much of the music had been composed amid the terror and hunger to which its population was to remain subject for 872 days, one of the longest sieges in history. The work had been premiered in Kuybyshev and New York, where the score had secretly been flown. But it was essential to perform the music in Leningrad itself, as a supreme act of resistance. The orchestra were starving; the drummer was rescued from the morgue:

'My God, how thin many of them were,' one of the organizers of the performance remembered. 'How those people livened up when we started to ferret them out of their dark apartments. We were moved to tears when they brought out their concert clothes, their violins and cellos and flutes, and rehearsals began under the icy canopy of the studio.'[35]

Before the concert, the Soviet Commander ordered a massive bombardment of the besieging forces to ensure their silence during the performance. The music was broadcast via loudspeaker to the German troops, as an act of spiritual resistance. Fifty years later, the BBC interviewed a surviving German officer, who stated: 'When I heard that music, I said to myself, we shall not win this war.'

Music is strength, the spiritual strength of a person and a people. 'The voices woke me in the darkness of the early hours,' my friend John Schlapobersky recalled. He was a prisoner subjected to torture in solitary confinement in one of Apartheid South Africa's most notorious jails. The singing, he discovered, came from those awaiting execution, 'literally on death row'. 'I understood why silence descended at dawn . . . They would sing as the community of the condemned to support those of their number facing execution at dawn.'[36] Song is solidarity and resilience; it survives even if those who sing it do not. Song cannot be enclosed within even the highest security jails; it defies imprisonment.

On their long journey into exile under Nebuchadnezzar two and a half thousand years ago the defeated Israelites sat down by the waters of Babylon and wept, saying: 'How can we sing the song of the Lord in a strange land?' (Ps. 137:4). Yet those very words became song. The only form of exile capable of silencing song is internal, when the mind becomes estranged from the spirit, when the singer can no longer hear the music of their own soul.

Precisely this is what troubled Kalonymus Kalman Shapira, the Rebbe of the Warsaw Ghetto: 'One can accept sufferings in love, and believe that everything is from God,' he wrote, with extraordinary faith and courage, in the winter of 1942:

> . . . but to sing at such a time, that is hard. For to sing requires one to make music from within the self, with one's very heart and soul. Even the prophet Elisha needed the inspiration of listening to a musician before the spirit of God would come to him; it was only after the music had entered him that the gift of prophecy was restored.[37]

That is why, he continued, in times of utmost hardship when morale is torn to tatters, leaders must be gentle and forbearing. Only in an atmosphere of fellowship and compassion is it possible to sing. No doubt he was addressing his own feelings of responsibility as a teacher in the unimaginable conditions of the ghetto. But he may also have been challenging God's leadership of the people.

The Torah does not actually say, 'God is my strength and my song;' a more precise translation is, 'My strength and God's song,' or, 'My strength is God's song.' Not all music is God's music. My grandparents well remembered being forced to listen to outbursts of the Nazi *Horst Wessel Lied*, hatred in rhyme, loutish cruelty posing as song.

Even the Song at the Sea, sung by the Children of Israel in the surge of relief after escaping entrapment between Pharaoh's chariots and the impassable waters, is not entirely God's song, at least not in heaven. In a poignant fantasy, the Talmud relates how God chides the angels when they try to join in: 'My creatures are drowning in the sea, and you dare to sing!' (Talmud, Sanhedrin 39b).

The ultimate song, God's true song, will not be a song of triumph over others, but over the enemies of all humanity: hatred, injustice, misery and cruelty. It will be a song of redemption for all the world. It will come, as Isaiah prophesied, from everywhere, 'from the corners of the earth' (Isa. 24:16). For true music is the outpouring of the spirit that flows through all life and cannot therefore be anyone's enemy. As Rabbi Abraham Isaac Hacohen Kook (1865–1935), the first Chief Rabbi of Palestine, wrote:

> There is one who sings the song of his own life and in himself finds everything, his full spiritual satisfaction . . . There is another who sings the song of his people . . . There is another who reaches toward more distant realms, and who goes beyond the boundary of Israel to sing the song of humankind . . . Then there is one who rises toward wider horizons, until he links himself with all existence, with all God's creatures, with all worlds, and sings his songs with all of them.[38]

Only when all these songs come together will 'this full comprehensiveness rise to become the song of holiness, the song of God'.[39] This, he declared, is the true mission of *Israel*, which means *Shir El*, God's song.

What freedom is for

The Children of Israel left Egypt *beyad ramah*, 'with a high hand, punching the air' (Exod. 14:8). They didn't behave like people in flight, commented

Abraham ibn Ezra, 'they had their weapons with them'. Nachmanides imagined that 'they made flags and banners, sang, beat the drum and played music, like people freed from slavery forever, not like slaves destined to return to their labours.[40] But, he added, all this was reported back to Pharaoh,[41] and so infuriated him that he determined to pursue his former serfs and bring them back by force.

After centuries of bondage and generations born into slavery, the Children of Israel had every reason to rejoice in their new-found liberty.

But freedom is only ever the beginning of the journey. It is never the sole or end goal. The Children of Israel's destination is not unconditional freedom but the service of God. This is made clear from the outset, from the moment God speaks to Moses at the burning bush: 'When you bring the people out of Egypt you shall serve God upon this mountain' (Exod. 3:12).

Unlike in the much-loved spiritual, Moses never says to Pharaoh: 'Let my people go.' The message is always: 'Let my people go so that they may serve me' (e.g., Exod. 5:1; 7:16). In Hebrew, the words for 'slavery' and 'service' are the same: their root, *avad*, means both to labour and to worship. But there is every difference between being forced to sweat for a tyrant in constant fear of one's life and being called to the service of God. The great eleventh- to twelfth-century Spanish Hebrew poet Yehudah Halevi summed this up in a deceptively simply verse:

Those who serve the things of time are slaves to slaves;
Those who serve the eternal God alone are free.

That is why on Passover night we conclude the Haggadah's long analysis of the Exodus not by thanking God for our liberty but by blessing God for redemption. For freedom itself is not freedom unless it's in service to redemption.

Nevertheless, the Children of Israel are entitled to celebrate their departure from slavery by 'punching the air'. They have finally attained 'freedom from'. It's a freedom desperately sought by millions across the world today: freedom from oppression, injustice, cruelty and indignity; from having one's rights trampled down by tyrants and denied in corrupt and perverted systems of justice; from the violence and contempt targeted at minorities and refugees by racists and vigilantes; from domestic violence, sexual abuse and the calculating cruelty of coercive control inflicted especially on women and children, but also sometimes on men, behind closed doors.

That is why the story of slavery and liberation is the meta-narrative of Judaism, *the* story par excellence, which encapsulates all the different struggles against the many kinds of oppression under which Jews and other peoples, as well as countless marginalised and humiliated groups and individuals, have suffered throughout history. It expresses our gratitude to God for our release from Pharaoh, and from Pharaoh's acolytes in many other lands and ages. It reminds us daily of humankind's universal hope for liberty and justice. It embodies our commitment to stand up not only for our own freedom and dignity but also for that of others. It requires us to challenge ourselves, lest we, too, cede to the allure of becoming oppressors.

But 'freedom from' must always be accompanied by 'freedom for'. As the desert opens out before the Children of Israel and the Promised Land remains distant, new struggles begin. Within three days of crossing the Red Sea, the people complain about the lack of food and drink (Exod. 16:2–3). They may have been slaves, but all they remember now is the ready availability of food and water in Egypt, the fish, cucumbers and melons. Forgotten are the misery, beatings and humiliations. Furious with Moses and frustrated with God, the people want a new leader who will take them back to the safety of servitude. The evidence of the daily manna and the promise of a land of their own fail to calm their anguish and restore their confidence.

The Children of Israel are not the last nation in history willing to exchange the uncertainties of freedom for the supposed security of authoritarianism. That is the undying appeal of populist nationalism: the abdication of the challenges of responsibility in favour of a clearly defined place in the world. This is particularly attractive in times of depression, when everything in every direction looks like trackless wilderness.

In *Darkness Over Germany*, a remarkable account of conversations with Germans during the 1930s, many conducted in secret, Amy Buller describes a disturbing talk by Karl Weber, a rising Nazi star. Weber wants foreigners like her to understand why so many find Nazism so compelling:

> I want to suggest to you that the younger generation in Germany needed above all the freedom that comes from security, the kind of security I mean is that which comes to those who give complete obedience to an authority they know they can trust.[42]

Making good use of our 'freedom for' is hard. Yet it is existentially connected with 'freedom from'. This is expressed in the Jewish calendar through the link between Passover and *Shavuot*, the festival of the Giving of the Torah. The relationship between them is apparent in the name the rabbis gave to *Shavuot*, *Atseret*, literally 'closure', since it marks the culmination of the journey out of slavery to the covenant with God at Sinai. A cynic might read this as the exchange of one kind of domination for another, subjection to God in place of subjugation by Pharaoh. Strict religious obligations are not exactly what many people understand as freedom. But Judaism has never taken liberty as the right to do as one pleases, even with the proviso that our choices must not cause harm to anyone else. Rather, the essence of freedom is the opportunity, and the concomitant responsibility, to do good. This is the freedom for the sake of which our ancestors were liberated from slavery, for which we must fight and which we must embrace, in every generation.

YITRO (18:1-20:26)

'I am the Lord your God'

A letter, written on 10 January 1947, by Charlotte Tuch in Berlin to my grandmother in Jerusalem, read:

> You dear mother wrote the following words: In spite of everything, my faith in God remains unbreakable. These words accompanied me through the long years of persecution and bombing when more than once our life hung by a silken thread, and gave me the strength to bear it all and come through.

I never knew my great-grandmother Regina, wife of Rabbi Dr Jacob Freimann. She died in Auschwitz-Birkenau, probably in July 1944. The nearest I came to a personal experience of her was when I stood on the Mount of Olives at the grave of her granddaughter Eva, who died young that same year, and saw, added to the original inscription, a memorial to her:

> Rebbetzin Rachel, daughter of Rabbi Yisrael Meir,
> Born on the 1st of the month of Shevat 5629 (1869)
> Murdered in the Holocaust, for the sanctification of God's name . . .

Soon afterwards the letter from Charlotte Tuch came, by chance, into my possession. Together with her husband she had survived underground, without papers or ration cards, in Hitler's Berlin. It had been hard, she wrote, to find the physical and emotional energy to reply to my grandmother's letter of enquiry which had somehow reached her in the bombed-out city. Sadly, she had no good news to share; no, she too had heard nothing from any of the relatives after whom my grandmother was asking. They had disappeared into the silence. There could no longer be any doubt; Regina, together with other missing family members, had been murdered.

But my great-grandmother's voice was not dead. Her words, spoken probably in the ghetto-town of Theresienstadt with astute awareness of what awaited her, had sustained Charlotte and her husband during the razzias and searches, the bombings, the final battles and the occupation of the ruined city by the Red Army: 'In spite of everything, my faith in God remains unbreakable.' This was something even the Nazis with all their might could not take from her. Ever since I first read them on that thin sheet of airmail paper, her words have spoken to me too.

The first of the Ten Commandments is not, like so many other of the Bible's injunctions, in the plural but the singular, addressed to each and every individual: 'I am the Lord your God, who brought you out of the Land of Egypt, the house of bondage' (Exod. 20:2).

In Hebrew, every letter of the alphabet is also a number. Noting that the numerical value of the word 'Torah' adds up to 611, a famous midrash on the verse, 'Moses commanded us Torah,' observes that of the 613 commandments, as they are traditionally counted, all but two were transmitted by Moses. The exceptions are, 'I am the Lord your God,' and, 'You shall have no other gods beside me.' These were spoken by God directly, without any intermediary (Talmud, Makkot 23b). The implication is clear: there are certain things that everyone has to hear for themselves. Tradition alone cannot convey them; they must be experienced by each of us personally.

When God first commands Moses to return to Egypt and speak to the Children of Israel, Moses asks to know God's name. God famously replies: '*I am that I am* . . . This is what you shall say to the Children of Israel: "*I am* has sent me to you"' (Exod. 3:13–14).

Then, as if reconsidering, God adds:

Thus shall you say to the Children of Israel: 'God, the God of your ancestors, the God of Abraham, the God of Isaac and the God of Jacob has sent me to you. This is my name forever, my remembrance from generation to generation.'

(Exod. 3:15)

These are two very different answers.

God's second response appeals to tradition; it is God's calling card through the ages. The God of our ancestors is at the centre of Jewish liturgy and spiritual history. Every daily prayer opens with an appeal to the God of Abraham, Isaac and Jacob; many today add the mothers, Sarah, Rebecca, Rachel and Leah. Learning what God has, and has not, meant to the family of Israel, to the scholars, leaders, poets, historians, martyrs and diarists, to the pious and to the sceptics, connects us to each of them in their understanding of and struggles with their inherited religion. Reflecting on what that faith has meant to our ancestors, up to and including our own parents, through all the blessings, challenges and griefs they faced in their journeys through life, is humbling and inspiring. It opens our heart to what God may be to us; it gives us rituals and a language in which to seek and understand our own experience. That is what so moves me in learning about my great-grandmother's ineradicable faith.

However, God's first answer speaks not to tradition but to personal experience. It is not a noun with an external point of reference. Even as a verb, it describes no action that can be visualised or imagined. Its meaning is thoroughly enigmatic: 'I am being,' or, 'I am becoming.' A simple re-arrangement of its four Hebrew letters, *yud*, *heh*, *vav*, *heh*, changes it into *ha-va-ya-ah*, existence.

Perhaps it's the very mysteriousness of this name that makes it so compelling. It calls us to seek God's presence within life's unfolding, through our own intuition and awareness. This God can never be defined, never stowed away in our mind as something known, a belief verified, a box ticked. By definition, it eludes definition; it is always a new becoming; perhaps, as the contemporary mystic Arthur Green suggests, it should be understood not as, 'I am that I am,' but as, 'I shall be that I shall be.'[43] We gain a momentary understanding only, before this escapes us, until at some unknown point in our future we have another, different encounter.

Yet this does not render whatever awareness we have gained irrelevant or merely tangential to our ongoing experience. For such moments of revelation – and, for most of us, revelation is probably momentary only – are sufficient to direct the course of our lives, just as a few stars in the sky seen even intermittently may be enough for a mariner to set the ship's course. Faith lies in the journey through the darkness in between.

God concludes by telling Moses that this is 'God's name *le'olem*, forever' (Exod. 3:15). Since the word is written in the Torah without the letter *vav*, the '*o*' in the middle, the mystics read it as *le'elem*, meaning 'that which is hidden'. This is the God whose name and presence no one else can reveal to us, which tradition alone can't teach. It cannot in truth be otherwise, for the faith that gives us strength, that enables us to endure sorrow and inspires us to sing, can only be our own, ratified in those hidden places where God's 'I am' and our 'I am' meet.

Revelation

Does revelation come from the outside in, or from the inside out? Is the place where God and humanity meet somewhere specific, or simply anywhere?

The Torah provides a dramatic account of the revelation at Sinai: smoke covers the mountain, thunder and lightning rage, the call of the shofar grows ever louder. Into this maelstrom, Moses is summoned. While he 'draws near to the thick darkness where God abides' (Exod. 20:21), the people stand back, afraid (Exod. 20:18). That, said Rebbe Nachman of Breslav (1772–1810), is the journey of faith; one must be prepared to traverse the deep inner darkness.

At Sinai, God the eternal descends into the world of place and time, setting out the principles and laws that are to govern all creation. The rabbis imagine God addressing all life, present and future: 'If you keep my Torah, well and good. If not, you'll be turned back into chaos' (Talmud Shabbat 88a). Without a moral order, the world cannot survive.

The scene is, and is intended to be, unforgettable, a unique and definitive moment in history. But to the mystics, the account is symbolic rather than, or possibly as well as, historical. For God is not a distant external other; the God whose divinity is revealed at Sinai also dwells within humanity. What we become aware of in the moment of revelation is not just the voice of God from without, but the quintessence of who we are, our true, core nature made known to us from the depths of our being:

[When God spoke at Sinai] the inner vitality of all nature was revealed. All nature became subservient to God alone, as will be the case once again in the time to come when God's name will be one. The Torah says, 'God descended on Mount Sinai,' which Onkelos translated as 'God was revealed': that is, the inner vitality within all created beings became manifest to them . . . When God said, 'I am the Lord your God,' every single created being experienced this as addressed to them.[44]

Thus the 'I' that is myself and the 'I' spoken by God meet and merge. In this moment of recognition, I am not other, a separate being with an independent will. I am part; God's 'I' embraces me, simplifying me into my most essential nature, a manifestation of the one. Moments later, revelation has passed and I, in my separateness and autonomy, inhabit once again the day-to-day world of moral choice. I am my 'I', my old familiar self once more.

But the impact of that personal moment at Sinai is not, and must never be, lost. Our ordinary selves and everyday lives are not 'ordinary' any more; they have been marked by the transcendent. Although the full intensity of the moment of revelation, or recognition, has passed, we carry what the Kabbalist mystics termed the *reshimu*, its residue or impact, with us always. We are bound to forget; daily preoccupations push the memory of what we felt and knew down to the bottom of the mind. But prayer and rituals remind us that we once had the experience and that it was real. The festival of *Shavuot*, marking the Giving of the Torah with the recital of the Ten Commandments, is intended not just as a commemoration of the revelation at Sinai, but also as an echo, even a restoration, of it. The voice that silenced all creation and filled every being with inner knowledge speaks once again, quietly, but not so faintly that it cannot be heard.

Furthermore, at any time, something, most likely something unexpected, may renew the experience in a different manner. A moment of realisation might come upon us suddenly, beneath a luminous night sky or surrounded by the meditations of the trees, silencing the noise in the mind. Awe takes hold of us and we become aware once again, not in theory but as lived experience, that an infinite vitality passes through us to which we truly belong. The minute-by-minute interactions with the material world that define our daily lives are not our final reality. There exists within us an immeasurably deeper 'I' which flows through all things, engulfing the 'I' of our fragment of consciousness. For these few moments of silence, our habitual 'I, me and mine' are not. For a short time afterwards, until once again the awakening is submerged, we know.

In his poem '*Ich und Du* – I and You', twentieth-century American-Polish rabbi Abraham Joshua Heschel describes just such a relationship with God. He was taking issue with Martin Buber whose famous book with that title categorises even the deepest relationships as essentially dialectic. For Heschel this is not the case; divine and human consciousness interpenetrate. Ultimately, the boundaries of 'I' and 'you' are transcended:

> Am I not – you? Are you not – I?
> My nerves are intertwined with yours.
> Your dreams have met with mine.
> So are we not one in the bodies of millions?
> . . . I live in Me and in you.
> Through your lips goes a word from Me to Me
> From your eyes falls a tear – which welled up in Me.[45]

A former student of Heschel told me how one day he asked the class: 'Why do you think the Torah is so opposed to making any image of God?' before answering his own question: 'Because God already has an image: you and I and every single human being are God's image.' In the words of the title of one of his best-known books, *God in Search of Man*,[46] God wants our consciousness. God lives in each of us, and that is the source of our deepest responsibility.

It has been argued that 'I am the Lord your God' isn't a commandment at all but simply a statement. It doesn't require us to do or not to do anything. But that's not true. It's the commandment at the heart of all other commandments, calling us to be conscious that we are commanded.

Carrying God's name

In Shakespeare's *King Lear*, Edgar, a former nobleman, now a fugitive disguised as a bedlam beggar, recites a summary of the Ten Commandments to a distraught King Lear in the middle of a terrible storm: 'Keep thy word justly; swear not.'[47] This is how the third commandment, 'Do not take the name of the Lord your God in vain,' is usually understood (Exod. 20:7). It's about refraining from swearing in God's name.

In biblical thought, name and essence are closely associated. When we invoke God's name in any cause or context, we draw attention to the significance God holds for us. To do so contemptuously suggests that God has no meaning for us. This calls our own integrity into account; if we're casual or dismissive about the God of truth, what remains in life that commands our respect? What's left in us that deserves to be respected in return?

Important as this is, there is a different and perhaps deeper level to the third of the Ten Commandments. The negative formulation, 'Don't take God's name in vain,' masks an assumption: that we do in some manner 'take' God's name. But 'take' is a misleading translation. The Hebrew *tissa*, from the root *nasa*, means 'carry'; we are carriers of God's name. Our choice lies not in whether, but how, we do this. This commandment requires us not to do so in ways that void it of meaning.

As in English, 'name', *shem*, also indicates reputation. 'Better a good name than fine oil,' says Ecclesiastes 7:1. The rabbis of the Mishnah taught that the greatest of all crowns is that of a good name (Avot 4:17). We are bearers not just of God's name but also of God's reputation. You have been entrusted with God's name, Moses tells the people, indicating both a privilege and a deep responsibility (Deut. 28:10). God's reputation in this world depends partly on us.

Kiddush Hashem, the sanctification of God's name, is generally associated with martyrdom. People murdered simply because they are Jews, whether or not they have any choice in the matter, are all regarded as *kedoshim*, holy martyrs who died 'for the sanctification of God's name'. Those are the words inscribed in memory of my great-grandmother on her granddaughter's gravestone on the Mount of Olives. She herself is part of the ash in the fields surrounding Auschwitz-Birkenau.

But *Kiddush Hashem* is not solely about how we die; it is also about how we live. That's why Maimonides codifies the principle in the opening section of his compendium of Jewish law, the *Mishneh Torah*, in which he sets out the underlying principles of Judaism, including what it means to be a good person, a good Jew:

When such a person speaks with people in a kindly manner, shows sympathy with their situation, receives them warmly, suffers humiliation without humiliating others in return, treats them with respect even when shown none, conducts all dealings with honesty and in good faith, avoids excessive chatter, is occupied with Torah, wearing tallit and tefillin, behaves with greater generosity than the law strictly requires, yet without being aloof or appearing critical, and draws widespread praise and affection, setting an example, such a person sanctifies God's name.[48]

The better known the individual and the more public the circumstances, the greater is the *Kiddush Hashem*, the sanctification of God's name.

But the converse is also true; when people behave rudely, high-handedly, with cruelty and contempt, they desecrate God's name. The more public this *Chillul Hashem*, literally voiding of God's name and reputation, the worse it is. As a marginalised and frequently targeted minority, Jews are highly sensitive to how we are perceived. We probably think of this more in terms of the reputation of Judaism than of God. We have an instinctive anxiety lest anyone or anything bring, or be seen or framed to bring, the name of the Jewish People into disrepute. But, alongside members of other faiths, we also carry a deep responsibility not to drag God, and religion as a whole, into the mud.

Carrying God's name has personal as well as public significance. A name is not arbitrary; in the Hebrew Bible name, character and destiny are understood to be intimately connected. 'Four things have the power to tear up God's decree' and change our destiny, the Talmud declares, among them not only improving one's conduct but also changing one's name. God modifies Abram's name to *Avraham*, 'father of many nations', and Sarai's to *Sarah*, meaning 'princess' (Gen. 17:5, 15). Only then are they able to have a child together (Talmud Rosh Hashanah 16b). To this day many observe the custom of adding a name like Nechama, meaning 'comfort', or Raphael, meaning 'may God heal', to that of anyone who is seriously ill, in the hope that this, together with good medical treatment, will bring them back to health.

This might sound like magical thinking, but many of us today still intuitively feel that there is a relationship between name and personality, though perhaps not destiny. My wife and I called our first daughter Libbi in memory of my late mother. Like so many parental choices, it reflects our family's history and memory. It is also, perhaps, an attempt at recapture, as if name and character are linked. Nobody calls their child after someone they didn't love or respect. Some mystics believe that to name a baby after a deceased relative is to re-embody their soul. So if God's name, secret and unknowable though it is, somehow expresses God's essence, the significance of being entrusted with carrying it must be profound.

This is especially true if we understand God's name not solely as extraneous to us, but also as within us. The Kabbalists saw in the vertical arrangement of the letters of God's secret name, *yod heh vav heh*, the shape of the head, torso, arms and legs of the human body, signifying the sanctity of every human life. Into this form, or name, God breathes the breath of life. Thus when, according to legend, the Maharal of Prague, Rabbi Judah

Loew ben Bezalel (1525–1609), created the famous golem, a figure moulded from earth, to protect the city's Jews from persecution, he brought it to life by writing God's name on its forehead and calling on God's breath to enter its inert body, imitating how God 'breathed the breath of life into the nostrils' of the first human being (Gen. 2:7). Some infinitesimal portion of God breathes in each of us.

It follows that we carry, or even embody, God's name not only when we swear but also in everything we say and do, and in the depths of who we are. It is hard to imagine a call to greater responsibility, from which there is no escape and no time out.

MISHPATIM (21:1–24:18)

Rapo Yerapeh – he shall surely heal

Rachel Remen, a remarkable doctor who devoted herself to caring for the carers, wrote of how she once asked a paediatrician who was struggling to find meaning in his work:

> 'Why did you choose it [paediatrics], Jon?'
> He drew in his breath: 'I thought I could become a friend to innocent life,' he said softly.[49]

How do healers find healing?

The Torah says *verapo yerapei*, repeating the verb for emphasis: 'He shall surely heal' (Exod. 21:19). I'd been searching for an interpretation that reads the words differently, as the Hasidic masters often do. Since only the consonants are actually written in the Torah, it's often possible to vocalise them in ways other than the accepted pronunciation. But I couldn't find a rabbi who read them as I wanted to: *verofeh yeirapei*, 'the healer shall be healed'.

Where does healing come from for hurts that are not to the body but to the soul, moral injuries, ravages of spirit and morale? From where do consolation and rehabilitation come after all the fear and grief that accumulate in the heart as it absorbs the tormented, unjust sufferings that afflict so many? Rachel Clarke, a palliative care doctor who transferred to a large hospital to help beleaguered colleagues as the coronavirus took hold across

Britain, wrote in her frank account of the pandemic: 'I fear, too, that the public is unaware of how exhausted, stunned – shell-shocked, even – many National Health Service staff and care workers remain.'[50]

The plain meaning of the Torah's words, 'he or she shall surely heal', form the core of Judaism's understanding of medicine: 'It was taught in the school of Rabbi Yishmael: From here we learn that permission is given to the healer to heal' (Talmud Bava Kama 85a).

Commentators have puzzled over why the Talmud refers only to 'permission' when the instruction to heal is clearly a command, not just a request. The issue is that the Torah has previously said: 'I am God, your healer,' indicating that God alone is entitled to heal (Exod. 15:26). If this is so, it would seem wrong to put one's faith in merely human interventions. Perhaps even the very attempt to cure illness might be counter to God's will.

The Talmud gives voice to this hypothetical challenge, but only in order to refute it, interpreting the emphatic repetition, 'heal, he shall surely heal', to mean that competent doctors not just *may*, but *must*, exercise their professional skills. Similarly, those who are ill, and loved ones acting on their behalf, have a responsibility to seek healing. The Talmud even says that just as one shouldn't settle in a community that has no teacher of Torah, so one shouldn't live where there's no access to a physician (Talmud Sanhedrin 17b).

In codifying the ruling that healing is a *mitzvah*, a commandment, Maimonides offers a further source for the obligation, the requirement that 'you shall return it to him' (Deut. 22:2). The reference is to lost property, but what loss, he argues, can be greater than that of one's health and what 'return' more important than its restoration (Talmud Sanhedrin 73a)?

The *Shulchan Aruch*, the authoritative sixteenth-century code of Jewish law composed by Joseph Caro (1488–1575), therefore rules: 'Permission is given to the healer to heal, and, moreover, it is an obligation, included in the commandment of *pikkuach nefesh*, saving life. If a healer refuses their services, they are considered guilty of bloodshed.'[51]

The *Turei Zahav*, a commentary on the *Shulchan Aruch* by David Halevi Segal (1586–1667), notes that, whereas healing should ideally come from God, we are unworthy of such direct divine intervention and must therefore depend on the physician's best understanding of those natural elements by which our earthly lives are governed. In a famous prayer attributed to Maimonides, the physician asks God for guidance in the sacred task of healing:

Thou hast endowed man with the wisdom to relieve the suffering of his brother, to recognize his disorders, to extract the healing substances, to discover their powers and to prepare and apply them to suit every ill. In Thine Eternal Providence Thou hast chosen me to watch over the life and health of Thy creatures. I am now about to apply myself to the duties of my profession. Support me, Almighty God, in these great labors that they may benefit mankind, for without Thy help not even the least thing will succeed.

Inspire me with love for my art and for Thy creatures.[52]

'Love . . . for Thy creatures' is surely an essential part of the healer's art. Rachel Remen, who devoted her life to working with terminally ill people and those caring for them, wrote of how she had once:

> . . . carried the belief that as a physician my love didn't matter and the only thing I had to value was my knowledge and skill . . . [But] Medicine is as close to love as it is to science, and its relationships matter even at the edge of life itself.[53]

Even if curing physical symptoms were 'all' doctors were called upon to do, it's an infinitely complex task, as this daily blessing indicates:

> You have formed the human being with wisdom, creating multiple apertures and organs; you know that if one of them opens which should be closed, or closes which should be open, we will be unable to get up and stand before you.

But healing is more than the treatment of physical symptoms; body and soul are inextricably interconnected. Traumatised feelings may remain long after physiological damage is repaired. The rabbis of the Mishnah understood the importance of this psychological dimension; anyone who caused injury had to recompense the victim not just for their medical bills, time off work and loss of future earnings, but also for their pain and humiliation. The repair of physical hurts had to be accompanied by healing of the spirit and emotions (Talmud Bava Kama 83b).

Rachel Remen therefore asks whether there isn't rather more 'to helping people recover than knowing the right diagnosis and offering the proper treatment? Did our relationship to our patients affect outcome as profoundly as our medications?'[54] She stresses how deeply not just knowledge and skill but also intuition and compassionate understanding are needed from healers. Such work, especially in times of crisis, cannot but have a profound impact on everyone engaged in it, from hospital porters to doctors, nurses and carers.

But who cares for them? Who, after their days, months and years of dedication, helps the healers find healing? What brings restoration to those who struggle constantly to save lives yet must often attend to the dying?

The truth is that we all share the responsibility for valuing and supporting those who care for us. If they give from their hearts, we should give them our heart-space in return.

Even so, there are depths of healing beyond our reach. A picture taken during the height of the Covid-19 pandemic showed a doctor watching the birds by a pond in a brief moment of reprieve from intensive care. Nature, like music, beauty and thoughtful companionship, is a form of God's healing, God's way of saying, 'I am God, your healer.' We cannot find our way into each other's hearts to cauterise our wounds and cure our sorrows. But we can protect those spaces in nature and society where God's presence may touch us 'with healing on its wings' (Mal. 3:20), and in this manner help our healers find healing. In so doing, we ourselves become both healer and healed.

Anshei Kodesh – people of holiness

At a birthday party long ago, the host suggested as an ice-breaker that we should share what we wanted to be when we were older. Someone I didn't know said: 'I just want to be a human being.' His answer has stayed with me through the years. Only, what does being a human being mean?

One of the most popular Yiddish words is *mensch*; 'so-and-so's a real *mensch*' indicates that they're decent and kind, the sort of person who would help anyone if they could. But the party guest used the Hebrew *ben adam*; there was something biblical in his response, as if he were trying to answer the implicit question, 'What does God want of me?' as in the much-quoted verse from Micah: 'You have been told, human beings, what God seeks from you; only to practise justice and the love of kindness, and to walk humbly with your God' (Mic. 6:8).

Probably no single verse is engraved more often on tombstones, and not only in Jewish cemeteries.

But how does that translate into being 'truly human' in daily life? The Torah teaches: '*Ve'anshei kodesh tiheyun li*, You shall be holy people to me' (Exod. 22:30). Literally translated, *anshei kodesh* means 'people of holiness', suggesting, perhaps, that the one is contingent upon the other: to be holy means to be human and to be truly human requires being holy.

'I have no desire for angels down on earth,' wrote the Hasidic Rebbe, Menachem Mendel of Kotsk (1787–1859), famous for his astute, sometimes acerbic, insights: 'I want you to be *people* of holiness: humane conduct, but with holiness.' The word here for people is not *am*, 'nation', but *enosh*, deriving from a root meaning 'weak' or 'vulnerable', hinting at our mortality. How, in our frailty, subject to all the accidents of everyday life, can we aspire to being holy?

Exodus 22:30(31) continues: 'You may not eat *terefah*, meat torn in the field; you must throw it to the dogs.' This hardly seems like an answer to a question about holiness. But at the most basic level who we are is, quite literally, what we consume. *Terefah* is generally translated as 'carrion', but the contemporary Israeli rabbi David Rosen, a committed vegan, notes that in rabbinical law it refers to any animal carrying an injury or illness which it cannot survive for more than twelve months. Therefore, 'Industrially farmed animals and their milk may be forbidden under this category due to the way that they are treated.'[55] The conditions in which they are forced to live in both the meat and dairy industries are likely to damage their internal organs to such an extent that they cannot be considered kosher, and 'if they are non-kosher, then their products are non-kosher and their milk becomes non-kosher.[56]

Therefore, if we want to be truly human, we must not consume unethically, without regard for the creatures whose bodies or products we eat, nor without regard for our fellow human beings on whose labour we depend. This may sound basic, but if we ignore such basics our humanity is flawed. Nachmanides comments on the verse, 'Be holy, because I, your God, am holy' (Lev. 19:2), that we must sanctify ourselves even with regard to what is allowed to us; otherwise we risk being 'gross with permission of the Torah'.[57] What and how we consume is the key issue as we face the climate crisis in the twenty-first century. It's not enough to avoid what isn't kosher; we have to consider the ethical and ecological footprint of what is permitted to us. Otherwise, while we may like to think of ourselves as decent people because we're nice to our immediate neighbours, we may in reality be helping to maintain grave injustices and unconscionable cruelties far across the world. Being 'people of holiness' requires us to behave with humanity and kindness in all our interactions. There is no 'somewhere' or 'sometimes', just as the much-quoted 'love your neighbour' doesn't contain the words 'some of'.

The context of the commandment in Exodus 22:30 is highly significant. It follows a series of laws about social justice: don't afflict a widow or orphan;

don't oppress strangers; don't exact interest when lending to the poor. It precedes a further sequence of rules about speech ethics: don't spread ugly rumours; don't follow the crowd to do evil; don't bear false witness. It's close to the words that mark the midpoint of the Book of Exodus: 'I shall listen [to the cry of the oppressed] for I am merciful' (Exod. 22:27).

Being human means that we too should have a heart open to this cry, as the rabbis explained: 'Be merciful, for I, your God, am merciful',[58] or, as the followers of Hillel, the much-loved sage of the first century BCE, expressed it: 'At all times one should treat one's fellow beings with sympathetic understanding.' (Talmud Eruvin 13b) While *beriyot*, 'fellows', is generally understood to refer to human beings, it actually means 'creatures', implying all living beings. We are less than truly human if we mistreat not just each other but animals too, as the Torah goes on to say: 'If you see your enemy's donkey collapsing under its load, you may not abandon it but must surely come to his assistance' (Exod. 23:5).

To be human means never to be indifferent.

None of this may sound particularly holy; it amounts to no more than how any decent person should behave. But that's the point; being 'religious' must be grounded in being ethical. The foundation of all genuine spirituality is how we treat one another. There is no such thing as being good to God and bad to each other. For God is not shut away in the distant heavens but present in the heart of all life. Being human is therefore both the beginning and the essence of being holy. If we treat life as sacred, life responds by allowing us to experience its preciousness. This in turn opens our hearts more fully and makes us more truly human.

'We shall do and we shall hear'

The rabbis lavished praise on the Children of Israel because in their response to Moses at Sinai, 'Everything God has said we will do and we will hear,' they put 'do' before 'hear' (Exod. 24:7). They imagined even the angels dancing with delight. But they also had reservations, like the challenge they put into the mouth of the heretic who, on seeing the sage Rava so immersed in Torah study that he unthinkingly crushed his fingers until they bled, rudely said: 'Rash nation, putting your mouth before your ears. Are you still so hasty? First you should have listened and only then, if you could, accepted' (Talmud Shabbat 88a).

The Talmud gives the line to a heretic, but the point is real: how can one commit oneself to doing what one hasn't yet been told, or subject oneself to demands before knowing what they are, even if they come from God? It's an acutely relevant question today when we prioritise individuality and autonomy and are reluctant to forgo any degree of personal choice without knowing, in detail and with assurances, what the benefits are likely to be. It does seem rash, if not downright irresponsible, to agree to be bound by a system of rituals and laws without understanding exactly what's involved, without possessing, let alone studying, the fine print. We expect to know what we're letting ourselves in for prior to making any commitments. We want to hear before we promise to do. Even then, most of us prefer to put our toe in the water rather than jump in. Jewish practices can seem alien or arcane, especially if we didn't grow up with them: how can anyone be expected to engage in them without a significant amount of prior explanation?

Yet the people's response at Sinai has remained paradigmatic for Jewish life throughout the ages. Judaism is primarily learnt by absorption and osmosis, not theoretical explanations. The willingness to follow a clear practice characterises the beaten path not only of Judaism but also of every serious discipline of body, mind and spirit. For the objective is not the transfer of knowledge so much as the communication of experience. To be more exact, it's not the experiences themselves, which always remain personal, but the route into them, the way to expose oneself to them, which religious traditions seek to convey. This cannot be achieved unless we are prepared to follow the necessary practices, and this inevitably requires trust. We have to commit, at least to some extent, before we can really hear. Then, as we live the experience, that hearing deepens, and opens up in turn new depths of experience.

Shabbat is a key example. A mother once said to me at the conclusion of a beautiful Sabbath full of prayer, music and discussion accompanied by good food: 'I wish I could just wrap this all up and give it to my children.' But we can't transmit the outcome of an experience; we can only share the pathway that leads towards it. We cannot know in advance what the journey will feel like for us, let alone for someone else. We have to trust, and encourage others to trust, the overall wisdom of those who over centuries established and refined the pathway. This means acceding to at least some of the preconditions, however countercultural they may currently seem, as, in the case of *Shabbat*, not working, shopping or switching on screens may appear to us today. In the classic language of Judaism, following the way of the commandments involves at least some degree of acceptance, although not unquestioningly, of the discipline they demand.

The effectiveness of religious practices and rituals depends on the willingness to follow them into the spaces they can help us find. Hallowed by the hearts, souls, aspirations and commitment of those who established and lived by them over generations, they have the power to awaken sensitivities we may not have realised we had. They can guide us into experiences we cannot otherwise access or know; the awareness, however fleeting and attenuated, of spiritual communion and the presence of God.

Throughout his career, Kalonymus Kalman Shapira, known subsequently as the Rebbe of the Warsaw Ghetto, was concerned with the question of inner growth. He returned repeatedly to the problem of how it is possible to transcend the limits of our cognitive mind and deepen our spiritual intuition. In a remarkable meditation on the meaning of 'we will do and we will hear', he begins by noting that even our physical senses require the appropriate stimulation to activate them:

> In truth, the human being needs to be revealed. For this he needs things which will reveal him. If he receives no such stimuli, then parts of his humanity will remain concealed from him. This applies even in the physical domain. If one wants to realise one's ability to see, one has to make use of one's sight, but if one shuts one's eyes one's ability to see ceases. Thus, visible objects reveal to us our capacity for sight. So it is with all our physical capacities and, all the more so, with our spiritual capabilities.[59]

But if we do not engage with the kinds of activities that have the power to awaken these capabilities within us, they will remain dormant. This doesn't mean that we don't have them, only that we are as yet unaware of them, because our experiences to date have not yet aroused them within us:

> If you know human nature, if you know your own self, the self you know is only the shadow of the world, those aspects of your humanity which certain kinds of experience have caused to be revealed out of [all] the human potentialities hidden within.[60]

We therefore need a spiritual education, not to impose the will of others on us, but to draw forth our own potential. This, he explains, is what the Children of Israel meant when they said: 'We will do and we will hear,' words he interprets in a radically original way:

> Had they had first said, 'We will hear,' who would have heard? – Their 'I'. But which 'I'? – Their 'I' in its [previous] state of understanding

which the [physical] world and its fullness had revealed in them. Hence, they would be able to recognise and hear only according to their physical capacities. This is not what Israel wanted. Therefore, they first said, 'We shall do.' Or, since in Hebrew 'do' is the same word as 'make', 'We shall make.' What shall we make? – Ourselves!

The Torah will bring forth from within us the hidden essence of our humanity and then 'we shall [be able to] hear' [more deeply than we could have done before].[61] What the Children of Israel say at Sinai is that they are ready to be made, to be guided and to be formed by their spiritual journey, even though they can't fully know in advance how this will feel or where it will lead. Without surrendering our critical faculties – an important qualification – we must do likewise if we want to follow a spiritual path.

'Do not abuse or oppress the stranger'

Both my parents were refugees from Nazi Germany. My father fled Breslau when he was sixteen after a tip-off that his father was high on the Gestapo list. 'We laid the table as if we were returning for tea, packed a small bag each, and left for ever.' Visas to Palestine saved their lives.

My mother's father was a rabbi in Frankfurt-am-Main. Urged to flee the country, he refused to leave his community, insisting that 'the captain is last to leave the ship'. But when he was interned in the concentration camp of Dachau after Kristallnacht, it was a question of flight or death. Fortunately, the family were able to obtain temporary visas to Britain with the help of the British Consulate, by means of which they procured his release. They arrived in England in April 1939.

During the war years they were hosted by a devout Christian couple outside London. When the time came for them to leave, my mother was at a loss as to how to express her gratitude. 'You don't have to thank us', the lady said. 'One day you'll do for others what we've tried to do for you and that will be our thanks.'

This story, together with our family history and the history of the Jewish People, has had a profound influence on me. Though Jews were sometimes made welcome in towns and countries across Europe, time and again through the centuries they were marginalised, ghettoised, persecuted, forced into exile and killed. Therefore, the fate of refugees feels very close to home. The Torah's commandment to love the stranger, repeated no less than thirty-six times, chimes with Jewish experience: 'Do not abuse or oppress the stranger, for you were strangers in the Land of Egypt' (Exod. 22:20).

The Biblical Encyclopaedia explains that a stranger, *ger* in Hebrew, is:

> One who dwells outside the land of their birth. Since migration from land to land is sometimes caused by economic or political troubles, there is an added nuance of seeking one's livelihood or asylum in another land. The root also has a public legal meaning and indicates the status of a member of another people resident among the local population.[62]

Evidently, the reasons that force people to flee their homelands have not changed significantly over the course of history: war, internal upheavals and economic collapse caused by drought and other ecological disasters (which are likely to become the main cause of mass emigration in our own day).

The mediaeval rabbis took the injunction to love and support the refugee to heart. Rashi, sensitive to the Torah's reminder that 'you have known the soul of the refugee', warns:

> If you oppress them, they can turn round and say back to you: you too are descended from refugees. [Therefore] don't accuse others of a blemish you also have.[63]

The twelfth-century Spanish-born grammarian and commentator Abraham ibn Ezra, himself a wanderer through many countries including England, insisted:

> When refugees agree not to practise idolatry, you must not wrong them in your land. This is because you have much more power than they do. Remember that you were strangers like they are now. Just as the Torah refers to the stranger who has no power, so it also mentions the orphan and the widow who are Israelites but have no power. After commanding, 'You shall not ill-treat' in the plural, the Torah says in the singular, 'If you mistreat'. For any individual who sees somebody mistreating an orphan or widow and fails to go to their assistance is considered as if he or she had personally mistreated them . . . If one person mistreats them and nobody comes to their aid, the punishment is collective.[64]

In other words, we have a shared responsibility towards refugees. We are not allowed to turn a blind eye or hide behind leaders who are hostile to migrants. Other people's racism or indifference cannot justify our own inaction. We have an obligation to aid the poorest in our society, and asylum seekers are especially vulnerable.

But ibn Ezra insists on one proviso: the refugee must abjure idolatry. It's interesting to consider what the contemporary equivalent might be. The rejection of idolatry and the affirmation of the oneness of God are the basis of Jewish faith and culture. Arguably, the parallels in democratic states today are the values of freedom and equality, including freedom of conscience and speech, and equality between men and women. A country is entitled to require those seeking safety within its borders to uphold these central principles.

For Nachmanides, the issues were even closer to home. He was forced to flee his native Catalonia after successfully defending Judaism against Pablo Christiani in a public disputation in Barcelona in 1263 in the presence of King James I of Aragon. He found refuge in the Holy Land which, despite its desolation, provided comfort to his spirit. But nothing could console him for the separation from those he loved:

'I am the man who saw affliction'. I am banished from my table, far removed from friend and kinsman, and too long is the distance ever to meet again . . . I left my family, forsook my house. There, with the sweet and beloved children whom I brought up on my knees, I left also my soul. With them, my heart and my eyes will dwell forever.[65]

His words should be read by everyone who has no place in their soul for refugees. 'I miss my brother terribly,' a young man told me, who had fled Iran and lived with us for many months.

'My mother and brother were killed in front of my eyes,' explained a woman from Ethiopia who stayed with us for just three weeks.

'And your father?' I asked, tentatively.

'I haven't heard for twelve years. Maybe he's dead; or maybe in prison . . .'

Nachmanides understood the Torah's words as an urgent warning to those in power that God always listens to the dispossessed and downhearted:

I see the tears of the oppressed who have no one to comfort them and power lies in the hands of their oppressors, and I protect every human being from the hands of those stronger than them. Similarly, you shall not afflict the widow or orphan, for I hear their cry. For all these people do not trust in themselves but put their trust in Me.[66]

Don't imagine God saved you from Pharaoh because you were special, he continues. God took your part because you were strangers and outsiders in Egypt. If you now afflict strangers in your land, 'God will surely have mercy on them just as God had mercy on you.'[67]

Few modern commentators have written as forcefully on this subject as Samson Raphael Hirsch (1808–88). After fighting for civil rights in the Moravian *Landtag*, he was called to Frankfurt in 1851 by a small orthodox congregation. He lived and taught there through the unification of Germany under Bismarck when Jews were granted a significant measure of civil rights. He believed that it should be possible to live as a strictly observant Jew while participating fully in a modern state that upheld the principles of equality of rights and opportunities:

> Your entire misfortune in Egypt was that you were 'foreigners' there, who, as such, according to the view of the nations, had no rights to land, home, or existence and towards whom everything was consequently regarded as permitted. As strangers you were without rights in Egypt; out of that grew your slavery and suffering. Beware therefore, so runs the warning, lest in your state you make the rights of anyone dependent on anything other than the simple fact of their humanity which every human being possesses by virtue of being human. With any diminution of this human right (*Menschenrecht*) the door is thrown wide open to the whole horror of the experience in Egypt of the wilful mistreatment of other people.[68]

Hirsch's warning reads like a premonition of the Nuremberg Laws of 1935, through which my parents and hundreds of thousands of others were stripped of all rights and rendered victims, rather than citizens, of the state.

In failing to stand up for others, especially those most vulnerable to abuse and contempt, we betray both their humanity and our own.

TERUMAH (25:1–27:19)

....

Make me a sanctuary

The heavens are my throne, and the earth is my footstool; what house can you then build for me and what space is my resting place?

(Isa. 66:1)

God, where shall I find you? And where shall I find you not?

(Yehudah Halevi)[69]

Moses is commanded to tell the Children of Israel to make a *mikdash*, a sanctuary, a *mishkan* or dwelling place for God. The specifications are so complicated that God resorts to telling him to 'look and do, as shown upon the mountain' (Exod. 25:40). The boards framing the tabernacle must be made of cedar wood, each plank ten cubits high by one and a half cubits wide. The sockets on which they stand, two for each plank, must be cast in silver. The curtains that cover the entire structure must be woven from threads spun from wool and linen intertwined, in colours of blue, purple and scarlet. The result is to be a palace, glorious yet portable, for a God who is manifest yet invisible.

There's an obvious irony to this focus on lengths, breadths and heights. For God has no need for a specific number of square cubits to be at home, or not at home, in the world. 'God is the place of the world, but the world is not God's place,' runs a Midrashic saying, indicating that God cannot be bound by space, let alone by any one specific location (Bereshit Rabbah 68:9). Isaiah's question goes straight to the point: 'What house can you then build for me?' (Isa. 66:1). It highlights the paradoxical nature of the Tabernacle and, later, the Temple: how can a space be created for what transcends space, for where the boundless meets the bounded, the limitless the delimited?

Yet experience suggests such locations exist; there are holy places where God and human beings have been felt to meet. Many are strictly personal. That isn't because they're protected by No Entry signs; they may be entirely accessible to everyone, but it is only to us that they have become holy. We encountered something there, or perhaps something encountered us, and the place became sacred – for us. Such spaces may be specific sites to which we return over and again in search of something other:

inspiration, consolation or simply the reminder that there still exists something beyond, a hidden dimension to life known only to the spirit. Perhaps like Jacob when, with stones for his pillow, he dreams of a ladder from earth to heaven, we suddenly alight upon God's place and, like him, say to ourselves, 'There's God in this place, but I hadn't known' (Gen. 28:16).

Therefore, for many readers, the Torah's lengthy account of the Tabernacle has to be taken figuratively; the objects described are not external furnishings but internal realities. The altar is where we place the offerings of our daily actions before God. The menorah is 'God's lamp, the human soul' (Prov. 20:27), illuminating the path to the holy. Its radiance extends to the curtain that separates the holy from the Holy of Holies, where we broach the domain of the heart. Here, in the innermost chamber, is the *aron ha'edut*, the Ark of the Testament, for it is there, in secret, that we know God. Like the high priest who enters just once a year on Yom Kippur, we find our way to this innermost sanctuary only rarely and, in the quiet, hear nothing but the articulate silence of the presence of God.

The journey to such places cannot be mapped out; it differs for each of us, and changes as life changes us. The path may elude us for months or years, as challenging experiences leave us distracted or numb. But suddenly we discover it; a flame from the inner menorah lights the way and we find ourselves in the Holy of Holies once again.

But the courtyards of our temples are more accessible. In fact, some of our sacred places probably look quite ordinary, even domestic, from the outside. 'Every day my daughter comes home from school, settles herself on the sofa next to the dog and tells her everything,' a mother explained to me. She's worried because the dog's getting old; what will happen when the animal dies? This is her daughter's holy space.

Gardens can be sacred spaces: we tend them with loving skill and patience; life answers with its glory of growth, flowers and fragrance finer than any fabricated incense. But for many of us it is nature in its purity that is our temple; like the psalmist, we find God by the quiet waters. Or perhaps our temple is the forest, as twentieth-century Jewish poet Chaim Nachman Bialik wrote in his magnificent poem, *Haberechah*, 'The Pool':

And I, in the days of my youth, best beloved of my days,
When the wings of God's presence first touched and stirred me
And my heart still knew how to long and yearn in silent wonder
And seek a secret place to pray,
I would betake myself in the heat of the summer
To the tranquil domains of the mighty forest

To the very thick of the woods . . .
There, behind the curtain of the leaves
Is an island, small and green, decked in fine lawn,
An island apart, a small world of its own,
A holy place, peaceful, hidden within the shadows
Of the ancient trees broad in canopy and bowed with leaves . . .[70]

Here, the furnishings of the Temple merge with the features of the forest. The rich cloths that separate off the Holy of Holies become curtains of leaves; the sacred ark where we overhear God's speech is guarded by trees.

Both joy and sorrow can lead us to sacred spaces. During the long months of watching over her comatose daughter, Isabel Allende wanders sleepless through the house, 'a raft without a rudder, adrift on a sea of pain', yet finds that she has been given 'the opportunity to look inside myself and discover interior spaces – empty, dark, strangely peaceful – I had never explored before. These are holy places.'[71]

She enters underwater caves inside in which, 'raw and bleeding,' she cries without tears.[72] Countless heart-torn people have found their way to such undersea refuges, though the route there is never the same.

Like the portable Tabernacle in the wilderness, our sacred spaces travel with us through life; they are both somewhere and nowhere. Their precise coordinates exist only inside us, when we find our way to them. Like the Tabernacle, too, they remain sacred as long as we feel God's presence hovering over them. When we lose the sense that this presence is there, we have to move on, to the next space where our spirit finds restoration.

In the making

Moses relays God's instruction to the people to 'make me a sanctuary and I shall dwell amidst them' (Exod. 25:8). This means, 'In the midst of the hearts of those who volunteer for the work,' observed Rebbe Shlomo of Radomsk (1801–66), noting that the Torah doesn't say 'in the midst of *it*' but 'in the midst of *them*'. The creation of holy spaces lies not in the structures built, but in the nature of the making. It's not just a matter of design and materials; the secret lies in the process. Any work of art, any sacred object, any place of grace and beauty is an embodiment of the spirit of its making.

That's why biblical Hebrew reserves for the artist the word *aman*. In the Song of Songs, the body of the beloved is described as *ma'aseh yedei aman*, the work of the hands of the skilled creator, God, the ultimate *aman* (Song 7:1). The true meaning of being made in God's image, suggests Dorothy Sayers, is that the godlike capacity for creativity has been bestowed on us.[73] *Aman* is composed of the same root letters as *ne'eman*, 'faithful', and the familiar *amen*, 'so may it be', for creating is a work of faith. Any artistic undertaking is an act of faith, a journey beginning with blank paper or with rough stone, with a rhythm in the head, with an intimation that only the silencing of all other thoughts can enable one to pursue. But it also requires keeping faith within the doing itself, an endeavour exacting the spirit's sustained attention. It demands the refusal to be distracted from listening to the often almost inaudible instruction which alone must guide the pen, the brush, the chisel, and which dictates in a language only the maker understands: this must be fashioned thus. Perhaps that is what the Torah means when, after Moses has been informed of their basic dimensions, he is told that all the component parts of the Tabernacle must be made 'according to what he has been shown upon the mountain' (Exod. 25:40). Such instructions can never be recorded; only the maker can know.

Since childhood, I've loved to watch artisans at work: the carpenter making fitted shelves, examining the grain of the timber, cutting precisely so; the French-polisher, dyeing the wood to bring out the natural beauty of the contrasting hues of umber and dark brown. I would sit, like Osip Mandelstam watching the preparation of wool, absorbed in their absorption:

A thing I love is the action of spinning:
the shuttle fluttering back and forth, the hum of the spindle.[74]

Later in life I would begin to understand what it can mean to become immersed in poetry or prayer, and what can happen when the words articulate me, not I them. It is within the action itself, in the quality of being in that action, when one loses oneself within it, that beauty comes to shine through. This may be why, in the many chapters devoted to the creation of a dwelling place for God's spirit, the Torah repeatedly describes the materials, their rich colours, the dyeing and weaving, the hooking and attaching of one part to another, throughout which the verb 'make' appears over and again, connecting all the elements together so that the very narrative imitates the smelting and moulding, sewing and stitching.

To oversee the work, God appoints Betsalel (Exod. 31:1). *Betsalel*, meaning 'in the shadow of God', is more than just a name. It describes the essence of the artist: the human being, created in God's image, *betselem*

Elohim, in turn becomes a creator when he or she stands *betsel*, 'in the shadow', underneath the wings of God's inspiration. This gift of creativity is our portion of divinity, a shadowing of God's creative power. Betsalel is both a particular individual, the master craftsman guiding all the welders, carpenters and tailors who devote themselves to the sacred task of building the tabernacle, and at the same time the embodiment of artistry itself. He is granted *ruach Elohim*, 'the spirit of God': just as that spirit first hovered over the inchoate planet guiding God to say, 'Let there be . . .', so the artist's intuition sees into the cedar wood, the metals and fabrics, and says, 'Let there be made . . .' God bestows on Betsalel 'wisdom, understanding and knowledge, to think thoughts and make' (Exod. 31:3). The thinking and making are so inseparably interconnected that one Hasidic master goes so far as to suggest that 'Betsalel established the Tabernacle in thought alone, and the thought became deed'. Between intuition and actualisation, nothing, not a single extraneous distraction, is allowed to intervene.[75]

Alongside Betsalel is Oholiav, 'master of my tent', named second because only beneath the shadow of God's presence can any human being find the mastery to create a space for God's spirit. It's not just their skill as artisans that is expressed in the work; the feeling and intention with which it is imbued during the process of creation remain within it, endowing it with qualities for which its physicality alone cannot account. 'There's magic in the web of it,' Othello warns his ill-fated bride Desdemona, demanding the return of the handkerchief which the wicked Iago will subsequently use to engineer their undoing:

A sibyl, that had number'd in the world
The sun to make two hundred compasses,
In her prophetic fury sew'd the work;
The worms were hallowed that did breed the silk.[76]

The soul of the artisan, the quality of his or her attention during the creative process, penetrates the raw materials and resides within what is made. Every object fashioned with purity of thought and loving dedication is, in and of itself, God's place, a refraction of the light from the infinite spirit that guided its creator. That's why Moses isn't instructed to procure somewhere for God to live, but rather to inspire the people to fashion a sanctuary. It is to be a manifestation of the sacred energy ceaselessly at work, yet hidden, in all that is. God will dwell not in the Tent of Meeting but in the creation of it; the 'meeting' is in the making.

TETSAVEH (27:20–30:10)

....

Carrying on one's heart

Wear it with pride, the yellow badge.
(Robert Weltsch, 4 April 1933)[77]

Clothes confer status; they indicate rank and position. We may betray the station they represent, or, if we are forced to wear them as marks of contempt, they may symbolise our betrayal by others. They express, but may also conceal, who we truly are, an ambiguity implied in the very word in Hebrew for garment, *beged*, derived from the root meaning deception.

The Torah devotes careful attention to the high priest's clothes. They are to be sewn from the choicest materials by artists endowed by God 'with the spirit of wisdom, to make Aaron's vestments, for consecrating him to serve me as priest' (Exod. 28:3). 'Wisdom' in this context denotes the skill of dedicated craftspeople. Coupled with 'spirit', it expresses an inner attunement, enabling them to communicate by means of their art something of the beauty and wonder of the sacred. This will in turn be transmitted to those who wear the garments, as Rebbe Yisrael of Modzhitz (1849–1920) explains: 'The thoughts of the wearer are linked to those of the maker, because what is made is imbued with the powers of the one who made it.'[78]

The exact details of the cut and composition of the clothing are difficult to follow. To try to describe them, Rashi, who had his eyes open to the world around him as well as being alert to every nuance of the text, refers to the jackets and gowns worn by French noblewomen. What is clear is that they were made from the finest cloth. The Talmud explains that the thread from which the priestly garments were woven was composed of six-fold bands of the colours blue, purple and crimson, and of fine linen, every band intertwined with a fine filament of beaten gold (Yoma 72a). The clothes must have been luminously beautiful. To don them must have felt at once a great privilege and a grave responsibility.

Nowhere is this more clearly expressed than through the precious stones set as jewels in the high priest's garments. The names of the tribes of Israel were engraved on two *shoham* stones, six on each, which were then attached to the shoulder pieces of the ephod, or tunic, like, says

Rashi, the epaulettes worn by the nobility. They were to be 'a remembrance of the Children of Israel' carried on Aaron's shoulders when he entered the presence of God (Exod. 28:9–12). The twelve names were also individually carved on twelve different gemstones that were set in gold on the breastplate. These he was to wear 'upon his heart before God always' (Exod. 28:21, 29–30).

Moshe Mordechai of Filov explains the two sets of stones as symbolising two levels of leadership responsibility (Midrash Moshe to Exod. 28:12). Carrying them on the shoulders represents sharing the burden of people's material needs and bringing them before God. A leader must be aware of the daily troubles faced by the community. When, in a story I often find myself revisiting, Rabban Gamliel, the somewhat authoritarian head of the Sanhedrin in the late first and early second century, went to apologise to Rabbi Yehoshua for treating him too harshly, he was shocked by his poverty. 'Alack,' said Rabbi Yehoshua, 'for the generation whose leaders do not know the struggles of ordinary people' (Talmud Berachot 28a).

Carrying the names of the twelve tribes on the breastplate over the heart represents the spiritual bond between priest and people. The priest has to be open to feeling the sorrows and fears, hopes and yearnings of the community in order to bring them before God in prayer. The stones serve as a constant reminder that both the material and spiritual needs of the people 'must be the very root and core of his existence, just as the heart is the source of human life' (Midrash Moshe to Exod. 28:30).

Rebbe Moshe Mordechai is clearly not just speaking about the role of the high priest in Temple times, but of everyone entrusted with the mantle of communal leadership. The robes of office, far from indicating rank and rights, symbolise connection and responsibility. Indeed, he may have in mind not only leaders but also each of us, and not just how we behave when we enter holy places but also the kind of person we need to be if we want the holy to enter us. If we care about whether those around us have safe homes, food security, a livelihood and access to schools for their children; if our heart is open to the troubles and aspirations of those with whom we interact at home, at work and in the street, then we are in God's place. If we can't be bothered, we profane both who and where we are. But if we do care, we help to make the place sacred, wherever and with whomever we may be. The deeper our commitment, the more holy the place may become.

Around his head the high priest wears a band of fine gold inscribed with God's holy name. '*Vehayah*, it shall be upon his temples *always*,' the Torah insists (Exod. 28:38). Rebbe Chaim Meir of Vischnitz (1887–1972) notes that this is the same word as we find in the verse, 'I set God before me *always*' (Ps. 16:8), and adds that the four Hebrew letters of *vehayah*, 'it shall be', are the same as those that form the divine name. The high priest should not just think about God as if this were one notion among many. Awareness of God must permeate his consciousness; he must try to recognise the sacred in every person and all life.

Significant as the symbolism of these garments may be, nothing is as important as the love that goes into their preparation. The wool, linen, gold and precious stones from which they are made are all gifts from the community. 'The depth and integrity of a priest's service depend on the love of his people within him,' observed Rabbi Levi Yizhak of Berditchev, known for his compassion towards everyone.[79] Putting on clothes made entirely from offerings of love should inspire a reciprocal generosity within the wearer. In the end, what most entitles leaders to represent their people is love; without it, spiritual leadership will never reach the heart.

The garments, the Temple itself and the rituals performed there by the priesthood are no more. But the role of caring for our communities, materially and spiritually, is as important as ever and now devolves upon us all. The precious stones are long gone, but not the care and concern they symbolise, which rests today upon all our shoulders. Whatever clothing we wear, or are forced to wear, even the yellow hat in the Middle Ages and the yellow star, nothing can strip us of these responsibilities, which define us as truly human.

KI TISSA (30:11–34:35)

Shabbat

It was late one Saturday night, after the end of a long midsummer Sabbath. We were in the New Forest, by a small body of water where we could see the reflection of the trees in the moonlight. There were twenty or so of us, four leaders and about eighteen young people in their early teens.

'What do you like about *Shabbat*? I asked them. That was thirty years ago, but I can still hear their answers.

'It's the one day my parents are never out.'

'None of us is allowed to answer the phone.'

'We always eat together; we get time to talk.'

'My grandparents always come; I love it.'

'We have my favourite food.'

Moses is instructed to tell the Children of Israel *la'asot et HaShabbat*, to *make* the *Shabbat* (Exod. 31:16). More than a hundred generations later this injunction still applies. The same words are still used, not only in the formal prayers and the *Kiddush*, the sanctification of the day over wine, but colloquially, when people say, 'I'm making Shabbes now.' Technically, this refers to the action that brings the day in, if sundown has not already automatically done so: most probably the lighting of the candles. But far more is involved: the shopping, cooking, baking of *challah*, inviting of guests and planning of dishes, and the challenges of having everything ready in time. Kindling the *Shabbat* candles indicates the moment of switch-off, when work is done, money put aside, screens shut down and the weekday rush is over. It marks that peace which, not always but sometimes, if there are no arguments or upsets, descends as the flame takes hold of the wick and the *Shabbat* candles burn.

The Jewish way is to measure out one's life not in coffee-spoons but Sabbaths. As the Talmud points out, the days of the week are named not according to qualities, let alone deities, of their own, but as lead-ins towards *Shabbat*: day one, day two, day three. If he came across a particularly delicious item of food, the first-century BCE sage Shammai would exclaim, 'It's for *Shabbat*;' whereas his colleague and contemporary Hillel had a different attitude: 'Blessed be God, day by day,' he would say, trusting that something even more special would be found for the holiest meals of the week (Talmud Betzah 16a).

Achad Ha'am famously observed that 'more than Israel has kept the Sabbath, the Sabbath has kept Israel'.[80] The 'success' of *Shabbat* is based not only on the Torah's repeated emphasis of its importance, but even more on how the rabbis turned it from a broad instruction into practical rules. Critical to their approach is the context of the commandment: 'Only, you shall keep my Sabbaths, for it is a sign between me and you for all generations, so that you shall know that I am God who sanctifies you' (Exod. 31:13).

This verse immediately follows the lengthy instructions about the Tabernacle and is introduced by the particle *ach*, 'but' or 'only'. Rarely can such a diminutive word have had so great an impact. Rashi explains:

Even though you must pursue the work [of building the sanctuary] energetically, do not allow it to override Shabbat. *Ach* and *rak* indicate exclusions; [here *ach*] excludes Shabbat from the tasks involved in making the tabernacle.[81]

Based on this juxtaposition, the rabbis of the Mishnah developed the detailed laws that govern the observance of the Sabbath to this day. The Ten Commandments simply said that it was forbidden to work on *Shabbat*, without specifying what kinds of work were included. There was clearly a need for closer definition. The teachers of the Mishnaic period therefore enumerated the different tasks involved in building the sanctuary, establishing thirty-nine *avot*, or major categories; some were connected with the preparation of fabrics, some with growing and cooking food, some with animal husbandry and the preparation of skins, while others involved construction itself. Each of these *avot* had *toladot*, or subcategories, which subsequent codes of law expanded through the centuries, especially as new forms of production, transport and communication were developed. Work itself they defined as *melechet machashevet*, intentional, purposeful work. But they also added the category of *shevut*, rest, that is to say activities that infringed on the obligation to rest, including what should be considered *oovdin dechol*, actions characteristic of weekday tasks, which, were they to be done on *Shabbat*, would risk making it feel like any other ordinary day.

The Talmud acknowledges that this complex agglomeration of rules is like 'a mountain hanging by a hair'. But the connection is less tenuous than it may seem. There is a deep reciprocity between the labour from which we are required to refrain on *Shabbat* and the work from which 'God rested on the seventh day' (Gen. 2:3). If the purpose of the days of creation was to fashion a world fit for human life and habitation, the objective of our weekdays is to make that world a fitting abode for God. This is expressed symbolically through the building of the *mishkan*, a metaphor for the wider struggle to establish societies based on justice, compassion and respect for all. As 'partners with God in creation', since God rested in order to appreciate and bless the work, so must we (Talmud, Shabbat 10a).

There is always the danger that the spirit of *Shabbat* gets lost amid the multitude of its rules. It's not hard to see why its many laws can make the day seem oppressive: there's much one's not allowed to do. But the aim is anything but negative: to ensure the safeguarding of sacred time. Hours set aside for calm and quiet are easily eaten away; there's always one more thing that needs doing. The rules around *Shabbat* are like lines put firmly around a date in the diary, blocking out the day. What's special must be protected, otherwise it ends up eroded by the pressures of the everyday. Nothing should intrude into this sacred time, except the saving of life; as the rabbis said: 'Break one *Shabbat*, so that you can live to celebrate many more' (Talmud, Yoma 85b).

The commandment to keep *Shabbat* is followed immediately by the story of the golden calf, the archetypal image of idolatry. In both narratives the word 'make' is key. In our world of doing and building, there is always the danger that we end up worshipping the results of our own ingenuity. The Torah warns sternly against proudly imagining that 'my strength and the power of my hands made me all this great wealth' (Deut. 8:17). In the five verses about *Shabbat* in Exodus 31:13–17, the word 'make' comes five times, four of them in the negative. We must not idolise the objects we produce or our capacity to manufacture them. Making should ultimately be an act of service. The Sabbath, wrote Abraham Joshua Heschel, is 'a day on which we stop worshipping the idols of technical civilisation':

In the tempestuous ocean of time and toil there are islands of stillness where man may enter a harbor and reclaim his dignity. This island is the seventh day, the Sabbath, a day of detachment from things, instruments and practical affairs as well as of attachment to the spirit.[82]

For one day in seven we are called upon to stop doing and instead appreciate creation. We set aside time to renew our awareness that there inheres in life a holiness that we must honour.

The last word in the commandment to keep *Shabbat* is *vayinafash*; it refers to God, who 'rested on the seventh day and was restored' (Exod. 31:17). *Nefesh* means 'life' or 'spirit'; Rashi explains that 'one restores one's soul and gets one's breath back by calming down from the pressures of work'.[83] He adds, with an implied exclamation mark, that 'God, who, Scripture says, "never tires and never wearies" prescribes such rest for himself to amaze the ears'.[84] If even God needs a day of restoration, how much more do we! Or perhaps God's rest is the same as ours; when we take time to appreciate God's world, God can rest too.

Religion and idolatry

The gods we worship write their names on our faces; be sure of that. A person will worship something . . . That which dominates our imaginations and our thoughts will determine our lives, and our character . . . Therefore it behooves us to be careful what we worship, for what we are worshipping we are becoming.

Ralph Waldo Emerson[85]

The polemic against idolatry runs through the Hebrew Bible from beginning to end. False gods, child sacrifice and pagan rites are constantly excoriated. But it is not just other nations who practise idol worship; its seductive power is the source of constant temptation to the Children of Israel. The kings of Israel and Judah are evaluated largely according to whether they did or did not remove these 'abominations', the local altars and shrines, the destruction of which God is consistently understood to demand.

It is the Children of Israel who commit the most notorious act of idolatry of all. The story of the golden calf is set in the middle of the account of building the Tabernacle. This is especially striking since the narrative need not have been ordered in this manner. Moses relayed the instructions about the Tent of Meeting only after he came down from Sinai; it was while he was away with God in the cloud-covered mountain that the people danced drunkenly round their idol. The narrative of the calf should really have preceded the description of the Tabernacle, but instead it is placed in its very centre. The difference between making a home for God and fabricating the god itself may be more subtle than we would like to think, the former readily degenerating into the latter.

The most dangerous objects of idolatry are not made of metal or stone. They are the images and goals we worship and pursue, though we would never admit to making them our gods. Status and money are obvious modern idols. Like King Midas in the legend, who loved gold so much that he turned everything he touched into it, including his own daughter, idolatry lures us into translating all things into its currency. In the process we, too, become transformed, remade in the image of the false gods we serve.

Maimonides understood idolatry as a process of decline. Instead of worshipping the God of all creation, humans began to adulate the parts of creation itself – sun, moon and mountains – until they become the ultimate objects of worship and the God who made them was forgotten.[86] The portion of creation we are in danger of idolising in this manner today are our own selves, whom we regard as set apart and elevated above the sanctity of all other God-given life.

Taking selfies is a harmless, iconic act of our age. Yet it symbolises how we have embraced a way of life in which it is overwhelmingly our self-image and our own interests that we serve. In practice, we often mistake the first commandment as if it reads not 'I am the Lord your God', but 'I', that is, 'Me and what I need and want' am lord and master of the world. Individually, as societies, but most dangerously as a species, we risk allowing our entire civilisation to become a cult of idolatry of self, into which we have so long, so subtly and so persistently been seduced that we struggle even to recognise that this is the case.

It's therefore tempting, in the manner of Hasidic creative misreading, to translate the opening words of the second commandment, *lo ta'aseh* lekha *fessel*, not as, 'Don't make an idol for yourself,' but as, 'Don't make your *self* into an idol.' This would be grammatically inaccurate, since the object 'you' is indirect, in the dative not the accusative. But it would be in keeping with the meaning of the words that we must not turn any object into the focus of our worship, and few things matter more to us than self-image.

More dangerous than the veneration of our individual selves is our collective worship of 'humankind', the assertion of our dominance over every other species, with the consequent desacralisation of nature and its subjugation to our uses. The ultimate price of this anthropocentric and self-serving attitude may be self-destruction, in which we drag down the rest of creation with us.

A particularly challenging aspect of the story of the golden calf concerns the nature of religion, for religion itself is liable to become a form of idolatry. We are unlikely to be tempted to bow down to wood and stone; the deeper danger is that we deify the details of our faith instead of God whom they direct us to worship. Then, instead of being guides and means to service, our holy texts and sacred rites themselves become its object. Symptomatic of this may be anger towards those who critique our holy books and traditions or interpret them in significantly different ways from us, as well as the oppression of people of other faiths who arrive at the worship of the same God by following different paths. Religion can be dangerous; pulpits can readily be misused to incite hatred and arm zealots, and they often are.

Paul Tillich, the twentieth-century Christian philosopher, makes a crucial distinction between 'myth' and 'broken myth'. By 'myth' he understands a core narrative through which we derive our deepest sense of meaning and purpose. A myth becomes 'broken' when we have significant evidence that it is not true in the literal, empirical sense. It can nevertheless remain the guiding 'myth', the central narrative of our faith, only now it is broken. It retains its symbolic 'truth' at the core of our religion, for, as

Tillich acknowledges, 'there is no substitute for the use of symbols and myths; they are the language of faith'.[87] But now it is, and should be, open to historical and sociological contextualisation and analysis. This can be experienced by traditional bodies as undermining their interpretive monopoly and power, leading them to suppress critical thought:

> The tool of repression is usually an acknowledged authority with sacred qualities like the Church or the Bible, to which one owes unconditional surrender ... The enemy of a critical theology is not natural literalism but conscious literalism with repression of and aggression toward autonomous thought.[88]

This is where religion risks becoming idolatry, when the authority of the institution displaces God as the ultimate concern.

Yet the issue of idolatry goes deeper still, to the roots of faith itself. Faith involves both the longing to know God and the understanding that we can never know. Such not knowing calls for deep trust. Mordechai Yosef Lainer (1801–54) explains that Hebrew has two words for 'I': *ani* and *anochi*. The Torah could have used the former in the opening verse of the Ten Commandments, to read: 'I, *ani*, am the Lord your God.' Instead, it employs the latter, *anochi*. The difference between the two pronouns is the letter *caph* (the *ch*) which, when prefixed to a word, indicates simile or comparison:

> *Caph* indicates that what was revealed was not perfect, only a similitude and likeness to the light which the Holy Blessed One will reveal in the future. The more depth people attain in the study of Torah, the more they realise that until now they have been in darkness. Day and night hint at this: day, because God opens the gates of wisdom to humankind; night, so that no-one should think they've understood everything perfectly, because everything so far comprehended is like night compared to the day which will follow, and so on forever.[89]

Frightened by Moses' long absence, the Children of Israel want a physical, tangible god which they can see. In their confusion, they turn the gold intended to adorn a home for God into their god itself. Similar anxieties may lie at the root of modern idolatry too: the fear of not knowing and the consequent need to place ourselves at the centre, defining and controlling. But God, and the soul's journey toward God, are unknowable and endless.

VAYAKHEL (35:1-38:20)

....

Who gives?

Building projects can either create division or bring people together. *Vayakhel* means 'he gathered together the community'; that is, Moses united everyone around the task. Key to how he achieved this was his attitude to gifts, as the Torah and its commentators make clear in early chapters about the sanctuary.

Before the word 'Tabernacle' is even mentioned, the Children of Israel are asked to donate to its construction. The sanctuary will be built out of giving. Yet God's instructions to Moses are to tell the Children not to *give*, but to '*take* my offering from everyone whose heart prompts them' (Exod. 25:2). Only later does the Torah substitute *give* for *take*: 'This is what they shall *give*, everyone who is counted' (Exod. 30:13). Is the people's contribution, then, a giving or a taking, or is giving sometimes taking and taking sometimes a deeper form of giving?

At university I joined a student helpline. During our training, we played a game in which we had to sit in a circle in silence with coins in our hands, nothing we weren't prepared to part with. In the first round, conducted in silence, we were asked to get up in turn and give one or more coins to whoever we chose. Afterwards we spoke about how we felt. People commented that it was nice to receive gifts; none of us seemed hurt that we were sometimes missed out and, fortunately, no one was given nothing at all. In the second part of the exercise we were asked to go round again, only now we could take from whoever we wanted. This time our reactions were different. We found it deeply upsetting to be passed over; it hurt to seem considered as having nothing to give. It made us feel as if we had no value.

The rabbis understood the creation of the Tabernacle to involve both giving and taking. Three separate contributions were required: a coin from each person to cast the bronze sockets on which the structure was to stand, a further coin from every person towards the funds for the communal sacrifices, and a voluntary donation towards the building of the Tabernacle itself. No one was to be deprived of the opportunity to participate; no gift was to be rejected. The only qualification for making an offering to the Tabernacle was that it should be brought by those 'whose heart prompts them' (Exod. 35:21). Hasidic commentators saw this as an opportunity to explore the meaning of giving. Taking typical liberties with the grammar, Rebbe Avraham of Slonim (1803–83) read the words *asher yidvenu libbo*, literally 'whose heart prompts them to give', as 'who is prompted to give their heart'. An offering that includes the heart is very different from something given casually, even if it's less valuable in strictly monetary terms. To Rebbe Avraham, a project only becomes holy when people put their heart and soul into it. It's the giving of ourselves that makes us most truly human: 'Who is truly a "person"? One who is prepared to give not just their possessions but their heart to God.'[90]

Rebbe Avraham of Sokatchev (1838–1910) notes that love from the heart is the most important aspect of the gift:

> The offering for the sanctuary was voluntary, not forcibly demanded or extracted, because what's needed for God's presence to dwell anywhere is the love of God, and the test of this is generosity.[91]

Rebbe Shalom of Belz (1781–1855) focuses on the fact that the most expensive donations, the precious stones brought by the heads of the tribes, are mentioned last: the contributions of ordinary members of the community take precedence (Exod. 35:27). He himself was famous not only for his generosity but also for participating alongside his congregation and carrying buckets of cement when a new synagogue was built in his town.

But what if a gift is brought for the wrong reasons? Rebbe Chaim Tsvi of Sighet (1884–1926) answers this critique by interpreting a comment from Rashi. The Torah's instruction is to 'take an offering *for me*' (Exod. 25:1). Puzzled by these words, since the gifts are intended for the sanctuary, Rashi understands them as relating to the giver's motives: '*For me* [means] for *My*, that is for God's name.'[92] The offerings have to be accompanied by the appropriate intentions. Rebbe Chaim Tsvi turns this explanation on its head:

> If the objective is indeed 'for my name's sake', then you should take my offering from everyone (and not just from those 'whose heart prompts them'), since 'out of acting from impure motives, a person learns to act from pure motives'.[93]

Rebbe Chaim Tsvi quotes the axiomatic rabbinic attitude to motivation: don't exclude those who appear to be acting out of ego and vainglory but trust the activity itself to transform the motives of those who engage in it.

The process of building the sanctuary will purify those who contribute to it. This view had already been expressed by his grandfather, Rebbe Yekutiel Yehudah of Sighet (1808–83):

> There are those whose hearts arouse them to give to the tabernacle. But there also exists a different category of persons: those whose offering, which at the time did not include the heart, subsequently arouses in them a new understanding of what they have done. Their gifts, too, must therefore be considered as 'what their spirit has prompted in them'.[94]

This accords with the Torah's instruction to 'take from *every* person whose heart prompts them'. It's cruel to treat someone's offering as unwanted, not because the gift doesn't meet the criteria of what's needed, but because the giver is unwelcome. I vividly remember how, during that game at university forty years ago, I felt that if no one were to take any of my coins, it would mean that I was worthless and that not just my money but also I myself was deserving of rejection. In instructing Moses to 'take from every person', God is insisting that no one should be made to feel superfluous to requirements. If, by extension, all the earth is God's temple, no contribution to making this world a sacred place should be rejected, no matter from whom or where it comes.

PEKUDEI (38:21–40:38)

Good and evil buildings

The book of Exodus begins with the building of store cities for Pharaoh and ends with the creation of a dwelling place for the presence of God. These two processes of construction epitomise the journey on which the book takes us, from slavery to freedom, from subjugation to tyranny, toward the service of God.

Important buildings always invite the question: on what and by whom are they built? Pithom and Rameses are the products of slave labour, from the casting of each and every brick upwards. Pharaoh's response to Moses' and Aaron's demand for freedom is telling: no longer will even the most basic materials be provided. Henceforth the Hebrew slaves must collect stubble for themselves while the daily tally of bricks will not be reduced.

They complain to their officers, fellow Hebrews, who are beaten by the Egyptian overseers because their squads fall short of their quotas. Perhaps the fate of these men in the middle is the worst of all, set, almost certainly through no choice of their own, against their own people. This is only one of many separations. The rabbis understood 'God saw our affliction' (Deut. 26:7) to refer to 'separation from the way of all the earth' (Talmud Yoma 74b), the tearing asunder of families, the enforced parting of husbands and wives. No doubt they knew what they were talking about since this has been the strategy of persecutors throughout history, down to the treatment of the Uyghurs in China in our twenty-first century.

The enslavement of the Hebrews brings divisions within Egyptian society as well. The Torah records that 'they were disgusted – vayakutzu – because of the Children of Israel' (Exod. 1:12). Rashi offers two possible interpretations: 'They hated their own lives. [Alternatively] our rabbis explain: the Children of Israel were like thorns – kotsim – in their eyes.'[95]

Why would Egyptian people hate their own existence? Maybe the Israelites were repugnant to them in their degraded state. Or perhaps they felt disgusted with themselves and their own society: they saw the injustice of the slave structure and they, too, felt oppressed and powerless before the tyrannical authority of their own leader. They knew intuitively that such patent wrongdoing, in which they were ineluctably implicated, would inevitably bring terrible consequences from which they were also bound in the long run to suffer.

The construction of the cities, intended for the holding of grain, heralds disaster. The plagues ruin Egypt; the whole project proves to be a social, economic, political and environmental catastrophe. Founded on tyranny, built through cruelty and injustice, the storehouses end up surrounded by wasteland, monuments to the futility of power, as in Shelley's 'Ozymandias':

Round the decay
Of that colossal Wreck, boundless and bare
The lone and level sands stretch far away.[96]

Pharaoh's Egypt is a warning to civilisations ever after. One wonders today what bones of slave labour lie buried beneath the foundations of stately buildings and under the tracks of miles of railways, silenced and forgotten by history's 'victors'.

In contrast, the mishkan, a dwelling place for God, is constructed with voluntary participation and from materials willingly donated. Moses appeals to all who are generous of heart to bring gifts, and to everyone 'whose heart prompts them to draw near to the work and do it' (Exod. 36:2). There is no compulsion. Unlike the constant shortage of bricks for the store cities, the people bring more wood, cloths and precious metals than are required, to the point where they have to be asked to stop.

Unlike the pyramids, the building of the Tabernacle brings the people together. The task creates a sense of collective purpose around which they can be united, as the Torah emphasises: 'Moses drew together the entire community of the Children of Israel and said to them: "These are the things God has commanded for you to make them"' (Exod. 35:1).

The Hasidic teacher Shlomo Yehudah Leib of Lantshna (1778–1843) understands 'make them' to refer not to the Tabernacle and its furnishings, but to the people themselves: the real objective is to create not so much a physical structure as a shared society.[97]

The Tabernacle is therefore a 'tent of meeting' even before it has been completed. There is a profound causal connection underlying the apparent disjunction in the Torah's instruction to 'make me a sacred space, and I will dwell in them' (Exod. 25:8). It would have been more logical for the second half of the verse to read, 'I will dwell in it.' The point is that what creates the true holiness in which God can be present is dedication to a shared creative purpose, symbolising the redemptive goal of bringing all humanity together to establish a world of justice, dignity and harmony fit for God's habitation.

Unlike slave labour, the instructions for building the Tabernacle are carried out enthusiastically. Noting the repetition in the verse describing the completion of the work: 'The Children of Israel *did* according to all God commanded Moses, *so they did*' (Exod. 39:32), Rebbe Yehoshua Heschel of Choliov comments:

> At first they 'did' because they were commanded by Moses, the master teacher of Israel. But afterwards they rose to the highest of levels and 'did the work' as if they themselves were personally commanded from the mouth of God.[98]

He imagines the Tabernacle being built with the same inner concentration as a work of art to which its creator has devoted heart and soul, every word, note or brushstroke the transmission of sacred inspiration. The result is in harmony with the world, as the Torah's careful phraseology implies. Just as 'the heavens and the earth were completed', so the tabernacle 'is completed' (Gen. 2:1; Exod. 39:32). Just as God 'saw all God had made, and behold it was very good', so Moses 'saw all the work and behold they had done it just as God commanded' (Gen. 1:31; Exod. 39:43). Just as God 'blessed the seventh day and made it holy,' so Moses 'blessed [the people]' (Gen. 2:3; Exod. 39:43).

The Tent of Meeting represents the human equivalent of God's creativity. In the final chapter of Exodus, the human and the divine come together. The Torah first states that the Tabernacle was 'set up', as if it constructed itself, then tells us in the very next verse that it was assembled by Moses (Exod. 40:1, 2). Rashi explains that Moses was given the privilege of carrying out this final task, but the boards and curtains were too heavy for any single person to manage. God therefore came to his assistance. Perhaps this is how artists feel when, exhausted and overwhelmed on completion of a piece of work, they look at it and think, 'Something other than I alone made this.'

Across the world there are cities founded on slavery and cruelty. There are also many kinds of dwelling place for God, created by people of all faiths. But, unlike the Tabernacle, the work is not yet finished and will not be complete until the whole earth is governed with justice. Only then will 'the earth be full of the knowledge of God', just as 'the cloud of God's presence hovered over the tent of meeting' at the close of Exodus (Isa. 11:9; Exod. 40:38).

THE BOOK OF LEVITICUS

וַיִּקְרָא

VAYIKRA AND TSAV (1:1-8:36)

The fire on the altar

Among Roman Vishniac's many remarkable photographs of what was soon to become a vanished world, destroyed by the Nazis, is a picture taken in 1936 of elderly Jews studying the mediaeval mystical texts of Kabbalah in a basement in Kazimierz, the once vibrant Jewish quarter of Krakow. On the table between them is a single burning candle, yet what illumines the darkness is the light reflected from the pages of the holy books and the glow on the faces of the old men pondering the sacred words. Read not, 'All night until morning the fire of the offerings shall burn *on it*,' i.e., the altar, observed Rebbe Moshe Yechiel of Ozharov (1889–1971). Read rather: 'the fire shall burn *in him*, the lover of Torah, who devotes himself to God. For when one is occupied with Torah one's whole being becomes like a burning flame and one's spirit like an altar, aglow from within'.[1]

Through centuries of exile and decades of darkness, through years of persecution and poverty, the fire on the altar, which, along with all the other furnishing of the Temple, existed in the external world no more, became the flame of Torah in the soul. Like the blaze that consumed the sacrifices in the Temple, it was to be 'a constant fire', never allowed to go out, neither by day nor by night (Lev. 6:13). It was nourished not by the limbs and fats of animal offerings, but by the devotion of mind and heart. The source of the flame was Torah; through dedication to its study and practice, the soul too would be set alight. 'This is the Torah of the *olah*,' taught Rebbe Menachem Nachum of Chernobyl (1730–97), reading *olah* not as 'burnt-offering' but, from the root *oleh*, as 'one who ascends', one who seeks to transcend spiritually the ceaseless challenges and frustrations of the daily struggle for existence:

> The Torah has the power to raise one up so that one can illumine the darkness until the obscurity of the night becomes the morning light of dawn.[2]

The Kabbalists called this inner illumination the *or haganuz*, the hidden light, the original light with which God created the world but then concealed from sinning humankind. Where did God hide it? they asked, before answering: In the world to come, in the Torah and all created things. Covered, but not smothered, within material reality, it awaits the seeker who learns to see the deeper life which abides within all being. For in truth, this secret light shines 'from one end of the world to the other' (Midrash Bereshit Rabbah 11:2). It is the hidden source of the vitality of everything, a radiance both one and indivisible, yet clothed in all the forms of earth's diversity. When the seeker encounters it through the study of Torah, a corresponding flame, long smouldering in the soul, often hidden even from the self, rises up, illumining the consciousness with that same light which is present, though latent, in us all.

We can discover this inner flame not only in spiritual texts but also through sustained love of the natural world, in attentive listening to people's heartfelt concerns and, beneath the noise of our plans and frustrations, within ourselves. Its light is modest; it leads us towards deeper awareness, humility, awe and compassion. It is against its nature to flame forth and seek to be seen:

> The fire on the altar should reside within the depths of the heart, in such a way that others don't perceive it.[3]

Often, though, the challenge is to feel it in ourselves. We may never have believed, or have lost all confidence, that it's there:

> I said, surely the darkness shall envelop me,
> And the light about me shall be night.
> Even the darkness is not too dark for You,
> But the night shines as the day,
> The darkness is as the light.
>
> (Ps. 139:11–12)

It's not clear whether the psalmist wants to hide away but the light insists on pursuing him even into the most intimate lair of consciousness, or whether the arrival of the light brings the comfort of inner illumination. Perhaps both experiences are simultaneously true, for the light is there, waiting for us notice it in the recesses of our own self.

The poet and novelist Ben Okri was asked at a meeting in my synagogue how he felt oppressed peoples reacted to inherited trauma. Either with anger or with spirituality, he answered. All but powerless to affect the outer realities in which they lived, Jews turned to the inner world, seeking the light within, not only as solace but as the source of profound creativity.

Quoting the line from her diary, 'Like a songbird in its cage', Nick Naydler wrote in honour of Anne Frank:

Here do I take pen
In this my cave of light,
this cage of heaven and hell,
in here unreel my life. I know
what is inside this jail;
this chapel my song is dawnlight;
I must sing.[4]

Combining the imagery of music and vision, his poem is a tribute to the inalienable creativity of the human spirit, God's light within us all. Often unheeded, unattended by our consciousness, in moments of contemplation, wonder or exaltation, it shines forth within us, illuminating the mind, uniting it with that infinitely greater light which travels from one end of the world to the other.

Sometimes this flame teases us like a distant, elusive signal from the depth of the forest. Sometimes we lose sight of it and despair of its existence. Then we have to begin the search for it all over again. But sometimes it burns steadily, like the glow from a woodfire on the altar of the spirit.

To the Jewish mystics, this fire represents the true Torah of the soul, reading not *Torat ha'olah*, 'the law of the burnt offering' (Lev. 1:2), but *Torat ha'oleh,* 'the Torah of the one who seeks to ascend'. As for the actual altar in the Temple, that's history. The true fire is the inextinguishable flame that burns in the human spirit.

Korban – sacrifice

The Torah devotes much of the first half of its central book to the sacrificial system. Most of us find this difficult. How can God want so many dead animals? What kind of God takes pleasure in fats and kidneys? We sympathise instinctively with the outrage of the prophets:

What do I need all your sacrifices for? I've had enough of burnt offerings, rams and sheep-fat; I don't want cow-blood, lambs and rams.

(Isa. 1:11)

We tend to forget that they are just as scornful of the perfunctory performance of prayer if our words make no impact on our conscience or conduct. But the question remains: what are we to make today of these chapters about burnt- and guilt-offerings, flours, breads and libations, when the Temple no longer stands, when the altar and its cult seem irrelevant, when the theology the sacrifices imply seems incomprehensible and even repellent and when the treatment of the animals involved feels cruel?

I don't pray for the restoration of sacrifices. A committed vegetarian, I cannot imagine wanting to slaughter a cow to honour God. I agree with the early twentieth-century Rabbi Abraham Isaac HaCohen Kook that should the Temple ever be rebuilt, it will only be as 'a house of prayer for all peoples' (Isa. 56:7), and that any offerings must be blood-free gifts of thanksgiving from the produce of the earth.

Yet it is as unwarranted to deride the biblical sacrificial system on account of modern sensibilities as it is to regard those sensibilities in turn as irrelevant to the understanding of God's will today. We cannot imagine ourselves back into the customs and ways of life of peoples two thousand years ago and should therefore be cautious of passing judgement over them. The Hebrew word translated as sacrifice is korban, from the root karov meaning 'near': the Bible sees sacrifice as a rite that brings us near to God. It is far from unthinkable that a peasant farmer, taking an animal he had personally reared to the Temple, would experience a deep sense of connection when he put his hands on its head and confessed his sins before delivering it over to the priests and the altar. Families may well have brought their festival offerings to Jerusalem with pride and feasted on their allotted portions with joy and gratitude. The meat of most of the animals sacrificed, all of which had to be kosher species, was eaten either by those who brought them or by the priests. Though animal lovers like myself may find it hard to stomach the details in the Bible's accounts, whatever happened at the Temple was as nothing compared to the immense suffering of billions of factory-farmed cows and sheep today, which scarcely see the daylight or a field, are hardly able to turn round in their pens and which, when fattened up sufficiently, are transported great distances, often without food and water, to be slaughtered in abattoirs built far from the gaze of those who cheerfully devour their meat. Unlike in biblical times, most of the population in wealthy countries is divorced from any relationship with the animals it consumes other than through buying them, chopped up and wrapped in plastic, in supermarkets.

But perhaps the most challenging aspect of the sacrifices is not what happens to the animals but the idea that they matter to God, that God enjoys their 'pleasing savour' (Lev. 1:9 and many other places). Here too the Torah has to be understood in its cultural and theological contexts. The numerous references in the Hebrew Bible to idolatrous practices, including the sacrifice of children, make it clear that such rituals were taken for granted as ways in which human beings courted the favour of the gods. This fact enables the outstanding twelfth-century philosopher and halakhist Maimonides to argue that the sacrifice of animals was not God's 'first intention'.[5] Rather, the Torah recognised the 'nature of man, which always likes that to which it is accustomed'.[6] The rules governing the sacrifices, the insistence that they can be offered only at recognised locations, that the blood be poured on the altar solely by the priests, and above all that there must be no human victims, form a tight series of regulatory measures. Under these conditions and with these stipulations:

> God suffered the above-mentioned kinds of worship to remain, but transferred them from created or imaginary and unreal things [i.e., idols] to His own name.[7]

But, says Maimonides, all this is a thing of the past; what God really wants is our devotion in prayer. Intriguingly, he adds that the notion of serving God without sacrifices would have been as unthinkable a millennium earlier as doing away with words and praying only in silent meditation would be to his own contemporaries.

Although Maimonides takes the cultural context into account and understands Judaism, including some of the commandments of the Torah itself, as educational measures in a developmental process, he unsurprisingly attributes this to divine intentionality rather than to the changing nature of human society. For Maimonides, the shift to the service of God through prayer was God's plan all along. A less pious historical account would see the change as prompted by this-worldly events, first and foremost the destruction of the second Temple in 70 CE followed by the dispersal of Jews around the Mediterranean and beyond. What began as a painful concession to necessity, with the Temple in ruins and the scattered nation in mourning, grew into one of the most profound processes of change in the history of Judaism. The view has long been discredited that prayer simply and suddenly replaced sacrifice; it had developed for centuries in parallel with the Temple cult. But during the post-destruction period, *avodah*, 'worship', transitioned almost entirely into *avodah shebalev*, 'worship in the heart', in an increasingly organised manner which was to become so irreversibly accepted that it became possible to argue that this had been the divine intention in the first place.

Yet the sacrificial system did not simply disappear; it left a profound imprint on the entire pattern of Jewish worship. The Talmud makes it clear that the three daily prayers correspond in their timing to the morning and afternoon sacrifices and the night-time rituals in the Temple (Berachot 26b). There are also deeper, more intrinsic connections, as Arthur Green suggests:

> Prayer comes in place of sacrifice. In true prayer, we give the only gift we have to offer: ourselves. *Va'ani tefillati*, says the Psalmist (69:14), felicitously mistranslated by later Hasidic readers as 'I *am* my prayer.'[8]

Instead of bringing animals to the altar, we give ourselves, writes Green, 'by opening our hearts, by being present to God's presence in our lives, by sharing with others, by generosity towards the needy, among whom God's presence rests'.[9]

Perhaps it is this focus on the heart that makes an undated mediaeval poem so mysteriously beautiful, with its chorus listing all the different kinds of Temple sacrifice:

> God, You are my God and my Redeemer; I place myself before You,
> God who was and shall be, God who was and is, truly Yours is all the
> earth.
> The Lord of hosts, with how many wonders He holds together his
> tent!
> In the paths of the heart He plants the heart's growth, the Rock
> whose work is perfect!
> And our thanksgiving, burnt- and meal-offerings, our sacrifices for
> sin and guilt, for peace and purification: we give them all so that
> you will draw us close.[10]

Adam asher yakriv – when a person offers

To the Hasidic rabbis of the late eighteenth and nineteenth centuries onwards, there was nothing revolutionary about reinterpreting the laws of the Temple sacrifices to refer to the inner dynamic of the giving of the self. That is how they understood the Torah anyway. Let history be; whatever happened took place long ago. The eternal message of the Torah concerns the relationship between the soul and God. In this light they 'reread' the Torah from beginning to end, frequently ignoring syntax and semantics in order to find in the hidden depths of the text hints of the secrets of God.

The second verse of Leviticus opens a series of general rules governing the types of animals that may be sacrificed. A pedantically literal translation would be:

> Speak to the Children of Israel and say to them: a man, when he brings near from you a sacrifice to God – from the domestic animals, from the cattle or the flock, shall you bring your sacrifices.
>
> (Lev. 1:2)

A number of creative Hasidic rereadings transform this basic instruction into an exploration of the essence of sacrifice. The early masters Dov Baer of Mezeritch (d. 1772) and Shneur Zalman of Liadi (1745–1812) focus on the words 'bring near' and 'from you'. They take it as given that the object to be sacrificed is not an extraneous being, a cow or sheep, but our innermost self. This understanding is rooted in the meaning of *korban* as an act of 'bringing near', of devoting one's heart and soul to God. Dov Baer, the great organiser in the early days of Hasidism, emphasises how it is only if one first dedicates oneself that one can become a guide for others:

> Before you can draw others to the service of God and '*bring near*', you must first bring yourself close and offer '*from you*', that is, *yourselves*. Only then can you succeed in drawing others near to God.[11]

True leadership lies not in eloquence or charisma but in the integrity with which one works on oneself. Such dedication may not make the headlines but communicates itself quietly but surely to those who follow.

Shneur Zalman of Liadi, known affectionately as the Alter Rebbe, the founder of Lubavitch Hasidism spells out what true devotion involves:

> The way to bring oneself close to God is to be prepared to offer one's entire self, with all one's feelings and all one's strength, as it says, *from you*, from your whole self, must come the *sacrifice*, the drawing near, *to God*.[12]

While the ritual at the altar may have had a cathartic effect, as if a weight was lifted from the heart, now it is the heart itself that must direct its thoughts and intentions to God in a lifelong journey of dedication. The Alter Rebbe's comment reminds me of how my grandfather understood the words in the *Shema* meditation, *bechol me'odecha*, literally 'with all your very-ness'. 'With all your effort,' he explained, 'requires using whatever talents you have and every opportunity life brings to serve God.' When I was a primary school teacher, I saw colleagues who year upon year would think each day of small things they could do, like bringing a favourite book from home, or giving regular individual attention, so that each of their pupils would feel personally cared for. Though they sometimes did this with a sigh, what motivated them was love. That is heartfelt commitment in practice.

Moshe Elyakim Beri'ah of Kozhnitz (1757–1828) considers how it can be possible for a mere human being to feel near to the infinite God:

> Despite being formed of clay, we are capable of coming close to God. This is because God comes to our help, as the Torah says, 'our sacrifice', that is, 'our coming near', is 'to', that is 'belongs to' God.[13]

Perhaps the most remarkable of all Hasidic insights comes from Rebbe Kalonymus Kalman Shapira (1889–1943), known subsequently as the Rebbe of the Warsaw Ghetto. Taking as a starting point the great mediaeval commentator Rashi's note on the opening word of Leviticus, 'And God called,' he observes:

> Rashi explains that '*calling*' is an expression of love. This is emphasised here, at the beginning of the book about sacrifices, to teach that even when you '*bring near as a sacrifice your own self*' because heaven has sent you sufferings, this is nevertheless an expression of God's love, for 'whom God loves, God chastises'.[14]

These words were written in the Warsaw Ghetto while his fellow Jews, his comrades in Torah, were being murdered every day. At first sight, it seems incomprehensible, even blasphemous, that he should dignify such abhorrent cruelties with any kind of theological meaning. What can such torments have to do with God's love? But, as a fellow victim whose own life was in daily danger, his purpose was not to justify the ways of God but to impart courage to those suffering alongside him by suggesting that even in this hell they could choose to understand what had been forced upon them by their enemies within the context of their own relationship with God. His aim was to enable his comrades to find renewed strength with which to endure their fate. In a sermon given in the Ghetto on 17 January 1941 he spoke about the *magrefah*, described in the Talmud as a ten-stringed musical instrument capable of producing a thousand different notes of such resonance and beauty that they could be heard as far away as Jericho. But in the context of the sacrifices, the same word refers to the shovel used to remove ashes from the altar:

> So it was precisely the instrument used for the ashes of the sacrifices which made the loudest musical sound. All temple music was a remembrance-offering to God in heaven . . . and the *magrefah* too had its effect on Heaven above, to arouse great compassion and immediate salvation for Israel.[15]

His words have a terrible resonance that he may not fully have known at the time. The death camps with their mass gassing facilities and crematoria had not yet been constructed on the industrial scale that was shortly to be planned and actioned. The Sonderkommando had not yet been given their unthinkable tasks and the ashes had not yet begun to pile up in the fields behind Belzec or Birkenau. The great deportations to Treblinka from the Warsaw Ghetto would take place in the summer of 1942. But that doesn't prevent the rebbe's words from testifying not only to immense courage but also to that combination of devotion, sensitivity and creativity which enabled him, and other teachers like him, to find in the Torah the strength and inspiration to confront their destiny and interpret it as a meaningful sacrifice, even in the bitterest and most nihilistic of circumstances.

Apologise! The sin-offerings

'If the whole community sins'; 'When the head of state sins'; 'If an ordinary person sins': these subheadings in the chapters devoted to sin-offerings make it clear that the need to apologise is universal. Jewish tradition concurs with Alexander Pope that 'to err is human'; even in the house of mourning, where one speaks no ill of the dead, the memorial prayers acknowledge that 'no one is so perfect as to do only good and never wrong'. Nobody, not even the occupant of the highest office, is exempt from the obligation to say sorry and make reparation.

Sometimes we are truly remorseful and long to apologise. The hurt we've caused sits on our conscience and we can scarcely wait for the opportunity to express our regret and make amends. But often apologising is hard, especially when it involves loss of face: the higher a person's station and the more public the incident, the greater the potential humiliation.

'Happy the generation whose leader brings a sacrifice for his mistakes,' observed Rabban Yochanan ben Zakkai, head of the community during and after the first-century siege of Jerusalem by the Romans. He was playing on words: the letters of 'when' in '*when* the head of state sins' together with the penultimate letters of 'head of state' form the word 'happy'. He continued:

> What then, you may say, of the ordinary individual? And if the head of state brings an offering for his unintentional mistakes what, then, about his deliberate sins . . .
>
> (Vayikra 4:22 and Talmud Horayot 20b)

That, explains nineteenth-century German Rabbi Samson Raphael Hirsch, is why the behaviour of the highest in the land is so important: 'How must the readiness of the king to listen to the voice of his conscience move ordinary citizens to listen to the voices of their conscience too.'[16] The converse is equally true: a corrupt and conscienceless leadership sets an example of moral bankruptcy for the entire nation. When challenged, they ruthlessly suppress those who try to call them to account.

Shakespeare's Lady Macbeth speaks for all tyrants when she admits in her sleepwalk to the murders she and her husband have committed: 'What need we fear who knows it when none can call our power to account?'[17] History shows that many leaders guilty of even greater crimes seem to suffer no pangs of conscience at all, even in the middle of the night.

The thirteenth-century commentator Nachmanides notes that the Torah specifically refers to the leader's transgression against 'the commandments of *God his Lord*', precisely because leaders are liable to think that no one has sufficient authority to challenge them:

> Although he is king and master and need have no fear of flesh and blood, he must still fear his God who is the Master of masters; he must lay it to his heart that above him is the One Most High, who holds his life and kingship in His hands.[18]

To this day it remains difficult for public figures, or anyone in a position of power, to apologise. Pride is always a barrier to the admission of wrongdoing. True penitence, Maimonides rules, involves apologising sincerely, striving to make good the ills inflicted, committing oneself to not repeating the offence and leaving one's familiar home 'because exile humbles the heart'.[19] Forced to flee his homeland twice, he well understood the suffering exile entails. But his words can also be taken metaphorically: when we apologise, we leave the safe precincts in which we see ourselves as right and good and enter the vulnerable and uncomfortable territory of acknowledging we've been wrong and hurtful. That's why apologising takes courage. People capable of saying sorry from the heart deserve respect. It is honest and brave to try to understand the world from the point of view of those we have injured.

It is especially important for parents to apologise to their children, and teachers to their pupils, when we've been wrong. Otherwise, we communicate to them that position and pride trump integrity and that status and authority preclude humility. It's the same when people with power and influence refuse to say sorry to those they regard as their juniors. In our capacity for making mistakes, in our frailty as human beings susceptible to selfishness and hurtfulness, we are all equal.

But there are added barriers in the way of prominent individuals. The jeering crowd of detractors and denouncers is never far away. Mistakenly thinking he was off air, the former British prime minister, Gordon Brown, made a dismissive comment about a woman who'd asked him awkward questions. On discovering that his throwaway remark had been broadcast, he insisted, against the advice of his staff, on returning to apologise. It was a rare national moment of decency. More often, politicians and public figures, including religious leaders, blame others, hide behind evasions or insist they were right all along, even in the face of the facts.

Leaders have to be able to admit that they've made erroneous decisions, as well as to confess to deliberate wrongdoing. 'I did once apologise to the House,' a senior parliamentarian told me. 'I acknowledged that the measures I'd been advocating had been proved mistaken and that from now on we would follow a different course. It was hard, but it led to the adoption of a better policy backed by all the organisations which had attacked my earlier position.' Then she added, 'Saying sorry is high-value currency in politics. You can only use it once, twice at most, in an entire career. Otherwise, you're out.'

Her comment is a worrying indication that the contemporary ethos has no place for confessing to being wrong. Clearly, leaders shouldn't remain in post if they make too many mistakes, let alone if they lie or deceive; there's a limit to the price society can pay. But it's a dangerous environment in which it is unforgiveable to be mistaken, not through dishonesty, contempt or negligence but through genuine error. It encourages people to justify their actions and prove themselves right even when the evidence points in the opposite direction and they themselves know it. This fosters a culture of shamelessness and prevents the resolution of errors in a spirit of truthfulness and humility.

Happy, indeed, the people whose leaders can admit to their mistakes.

Me'ilah – the sin of inadvertent misappropriation

In this era of climate concern, an unusual category of sacrifice may prove strangely relevant. As we take cognisance of the damage we've done to the natural world and impoverished and threatened communities and begin to work seriously on redressing climate injustice, rewilding, reforesting and rebirding, we also need to rediscover and recognise the sacred in the world.

One of the most obscure of all the Temple offerings is the *asham me'ilah*, the ram of atonement for the misappropriation of consecrated property. It must be brought if one 'inadvertently commits a trespass [by misappropriating] items sacred to God'; in other words, if one takes some of 'God's things' without realising to whom they actually belong (Lev. 5:15). The very notion that God has 'things' sounds strange. What the Torah is referring to are items such as animals dedicated for sacrifice, wood donated to the altar or funds provided for the upkeep of the Temple. Anyone who, unaware of the status of these items, makes personal use of them must pay back their full cost, with an additional one-fifth, and offer a 'ram of atonement'.

Like all sacrificial rites, this ceased when the Second Temple was destroyed. One might therefore have thought it would remain of historical interest only, but the Talmud offers an astutely contemporary application:

> The rabbis taught: it is forbidden to derive benefit from this world without first reciting a blessing. Anyone who nevertheless does so is to be regarded as if they had committed the sin of *me'ilah*, misappropriation.
>
> (Berachot 35a–b)

The category of *me'ilah* applies exclusively to the inadvertent misuse of what belongs to God. The inference is clear: the gifts of this world are not ours by right. They are to be considered as God's property and we are not entitled simply to take them without according due recognition and asking permission. The Talmud elaborates:

> Whoever derives benefit from this world without saying a blessing is like someone making personal use of objects consecrated to heaven, as the Bible says: 'The earth is the Lord's and the fullness thereof' (Ps. 24:1).
>
> (Berachot 35a–b)

What difference, though, can a blessing, a mere verbal formula, make? The Talmud continues:

> Rabbi Levi noted a contradiction: It's written that 'The earth is the Lord's and the fullness thereof.' Yet it's also written that 'The heavens are the heavens of the Lord, but God has given the earth to humankind.'
>
> (Berachot 35a–b)

As ever, the Talmud presents the problem only in order to resolve it: 'The former verse applies until we recite a blessing, the latter after we have done so' (Berachot 35a–b).

To say a blessing is to recognise that the produce of the earth is not ours by right; it is a gift not to be snatched at but received with gratitude. A blessing represents acknowledgement and appreciation. A mediaeval commentary offers an example of good domestic practice:

> When they laid the table, they would chant, 'The earth is the Lord's and the fullness thereof.' When they cleared everything away, they would sing, 'The heavens are the heavens of the Lord, but the earth God has given to humankind.'[20]

When I was a child, I was given a 'from below to above' explanation of blessings: we say them to raise things up. Before, this was just an apple, a mere object; now it's been made special. The Talmud understands blessings in the opposite way, from above to below: in saying them, we recognise that the items concerned are not unconditionally ours but bounty from God's altar, from life. Blessings are more than pious formulae; they express an attitude profoundly different from that of our prevailing culture of consumerist entitlement, epitomised in the words, 'Let me just grab . . .'

Me'ilah applies only to inadvertent acts. Is it fair, though, to punish people for what they didn't even realise they were doing? There are certainly situations in which ignorance is exactly that – plain ignorance – and should be recognised as such. But in this instance, it's precisely the ignorance that constitutes the sin. We ought to know that the gifts of this world are not all ours by right. There are indeed 'rights' to which we should regard every person as entitled: to food, drink, clothing, shelter, health care and education. But that is very different from promulgating a culture of entitlement in which we have the automatic right to arrogate to ourselves whatever our money can buy. In living in such a way, we reduce the world to a trade market of commodities in which nothing is sacred.

Our relationship to food products is overwhelmingly transactional. We find them in the supermarket or online and pay at the automated check-out. We hold that in this manner we have acquired them: we didn't steal them, so legally they are now ours.

Farmers and gardeners think differently. They know the uncertainties that accompany the progress of the spring sowing into the autumn's yield. Will the seed germinate? Will the young plants thrive? Will the blight spare them until the green tomatoes have turned red? But most of us have lost these relationships. We relish good food, but we don't understand or honour its complex journey and the labours of those who care for it until it reaches the shelf from which we drop it into our trolley.

The Talmud asks what we should do if we've failed to bless our food. 'Go to a wise person and learn the blessings,' it answers. 'Isn't that too late?' it argues back, to which the obvious response is, 'Learn for next time.' But the Talmud may also be saying something deeper. What we have to learn is not just the wording of the blessings: that's easy. What we really need to understand is why blessing, appreciation and not taking things for granted are so important. That requires a far deeper process of relearning than the acquisition of a few formulae. As the poet Osip Mandelstam wrote:

Tell me who it is I must thank for giving
The quiet joy of breathing and of living?[21]

SHEMINI (9:1–11:47)

....

Aaron's silence

The Hebrew Bible knows many kinds of silence. There is the silence of God and the silence of bewildered humanity. There is the silence of grief, the silence of compassion, the silence of horror and the silence of awe.

Aaron is silent. His two eldest sons have just been devoured by flames from heaven in the middle of the great public dedication of the Tabernacle because they brought 'strange fire' not commanded from on high (Lev. 10:1–2). Aaron was rewarded for his silence, explains Rashi; perhaps he had in mind the Talmud's wise observation that 'the reward of the house of bones is silence' (Berachot 6b).

What can one say in the face of tragedy and pain? So long as they don't talk, even Job's so-called comforters provide consolation. They sit in the dust in silent solidarity with him in his shock and grief at the deaths of his children and the decimation of his entire world. It's only when they begin to speak, claiming to know God's ways and counselling him with their superficial explanations, that their relationship sours. Shut up with your pious justifications and implied accusations, he eventually tells them. To this day, the custom in a house of mourning is for the visitor to remain silent after the traditional greeting, 'May the All-Present One bring you comfort.' One waits until the bereaved begin to speak. Nowadays that can feel awkward, so many people prefer to share a memory or offer a general comment such as, 'He was such a special man,' before listening for where the mourner chooses to lead the conversation.

Silence is not easy. This is not because it may seem like not caring; the difference between distracted vacuity and the quietness of fellow feeling is readily communicated. It's because the pressure to suggest reasons, to hold out comforts, to offer something – anything – is so great. Is there nothing to be said in the face of tragedy; is there really no moral or theological consolation? Are we that empty, that useless? It's a hard feeling to bear, so we resort to words. Moses turns to his older brother with the best possible of explanations: 'This is what God meant when God said, "I shall be sanctified by those close to me and honoured in the presence of the whole people"' (Lev. 10:3).

But Aaron is silent. Maybe his brother's words have touched him. He is indeed comforted, explains the Italian commentator Ovadiah Sforno

(1470–1550). He's been weeping out loud, but now he falls silent, observes Nachmanides. Or maybe silence is the only response he can manage to the inadequacy and ineptitude of even the most well-intentioned explanations at such a moment. Maybe he's feeling like so many parents, who, purportedly comforted by the notion, 'Your child was so good that God wanted her among the angels,' would infinitely rather have her back down here, playing in the garden.

Yet sometimes we may have to break the silence or try to probe its possible meanings. A person's heart may be sealed in wordless loneliness and reachable only by breaching that invisible membrane. As Ecclesiastes 3:7 says, 'There is a time to keep silent and a time to speak.' The Talmud records how Rabbi Yochanan, famous for his radiant good looks, visits his impoverished pupil Rabbi Elazar who has fallen ill. Noting that he lives in a dark basement, he bares his arm and the room fills with sufficient light for him to see that his student is quietly weeping. Rabbi Yochanan wants to know why:

> What are you weeping for?
> If it's because you haven't studied much Torah, we've learnt that, 'It's the same whether one does much or little so long as the heart is directed toward heaven.'

Rabbi Elazar doesn't answer, so Rabbi Yochanan tries again:

> If it's because [you can't afford] much food, not everyone merits two tables.

There's still no response, so he breaks the silence one more time:

> If it's because of what happened to your children, this is the bone of my tenth child.

Finally, Rabbi Elazar, vexed perhaps by these probes into his feelings, answers:

> It's because beauty like this (he indicates Rabbi Yochanan) must perish in the dust that I weep.
>
> (Talmud Berachot 5b)

At that, they both cry. Then, in the spirit of their re-established understanding, Rabbi Yochanan holds out his hand and, symbolically, helps Rabbi Elazar rise up.

But there are other times when intuition guides us to refrain from words and simply sit quietly by. Such silence, if it's to be of comfort, is never the silence of absence. It's a presence, a creating of shared space, a communication without words that we are here, open, attentive. It's a human version of the Kabbalistic idea of *tsimtsum*, which is usually said of God: contraction, a conscious making room for the other, their quiet, their unspoken feelings, their words when they begin to speak. As Joan Halifax notes in her moving book, *Being with Dying*:

> Often we feel that silence and stillness aren't good enough when suffering is present . . . [but] in the shared embrace of meditation, a caregiver and a dying person can be held in an intimate silence beyond consolation or assistance.[22]

Therefore, the questions is:

> Can I relax and trust in simply being here, without needing my personality to mediate the tender connection we share?[23]

But it's by no means only in the context of suffering that presence in quietness is so important. One of the most powerful experiences of silence is the revelation to Elijah on God's mountain. After the storm, earthquake and fire have passed by him, Elijah hears God in 'the voice of fine silence' (1 Kgs 19:12). Where does this silence come from? Is it not there until after the storms and tremors? Or is it always present, only Elijah isn't able to feel it until all the drama is over, until he's exhausted from the meaninglessness of all the words and all the noise?

Maybe we, too, wearily letting go for a while of all our wants, plans, protestations and justifications, and even perhaps of the effort of listening, may sometimes get to hear the same sacred silence in the eternal flow of being.

Darosh darash – the search for meaning

Traditional printed editions of the Torah have a small note next to Leviticus 10:16. The context is Aaron's failure to bring the sin-offering required for the ritual dedication of the Tabernacle owing to the sudden death of his two older sons Nadav and Avihu. Moses *darosh darash* – 'urgently enquires' – why this has not been done. The note reads: 'This marks the halfway point of the Torah in words, [with *darosh* on this side of it and *darash* on the other.]'

Needless to say, the matter is disputed, and I've never tried counting myself. But, accurate or not, the idea that these words are the midpoint of the Torah is gripping. *Darash* means 'seek'; *darosh darash* is the emphatic infinitive absolute form: 'seek and seek again'. That the halfway point in the Torah should be the empty space between 'seek' and 'seek again' begs consideration.

Darash has an extraordinary range of applications. It can refer to matters as mundane as lost sheep, which must be looked after until 'your brother *seeks* them from you' (Deut. 22:2). In a legal context it can mean the need for evidence, as in the instruction to '*pursue*, question and investigate thoroughly' (Deut. 19:18). It may indicate concern, or the lack of it, for others, as in the psalmist's complaint that no one *doresh lenafshi*, 'nobody cares about me' (Ps. 142:5). It may refer to the urgent need for peace, as when Jeremiah advises the exiles taken to Babylon by Nebuchadnezzar to 'pursue the peace of the city' because they're going to be there for a very long time (Jer. 29:7).

But across the Hebrew Bible, *darash* most often refers to God. We seek God, and God seeks us; God searches our heart and conscience. As Reuben reminds his brothers when they stand guilt-stricken before Joseph in Egypt: 'Didn't I tell you not to sin by the child! His blood is now *required*' (Gen. 42:22). There exists a God who calls us to account. But God doesn't only challenge us; God needs us too. As the title of one of Abraham Joshua Heschel's works states, God is also 'in search of man'.[24] As if this weren't enough, *darash* takes on a further meaning in rabbinic Hebrew, where it refers to the pursuit of meaning itself. *Lidrosh baTorah* is to seek out the meanings of Torah; a *derashah* is an exploration of the moral and spiritual implications of anything from a single letter to an entire section of the Bible. Therefore, it could scarcely be more significant that this word *darash* should be the midpoint of the Torah. It represents the overriding importance of quest, the pursuit of meaning.

Yet it's not the word itself that occupies the centre of the Torah but the space between its two forms, the gap between *darosh* and *darash*. Who owns that empty place? The answer is everyone who engages with Torah, past, present and future, including you and me. We are here in the midst of it, pursuing its meanings and being pursued by them. We ceaselessly ask why; and Torah and life ask why of us in return. The gap between 'seek' and 'seek again' is where we negotiate between experience and Torah.

As a noun, 'Midrash' signifies the genre of rabbinic interpretation that searches out every opening and opportunity in the text for its potentiality for meaning. As the American scholar of Judaism and rabbinic literature Michael Fishbane writes, an apparent disjunction, a seemingly redundant word or letter, a gap in the narrative, offers the space in which the reader:

> . . . opens new pathways in the texture of scripture, and reveals new patterns in its warp and woof. The interpreter is like a new Moses, standing within the words of scripture and enunciating new revelations from its midst.[25]

Midrash is central to what makes the Torah eternally immediate. While Midrash Halakhah, the derivation of laws, had to be rooted in what the rabbis regarded as authentic tradition, the world of Midrash Aggadah, homiletic 'storytelling' Midrash, was, and remains, wide open. In a remarkable combination of creative imagination, sharp insight into each specific context and lateral reading in which every word of the sacred text was understood as in potential relationship to its usage anywhere and everywhere else in the canon, the rabbis of the world of Midrash expanded the possibilities of Scripture to address the constantly changing 'now' in which they found themselves. This process has never ceased. A well-structured *derashah* is neither now nor then, but both; the contemporary is brought into relationship with the Torah, into the space between 'seek' and 'seek'.

A reviewer once scathingly described a book as 'filling a much-needed gap in the literature on the subject'. Just as Midrash occupies gaps in the text of Torah, so it also vacates them. The place always remains free for further possibilities, the issues of the future. A defining characteristic of Midrash is that it doesn't totalise; it never claims to be the only valid interpretation. It doesn't shut down alternative possibilities; it never forecloses on what others may bring to and take from the text. Fishbane continues:

> Nothing so much characterises the rich collections of theological midrash from late antiquity as the recurrent phrase 'another example' (*davar acher*), for the voice of Sinai was ceaseless, unendingly turned over to find all that was in it.[26]

That voice continues through every generation.

This is true not just across history but also in our own lives. What a verse means to us at a certain moment, how it strikes against our experience when we are twenty, isn't and shouldn't be the same as when we are forty. Just as a line from a song may pass through our mind and we think, 'I never understood that until now,' so the meanings of Torah should grow and change within us as we change and grow. Understanding is always provisional. We should experience the same sense of discovery at fifty as at thirty, and again at sixty. Neither interpretation invalidates the other; they differ simply because we are now different.

Perhaps, though, beyond everything else, there lies a still deeper meaning to the wordless empty space at the centre of Torah: the unknowable, unnameable God, the *Ein Sof*, the endless, and the unfathomable mystery at the heart of the quest to understand.

TAZRIA (12:1–13:59)

Caring for the sick

How a society cares for its sick is indicative of its spiritual as much as its physical health. Britain is justly proud of its National Health Service, free at the point of delivery, despite the constant need for more funding and staff. Behind its philosophy lies the core value mandated in Judaism as *Bikkur Cholim*, the obligation to care for the ill, a responsibility stressed in every single prayer service of the working week.

Some find the chapters of Leviticus that address these issues dull; to me they're fascinating. They describe in lurid detail symptoms varying from infected white sores on the body to bluish-green marks on houses and patches of rot on clothes. These are all understood as indications of different forms of *tsara'at*. Though generally translated as 'leprosy', it's impossible to be certain about the exact nature of the illnesses described.

The Torah explains how society is expected to respond to those who show the telltale symptoms. The burden of care falls mainly to the priests:

> When a person has a swelling, scab or pale spot on the skin of their body and it develops into an infection of leprosy in the skin of the flesh, they are to be brought to Aaron the priest or one of his priestly descendants.
>
> (Lev. 13:2)

The word 'brought' invites speculation: didn't people go of their own accord? Did fear, for themselves or their families, keep them awake night after night as they stared at their developing symptoms, mercifully not visible to anyone else – or at least not yet – until anxiety drove them to make the fateful appointment with the priest-cum-doctor? Did a compassionate friend, intuiting their worry, offer to accompany them to this assignation with destiny, from which there might be no return for weeks, for years or maybe forever? Were the victims effectively hunted out of their homes by relatives or neighbours terrified of the risk of infection and dragged against their will to the appropriate authorities? Would they be put in quarantine, once or, as the Torah instructs if the symptoms remain unclear, for a second even more anxious week? What if the diagnosis were to prove positive: would they be expelled from the camp? Would they ever be healed? There is no reason to suppose that people's fears back then would have been different from our own today, or that the words, 'I'll come with you,' spoken quietly but firmly to brook no contradiction, would have sounded any less kind in former ages than now.

The sufferers must have wondered in trepidation what kind of human being the priest would prove to be before whom they would have to uncover their body and disclose their symptoms. Those *cohanim* were doubtless no less different one from another than medical staff are today. People often tell me about their experiences with the latter:

> The doctor was extremely kind; she explained everything in straight-forward terms and promised to call as soon as the results came in.
>
> We asked about the prognosis: his response was, 'I wouldn't expect to see you here this time next year.'
>
> She lacked the human touch.

I've learnt, too, that there is likely to be a considerable degree of variance between what people hear doctors say, particularly when they're anxious, and what the doctors think they've said, especially regarding tone of voice.

Rebbe Shlomo of Radomsk (1801–66) read great importance into the fact that the priests were all descendants of Aaron, who had a reputation for gentleness and compassion: 'The sacred qualities of Aaron, a man of faithful kindness who loved and pursued peace, endure down the generations forever.' Such qualities of calm and kindness, he added, 'have the power to purify every person of their diseases'.[27]

He no doubt believed that healing ultimately comes from God. But this wouldn't necessarily have entailed the rejection of human intervention.

Many rabbis were themselves physicians or had close relationships with members of the medical profession. Yet, as Rabbi David Halevi Segal (1586–1667) explains, commenting on the wording in the *Shulchan Aruch*, 'The Torah *has given permission* for doctors to practise healing, *and it is an obligation.*'

> True healing is attained through praying for God's mercy, since healing comes from heaven . . . But because people are not worthy of such [divine intervention] they must therefore seek healing according to the laws of nature.[28]

Doctors are obliged to offer such healing as lies within their power. The rest is in God's hands; healing always has an emotional and a spiritual dimension.

Perhaps this is what the rabbi of Radomsk had in mind: the kindness that softens the edge of fear and enables the patient to feel less in the grip of a remorseless process of examination and exclusion and more in the embrace of understanding and compassion. Such thoughtfulness and love, which mercifully often seems to permeate the atmosphere of hospital wards and hospices, may not in itself have the power to effect a physical cure, but it can bring a deep measure of reassurance to the anxious heart.

Writing about her experiences as a nurse in her aptly named book *The Language of Kindness*, Christie Watson describes how she takes Betty, an elderly lady suffering from sudden chest pains and whose temperature is falling sharply, across the hospital to where she can offer her a 'bear-hugger' machine to blow hot air and warm her up. The fabric-like paper on the instrument reminds Betty of the wartime parachute silk out of which she sewed her wedding dress. Despite the pressure of other duties, Christie sits for a minute and, as she listens to the story, 'I stop seeing a frail old woman alone on a hospital trolley, and instead finds herself looking at a young woman in a dress made from parachute silk, dancing with her new husband, Stan'.[29] For Christie, Betty is no longer a patient requiring time she can scarcely spare, but a person with a unique and engaging history.

In a similar vein, the Torah doesn't say, 'When a patient' but rather, 'When a person' develops symptoms (Lev. 13:2). Rabbi Pinchas Menachem Elazar of Pilin notes that in the same verse in which the priest is instructed to 'look at the disease', he is also required to 'see him', the human being: 'because it's not enough to examine the infection; he needs to consider the whole person, for it is in this way that he can be healed'.[30]

Perhaps today, too, those who accompany us to our appointments, as well as the nurses, doctors and therapists who see us, can help to ensure that we aren't instantly turned from a person into being an illness. Even if they can't fully cure us, maybe through their kindness and encouragement they can help us to find the stamina and inner wholeness to live with whatever illness we may be found to have.

'Alone shall he sit'

'Most people don't die of the cancer,' a therapist working with the dying told me. 'They die of the loneliness, from the feeling that they don't belong any more, that nobody wants them, that they're worthless. They turn their face to the wall and die.'

There can be little loneliness like that of the leper:

> His clothes must be torn, his hair let loose, his upper lip covered; and he must cry out 'impure, impure' . . . *Badad yeisheiv* – Alone must he dwell; his place is outside the camp.
>
> (Lev. 13:45–6)

It's impossible to capture the force of the original language; no one familiar with the Hebrew Bible can read these words without hearing at the same time the opening words of Lamentations: *Eichah yashvah badad*: 'How she sits solitary, the city once filled with people.' The anguish of the leper in his isolation has become the symbol of the desolation of Jerusalem, forsaken by all her former friends. It's an abandonment many still fear today. 'Many don't dare tell their family,' a doctor working with leprosy patients in southern Asia told me.

It's the leper's own fault, the Talmud suggested (Arachin 16b); it's measure for measure. Leprosy, *tsara'at*, is a punishment for *lashon hara*, slander. Hence the fate of Moses' sister Miriam whose flesh turned instantly leprous after she spoke denigratingly about his wife (Num. 12:1–10):

> The leper caused division between man and wife with his slanderous accusations, separating people from their friends; therefore he must now be separated from society.[31]

Lepers were not even allowed to join with others who found themselves outside the encampment for different reasons, such as ritual uncleanness through contact with a corpse. They were excluded from any and every form of company.

The Talmud's rationalisation reads like an attempt to justify suffering by blaming the victim in order to preserve the notion of a righteous God. It feels cruel and makes little moral sense.

If lepers are completely isolated, to whom is their cry, 'unclean, unclean,' addressed? It sounds like the infamous bell with which, across mediaeval Europe, they warned wayfarers out of their path. Samuel David Luzzatto (1800–65) suggests that they called out the words as they left their home. In her novel *The Island*, set in the leper colony of Spinalonga off the coast of Crete, Victoria Hislop describes how a young woman recently infected with the illness can see her former house from the shore.[32] She is tormented by the knowledge that she may never again share the companionship of the family she so deeply loves. The colony was not closed until 1957. It was around that time that Rabbi Aryeh Levin, renowned for his compassion, entered the leper compound in Jerusalem. The men and women thronged round him, deeply moved by his visit. 'No one has ever come to see us before,' they told him. After that, there wasn't a week in which he failed to go.[33]

The Talmud groups together three categories of persons: mourners, lepers and people under the ban, that is, excluded from the community for refusing to abide by its rules (Mo'ed Katan 14b onwards). All three groups have to tear their clothing, let their hair grow long, cover their lips, sit on the ground, eschew company and keep silence. The link between lepers and mourners reflects their loss and grief; the comparison with those under the ban implies sin and punishment. The leper is not just isolated by his suffering but is also made to feel guilty and rejected. In the silence surrounding him, it's hard to imagine how he can have escaped the inner 'why?', which must only have added to his torment. It's a question so many people suffering from physical and mental illness experience. It eats away at one's morale. It draws one down into bleak inner chambers where bewilderment, anger, self-blame and hopelessness have free rein to torment the consciousness. This is a world within worlds, which exists only in the mind yet may exact greater credence than the sound of an encouraging voice, the joy of sunlight or hope itself. It is a world known all too well to many who suffer from illness and depression. Isolation only makes it worse.

Today we like to pride ourselves on inclusion. Yet bitter loneliness remains the reality for many, perhaps at times for all. 'The greatest cruelty,' wrote palliative care doctor Rachel Clarke in her book about the Covid-19 pandemic, is:

The unspeakable pain for so many families of being unable to be present when their loved one dies, or to mourn together afterwards. So often, I find I am updating anxious spouses, sons or daughters by telephone who are themselves self-isolating. They have no one to hug, no warm human presence to cling to.[34]

Even when people are not required to isolate physically, loneliness may still be their inner reality; a person can be surrounded by others yet feel utterly apart. Listening to people's pain has taught me to avoid the words, 'I know how you feel.' We never do.

Mercifully, the Talmud offers an alternative explanation for the leper's cry:

> It teaches us that they should make their suffering known to the community, so that the community can pray to God to show them mercy (and heal them).

> (Mo'ed Katan 15a)

Rabbi Baruch Halevi Epstein (1860–1941) explains that on hearing them weep, especially at night, others will weep with them and beg God to send them relief.[35]

The assumption is that we're within hearing, which implies that we have a responsibility to remain in communication. No one should be left to suffer alone. In the traditional prayers for the sick, we name the specific people we know who are unwell and then include them 'among all others who are ill', because community does not end at the threshold of the healthy. It needs to embrace everyone, especially those who feel most isolated.

The Torah repeats over and again how it is the task of the priest-cum-doctor to see. He needs to examine the symptoms; if after seven days they have not healed, he must look a second time. But he must also see the person. In the Bible and rabbinic literature, seeing is not just an act of the eyes; it means perceiving with compassion, like God who 'sees to the heart' and who 'saw the suffering of the Children of Israel' when they were enslaved (1 Sam. 16:7 and Exod. 2:25). Though the priest had the unenviable duty of determining when a person needed to be excluded from the camp, his deeper task was to look again, and yet again, until such time as the sufferer could be brought back into the community. Even if the symptoms persisted, he had at the very least to continue to include the suffering person within the circle of compassionate awareness.

Why? – and the need for meaning

In *Being with Dying*, Joan Halifax distinguishes between pain, which she defines as physical discomfort, and suffering, the story we form around our pain:

> I had made the very human mistake of following the arrow of pain with the arrow of suffering. The first arrow, the sensation of pain, is bad enough. But it's the second arrow – the story we tell ourselves about our pain – that's the real trouble.[36]

Most of us cannot help but create a story in order to try to make sense of our experiences, especially illness and pain. We probably don't compose it consciously and it never takes a final form. It is the unfinished product of our previous experiences, of the night hours when sleep eludes us, of our dreams and nightmares and, if we are fortunate, of the immeasurable and inextricable impact on our thinking and feeling of those who love us. The story we weave holds for us the meaning of our illness and health.

The critical issue is what kind of story this is. Is it helpful? Does it enable us to learn from what is happening to us? Is it generous towards ourselves and others? Is it soured by guilt, spiked with blame or made bitter by anger? Perhaps at different times, in the gentler moments of the day or the crueller hours of night, it is all of these.

There is every difference between the creation of an inner, subjective narrative by the person who is suffering and the imposition on him or her by others of their view of why this has happened. The Talmud reserves severe criticism for anyone who speaks to a sick person in the way Job's so-called comforters addressed him, rebuking him and demanding that he 'consider what innocent person ever perished' (Job 4:7). It classifies this as *ona'at devarim*, 'verbal abuse' (Bava Metsia 58b). Heartless moralising about another person's pain is a form of cruelty. Suffering calls for compassion, not judgement. Life brings all kinds of hurts; sometimes we do contribute to our own afflictions, but often they have no more connection with what we've done than that we were unfortunate enough to be in the wrong place at the wrong time. Neither blaming the victim nor blaming God is helpful.

Yet the compulsion to do either, or both, is strong. We instinctively want life to be meaningful; the words 'fair' and 'unfair' are part of our earliest vocabulary. It's hard to acknowledge that 'why?' may have no answer. It's especially tempting to use God to fill in uncomfortable gaps, especially since there's a long tradition of doing precisely that: since God is just, and all things come from God, those who suffer must deserve their afflictions. Both the Torah and the Talmud offer plentiful texts that can be understood in this way. Additionally, attributing other people's misfortunes to their faults allows us to suppose that if we avoid such behaviours the same afflictions won't affect us. 'So long as we keep our noses clean,' I heard someone who should have known better say in a lecture at a hospice. But having a clean nose is no proof against Parkinson's, motor neurone disease or cancer. The poet John Keats better understood the dangers of theorising and theologising when he coined the phrase 'negative capability': 'when a man is capable of being in uncertainties, mysteries, doubts, without any irritable reaching after fact and reason'.[37] What others need is our kindness and attentiveness, not our explanations and moralisations.

Yet we are almost inevitably drawn to try to answer the 'why?', even when we know it's unanswerable. As the scholar of rabbinics David Kraemer notes:

> We, as human beings, seek to give meaning and structure to our experience, and suffering is the phenomenon that perhaps most effectively challenges meaning and undermines our sense of order.[38]

In a succinct but profound passage, the Talmud considers the processes by which we try to restore our sense of meaning. It begins: 'When someone sees that afflictions have come upon them,' which clearly locates the thought process within the mind of the sufferer, not in some external observer moralising over another person's troubles (Berachot 5a).

There follow three putative 'explanations' for suffering: the first two are challenges; the third is an observation: '[In the first instance] one should carefully examine one's deeds . . .' The inference is clearly that our troubles must be the result of something we've done. This is one of the first questions many people ask themselves. Sometimes the answer may be yes, as in the case of the man who told me after a severe heart attack that he had drunk and smoked a lot, worked all hours, rarely exercised and failed to look after his family. 'That's all now going to change,' he concluded. What I couldn't know was whether this was really true or whether, as so often when misfortune strikes, it was a case of trying to reclaim some sense of agency by blaming oneself. Far more often, though, the illness has little or nothing to do with anything we've done.

The Talmud frames the next challenge in equally pious terms: '[If one finds no cause in one's conduct], one should attribute one's suffering to neglect of Torah . . .' This can be interpreted as: what have I neglected that is really important? It's less about self-blame and more about values. Illnesses and bereavements do change how we live, and not just because of what we may become unable to do. They prompt us to rethink our priorities. 'I want to spend more time with my family.' 'I'm going to devote myself to what I really care about.' 'I'm not going to waste the precious time I have left on things that are unimportant.' 'My friends have been so good to me; from now on I'm determined to be a better friend myself.' I often hear such words.

This leads to the Talmud's third observation: 'If one is unable to attribute one's sufferings to either of the above causes, then it's well known that they must be sufferings of love . . .' But what are 'sufferings of love'? Love of God, love of fellow human beings, sufferings that only love can help us negotiate, sufferings that deepen the love within us, sufferings that draw the love of others towards us, sufferings where love becomes the central value, the only thing that really matters? The Talmud provides a proof-text from Proverbs 3:12: 'whom God loves, God chastises', but fails to offer any explanation of what it understands by 'sufferings of love'. However, it does add a significant qualification: sufferings only become 'sufferings of love' if a person receives them as such. In other words, no one can preach to anyone else that what they're going through is all about love.

I've met people who meet the Talmud's criteria; they somehow find the capacity for love within their sufferings. A woman whose illness was not only shortening her life but also making even the smallest actions progressively harder once told me:

> You reach a place beyond why and wherefore, beyond accusation and self-blame, where the question becomes: can I turn this into love? Have I got enough love in me to keep going?

My own experience as a rabbi bears out Ira Byock's observation:

> Ask a person who is on a heart or liver transplant list, or someone facing cancer chemotherapy for the third or fourth time, 'What matters most?' and the answer will always include the names of people they love.[39]

METSORA (14:1–15:33)

....

When the illness has been cured

None of us can become the person we were yesterday. We can go to the same supermarket and make the same kind of coffee, but we can't become who we used to be. There's no way of undoing what experience has made of us; life allows no *status quo ante*.

The Torah describes the complex purification rituals that must be undergone 'after the plague of leprosy has been healed from the *leper*' (Lev. 14:3). The choice of words is puzzling: if the illness is cured, why is its former victim still referred to as a leper? They should simply be called *adam*, a person like everyone else, just as they were before becoming sick, yet the Torah still labels them a leper. Will they never, despite the offerings they bring and the week-long probation period during which they have to sit outside their tent, be allowed to escape being known by the condition that once banished them from the community?

Rebbe Yehoshua of Ostrovo (d. 1873) explains that the Torah wants to tell us that even after people are healed in body, they may still be suffering spiritually.[40] Inner healing takes time; the physical symptoms may have gone, but the psychological impact remains. 'It takes most people a year or more to recover emotionally from a major illness,' a therapist told me.

Of course, there is the joy of returning health, energy and, hopefully, zest for life. 'The sky overhead was very blue, very clear and very, very high. Not, I thought, the heaven, but a heaven of heavens,' observed Rabbi Milton Steinberg on leaving hospital after surviving a serious heart attack.[41] Hospitalisation may be the modern equivalent of being 'outside the camp', confined in a world set apart from the familiar contexts of everyday life which may seem not just a few streets, but worlds, away. He understood how fortunate he was to be able to step back into the daylight which those who have never come close to death so heedlessly take for granted. There's a special thanksgiving blessing to God 'who bestows goodness upon the unworthy', which people who have recovered from serious illness recite in the presence of the community to affirm their return to normal life.

Yet that return is also challenging. It's often only partial; the mind remains preoccupied. Will my health last? Is this release, or merely reprieve? For how long will I be in remission, and will I ever get out of it? Can I allow myself to be carefree? Or has the angel of death only retreated from the bedside to the bedroom door? It's not surprising that many people determine to make far-reaching changes after surviving a life-threatening illness: 'From now on I'm taking nothing for granted. I'm determined to do what's good and what I enjoy.'

The Torah's seemingly ungenerous choice of words is in fact disturbingly accurate. A person returns to her former life and home, but the shadow of having been a leper, a cancer patient, the survivor of a stroke or a traffic accident, hovers for a long time over everything she thinks and does. Maybe she now chooses to sit at the back of the church or synagogue, or to remain near the doorway at a party, pensive, as if voluntarily resuming for some moments that solitariness to which illness had confined her. She's left that place behind, yet it travels with her. Perhaps that's why it may be hard to accept friends' well-meaning invitations. But then they begin to talk: 'Isn't it time she moves on? It's a whole year now and she's still so down. We have to help her let it go; what she needs is closure.'

But 'closure' is at best an overused term. Some years ago, I shared a panel with a lawyer who had represented the families of children massacred at Dunblane when a gunman murdered sixteen pupils and their teacher at the local school. 'I don't believe in closure,' he said, 'there's no such thing.' I agree; life knows no closure. Minor issues can, and usually should, be put behind us. But when it comes to major events such as illness or the loss of those we love, our feelings don't 'close'. On life's unrelenting onward journey, we take with us everything that ever happened to us, whether we like it or not. The challenge isn't closure, but openness: how do I carry with me all my experiences, including the most challenging? Can they open my heart to deeper empathy with life in all its vulnerability? Can they sensitise me to others in their struggles with life's journeys?

These concerns are reflected symbolically in the sacrifices people cured from leprosy had to bring before they could rejoin the camp. The priest had to take on their behalf 'two living, pure birds, cedar wood, scarlet and hyssop' (Lev. 14:4). The first bird was slaughtered over 'an earthenware vessel and living waters'. The second was dipped, together with the cedar, scarlet and hyssop, in the blood of the first bird, over 'living water'. The same mixture was then sprinkled over the leper seven times to purify him, after which the live bird was set free across the fields. The words 'live' or 'living' occur five times in the brief description of this ritual.

This strange but evocative procedure had a particular resonance for me at the time of writing, when across the world people were moving out of lockdown back into 'normality', returning from 'alone shall he dwell' to the camp of community. Rites express emotions symbolically, without bringing them overtly into consciousness. Their power lies in their capacity to articulate experiences subliminally without exposing strong and haunting feelings to analysis by our rational self. The ritual of the dead and living birds somehow captures this transition from a world of apartness and closeness to death, back into the world of 'living, vital waters' (Lev. 14:6) and free movement. The first bird is slaughtered: the leper has been to death; for certain he has experienced a period of social death. During those days of aloneness, he must have felt mortality sidle closer, staring at him from his heart's fears. Perhaps others, whose lonely cry of 'impure, impure' he used to hear in the distance, have meanwhile succumbed to the disease and died. Maybe he never imagined that he himself would emerge alive. Even though he now finds himself back on the threshold of health and freedom, there is spilt blood on the margins of his mind; his spirit has been dipped in it. Like King Lear, his hand 'smells of mortality'.[42] Wherever he goes, he will carry that awareness of the proximity of death with him; he knows truly what everyone knows in theory. Will my end come sooner, or later? Perhaps he can push such thoughts away, but he will never be the same again. Liberty itself, if it comes, when it comes, will always be accompanied by the shadow thought: when will I fall from the sky? Yet life has reasserted itself within him; he's going to live.

Rebbe Yitzhak Meir of Ger (1799–1866) taught that the earthenware basin used in the purification ritual represents the human body, which is likened in the High Holyday liturgy to 'fragile pottery and floating dust'. However, the bowl contains not only blood but also waters, and not just any waters but *mayyin chayyim*, living, vital waters, like the rivers that flow out of Eden from the source of life itself. The second bird is dipped not only in blood but also in this elixir; the life urge is restored (Lev. 14:7). This bird-spirit is not just allowed to fly off but is 'sent off and away' across the fields of freedom. One imagines it rising with the currents of air, rejoicing in the newly restored joy of unrestricted flight, for the spirit is eternally in love with the boundless wonder of life.

But on its wings are the red-brown marks of drying blood.

ACHAREI MOT (16:1–18:30)

....

Entering the Holy of Holies

It was the ultimate encounter. No one but the high priest ever entered the Holy of Holies, and even he only on Yom Kippur, the holiest day of the Jewish year. He had to follow to the last detail the complex rituals described in the Torah, elaborated in the Mishnah and Talmud and outlined in the High Holyday liturgy used to this day. Five times he bathed and changed his garments from purple to white, entering the holiest precincts in simple linens; ten times he washed and 'sanctified his hands and feet'. Three times he stood alone before God, first to seek atonement for himself and his family, then for the tribe of Levi and finally for the whole house of Israel. What was at stake was the destiny of the Jewish People in the coming year.

The elders would carefully rehearse the order of the sacrifices with him, but in the essential moments the high priest was alone before God. What was in his thoughts at that time? What would we say if we had just three brief moments to make our peace and express everything on our minds before the ultimate?

That his duties inspired both awe and plain fear is implied in a painful interchange that took place each year on the eve of the sacred day:

> The elders said to him: high priest, we are the emissaries of the rabbinical court and you are our emissary and theirs. We call on you to swear by God who caused the divine name to dwell in this house that you will not alter anything of what we have told you.
>
> (Mishnah Yoma 1:5)

They would weep as they left the high priest because they doubted him; because they may have suspected an innocent man.

The Talmud explains the issue: the high priest had to pass alone through the curtain that separated the area designated as holy from the Temple's most sacred chamber, the Holy of Holies, which was empty except for the Ark of the Covenant. This was the abode of the presence of God, before whom he was required to make atonement. No one else ever entered this chamber; he alone had to do so once a year on this most awesome day. He could bring with him nothing except the specially prepared incense, the firepan filled with hot coals on which to burn it and the blood of the sacrifices to be sprinkled before the ark. The Sadducees, the religious sect to whom the high priest belonged, understood the Torah as instructing him to put the incense on the censer outside the dividing curtain, so that he would enter the Holy of Holies only as the smoke began to rise. But the elders insisted that he wasn't to place it on the coals until he was already inside the curtain, alone with God.

At stake were not just minutiae. The Sadducees may have believed that God was present in some perceptible form in the Holy of Holies and were therefore understandably fearful of approaching without the protection of the cloud of incense. The elders were insistent that the high priest enter without any such shielding because they held that God, the One who sees but cannot be seen, was incorporeal and invisible. They therefore made the high priest swear to follow their rules without deviation. There may also have been a less theological but more human reason: to stand on one's own, mortal, unprotected and burdened with such huge responsibilities before the all-knowing God must have been not just awe-inspiring but also terrifying. The incense would have provided at least a notional layer of cover.

What would it be like to encounter the God of all flesh? The Talmud records a surprising testimony. Rabbi Yishmael ben Elisha, who had served as high priest, recalled how:

> . . . once [on Yom Kippur] I entered the innermost sanctum, the Holy of Holies, to offer incense, and saw [in a vision], the Lord of Hosts, seated upon a high and exalted throne. He said to me: 'Yishmael, my son, bless me.'
>
> I said to him: 'May it be your will that your mercies overcome your anger and prevail over your other attributes. May you treat your children according to this attribute of mercy and conduct yourself towards them beyond the strict letter of the law.'
>
> The Holy Blessed One nodded his head.
>
> This teaches us that we should never take the blessing of an ordinary person lightly . . .
>
> (Talmud, Berachot 7a)

The scene is strangely touching. Rabbi Yishmael enters to seek God's forgiveness on behalf of his people, yet God seems to need him as much as he needs God. God is in pain; God, too, suffers from the hurts and injustices of earthly life. After the destruction of the Temple, God also feels the loss: 'Alas for the father who exiled his children; alack for the children exiled from their father's table' (Berachot 3a). This is not just a case of blaming the victim, or of a parent telling a child as he beats him that 'this hurts me more than it's hurting you'. God, too, wants a better world, a place of unbroken, healed relationships. Yet this lies beyond even God's power, for God is as dependent on what humans do as humans are on God. Therefore, when Rabbi Yishmael ben Elisha enters to seek forgiveness on behalf of the Jewish People, God, albeit indirectly, appears to ask forgiveness from him. Just as humanity needs God's blessing, God needs the blessing of humanity.

When I was growing up, my teacher, Louis Jacobs of blessed memory, would read every year before the section of the liturgy recording the high priest's service a meditation from Ansky's play *The Dybbuk*. It opens with an evocation of the uniqueness of the occasion: the holiest place in the holiest city is the Holy of Holies in Jerusalem; the holiest person is the high priest; the holiest moment is the Day of Atonement and the holiest language is Hebrew. Just once each year while the Temple still stood, these 'four sanctities' would meet. But now that it exists no more:

> Every place where a person raises their eyes to heaven is a Holy of Holies. Every person, having been created by God in God's own image and likeness, is a High Priest. Every day of a person's life is a Day of Atonement, and every word spoken with sincerity in God's name is the holy tongue.[43]

Therefore we also, like the high priest, stand before God in the Holy of Holies. We, too, must enter unprotected. If we hide behind a smokescreen of self-justification, we will lack the openness of spirit which alone can elicit mercy and pardon, whether from God or from our fellow human beings. What, then, do we say in our most naked moments before the One who knows? Perhaps we say, if not in words then through the unspoken feelings in our heart, 'I am sorry for all the pain in this world, and for all I have done that has hurt others, and all I have not done to bring healing where I could.' Or maybe we say, more simply, as Abraham and Moses did, '*Hinneni*, I'm here.' For God surely knows our frailty, faults and longing to do what's good and right. Or perhaps, like the boy in Paul Gallico's *The Day the Guinea Pig Talked*, when the strokes of that magic midnight finally sound during which they've been promised that they'll be able to speak to one another, all they manage to say in those brief, longed-for moments is, 'I love you.'[44]

For love, if it is real, is deeper than all angers and frustrations, and forgiveness and atonement are its blessings.

Scapegoats and scapegoating

The original scapegoat really was a goat. It was one of an identical pair over whom Aaron cast lots on the Day of Atonement. The goat over which the lot 'for the Lord' was drawn was sacrificed as a sin-offering to God. The goat whose destiny was 'for Azazel':

> . . . was stood alive before God to be atoned upon, then sent away into the wilderness to Azazel.
>
> (Lev. 16:8, 10)

The high priest would confess the sins of the nation over its head, then the animal was led from outpost to outpost until it was pushed over a cliff to its death in the desert. The passive verbs 'stood alive' and 'sent away' emphasise the haplessness of the creature upon whom the burden of collective guilt was placed, prefiguring the inescapability of the projections that later metaphorical scapegoats would have to bear.

I've always felt sorry for both those animals, especially the goat for Azazel, destined 'to carry off all the sins of the Children of Israel into a deserted land' (Lev. 16:22). The Mishnah records what would happen to it:

> What would the man do [who drove the goat into the wilderness]? He would divide the [red] thread the High Priest had attached to its horns into two. One part he would fasten on the rocks; the other he would tie between its horns. Then he would push the animal backwards [over the cliff] and it would fall, rolling over and over, not reaching halfway down before it was torn limb from limb.
>
> (Mishnah Yoma 6:6)

The Talmud explains that half the thread was fixed to the rocks so that the emissary who dispatched the goat could watch it turn from bright red to white, signalling that the sins of the people were forgiven as the animal met its death. This information would then be relayed to the high priest by a series of semaphore signals, though, according to Rabbi Yishmael, that was unnecessary, since:

A crimson thread was also attached to the entrance to the Temple which, when the goat reached the desert, would turn white.

(Mishnah Yoma 6:8)

In this manner, Isaiah's words would be fulfilled:

Though your sins are as scarlet, they shall be white as snow; though red as crimson, they shall be like wool.

(Isa. 1:18)

One can only imagine the anxiety of the crowds as they watched, and their relief when the ribbon changed colour.

The Torah ominously describes the place where the animal met its fate as *eretz gezerah*, 'a land of decree'. Rabbi Samuel ben Meir (1085–1158) explains this as 'a desolate land where nothing grows, set apart by decree as devoid of all good'.[45] The world has since been shown to contain many such places where scapegoated victims are driven to the slaughter.

It's hard to think of this strange rite, so at odds with Judaism's principles of personal and collective responsibility, as anything other than a remnant of paganism. It ceased forever with the destruction of the Second Temple. Yet the traditional liturgy for Yom Kippur records it in close detail. To this day we prostrate ourselves as we recall how the throngs gathered in the Temple courtyard would bow to the ground when they heard the high priest utter God's name 'in holiness and purity' before the goat loaded with their sins was sent away. Even this verbal recollection carries a strange cathartic power.

But there are no goats today to carry off our sins. The Mishnah makes it abundantly clear that Yom Kippur only brings atonement if we repent sincerely and determine never to repeat our wrongdoings:

Regarding sins between persons, Yom Kippur does not affect atonement unless one has first made peace with one's fellows. Rabbi Elazar ben Azariah taught: 'From all your sins *before God* shall you be purified.' Yom Kippur atones for sins before God; Yom Kippur does not atone for sins against other people until one is reconciled with them.

(Lev. 16:30 and Mishnah Yoma 8:9)

This, the rabbis explain, can only be achieved through sincere confession, apology and restitution, 'even if one has only upset the other person with words' (Talmud Yoma 87a). There are no shortcuts to forgiveness.

The Temple rite exists no more, but scapegoating, which is the exact opposite of taking responsibility, thrives. It's a byword for blaming others for our own and our society's shortcomings. We project onto them, usually in grossly exaggerated form, characteristics we dislike and behaviours we don't want to own in ourselves or our community. We blame them for all the ills of our nation. Once we've loaded these faults onto our victims, we feel entitled to mock and despise them. We consider ourselves justified in driving them out from our country for our own good, as an act of self-protection. Our world knows of many kinds of *eretz gezerah*, godforsaken locations from where no witness is supposed to return to tell the tale of what was done to them there. The bones of the millions who have suffered this fate, generations of Jews among them, are scattered beneath the cliffs of history. The societies that despatch them to such places do not thereby become guiltless of sin. They have blood on their hands and the ghosts of their victims haunt humankind.

At the close of Shakespeare's *The Tempest*, as the characters partner up, Prospero, who has orchestrated this benign and forgiving outcome, turns to Caliban, the play's evil genius, and says, 'This thing of darkness I acknowledge mine.'[46] His words can be understood as simply racist, a grudging concession that those whom the Elizabethan world regarded as 'savages' do indeed belong to the human race: Caliban is an anagram of *canibal*. But I take from Prospero's admission a different insight, a profound recognition that the impulse to hurt and the temptation to betray are part of us all. Only by owning them can we govern them.

We have to recognise the impact of how we see and portray others, and make ourselves aware of the prejudices and projections with which we burden them and the evils we place on their heads. We must not evade the challenge of owning our faults and wrongdoings. Far from sending them away into hidden places, we must take back upon ourselves the responsibilities for the ills we offload on to our 'others'. For, as Jacques Derrida wrote, 'Every culture is haunted by its other . . . identity presupposes alterity.'[47] How we relate to those others defines us, both as individuals and as societies. Unless we do so with honesty and integrity, there can be no atonement, no at-one-ment, and no healing in our violent, divided world.

Homosexuality – what the Torah has to say

I hold on to one of the handles of the scroll for balance. I am surprised
to find the words ominously poetic. Thou shalt not uncover the
nakedness of thy father's wife, the nakedness of thy sister, the nakedness of thy daughter-in-law. And then it comes. 'Thou shalt not lie
with a male as one lies with a woman, it is an abomination' (Leviticus
18:22). To my surprise, when it is read, I no longer feel pain or threat
or even accusation. I feel strangely empowered. In exposing myself to
this verse, it has become exposed to me.

Steven Greenberg[48]

Rabbi Steven Greenberg bravely chooses not to walk out of the synagogue
on the afternoon of the Day of Atonement. Instead, he asks to be called to
the Torah to confront and be confronted by that key verse about homosexuality which comes twice in Leviticus (18:22; 20:13) and is read a third
time during the afternoon of Yom Kippur. There are other morally challenging passages in the Torah, but few verses, if any, cause so much
contemporary pain:

> The discomfort is difficult to convey. I remembered vividly a video of
> ISIS throwing a young gay man from a tall tower to his death as
> punishment – the camera is watching his fall from the top – it was
> horrendous. Is this our beautiful Torah that encourages or approves of
> such atrocities – 'it is an abomination: they shall surely be put to death;
> their blood is upon them'?[49]

The Torah's words cannot simply be bypassed by reading them quickly;
gay members of our communities deserve better than our passing over
these verses in rapid semi-silence. If nothing is said, an LBGTQ+ person
might justifiably conclude that the absence of comment implies approval.
People who are gay are no less God-seekers than anyone else and deserve
an open, welcoming and equal place in life, including religious life, in its
sorrows, celebrations and leadership.

What, then, does one do with these verses? How that question is
addressed probably depends on how we read the Torah in general. Chaim
Rapoport raises this issue in *Judaism and Homosexuality: An Authentic
Orthodox View*, a frank and sometimes hard-hitting account of traditional
thinking, intended to awaken deeper understanding and greater compassion for the challenges faced by orthodox Jews who are gay:

[For] one who . . . maintains that the Torah's commandments contain 'harmful' ones and that some of the commandments were the product of primitive man, there is indeed no binding reason to keep any of the Torah's commandments. For, if the commandments under discussion are considered to be morally unacceptable, according to the subjective perspective of the individual or the collective *zeitgeist* of society, they would have to be disregarded, if not repudiated.[50]

He references Louis Jacobs, who, in his *A Jewish Theology*, includes a subsection, 'The Harmful', in his categorisation of the commandments. Jacobs notes that for the non-fundamentalist:

The laws were formulated by human beings in response to human conditions, under the guidance of God, to be sure, but subject to error like all other human institutions. The rationale for present-day loyalty to the law is that it preserves values, among them those of justice and equity. Where it patently does the opposite, it can have no claim on the allegiance of the Jew.[51]

He notes that the instances of 'harmful' commandments in the Torah are extremely few, mostly connected with the inferior status of women. Jacobs concludes that the non-fundamentalist Halakhist, who affirms the validity and importance of Jewish law but does not ascribe to the doctrine of the Mosaic authorship of Torah, will 'endeavour to mitigate the effects of the harmful without destroying the system as a whole'.[52]

Jacobs was my teacher and I endeavour to study the Torah according to the position he articulates here. It is both necessary and enriching to appreciate that the Torah was not composed in a void but amid literary, legal, social and cultural conditions which it inevitably reflects. If these are not acknowledged, one runs the risk of promulgating as God's eternal word what may in fact derive from the specific mindset of a particular time. That does not render the Torah a purely human document; rather, it acknowledges that, even with the deepest spiritual intuitions, our understanding of God's will suffers from the inevitable limitations of human thought, which can never entirely escape its historical and intellectual contexts. As a culture of loving and painstaking interpretation, rabbinic Judaism has never taken a red pencil to the Torah. But it has frequently reread verses, often radically, and in this manner, without ever regarding the Torah as merely a 'document of its time', taking history and its changing religious, societal, economic and legal circumstances into account.

How, then, might the verses in Leviticus be interpreted? Rapoport documents classic rabbinic responses:

> The Talmud makes much of the fact that the Torah places special emphasis on homosexual intercourse as an abomination. For the term 'abomination' is used only collectively with regard to other sexual aberrations, whereas homosexual intercourse is singled out as a *to'evah* . . .[53]

He references the mediaeval Talmudic commentaries of the Tosafot and the Rosh, who read *to'evah*, 'abomination', as *to'eh attah bah*, 'you go astray in it', meaning that 'men leave their wives and pursue homosexual intercourse'.[54] Maimonides writes that 'as soon as the penetrative act has begun, if they were both adults, they are to be stoned' (a penalty which was almost certainly never imposed).[55]

This is the critical point in a key responsum of the New York Committee for Jewish Law and Standards of Conservative Judaism. Its authors' interpretation is that the Torah does not universally condemn same-sex relationships; it only specifically forbids a man from lying with another man 'after the lyings of a woman', that is, penetrative sex (Lev. 18:22). The responsum therefore holds that this, but only this, act remains prohibited.

However, the responsum argues, other forms of same-sex intimacy are only rabbinically forbidden. Therefore, the widespread principle of *kavod haberiyot*, 'the dignity of persons', can be invoked to override this prohibition. Indeed, the Talmud employs precisely this ruling in a number of other situations in which strict interpretations of Torah would be degrading to human dignity.

This approach is all the more warranted since, as is now widely recognised, a person's biochemistry may determine sexual orientation in a manner over which he or she has no control. To condemn gay people to a life of celibacy and aloneness, to deny the joy of intimacy, partnership and full family life and to withhold recognition from such relationships must then be seen as a form of cruelty.

Speaking for myself, I didn't grow up knowing many gay people and I wasn't raised, in this regard, with a particularly inclusive attitude. What has changed me is people, friends. One conversation with a gay man, who hadn't yet come out publicly, will always stay with me:

It's taken me years of anguish, but now I can finally say the blessing for 'making me according to God's will' and know that God accepts me and that I can accept myself.

I can't count the mornings, when saying my own blessings, I think of this man who struggled for decades with feelings of self-questioning and self-negation as if he, unlike others, was not created according to God's will.

The knowledge that it is our very religion, through the words read from the Torah in the synagogue, that incites or exacerbates such hurt now fills me with sorrow. It leaves people in conflict with the unchosen chemistry flowing through the heart and veins of their very self, and with the burden of feeling, or being made to feel, that they should somehow deny, excise or therapeutically 'cure' an intrinsic part of who they know themselves to be. This cannot be right. Rather, in the words of a colleague, our aspiration should be for LGBTQ+ Jews:

> ... to find other Jews with whom to make lives together ... to commit to one another and treat that committed relationship as sacred. I want to support such couples as they build *battim ne'emanim b'Yisrael* – faithful houses in Israel, and if such couples are blessed with children, through means natural or assisted by science or adoption, I will do everything I can to support the children growing as committed Jews who feel rooted and inspired by their Jewish families and tradition.[56]

Today, we read a message to my congregation before the difficult verses from the Torah are recited, acknowledging that they have:

> ... caused great, often hidden, pain and profound suffering to many of us, and to numerous people over many generations. We hold everyone to be equal and believe we are judged not by the chemistry of how God made us, but by how we conduct ourselves and how we treat one another, by the respect, faithfulness and loving-kindness we show in all, especially the most intimate, of our relationships. We want to acknowledge the injury which has been caused and to welcome and celebrate everyone across all our communities.

KEDOSHIM (19:1–20:27)

....

Don't curse the deaf; don't place a
stumbling block before the blind

My father told me that during the years of poverty in Mandatory Palestine, where he and his family fled in 1937, he would never buy art or valuables from any of his friends, even if he could have afforded it. Refugees from Nazi Europe, like himself, had arrived virtually penniless and were forced to sell off the few family heirlooms they'd been able to bring with them for next to nothing to buy food. 'I never wanted to take advantage of their distress,' he explained. Though he had little, he tried to help them in other ways.

'Those who mock the poor scorn their creator' (Prov. 17:5): these words came to mind one autumn morning while I was in the old Jewish cemetery in Bingen, near Mainz, above the River Rhine. I stood there among the dead, many of whom had been killed in the First World War or under Hitler, and now lay in this beautiful graveyard carefully tended by the local, non-Jewish community. I hadn't yet said my morning prayers, so I put on my *tallit* and *tefillin*, my prayer shawl and phylacteries, and began to recite the familiar liturgy. Then I recalled the scene in the Talmud in which Rabbi Yonatan was walking through a cemetery, the fringes of his prayer shawl trailing over the gravestones. 'Lift them up,' his companion chided him, 'lest the dead say, "Today they mock us [by keeping the commandments, which we can no longer do]. But tomorrow they'll join us"' (Talmud Berachot 18a).

The Torah forbids exploiting people's disabilities and vulnerabilities:

> You shall not curse the deaf, nor put a stumbling block before the blind, but you shall fear your God; I am the Lord.
>
> (Lev. 19:14)

Nachmanides notes that the Torah has already forbidden cursing judges and leaders; now it commands us not to mistreat even the humblest of people. Samson Raphael Hirsch comments:

> Even when the other person cannot hear and the curse doesn't have the slightest effect in producing a painful feeling in its object, the commandment still applies. It is no less forbidden to curse oneself.[57]

We have to treat not just the disabilities of others with compassion, but also our own injuries and limitations.

It's questionable whether cursing the deaf really does have no effect. People who are deaf can probably tell by our body language when they're being treating with contempt. They're likely to be especially attuned to what people are saying about them, just as we're all particularly sensitive regarding our physical or emotional weaknesses. There is also the indirect effect of how we behave: mockery teaches others to mock, fostering a culture of denigration and contempt. This is further encouraged by a sense of impunity: the blind can't see and the deaf can't hear so they'll never know it was me. This epitomises the moral cowardice that underlies so much bullying. The Torah therefore reminds us to 'fear your God', that there is indeed One who knows, and that we cannot escape accountability.

The rabbis understood the instruction not to put a stumbling block before the blind not just literally but also metaphorically as a commandment never to exploit another person's ignorance, either cynically or through carelessness:

> What does 'before the blind' mean? – Before a person blind with respect to that matter. If someone asks you for guidance, don't give unhelpful advice. Don't say, 'Set off early in the morning,' so that bandits can seize him, or, 'Set off in the afternoon,' so that he gets terribly hot. Should you then [make excuses for yourself by claiming], 'I was only giving the best advice I could!' understand that this is a matter known to the heart, concerning which [the Torah says], 'You shall fear your God, I am the Lord.'
>
> (Torat Cohanim)

Those who innocently follow guidance assumed to have been offered in good faith aren't aware that they've been framed, just as a blind person doesn't know who put the brick in their path.

The Talmud extends this principle to misleading others not just in practical but also in moral concerns:

> Rabbi Natan used to say: from where do we know that one shouldn't offer a glass of wine to a Nazirite, or a limb torn from a living animal to a descendant of Noah? The Torah teaches: 'Don't set a stumbling block before the blind.'
>
> (Pesachim 22b)

Nazirites have made vows not to consume any product of the vine; offering them a drink is either a thoughtless or a deliberately mean-spirited way of placing temptation in their path. It's like encouraging all the guests to have a drink at a gathering, knowing that some of those present are struggling with an alcohol addiction. Tearing a limb from a live animal was regarded as the apogee of cruelty; avoiding causing wanton suffering to animals is one of the seven laws the rabbis understood as universal. Offering such food to anyone, Jew or non-Jew, ignorant of its provenance would be the height of cynicism.

How far should this responsibility to avoid abusing others be extended? *Lifnei iver*, 'before the blind', is rabbinic shorthand for not exploiting people's ignorance or doing anything, even inadvertently, to mislead them into wrongdoing. But what about 'before' 'before'? Is it permitted to sell to customers who, though not making any forbidden use of the products themselves, might subsequently sell them on to less-scrupulous third parties? Are we responsible for our client's sin of setting a moral stumbling block before the blind, or does our liability end with our own immediate actions? A case in point might be the sale of military hardware. Countries frequently make arms deals on condition that weaponry will not be resold to enemy states or terrorist groups. But what if there is reason to fear that such an agreement might not be upheld? Conditions in the contract may be no more than sops to the conscience, while everybody knows where the guns and bombs are likely to end up. Is the original seller in any way answerable for the fate of the child whose legs are blown off while playing in a field, even though he himself would never have placed the mine there?

The commandment not to curse the deaf or trip up the blind does not only teach us to curb whatever sadistic impulses may take hold of us to mock others for their vulnerability or ignorance. It also requires us to take a far-sighted view of the consequences of our deeds and dealings. Even if they don't appear to hurt anybody right now, we have to consider whether they are likely to cause future damage, physical or moral, to the dignity and lives of people to whom our actions may come to feel like casual contempt.

Love your neighbour

There are three love commandments in the Torah: to love our neighbour, to love the stranger and to love God 'with all your heart, with all your soul and with all your might' (Deut. 6:5). Of these, 'Love your neighbour' is the most frequently quoted. Popularised as the quintessence of Christian teaching, it's sometimes forgotten that it originates in the Torah:

> You shall not hate your brother in your heart; you shall surely rebuke your neighbour, and not bear sin on their account. You shall not take vengeance, nor bear any grudge against the children of your people, but you shall love your neighbour as yourself, I am the Lord.
>
> (Lev. 19:17–18)

Almost always cited in isolation from its context, in the Torah love of our neighbour is the culmination of a series of laws about treating our fellow human beings justly and fairly, without resentment or rancour. Nevertheless, the word 'love' takes the injunction to a higher level, appealing not just to the will but also to the heart. It's a commandment easier said than done, as underlined by Dolittle's good-humoured parody in *My Fair Lady* in which he says that 'with a little bit of luck' our neighbour won't be in when we come home.[58]

How, though, can love be commanded? 'Love' is not an action but a feeling, and emotions can't be summoned on demand. Yehudah Aryeh Leib of Ger (1847–1905) offers an appealing answer: the heart is naturally filled with the love of God; were it not for the distractions that get in the way, we would experience that love all the time. The commandment isn't therefore to *feel* love, since it's there within us already, but rather to remove the jealousy, anger and confusion that prevent it from coming to the fore.[59] Transposing this into the realm of human relationships, here, too, perhaps what prevents us from caring more deeply for others is not the absence of good will, but the focus on self and all those other preoccupations that divert us from what's truly important.

However, most commentators take a less emotive and more down-to-earth view of what loving our neighbour means:

> 'Love your neighbour' needs to be understood as hyperbole, because the human heart won't accept that one can love one's fellow human being in the same way as one loves oneself. For, as Rabbi Akiva taught, 'Your own life takes precedence over the life of your fellow.'[60]

Nachmanides isn't trying to minimise the importance of the commandment here. He was far from unfeeling. After being forced into exile for vindicating the cause of Judaism in public disputations with Pablo Christiani in Barcelona in 1263, he wrote heart-rending letters home, full of his longing for 'the sweet and beloved children whom I brought up on my knees . . . With them, my heart and my eyes will dwell forever.'[61] Nachmanides was simply being down to earth:

[What] the Torah commands [is] that one should love one's neighbour with regard to all practical matters just as one loves oneself in wanting all that's good.[62]

Noting the often-overlooked grammatical detail that the object of the verb 'love' is not in the accusative but the dative, he stresses how we should show love *towards* others in every sphere of life:

Sometimes a person may love their neighbour in certain respects, wishing the best for them in wealth, but not in wisdom, and so forth. But if one loved them with reference to all things, one would wish one's beloved neighbour to merit wealth, possessions, honour, knowledge and wisdom without seeking to be equal to them. Rather, one's heart's desire would always be for one's neighbour to have more of everything good than one has for oneself. Scripture commands us not to harbour in our heart the corrosive feeling of jealousy, but to love our neighbours and desire them to prosper in every way, just as we want for ourselves. We should not set a limit to love.[63]

Six centuries later, Samson Raphael Hirsch (1808–88) translated this into terms that could be understood as defining the role of the citizen in a democratic state. After fighting for equal rights in the Moravian Parliament, he was called to Frankfurt, where he lived through tumultuous years culminating in the attainment of a significant degree of civic equality for Jews under Bismarck. Writing in German, meaning that his commentary was also accessible to non-Jews, he explained that loving one's neighbours has nothing to do with whether or not we happen to like them. Rather, it entails demanding precisely those same rights and opportunities for them as we want for ourselves. He opened with the same grammatical point as Nachmanides: 'neighbour' is not in the accusative but the dative:

['*To* your neighbour' means] not the person himself, but everything that pertains *to* his person, all the conditions of his life, the weal and woe which make up his position in the world. To this, his weal and woe, we are to give our love as if it were our own; we are to rejoice in his good fortune and grieve over his misfortune as if it were ours. We are to assist with everything that furthers his well-being and happiness as if we were working for ourselves and must keep trouble away from him as assiduously as if it threatened ourselves. This is something which does lie within our capacity, and which is required of us even towards somebody whose personality may in fact be antipathetical to us. For the requirement to show such love is something which lies quite outside the sphere of the personality of our neighbour and is not connected to his qualities. The reason given as the motive for this commandment is 'I am the Lord'. It is something that is expected from us towards all our fellow men in the name of God who has bestowed on all men the mutual calling of *re'a*, 'neighbour': everyone is to find and recognize in everybody else his *mir'eh*, 'the pasturage of his life' [his co-partner in], the furthering of his own well-being, the conditions for his own happiness in life. Nobody may look on the progress of another as a hindrance to his own progress, or look on the downfall of another as the means for his own rising, and nobody may rejoice in his own progress if it is at the expense of his neighbour's disadvantage.[64]

Hirsch became known for his philosophy of *Torah im derech eretz*, 'Torah together with the way of the land': commitment to the scrupulous observance of Jewish law coupled with full participation in the life of the country of which one is a citizen. He understood 'neighbour' universally, as referring to any and every fellow human being. In this he was harking back to an ancient dispute:

> 'You shall love your neighbour as yourself.' Rabbi Akiva said: This is a great principle in the Torah. Ben Azzai said: 'This is the book of the generations of man' (Gen. 5:1) is a greater principle than that.
>
> (Sifra, Kedoshim 4)

Ben Azzai's disagreement with his teacher probably derived from precisely the question of how 'neighbour' should be understood. Since the first part of the verse referred specifically to 'the members of your people', it might be thought that 'neighbour' in the second half also meant our co-religionists only. He therefore chose an unquestionably universal text in order to emphasise that the Torah's commandments about justice and compassion applied to every human being, all our neighbours without distinction.

For different reasons, the twentieth-century French Jewish philosopher Emanuel Levinas (1906–95) took a similarly universalist approach.

Disillusioned by the abstract language of western philosophy, and specifically by the inability of his teacher Martin Heidegger, who embraced Nazism, to manage the most basic of distinctions between good and evil, Levinas sought to ground ethics in the immediacy of the encounter with our fellow human beings:

> ... the *human* first emerges in the ethical face-to-face. The human emerges not as a genus or the specification of a genus, but as responsibility for the other ... The priority of ethics does not come from choosing the right theory or from choosing to be good. Rather, ethics comes first because *the other person comes first*. The priority of the other person, putting the other before the self, is what constitutes ethics in the first place ... One does not know ethics, one undergoes it. And one only undergoes it in the first person singular, in the face-to-face relation with the other person, responsibly.[65]

Levinas' intention was not to reduce the commandment to a purely humanistic plain; it is not in the abstract but precisely in our neighbour that we encounter the presence of God.

He might have applauded the entirely different explanation attributed to the founder of Hasidism, the Ba'al Shem Tov. Repunctuating the famous verse, he's said to have read it, in typically creative Hasidic fashion with no regard for grammar, as: 'Towards your neighbour – as you are, so shall I, God, be [towards you],' leading him to the understanding: 'As you behave with love towards your neighbour, so, measure for measure, will God show love towards you'.[66]

What if I don't love myself?

I often think of this disturbing verse by the Scottish poet Olive Fraser:

> I was the wrong music
> The wrong guest for you ...
> I was the wrong music
> And why I never knew.[67]

In virtually every discussion I've ever had of what must be the Bible's most widely quoted precept, 'Love your neighbour as yourself,' someone asks, 'But what if I don't love myself?' It's not just a theoretical question, an intellectual quibble with the assumptions of the text. Who's to know whether there is someone in the room who's self-harming, for whom those bleak moments when thoughts of 'I could end this' are coming daily, or who has prepared a mental plan of how and where to do it? Self-harm takes many forms, most of which don't go directly by that name: binge eating or drinking followed by self-loathing, staring at one's body in self-disgust, cutting oneself and then despising oneself for doing so.

It's important to say that the fact that we may sometimes feel this way about ourselves doesn't mean we don't care about our neighbour. There are many people who are generous and thoughtful towards others yet harbour lacerating doubts about themselves and who find in acts of kindness a release from depression and self-hate.

There are sound moral and theological responses on the importance of self-love. The classic Jewish attitude is that we are no more allowed to loathe ourselves than we are permitted to hate anybody else. We, like our neighbour, belong to God's creation; that this particular part of it is me constitutes no sufficient reason to despise or injure it. Judaism does not regard us as sole owners of our minds and bodies; rather, they are entrusted by God to our care. In this most basic sense, our lives are not our own. In the words of American rabbi Elliot Dorff:

> God lends our bodies to us for the duration of our lives, and we return them to God when we die. Consequently, neither men nor women have the right to govern their bodies as they will.[68]

Samson Raphael Hirsch may therefore be technically correct in his comment on 'as yourself':

> Self-love, too, is only a consciousness of duty. [A person] sees in himself only a creation of God, entrusted to attain that bodily, mental and moral perfection for which God has designed him and placed him in earthly existence, and for which He has given him directions in His Torah.[69]

But in our moments of misery and self-contempt, such pious words will probably sound as if they came from a different universe, full of theory and void of empathy. For self-disgust infiltrates the consciousness from below, from some Cerberus-headed fifth column within, from where it rises up to seize and threaten the mind. A high moral tone is hardly likely to help us cope with the feeling that despair is about to ambush us from behind the nearest tree. It's about as helpful as telling us to 'snap out of it'. It's liable only to aggravate the sense of shame that this is simply not how we feel about ourselves, that, once again, we've failed.

There are many reasons why we may not love ourselves. The capacity for love may be inborn, but it certainly also requires nurture. Wordsworth describes this process in *The Prelude* in ways that pre-empt object-relations psychology:

> Bless'd the infant Babe . . .
> blest the Babe,
> Nurs'd in his Mother's arms, the Babe who sleeps
> Upon his Mother's breast, who, when his soul
> Claims manifest kindred with an earthly soul,
> Doth gather passion from his Mother's eye!
> . . . Thus, day by day,
> Subjected to the discipline of love,
> His organs and recipient faculties
> Are quicken'd, are more vigorous, his mind spreads.[70]

What happens, though, if a child does not receive the blessings of such love? That's what another great poet of nature, John Clare, described when he wrote, perhaps with deliberate reference to Wordsworth:

> E'en nature frowns upon the orphan child
> On whose young face a mother never smiled
> Foolhardy care increasing with his years
> From friends & joy of every kind exiled
> Even old in care the infant babe appears
> . . .
> Love is dead
> With him & will be all his whole life long
> Lone child of sorrow & perpetual wrong.[71]

No less bad is the fate of a child subject to abuse: 'My father said he had never wanted me. So he sent me to my mother who said the same.' Such cruelty penetrates the very core of being. It lacerates the inborn faculty for love; it punctures the receptacle in the heart where the feeling is stored and nurtured that we are lovable and deserving of love. These wounds may never heal; any subsequent affirmation of goodness and lovableness is liable to drain away through these holes in the invisible membranes in which our self-worth is held. Even the conscious, intellectual knowledge that we have real achievements to our name, that there are people who care genuinely and deeply for us, may never reach the ravaged place where goodness leaks out and self-doubt and anguish pour in. To remind a person living with such inner distress that the Torah commands us to love ourselves may be not only fatuous but also cruel.

From whatever cause, many of us have tasted moments of self-disgust. We may experience this as feeling too short, too tall, not muscular, not handsome, not beautiful, not intelligent; we may take out our frustration on our body. But our real desire may be to immolate our soul.

What, then, is the point of commanding us to love ourselves? It might be wiser to say that we could begin by learning to accept ourselves. Perhaps the reference to love is a roundabout way of telling us to seek help in our times of inner bleakness. Or perhaps it implies a commandment that underlies love of both self and neighbour: that we treat people – above all, children and especially young children – in a way that enables them to absorb the awareness, subconscious and conscious, that they are lovable and deserving of our attention and affection, so that they grow up to love themselves, and others, too, in turn.

EMOR (21:1–24:23)

. . . .

On mourning

'I'm not just grieving; I feel like I've been torn in half.' We're standing in the cemetery before the funeral of my colleague's wife, who died suddenly and unexpectedly. I don't understand how people manage to go on living when their life has been a symbiosis for twenty, forty, fifty years; when their cups of tea, daily plans, long-term hopes and midnight confidences have made them as one. How does a person begin to cauterise the wound when half of their very self has been pulled away forever?

Or if it's one's child? 'I went into the room and burst into tears,' the vicar told me in the Yorkshire village where we spent a heartfelt evening exchanging notes, rabbi and priest. 'Her father gave her the bike for Christmas. She was hit by a car on her very first ride. I had no words; all I could do was weep.' This was probably the only comfort it was possible to offer.

Judaism has a precise definition of who formally constitutes a mourner. According to Jewish law, one becomes a mourner for one's mother, father, son, daughter, brother, sister and spouse. The rabbis derived the list from those categories of relatives for whom the priests were allowed to forgo their state of ritual purity and participate in the burial rites (Lev. 21:1–3). But, as they were well aware, there are others for whom one grieves. They therefore added a wider circle: whoever one mourns for, one mourns with. A grandchild mourns in the presence of her mother when her grandmother dies; a husband follows the laws of mourning when in the presence of his wife who is mourning for her father.

Yet relationships rarely fit into such neat patterns. What of the ex? Or the lover? Or the friend who was, in truth, closer than family? Or a carer? Those rings of grief encompass many more people, some of whom may be known only to themselves. As Yehudah Amichai wrote in 'The Diameter of the Bomb':

> The solitary man mourning her death
> at the distant shores of a country far across the sea
> includes the entire world in the circle.[72]

Judaism offers a close structure for the process of mourning: interment as soon as the family can gather after death, since it's considered disrespectful to leave the dead unburied; seven days of formal mourning, the first three more intense than the rest; a month of grieving, extended to a year for parents; the recitation of the Kaddish at every prayer service. The Kaddish is a litany that includes not a single word about death but much praise of God and life; it brings the mourner back into community because its recitation requires a *minyan*, a quorum of ten. Through all these stages it is a *mitzvah*, a commandment incumbent upon the entire congregation, to honour the dead and support the mourners. These rituals function like banisters on a steep, long staircase; they are something to clasp in order to prevent one from falling all the way down to the invisible bottom.

Yet grief fits no schedule and defies all timetables. Ask a mourner, 'Does it seem long since she died?' and he's likely to say, 'Like yesterday and like forever ago.' The heart does not keep linear time.

Over the years I've witnessed much pain: slow illnesses, sudden deaths, bereavements timely and untimely; people parted cruelly from those they love; young children losing parents; worst of all, parents losing their children. I never pass unthinking over the words in the memorial service: 'Our children, in whom are garnered all our love and hope.' All this is in peacetime, without the horror of war which so many generations have had to endure with the gritty determination to keep on going.

I often wonder how people whose hearts are broken can find enough love, purpose and healing to live with wounds that cannot be taken away. I know that life, which visits us with blessings, will inevitably bring us sorrow, unpredictably, unequally. We will all come to know what we don't and cannot know until it befalls us. Therefore, my hope for us all is that when a loved one with whom our life has been intertwined passes through the gateway of death where the living cannot follow and the dead cannot turn back, there will be enough love to support us amid our tears, to share our memories and to stay present with us in the silence.

I hope that in the numb days when it's hard to believe it really happened – 'It feels so unreal; I can't take it in' – there will be attentive friends who understand how fatuous it is blandly to ask, 'How are you?' I hope that when the daily rush has reabsorbed everyone into their customary preoccupations and the community has moved on to the next bereavement, festival or wedding, steadfast friends will do better than merely leaving a message, 'Feel free to ask if there's anything you need,' and say rather, 'I'm taking you out for coffee tomorrow, if you feel up to it.'

I hope that over the strange months when it's impossible to know round what corner or inside what envelope memory waits in ambush with new pain, it may somehow be possible to begin to rediscover purpose: 'That mattered to her so deeply; now it's up to me to care.'

I hope that God will speak, not the 'this happened because' God, not the 'He wanted her in heaven' God, not the rationaliser or the blamer's God, but the God of life, who talks through the moonlight when it's impossible to sleep, and through the loud wren's song at dawn; the God whose hidden, all-present language translates simply as, 'I am here.'

I hope that slowly, over years, those we love, who once held our hand, traverse into our heart and speak to us from there, retelling us their wisdom and their bad jokes, listening when we need them to hear us, and answering in the immortal language of, 'She would have said . . .' There are things my father used to say which he tells me now more often and more clearly, long after he's been gone.

I know there's no gainsaying the dread of reaching for the key to unlock the front door to the empty house, the unoccupied place at the table when out of habit one's laid for two, the shadow space beside us that accompanies us wherever we go. I know that there is always the fear that some sudden association, against which there's no protection, will trip us up and make us fall back down into the cellar of pain.

Yet I hope that, somehow, there'll be enough purpose, enough love, to keep on going and live.

Disability

Some years ago, I'd almost completed my training for the Jerusalem marathon when I suffered a back injury which left me hardly able to walk, let alone run, for many weeks. Nevertheless, I made it to Jerusalem where, unable to compete, I decided to watch the 180-metre race for children with disabilities. They set off, each with their personalised mobility aids and attended by a dedicated team of family, physios and specialist staff. Every step was an achievement. It took some of the children more than an hour to complete the course. There was probably more love, courage and endurance in evidence there than in the sum total of all the other races that day.

I therefore find it painful to read in the Torah how Moses is instructed to tell Aaron that any priest afflicted with a 'blemish' may 'not approach to offer the bread of his God . . . a blind or a lame man, or a man with a flat nose, or anything superfluous, or a man who is broken-footed, or broken-handed, or hunchbacked, or a dwarf' (Lev. 21:16–20). Even though these rules applied only to the priests, and solely while they were engaged in the sacrificial rituals of the Temple, they nevertheless convey a deeply hurtful attitude towards physical disability.

It's been argued that 'God whose ways are perfect' has the right to expect perfection from those who serve at the altar. But what human being is perfect? Isn't imperfection what characterises us most deeply? Why then preclude people from officiating as priests simply because their 'blemish' shows physically as a broken hand or leg? This feels both cruel and wrong; just as God 'is near to the broken-hearted and saves those crushed in spirit', so God is surely equally close and compassionate to those who suffer in body (Ps. 34:19). Perhaps, like Isaiah's wounded and struggling servant, it is precisely in the humility and vulnerability of our injuries that we should come before God. And maybe God's perfection lies in accepting and welcoming us as we are.

Judaism insists that every human being, irrespective of physical appearance and mental capacity, is created in God's image and is of unique value before God. There are no exceptions, as the following chastening story makes clear:

Rabbi Eleazar son of Rabbi Simeon was coming back from Migdal Gedor, the home of his teacher, riding by the riverside on his donkey. He was in cheerful mood, his heart full of pride on account of all the Torah he'd learnt. There 'chanced' to meet him an exceedingly ugly fellow who said to him, 'Peace be upon you, my teacher.' The rabbi didn't return the greeting but said loudly instead, 'What an ugly man you are! Is everyone in your town as ugly as you?' The fellow replied: 'I don't know. But go and tell the craftsman who made me, "How ugly is that vessel which you made."'

(Babylonian Talmud Ta'anit 20a-b)

The brilliant rejoinder by Rabbi Eleazar's anonymous interlocutor strikes home. To his credit, Rabbi Eleazar instantly dismounts from his donkey, prostrates himself and begs to be forgiven. After all, is not every human being God's creation?

We are unlikely to make as outrageous a remark as Rabbi Eleazar. But there are many ways in which we may be unintentionally hurtful. Often this is because of a lack of basic sensitivity, as in the classic comment, 'Does he take sugar in his tea?' What's the basis for the assumption that *he* can't speak for himself? It's a simple matter of respect to address people directly, so that they can tell us what to do. More broadly, just as it's a legal require-ment for buildings to be constructed with disabled access, so it's a moral imperative to create communities with disability awareness. Our society is on a journey towards greater understanding, more inclusive attitudes and more sensitive language around disability, but we have a long way still to travel.

The Talmud shows deep respect for people who are blind, using the euphemism *sagi nahor*, a person of 'great light', a term that became the idiomatic phrase for 'euphemism' itself. The Talmud has words for pros-theses and even for the ancient equivalent of a Zimmer frame. But it shows much less empathy for people who are deaf, probably because the culture was largely oral, and because there were fewer known ways of engaging with, and less understanding for, those with profound hearing impair-ments. A lot has been learnt since then, but we undoubtedly have much more still to learn, with opportunities to develop technologies to facilitate communication and enable us to be more fully inclusive as a community.

This societal responsibility implies a concomitant personal obligation to educate ourselves towards a basic level of sensitivity about the more prevalent challenges many people, and possibly we ourselves, may face as we go through life. A key step towards recognising God's image in every person is to learn to see, listen to and engage with the *person* in every person. I remember bending down to speak with a gentleman in a wheelchair who took one look at me and said: 'Please see me, not my disability.'

But it's hard not to see the disability, at least at first. In fact, we probably need to see it in order to see the person. But that's different from making it our central focus, unless we're a therapist or doctor. Perhaps it's in this light that we should understand the *Shulchan Aruch*'s ruling concerning which priests may officiate today. The Temple and its sacrifices are long gone, but in many synagogues across the diaspora the priests stand before the ark on festivals, and in Israel every day, to invoke God's blessing on the congregation. After stating that a *cohen*, a priest, with certain visible wounds or disabilities should not participate, the *Shulchan Aruch* continues:

> But if . . . people are accustomed to this person and everybody knows he has this blemish, then he should lift his hands (i.e. say the blessing), even if he is blind in both eyes.
>
> (Orach Chaim 128:30)

The key word is 'accustomed'. It can be hard not to see a person's disability the first time one meets them; one is tempted to see them as 'the woman in the wheelchair' or 'the man with the white stick'. Maybe this is only human. But it shows a lack of humanity to leave it at that. We need to connect with the actual person. Isn't that what we all want, to be recognised and welcomed for who we are, blemishes included, perhaps most of all when we stand before God?

BEHAR (25:1-26:2)

To whom the land belongs

'The land shall never be sold in perpetuity, for the land is mine and you are *gerim*, passers-through, and sojourners with me' (Lev. 25:23). These words define the relationship between God, humanity and the earth. We may call land ours, but we never own it absolutely, for we ourselves are only temporary, now here, now gone, while the earth belongs in eternity to God.

222

This is well expressed in the story of the two men who agree to resolve their quarrel over the ownership of a piece of ground by listening to what the land itself has to say. They each bend their ear to the earth and then compare notes. What they hear is exactly the same: 'You don't own me,' says the earth. 'I own you.'

The laws of the sabbatical and jubilee years, outlined in this portion, are among the most socially radical in the Torah. The sabbatical is far more than a year of rest for the land. If this was all the commandment amounted to, it could be understood solely as a rule to protect the soil from over-exploitation. Such measures are important: archaeological records indicate that well before the Common Era parts of the fertile crescent between the Tigris and the Euphrates had already been turned into saline semi-deserts by the excessive cultivation of wheat. Equally, the seventh year represents more than an acknowledgement that people need a break from the cease-less cycle of ploughing and harvesting. Though this is undoubtedly the case, it too is a functional explanation, as if the sabbatical were there only to serve us.

Instead, the Torah teaches that the land must rest 'unto God', with whom it has an intrinsic relationship independent of human mediation (Lev. 25:4). Like the instruction to Adam and Eve to work the earth and serve it with reverence, the sabbatical year reminds us to treat land with deep respect because it is only ours on trust and must not therefore be misused.

It may seem strange that the earth is of itself precious to God. Does soil have a soul? Yet in the daily morning prayers we bless God, 'who has mercy on the earth and is merciful to all creatures'. Such thoughts may have been only natural in an age prior to the desacralisation of nature, when God spoke from mountaintops, when the trees of the field clapped their hands and when songs were heard from the corners of the earth.

In the sabbatical year, gates must be opened and barriers taken down. For the other six years of the cycle we are entitled to exercise the legal prerogatives of ownership, but for the duration of the seventh year 'our' land is no longer solely ours. Active cultivation is forbidden, as is harvesting for sale or storage. Rather, what the land produces naturally may be taken as 'food for you, your servants, your maidservants, your hired workers, the resident and the stranger living with you, and for the domestic and wild animals in your land' (Lev. 25:5–6). Rashi summarises:

Even though I've forbidden the produce to you, I haven't forbidden you to eat or enjoy it, only that you may not behave as if you owned it. Rather, everyone is equal with regard to it.[73]

Nachmanides explains that storing the produce of the seventh year is forbidden, but we are permitted to eat it 'together with the poor, the needy and the wild and domestic animals'.[74]

Throughout the biblical, Mishnaic and Talmudic periods, people lived in close relationship with the fauna and flora of the land. They knew the needs of the oxen and donkeys on whom their livelihoods depended: 'A righteous person understands the life of his animals' (Prov. 12:10). Rich and poor lived in closer proximity. Refugees and the homeless were entitled to the corners of the fields and to glean among the harvesters. The Torah repeatedly commands their inclusion in festive gatherings. The Bible presents a society that understands the impact of drought, flooding and plagues of locusts and other crop-destroying insects. As Ecclesiastes warns, even 'the king is subject to the soil' (Eccles. 5:8, though the verse is often translated differently).

Nevertheless, the sabbatical year must have brought a rediscovery of relationships, the restoration of a deeper awareness of community and the interconnectedness of all life in its shared dependence on the earth. It would have been harder to carry on afterwards as if one neither knew nor cared who else existed. The seventh year served as a reminder that a just society must include the poor, the homeless, the lonely, the refugee and 'the wildlife in the land' (Lev. 25:7).

Congruent with this objective are the measures to restore economic equality: interpersonal loans, which the Torah stipulates must be interest-free, had to be remitted at the beginning of the sabbatical. Those forced by poverty to sell themselves into bondage could go free; their former masters were required by the Torah to provide them with a 'start-up kit' of sheep or goats, grain and oil to afford them a proper second chance (Deut. 15:13–14).

But the most radical redress was left for the fiftieth year, the jubilee, when freedom was proclaimed across the country for all its inhabitants. In the Torah, liberty and social justice are integrally connected. In the jubilee, land had to be returned to its ancestral owners to whom it was distributed when the Children of Israel conquered the country under Joshua. The wealthy had to forfeit their gains while the poor were restored to their family holdings. There were exceptions: the original owners had just one year in which to buy back houses in towns surrounded by walls, perhaps an indication of the early impact of urbanisation. But these were special cases. The jubilee was a 'return to Go', a restoration of the *tabula rasa* of equal opportunity. That, at least, was the theory. There exists no evidence that its rules were ever fully implemented; the redistribution of wealth they demanded may simply have been too great. But many of the precepts of the sabbatical were, and are to this day, observed.

It is no accident that in his magnificent encyclical *Laudato Si*, published in advance of the Paris Climate Conference in 2015, Pope Francis draws repeatedly on the Hebrew Bible, from the understanding that human beings are not masters but stewards of God's earth to the profound connection between environmental and social justice:

> I will point to the intimate relationship between the poor and the fragility of the planet, the conviction that everything in the world is connected, the critique of new paradigms and forms of power derived from technology, the call to seek other ways of understanding the economy and progress, the value proper to each creature, the human meaning of ecology.[75]

The laws of the sabbatical and jubilee years are followed in the Torah by a short list of beautiful blessings and a long litany of terrifying curses, culminating in exile from the land which then will 'through all the years of desolation keep its sabbath's rest, which you did not observe when you were in it' (Lev. 26:34–5). This is not an arbitrary act of God but a basic truth: if we fail to respect the earth and all the forms of life that depend on it, and on which we in turn depend, it will eventually cast us off into a barren wilderness devoid of sustenance. In 1991, just days before his death, the moral philosopher Hans Jonas issued the following warning:

> The latest revelation – from no Mount Sinai, from no Mount of the Sermon, from no Bo (tree of Buddha) – is the outcry of mute things themselves that we must heed by curbing our powers over creation, lest we perish together on a wasteland of what was creation.[76]

In the words of Inger Andersen, executive director of the United Nations environment programme, 'We need to make peace with nature. Because nature is what sustains everything on Earth.'[77] Put in Jewish terms, we need to end our exploitation and return to partnership with God in the work of creation.

Redemption

In Judaism, the goal of history is not freedom but redemption. Freedom itself is in service to redemption. Even on Passover, the festival of freedom, when we tell the story of the Exodus from Egypt and rejoice in our liberation from slavery, we bless God not for our freedom but for our redemption. Redemption means that every nation, person, even house and field, has its rightful place in an integrated, interdependent world in harmony with itself and with God. Redemption is the fulfilment of the messianic dream.

The Hebrew for redemption is *ge'ulah*. The classic dictionary of biblical Hebrew gives the root meaning as 'redeem; act as kinsman; do the part of next of kin'.[78] The numerous references throughout the Hebrew Bible indicate that to redeem someone or something signifies restoring it to its proper position. Almost anything can be redeemed, from an object to an entire nation. 'I shall redeem them with an outstretched arm,' God promises Moses at the lowest moment in his early career when his interventions with Pharaoh have brought nothing but increased suffering (Exod. 6:6). But redemption, especially in the later books of the Hebrew Bible, is also personal: 'My redeemer yet lives, and from my flesh I shall see my God,' cries Job, when, taunted by his supposed comforters, he wrestles with his tormented thoughts on the ash heap of his calamities (Job 19:25). Thus, the object of redemption moves from the practical and physical, through the political and historical, to the metaphysical and intangible, God's redemption of the soul. The beautiful mediaeval poem *Adon Olam*, with which many Jews begin their day at dawn and close it before sleep, expresses the faith that:

> He is my God and my life's redeemer,
> My rock and my portion in times of trouble.

These words encapsulate the hope that we are not abandoned to random mischance and future oblivion but will in the end be saved from the absolute annihilation of death.

Though God is the ultimate redeemer of both the individual and humanity, the work of redemption is not exclusively, or even chiefly, heaven's task. It begins and largely rests with humanity; it is our responsibility. It starts, literally, from the ground up, with our attitude to the soil. The land itself is never entirely ours; we are merely trustees and, as such, are not permitted to stand by while the rich get richer and the poor become destitute. If the original owners are forced to sell their ancestral holdings, it is society's role to help them buy them back. If they are unable to find sufficient funds, those properties revert to them automatically in the jubilee year. Redemption begins with social justice.

More important than the return of land is the redemption of people. The words, 'If your brother falls low,' recur three times in Leviticus 25, describing four situations of increasing adversity. In the first, 'your brother' has to sell off part of his ancestral holdings; in the second, he falls into deep poverty; in the third, he is forced to sell himself into servitude to a fellow Israelite, and in the fourth he is sold as a slave to a foreign people. In every case the Torah insists that his *go'el*, his 'redeemer' must act on his behalf. We are not allowed to abandon our brothers or sisters to subjugation by strangers, nor may we wait passively for God to help. We are required to take personal responsibility, and the sooner the better, as Rashi explains:

> Strengthen them from the moment they begin to fall. To what can this be compared? To a burden on a donkey. So long as it's still on the donkey one single person can take hold of it and right it. But should the donkey collapse under its weight, five people are not sufficient to help the animal back up.[79]

In his famous description of eight levels of charity, Maimonides writes that the greatest:

> . . . is to support a fellow Jew by endowing them with a gift or loan, or entering into a partnership with them, or finding employment for them, in order to strengthen their hand so that they will not need to be dependent upon others.[80]

In a pluralist, multicultural world, we should apply this to everyone across society as a whole.

In the non-egalitarian world of the Hebrew Bible, women had little opportunity for economic independence. A childless widow was particularly vulnerable. It was therefore the duty of her deceased husband's brother to 'redeem' her and restore her to a protected place in the admittedly male-dominated social order. In the book of Ruth, the widowed heroine, a Moabite by birth, follows her grief-stricken mother-in-law Naomi back to Israel, where she gleans among the reapers during the grain harvest. But Ruth and Naomi are not abandoned to their misfortunes. They have a redeemer, Boaz, who has not merely the privilege but also the obligation to buy back Naomi's deceased husband's ancestral holdings and return them to the family, and at the same time to marry Ruth and restore her to her place as wife and, soon afterwards, mother. Her great-grandson will be King David, the ancestor of the Messiah, indicating that human acts of redemption and loving kindness have the power to bring the ultimate redemption closer.

Exiled from the land and subject to the frequently cruel hegemony of others, for almost two thousand years redemption could only inhabit the landscape of liturgy. The word 'redeemer' features three times in the daily *Amidah* prayer: the opening blessing affirms that God will ultimately bring redemption, an entire paragraph is devoted to the affirmation that God is and shall be Israel's redeemer, and the closing meditation includes a request to find favour before God, 'My rock and my redeemer'. In the long rivalry with Christian supersessionist theology, in which Israel was seen as the abandoned divorcee and the church as God's new bride, Jews affirmed in heartfelt prayer and passionate poetry that God was, is and shall be our eternal redeemer.

Many prayers for the State of Israel today refer to the country as 'the beginning of our redemption', since the Jewish People have been brought home from among the nations to their ancestral land. Sceptical of the messianism latent in this idea, I prefer to interpret it as an expression of longing for a world in which the political and social order reflects God's vision of justice for all peoples and peace for all the earth. For redemption will only come when every nation, each person and all creatures have their fair and rightful place in an ecology of interdependence in which all life is honoured and respected.

Sadly, the fulfilment of this dream seems not only to be far off but also to be getting even more distant. Perhaps it was because they felt similarly that the editors of the Talmud included the saying, much quoted since, that the messianic age will commence at the very moment when the world is at the nadir of its fortunes. In the meantime, though, we are not permitted to desist from fulfilling our own portion of the seemingly unending task of redemption.

BECHUKKOTAI (26:3–27:34)

··

The way of chance

Beschert is a key Yiddish word but, unlike *chutzpah* or *schlepp*, it hasn't quite made it into the English language. It means:

> . . . 'inevitable' or 'preordained'. It can apply to any happening which appears to bear the fingerprints of divine providence, such as bumping into an old friend you were just thinking about.[81]

Sinclair's example is telling. People invariably say *beschert* when something good happens, especially when two people 'destined' for each other meet and marry. One's *beschert* is 'one's intended', the person ordained by God to be one's partner, to whom dating agencies from matchmakers to online apps have sought to direct romantics through the ages.

But one never hears the word used when something bad occurs, though if God directs providence when good things happen, it's only logical to conclude that painful events also come about according to God's will. The Talmud insists that we must bless God for the bad just as for the good; we have to accept pain and misfortune as part of life. But I don't believe we're asked to see bad and good as equally *beschert*. Rather, the message is that we should try to respond positively to life's misfortunes and turn them, if not into blessings, at least into experiences from which we can learn. This stops short of insisting that we explain them as part of God's intended purpose. After all, who would be so cruel as to say, 'God wanted that to happen,' on hearing that a friend had been run over? Even Job's famous response when he learns of the decimation of his family, 'God has given and God has taken away; blessed be God's name,' is, I think, more an acceptance of the fact than an affirmation that God wanted this to happen (Job 1:21). Most of us believe in providence selectively, when it suits, which means perhaps that we don't believe in it at all.

Maimonides sees danger in such a theology of convenience. He bases his comments on the word *keri*, which appears in the Torah in that form solely in Leviticus 26, where a series of beautiful blessings is followed by a frightening list of punishments if we fail to obey God's commandments. These are typical of the concluding clauses of ancient suzerainty treaties between sovereigns and their vassals which balance reward for compliance with shocking punishments for disobedience. In these terrifying verses the word *keri* comes seven times, in every instance accompanied by the verb *halakh*, go or walk: if you walk *keri* with Me, warns God, then I will walk *keri* with you, only more so.

But what does *keri* mean? Rashi tells us his teachers understood it as indicating haphazardness, hence 'walking in the way of the commandments from time to time only'.[82] The mediaeval poet and grammarian Abraham Ibn Ezra notes that some take the word to imply defiance, 'like one who hardens his heart and has no fear of being vanquished', while others relate it to *korot*, mere occurrences, pure happenstance.[83] Elsewhere in the Bible, the same root, though not the same form of it, is used to describe Ruth's 'happening' upon the field of Boaz, her future husband, to glean during the harvest (Ruth 2:3). The narrator tells us that *vayiker mikreha*, 'her chances chanced', emphasising the word in a way that makes us question whether this really is fortuitous or whether destiny is at work.

Taking *keri* in this sense of 'chance', Maimonides reads the passage from Leviticus as a warning that if we interpret the disasters that befall us as mere happenstance and refuse to see in them God's chastising hand, God will remove from us the full protection of providence and abandon us to the random cruelty of events:

> This is the meaning of [the Torah's] dictum: [And if you] walk with Me in the way of chance, then I will walk with you in the way of furious chance.[84]

In other words, the denial that the evils foretold are sent by God and their reduction to mere occurrences is itself a further sin. The unwillingness to see God's hand in what happens makes it impossible for us to take responsibility and see that it's our own actions that have forced God to respond in this manner. If we aren't prepared to be accountable before God, God will refuse to be accountable to us.

Must we then interpret terrible events as divine punishment for wrongdoing, as the authors of the curses in Leviticus and Deuteronomy warn us to do? The question becomes even more disturbing if we consider that they were writing not just as lawgivers but also as witnesses to history, since it is evident that they knew all too well from the world around them the horrors they described: starvation, disease and, worst of all, watching helplessly as one's home is destroyed and one's children taken away:

Your eyes will yearn for them all day long and there'll be nothing you
can do . . . Your life will stretch out before you; you will be afraid both
day and night . . . In the evening you'll say, 'If only it was morning'
and in the morning you'll say 'if only it was evening' because of the
terror in your heart and the sights your eyes have seen.

(Deut. 28:32, 66–7)

In my community, we read these words from the Torah on *Yom Hashoah*,
the Hebrew date for remembering the martyrs and heroes of the Nazi
Holocaust.

In bringing God into our account of history, do we deepen our
awareness of the urgency with which we need to learn from it? Or, in
attributing events to the hand of God, are we liable to end up making
facile and morally odious claims which all too often blame the victim,
like those who want to explain the Holocaust, the Asian Tsunami,
AIDS or even Covid-19 as acts of divine justice? Yet, if we are too quick
to regard disastrous events as mere misfortunes, we risk avoiding reflecting on what provoked them and may well fail to heed the warnings they
pose.

It seems both wiser and more compassionate to focus not on God but
on the human causes behind events, for as George Santayana famously
warned: 'Those who cannot remember the past are condemned to repeat
it.'[85] And, as Hugo Gryn wrote about his experiences in concentration
camps: 'The real question is "Where was man in Auschwitz?"'[86]

Yet the God question is hard to avoid. The issue may be how we put it:
'What might God want from us in the midst of all this?' may be a better
way of framing it than, 'Why is God doing this to us?' It appeals to our
sense of responsibility without risking justifying disaster in God's name
and turning God into a vindictive deity. Rather, it invites us to see God
and God's hopes and dreams for creation as one of the victims of war,
famine, disaster, evil and folly. For, again in the words of Hugo Gryn, 'I
believe that God was there Himself – violated and blasphemed.'[87]

Yet the theological legacy of a God who, in Isaiah's in-your-face phrase,
'creates evil', words so strong that the editors of the daily liturgy changed
them to 'who creates all things', haunts Jewish consciousness (Isa. 45:7,
and the daily morning service). It can be felt in every festival service when
we say, 'On account of our sins we have been exiled from our country and
distanced from our land.' The Hebrew for the opening words, *mipnei
chata'einu*, 'for our sins', has become shorthand for this entire theology of
guilt and divine retribution.

But even within the Bible itself, let alone in the Talmud and Midrash, the poetry of the Crusades and the literature of the Holocaust, this theology is frequently challenged and, sometimes forcefully, rejected. In a striking passage, God is seen as suffering too, saying every day:

> Alas for the father who has sent his children into exile, and alas for the children exiled from their father's table.
>
> (Talmud Berachot 3a)

God feels sorrow for the destruction of the Temple, God's home on earth which lies in ruins. How do humans mourn, God asks the angels? They put on sackcloth, sit on the ground and weep, the angels reply. Then I'll do the same, God replies (Midrash Echa Rabba 1:1). The God who chastises has become a God who suffers alongside us amid the cruelties of human evil. God is not just the shaper of history, but history's victim too. Almost two millennia later, the Rebbe of the Warsaw Ghetto wrote on 14 March 1942, touching on the source of his extraordinary spiritual strength:

> God, blessed be he, is to be found in His inner chambers weeping, so that one who pushes in and comes close to Him by means of studying Torah, weeps together with God, and studies Torah with Him. Just this makes the difference: the weeping, the pain which a person undergoes by himself, alone, may have the effect of breaking him . . . But the weeping which the person does with God – that strengthens him. He weeps – and is strengthened; he is broken – but finds courage to study and teach.[88]

Through all theological insights and pitfalls, one thing remains: relationship. We never abandon the fundamental premise that we and God are bound to one another. We may not understand the dynamics of the partnership, but we know that it entails deep suffering, unending hope and constant responsibility.

I shall remember my covenant with Abraham

I loved and admired my grandfather. Though he died almost fifty years ago, in my heart he is as present as ever. I inherited his kiddush cup, his *becher*, as he would have called it, a silver goblet with the Hebrew inscription, 'Remember the Sabbath day to keep it holy.' I don't know if it was one of the few items he was able to bring with him when he fled Nazi Germany. But I imagine him taking it in his hands to say the blessings on the Friday night after his release from Dachau concentration camp in late November 1938 and again at the first opportunity in that unknown country, England, where he found refuge in April 1939.

Though I use the *becher* every week; on two occasions I have held it especially close. The first was on the Friday after 9/11, when the very world seemed to shake. The second came during the coronavirus pandemic, after the Prime Minister announced the UK lockdown and our civilisation entered possibly the greatest period of unknowing since the war. Holding that cup made me feel safer; it represented faith and courage. We've lived through other troubles, it seemed to say, and together we'll come through this. Like *Shabbat* itself, of which Achad Ha'am famously wrote, 'More than Israel has kept the Sabbath, the Sabbath has kept Israel,' it embodied the resilience of the Jewish People, the strength of community and loyalty to the covenant with God, whichever way society, politics and the fickle *zeitgeist* might turn.

That word 'covenant', *brit*, occurs five times within just four verses at the end of the terrible curses near the close of Leviticus. In one single verse it is repeated three times, matched by three mentions of 'remember':

> I shall remember my covenant with Jacob; also my covenant with Isaac, also my covenant with Abraham shall I remember, and I shall remember the land.
>
> (Lev. 26:42)

I've often had the privilege of chanting that section of the Torah. The established custom is to read the blessings slowly and loudly, but the curses quietly and fast. However, when one reaches this verse, its rhythm slows one down, deepening the impact. It's as if God's arms have opened to receive us back, for, as the Torah continues:

> Even then, when they were in the land of their enemies, I didn't despise, loathe or intend to destroy them, breaking my covenant with them, because I am the Lord their God. I remembered the covenant with their earliest ancestors.
>
> (Lev. 26:44–5)

The unknown composers of the ancient New Year liturgy placed the verse containing this threefold repetition of covenant at the heart of its most moving section, the *zichronot*, the meditations on memory. To partner it they chose the words of Jeremiah:

> I remember unto you the faithful devotion of your youth, the love of your bridal days, when you followed me into the wilderness, through a land unsown.
>
> (Jer. 2:2)

I don't know if it was because of his deep love for my grandmother, with whom his bridal days were delayed for four long years on account of the First World War, or because he too had to travel with her to an unknown land, but my grandfather cherished those words. When my grandmother died, I chose them for the inscription on their shared tombstone. The words epitomised their faithfulness to each other, to the Jewish People, to goodness and justice and to God.

Brit, 'covenant', embraces a series of concentric relationships, between all life on earth and its creator, between God and all humanity, between God and the Jewish People, between individual and community and between person and person. It is frequently accompanied by the word *hesed*, meaning devoted, enduring loving kindness.

The very first *brit* is the most embracing. It is God's covenant with Noah and all living beings ever after, as they emerge from the ark into a world of barren mudflats haunted by memories of a drowned and annihilated civilisation. It's a promise between God and the earth, marked by the sign of the rainbow, that God will never again 'bring a flood to destroy all life' (Gen. 9:13–15). As Job later declares, it's a bond with existence itself:

> Who barred the sea behind double gates
> as it was gushing out of the womb?
> . . . and said, 'This far, no farther!
> Here stops your breakers' surge.'
>
> (Job 38:8, 11)[89]

God's most primal pact is with nature itself, with day and night, earth and water, land and sea: it's as if God, who, according to Midrash, had previously been making and destroying other worlds, has come to recognise that there is no Planet B and that, should the relationship with humankind and creation fail, the creator would somehow fail with it too.

God's relationship with humanity deepens with the family of Abraham. This is founded on the responsibility to share God's blessings by 'practising righteousness and justice' (Gen. 18:19). It is ratified with Abraham and Sarah's descendants at Sinai and enshrined in the *aron habrit*, the Ark of the Covenant, likened to the heart in the body. It travels with the people through all their wanderings and is symbolised, after the destruction of the Temple, by the *aron hakodesh*, the holy ark in which the Torah scroll is kept in every synagogue.

Though formalised as an objective code of laws and sealed with the promise of peace and security if obeyed and the threat of collective punishments if disregarded, this covenant is also deeply personal:

> This is the covenant which I shall make with the Children of Israel after those days: I shall set my Torah in their innermost being and write it on their hearts.
>
> (Jer. 31:33)

It is a bond with existence itself, experienced intuitively in our moments of attunement when we understand that all life is sacred and that we must do our utmost never to harm it. It is this that the three times repeated *zachor* conveys in that beautiful verse at the conclusion of the curses: a remembering, a mutual mindfulness between us and God across and despite the challenges and ravages of history, a loving partnership of tenderness and hope, a tough, enduring bond of resilience and faith.

THE BOOK OF NUMBERS
בְּמִדְבַּר

BEMIDBAR (1:1–4:20)

Counting, and making count . . .

The rabbis were not inventive about names; they called the books of the Torah after the first significant word in their opening verse. But although on this basis its formal title is Bemidbar, In the Wilderness, the rabbis referred to this fourth section of the Torah as Chumash HaPekudim, the Book of Numbers.

It's been said that readers of the Bible fall into two groups: those who like reading lists and those who don't. When it comes to Numbers, the former fare better. Why, though, does the text have to tell us the exact headcount for each tribe of Israel? The figure isn't even complete since only males above the age of twenty are included, making the section not only dull, but ageist and sexist as well. What do such uninspiring verses have to contribute to our understanding of the world?

My attitude changed when I heard a youth leader preach. 'I often have to count out numbers,' she explained. 'When you're travelling to summer camp in a convoy of coaches with 185 children on board, you really don't want to find that you've left one of them behind when you stopped for a comfort break.'

'Seriously, though,' she continued, 'what's more important than counting people is making sure that people count. Each child matters. Every one of them needs to know that they are special. Every number is a unique person.'

Her comments were pre-empted a thousand years earlier by the great eleventh-century biblical commentator Rashi, though in rather different terms. Asking why the Torah records yet another census when the people have already been counted after leaving Egypt, he answers: 'Because they're so precious to God, God counts them every hour.'[1] Developing this thought, Rebbe Yitzhak Yaakov of Biale (1847–1905) notes:

God's love is not just for the collective, but towards each and every individual, since the way one person worships differs from how others worship, therefore no comparisons should be made. God counts them every hour to stress the value and importance of each particular person.[2]

His insight has its roots in the Bible's earliest reference to humankind, the creation of each human being in the divine image. Over the millennia, interpreters have debated what 'divine image' means: intelligence, the gift of speech, conscience, imagination, power. But this is secondary to the essential point: carrying God's image is the endowment and birthright of all human beings, without exception. Yet, as a famous Mishnah notes, God created the human being *yechidi*, a word meaning both 'single' and 'unique' (Sanhedrin 4:5). Every individual is irreplaceable. Each person brings sensitivities and insights into the world which no one else can fully replicate. No two people pour out their souls in the same way.

This uniqueness brings both privileges and responsibilities. 'Every person needs to be able to say, "The world was created for my sake,"' the Mishnah continues. No one else can experience it or contribute to it in the same way.

Counting every person therefore calls for deeper skills than basic arithmetic. This is reflected in the semantic range of the verb *pakad*, translated here as 'count'. It can mean 'visit' in the positive sense of bringing blessings and deliverance, as when God 'visited' Sarah and enabled her to conceive in old age (Gen. 21:1). Conversely, it can indicate punishment, as when God 'visits' the consequences of their sins on wrongdoers, emphasising the biblical understanding that being counted entails being accountable (Exod. 20:5). *Pakad* can also signify remembering, as when Joseph insists on his deathbed that God '*pakod yifkod*, will surely visit you' and bring you up out of Egypt (Gen. 50:24). In the passive, *nifkad* indicates absence, as when David's seat is empty at the feast of the new moon, infuriating King Saul (1 Sam. 20:24–7).

Pakad isn't therefore merely a matter of 'counting off' a list of people at roll call, but of appreciating how each person counts and what their presence, and absence, can mean. The Nazis turned people into numbers and made them stand for hours in rows at *appel* (roll call) in order to annihilate their identity. The purpose of biblical counting is the exact opposite.

Writing in *The Guardian* in 2018 about the future prospects of children growing up in care, Daniel Lavelle, who was taken into care himself, described how his efforts to locate his former companions met with limited success.[3] He hadn't seen most of them since, decades earlier, he watched them driven away in police vans. Out of several whose names he still remembered, he was only able to track down two or three. But nowadays people don't just vanish without a trace. Why, then, couldn't he find them? This, he argued, pointed to something deeper than his lack of skill in discovering their whereabouts. They hadn't just fallen out of address lists; they'd disappeared from society.

The two or three he did manage to locate had somehow managed to make good. It emerged that they had one thing in common: someone, somewhere, noticed them; somebody believed in them. It might have been a teacher, a social worker or an employer, but someone had showed faith in them. As for those, and he listed five or six former mates, whom he'd been unable to find, 'I guess no one believed in [them].'

The Children of Israel are counted both at the beginning and at the close of the book of Numbers. In between come the long years of wandering through the wilderness, during which the entire generation who left Egypt dies. The book represents life's journey: on that pilgrimage we, too, have the responsibility to count. The best way to do so is by enabling others to know that they truly count. That's why I was so moved by a letter to an aid agency from a family twice displaced by the war against Ukraine:

> The boxes [you sent] were packed with great respect for human dignity. Chocolate, tea, coffee! We feel abandoned, homeless, desperate. But in your parcel there is a message. It is paramount, even when one is a refugee, to feel like a human being! Who is complete!!![4]

The Tent of Meeting was in the midst

Leaders, it's said, should lead from the front. Otherwise they're either cowards who lack the courage of their convictions or ego-trippers devoid of both courage and convictions. Leaders who fail to walk their own talk rarely engender commitment to the values they claim to embrace. The head, and feet, which remain behind the parapet, don't inspire others to cross the uncertain ground that lies ahead.

But leading from the front is not the only secret of true leadership; totalitarians also often lead from the front. It all depends whose front it is and who's set to gain from going forward. The art of leadership lies no less in understanding, representing and leading from the centre.

The description of the encampment of the Children of Israel in the wilderness is idealised. But it's not intended as an eyewitness account; it presents a picture of how the Torah believes society could and should be structured. The tents of each of the twelve tribes are grouped symmetrically around the camp of the Levites, which includes the families of Moses and Aaron. In the centre is the *Ohel Mo'ed*, the Tent of Meeting, from where God instructs Moses what to tell the people.

This focal point, where God, community and leadership meet, is situated not at the front but *betoch*, 'in the midst of' the encampment (Num. 2:17). This accords with God's initial instruction to build a Tabernacle not so that God can live inside it in secluded privacy, but so that God can dwell *betocham*, amid the people (Exod. 25:8). Similarly, the human leaders are not located apart from the community but in its midst. It's impossible to inspire and guide those from whose concerns one is set apart by physical, social and emotional distance and whose voices one doesn't hear.

The same word, *betoch*, appears earlier in the Torah when Abraham argues with God over the fate of the evil city of Sodom. Warned of its impending destruction, Abraham confronts God, 'the Judge of all the earth', for failing to practise justice. 'Maybe there are fifty righteous people *betoch* – within – the city,' he challenges: shouldn't you spare the place for their sake (Gen. 18:24)? Israeli Bible scholar Nehama Leibowitz underlines the centrality of this word, seemingly superfluous since we know what city we're talking about: only if the few are truly ' "*within* the city", taking a prominent role in public life and exerting their influence on its many fields of activity' can they make a difference. Otherwise, they may possibly save themselves but 'will certainly not possess the spiritual merit capable of protecting' their society.[5]

No one, leaders included, can fully understand how life feels to other people: 'Do not judge others until you stand in their place,' warns the great first-century BCE sage Hillel.[6] But they must at least try to be aware of the challenges that face them. The Talmud records how Rabban Gamliel, the somewhat authoritarian head of the Sanhedrin at the close of the first century, offends the popular scholar Rabbi Yehoshua. Visiting his home to offer his apologies, he's shocked by the poverty in which Yehoshua lives:

> 'I can see from the [blackened] walls of your house that you're a charcoal maker,' he says. 'Alas for the generation whose leader you are,' Rabbi Yehoshua replies. 'You know nothing about the troubles faced by students of Torah, their struggles to make a living and get enough to eat.'
>
> (Talmud Berachot 28a)

But seeing alone is insufficient; one also has to care. One can live in the middle of a town, yet with a closed door and sealed heart. People who assume the prerogative of leadership as if it were theirs by virtue of their privileged background and education are prone to ignorance of the privations, challenges and temptations that confront people who have had none of the opportunities that propelled them to the top. One of the greatest frustrations of marginalised groups is the difficulty of making their voices heard. Living like Moses and Aaron in the middle of the camp means being personally accessible; it represents true commitment, body and soul.

Even for leaders from the centre, there's a stage in the process prior to action. They have to listen, with heart and mind. One can't understand, let alone represent, the concerns of the community if one doesn't care or dare to hear what they are. The rabbis saw Aaron as such a leader, a man who 'loved peace and pursue[d] it' (Ps. 34:14), a good listener, able to understand people's troubles and help them in turn to see the points of view of others, fostering a spirit of conciliation.

Moshe Mordechai, father of the famous Abraham Joshua Heschel who marched with Martin Luther King in Selma, Alabama, was considered a master of prayer. People poured out their hearts to him. Asked why his words seemed so often to be heard on high, he replied that he really didn't know. But every day he listened to the anguish of countless people and each story made a hole in his heart. When he prayed, God saw those wounds, and, as the Psalm says, 'God doesn't despise a broken or contrite heart' (Ps. 51:17).

Leadership isn't only about deeds, or even words. Sometimes it's simply about presence; action follows later. When Queen Elizabeth II visited Aberfan in 1966, after the disaster in which 116 children and twenty-eight teachers and assistants were killed when a mountain of coal slag smothered the local school, she made a deep impact. Her presence symbolised recognition at the highest level of the grief engulfing the town. She is said to have regretted not going sooner; the experience made an ineradicable impression on her too.

Even God needs to show empathy. The rabbis ask why God chose a thornbush in which to be revealed to Moses. To show solidarity, they answered; to demonstrate the psalmist's words, 'I am with them in their trouble' (Ps. 91:15). 'I know their pain,' God tells Moses afterwards (Exod. 3:7). Presence matters. That may be why one of the most frequent rabbinic names for God is *HaMakom*, the Place, the All-Present One.

The Tent of Meeting is pitched in the midst of the encampment, not only so that God's word can radiate outwards, but also so that the concerns of the people can travel inwards and be heard. In a vital society, communication is not just from the centre to the periphery, but also from the periphery back to the centre, so that the everyday troubles of its members reach the conscience of its leaders, even God. A leadership that doesn't listen cannot lead.

Ultimately, good leadership from the front depends on good listening from the centre.

NASO (4:21-7:89)

Suspicion . . .

Mercifully, the ritual of the *sotah* fell into disuse in the first century, with the collapse of the moral order under Roman oppression:

> When murderers grew many, the ritual of breaking the heifer's neck was abolished; when adulterers grew many, the bitter waters ceased.
> (Mishnah Sotah 9:9)

The reference is to the bitter waters which the *sotah*, or 'deviant' wife, was made to drink by her husband, if, possessed by 'a spirit of jealousy', he suspected her of intimacy with another man with whom he had previously warned her not to be cloistered alone.

The entire process is truly bitter; cruel and humiliating for the wife as well as degrading for the husband, who, in resorting to such measures, also exposes himself. He takes her to Jerusalem where a priest 'brings her before God', dishevels her hair, makes her swear that she hasn't been unfaithful and warns her of the disfigurement and death that will follow should she be lying. Who else but an extremely angry or abusive husband would force his wife to submit to such a procedure? The priest then prepares the bitter concoction, mixing dust from the Temple compound with water in which God's name has been dissolved, before making her drink (Num. 5:11–31). Should she be guilty, the liquid turns to poison inside her, swelling her stomach and causing a lingering death. If she's innocent, the potion makes her conceive, whether she wants to be pregnant or not.

The account concludes with words that serve only to emphasise the imbalance of power between husband and wife: 'The man shall be innocent of sin; the woman shall bear her iniquity' (Num. 5:31).

In a gesture towards lessening the inequality, the Talmud reframes the verse to mean that the entire ritual will only work if the man concerned is himself entirely innocent of wrongdoing. Only then will the bitter waters, acting as God's agents, expose his wife to the consequences of her misconduct (Sotah 47b). It's a small indication of the direction of travel of rabbinic legislation in limiting the degree of control men had over women, and in trying to ensure that wives had some, if by no means equal, rights.

A frequently quoted passage suggests that the outcome of the process was a return to marital harmony:

> See how great is peace! For God, whose name may not be erased, allows it to be dissolved in the bitter waters for the sake of restoring peaceful relations between husband and wife.
>
> (Midrash Yalkut Shimoni to Psalms, no. 711)

But it's hard to see how this could be the case. How would a woman forgive such treatment? Why should she want to, after being humiliated in such a brutal manner? Would the 'reward' of pregnancy, leaving her even more dependent on the man who had maltreated her, be sufficient? It's hard to see what good the entire ritual could possibly achieve. Paradoxically, one wonders if a wife might ever resort to the process deliberately, if cunningly, in order to expose her husband for his jealous and threatening behaviour and force him to acknowledge the God-given, irrefutable proof of her innocence. Even then, though, would the man actually believe the outcome, or might the 'wind of jealousy' that overcame him in the first place return, probably sooner rather than later? As Emilia wryly tells Desdemona in Shakespeare's *Othello,* men 'are not ever jealous for the cause, but jealous for they are jealous'.[7]

As if all this was not bad enough, the Mishnah introduces a further factor which, though it sounds supportive towards the woman, is likely to have had the opposite effect: 'If [the wife] possesses merit, her sentence is suspended. There is a degree of merit which causes suspension for a year, or for two years, or for three' (Mishnah Sotah 3:4).

This effectively undermines the entire purpose of the whole ugly process, which is intended to be definitive. Now, though, the husband, and any other witnesses, are free to say, 'Of course she's guilty; only she's scraped together enough good deeds for the effects of the waters to hold off for a while. Just wait and see.' It's precisely for this reason that Rabbi Shimeon objects to his colleague's notion of deferred outcomes, questioning how an innocent woman is then supposed to be able to clear her name (Mishnah Sotah 3:5).

The Mishnah's argument probably conceals an altogether different concern. The *sotah* ritual depends on the belief that God is 'hands on' and engages directly in human affairs down to the last domestic details of their private lives and, at least in the Temple, responds promptly in real time. The waters therefore put not just the woman but also God on trial. If a woman were to drink and nothing happened, this could be construed as public disproof, perhaps not of God's existence, but of God's involvement in the affairs of this world.

It's possible that the rabbis of the Mishnah no longer believed in such an interventionist God – or at least wanted to avoid putting the question to the test. The Mishnah notes not that the rabbis formally abolished the rite but that 'the bitter waters ceased'. The reason given is that public morality and the rule of law collapsed in the chaos of the Roman wars. But maybe the ritual was also suspended because the miseries of the Roman persecutions provoked a profound rethinking of God's relationship with humanity and history.

Behind the *sotah* process lies a challenging question: can suspicion ever be removed? Is there ever any smoke without fire? The charges levelled by men against women have varied through the ages, from adultery to witchcraft. Today, in a somewhat less unequal world, men are often, and frequently rightly, accused of misconduct. As the *#MeToo* movement has proved, accusations of abuse are all too likely to be accurate, and it is essential that victims, overwhelmingly but not exclusively women, are supported in speaking out.

But what happens if they're not true, if the press and social media destroy an innocent person's reputation? It's easy to brand someone an abuser. Truth often becomes hostage to popular presumption. Trying to halt the momentum of fake narratives once the crowd has got hold of them is as futile as King Canute's attempt to beat back the tide. It's all but impossible to undo the reputational damage.

The rabbis labelled slander, including casting aspersions by telling truths in a manner intended to imply the opposite or to provoke negative reactions, as *lashon hara*, the evil tongue. They added that, even when false accusations are withdrawn, they leave *avak lashon hara*, the dust of the evil tongue, in their wake (Tosefta Avodag Zarah 1:4). The taint remains.

At least the ritual outlined in the Torah forces the drama of suspicion and vindication to be played out in the structured environment of the Temple, managed by priests (all male!) under the arbitration of God. For centuries since, up to and including in our social media age, such accusations are cast before the fickle judgement of public prejudice.

But the Mishnaic qualification undermined the potential of the ritual to clear the woman's name. People would very likely not say, as she left the Temple precincts unharmed, 'She was innocent all along,' but rather, 'Of course she's guilty. Just wait, time will prove it; she'll be dead inside five years.' Since lifetimes were shorter and mortality rates high, she might well have been gone by then, dying in her humiliation, watched by an unforgiving husband.

May God bless you and keep you

May God bless you and keep you;
May God's face shine upon you and be gracious to you;
May God's face be turned towards you and give you peace.

(Num. 6:34–6)

The priestly blessing, consisting of just fifteen words in the Hebrew, is beloved across Judaism, Christianity and beyond. It is with these three verses that parents and grandparents bless their children on Friday night before the *Shabbat* (Sabbath) meal. I see in my memory my grandfather raise his hands, unsteady with age, and place them on my brother's head and mine before saying the Hebrew words with his heavy German accent. I recall, too, how on the eve of Yom Kippur in what we knew was probably the last year of my father's life, I knelt by his side while he put his hands on my head, because he was no longer able to stand. That blessing is with me still. 'The power of our blessing is not diminished by illness or age,' wrote Rachel Remen. 'On the contrary, our blessings become even more powerful as we grow older. They have survived the buffeting of our experience.'[8] Even now, when they are long gone from this world, my father and grandfather touch me through those ancient rites.

Blessing is a mystery. The word *barekh* has the same root letters as the Hebrew for knees, *birkayim*; the connection may be that blessings used to be recited on one's knees, metaphorically as much as physically, because blessing requires humility and generosity of heart. *Barekh* may also be related to *berakhah*, a pool of water. It's been suggested that a *berakhah* was so named because it was to the local well that the camels would be taken to drink and kneel down to rest. Whatever the case, there is a spiritual kinship: a *berakhah* is an appeal to the source of life, a call for the life-giving spirit to flow into our minds and fill the cistern of the heart. The Zohar, the key body of Jewish mystical texts, imagines a well on high, a great reservoir of intuitive knowledge and creative possibility, from which the sacred vitality overflows, sustaining all existence (Zohar III, 70a).

To say a *berakhah* is to make a connection with God, the source of all life. But a blessing also carries something of the tone and qualities of the person who offers it. This balance between the transcendent and the personal is apparent in the Torah's seemingly contradictory instructions: God first tells the priests, 'Thus shall *you* bless the Children of Israel,' but continues, 'You shall place my name upon [them] and *I* will bless them' (Num. 6:23, 27). Who, then, is doing the blessing, God or the priests? Both, explains Rashi: 'I,' says God, 'will affirm what the priests say.'

In other words, the *cohanim* speak the words and God ratifies them. But, adds the *Siftei Chachamim*, a commentary on Rashi's commentary by Rabbi Shabbetai ben Joseph Bass (1641–1718), it's not just God who gives the blessings, otherwise what point would there then be in involving the *cohanim*?

This corresponds to my own feelings. It's my father's blessing I still feel each Yom Kippur. I think of him specifically, a refugee in Jerusalem in his teens, then a parent in his thirties walking three miles home through Glasgow snow because the last train had left before he finished his evening classes to gain his degree. I see him, soon afterwards, a young widower, at the *Shabbat* table of the friends who looked after us, saying that blessing through which this resilient heritage is transmitted. It's not just God's grace but my father's strength of character, too, which is conveyed to me through those ancient words.

'May God bless you' connects us with the sacred energy within creation. It's a call to receptivity, an appeal to faithfulness towards life, so that life in turn may nourish us with its companionship. 'And keep you,' is a petition for protection from harm. But with a small play on words it can be stretched to mean, 'May God make you a keeper.' In the Torah, being a keeper involves taking care of other people's possessions and sometimes their persons. It requires us to do the opposite of Cain who, with his notorious denial, flung back at God his rejection of any responsibility: 'Am I my brother's keeper?' (Gen. 4:9). If we want God to keep us, we must become partners with God in keeping others, by showing generosity and kindness and by helping to protect and support them during life's crises and afflictions. As Arthur Green writes:

> The flow of life as we experience it is morally blind. But as humans we are here to direct that flow of life, to lead the divine energy in the world in the direction of compassion.[9]

It is through this capacity for compassion that we become a *shomer*, a guardian and trustee of the life around us.

The second verse, 'May God's face shine upon you and give you favour,' is an appeal for inner illumination, a call to nurture the sacred light that dwells within us and constitutes our deepest endowment as human beings:

> Rabbi Nathan explains that this refers to the light of the divine presence. [God will be] 'gracious to you,' [granting you] understanding, insight, moral intuition and wisdom.
>
> (Bemidbar Rabbah 41)

I imagine this light to be like the glow that illumines the sombre colours of so many of Rembrandt's portraits with such mysterious power. It's that radiance which transforms the faces of certain elderly people, a luminosity in and around the eyes expressing a balance of wisdom and kindness formed of experience and humility. This second part of the priestly blessing is an appeal to that light, a call for it to shine upon our path and be our guide.

'May God give you peace' is an invocation to *shalom*, harmony, a prayer both to receive it and to have the gift of sharing it. No blessing is more sought after, or more elusive. As the world stands, we cannot hope for a life free from conflict. The rabbis disapprove of those who try to avoid all stress and contention; they want the benefits of heaven while still here on earth. Ours is a world of struggle in which we are not at liberty to remain detached. This blessing is a plea for equanimity, for help in finding and maintaining an internal space of stillness despite the turbulence of fortune. We can't expect to inhabit that place all the time; we have to engage with the issues of our society. We're forbidden to ignore injustice and cruelty, to stand aloof from the suffering of others. To sustain us we need the ability to return to a place of inner sanctuary. Finding our path back to it is not easy; at times we may feel that we've lost the way there forever. But *shalom* is one of God's names, and a place of *shalom* within us is our own personal temple, our meeting place with God, which cannot be defiled. That's why *shalom* is the ultimate petition, concluding and including all other blessings.

Hearing God's voice

One has to be patient. After all the ceremony, gift-giving and tally-taking comes the moment of intimacy that makes it all worthwhile.

Chapter 7 of the book of Numbers is the longest and most repetitive in the entire Torah. It recounts in precise detail the offerings of the heads of each of the twelve tribes: one silver bowl, one silver basin and one golden spoon; one ox, one ram, one yearling lamb and one he-goat; plus, for the peace-offering, two more cattle, five rams, five he-goats and five more yearling lambs. This list is repeated twelve times in identical detail, after which the reader is not spared the sum totals of all the sacrificial animals and accoutrements for the altar.

But then comes that moment. The formalities are finally over and Moses enters the Tent of Meeting to encounter the presence of God. Midrash plays on the word, 'On the day Moses *kallot*, completed, setting up the tent,' reading it instead as *kallat* – 'On the day Moses was bride' (Num. 7:1). Moses and God are alone together at last, like bride and groom after all the speeches are done and they're finally left to themselves:

> Moses went into the Tent of Meeting to talk with [God] and heard [God's] voice speaking to him from above the cover that was over the ark of testimony, from between the two cherubim; and God spoke to him.
>
> (Num. 7:89)

Rashi explains that God's voice could not be heard outside the tent; it ceased at the entrance. It was audible only to Moses as God addressed him in the privacy of their shared holy space.

But this isn't exactly what the text says. God doesn't speak directly, even to Moses. *Medabber*, 'spoke' is not punctuated in the usual manner; instead, the first vowel is lengthened, giving *meedabber*, the reflexive form of the verb. God indeed speaks, but not specifically to Moses, at least not initially. What Moses hears, or rather overhears, is God speaking to God's own self. As the sixteenth-century Italian rabbi Ovadiah Sforno explains:

> 'Speaking': with himself. It's in this manner that God imparts knowledge and goodness to others through a limitless overflow of generosity, through which God's work is revealed in the making to each person

according to their understanding. This is the meaning of all speaking referred to in the Torah, whenever it says, 'And God spoke.'[10]

It is this divine soliloquy that Moses overhears. He is privileged to listen in on God's communication with God's self, the sacred speech of the divine in its eternal utterance.

What does it mean to listen in this way? This is exactly the issue Rebbe Kalonymus Kalman Shapira addresses when he considers why God's voice, which can be heard throughout creation, remains inaudible to so many. He begins by noting that hearing requires an affinity of spirit:

Since speech comes from the soul . . . it is only when the listener is able to understand the soul of the speaker and is close to him in spirit that he truly hears. If that is not the case, then he will be unable to comprehend even the speech of a being lesser than himself. We see this with the speech of animals and birds, which are lesser creatures than human beings, yet humans don't understand them, even though other animals and birds do. This is because their souls are close to each other; making them receptive to and able to understand each other. This is not the case with regard to humans who, although higher than them, are spiritually far removed from them and in consequence can't comprehend them. Hence there is nothing surprising about why people don't hear the call of all the worlds . . . and of all the angels who perform God's will and cry out constantly, 'God is one and God's name is one' . . . This is because people don't focus their attention on listening. But those whose spirit is firmly attached to God's holiness, who are not given over to material things and whose sole desire is God, their souls are attuned to holy speech and the speech of holy beings, and they do hear their voices.[11]

Perhaps some people can hear God speaking to them personally and directly. But it's wise to be extremely cautious, noting the Talmudic pronouncements that the age of prophecy is long over and that we pay no attention to voices from heaven. Scepticism is essential in trying to distinguish between what is truly sacred and what is loudly claimed in God's frequently abused name.

What we may be privileged to hear, though, what we might apprehend in moments of attentiveness, is God's voice speaking to itself. Always humbling, always opening us to new depths, this is God's speech as it can be known to us humans.

Maybe that was the 'fine silence' heard by Elijah after the tumult of the thunder and earthquakes, which made him cover his face with his mantle as he felt himself interrogated in the depths of his being by the presence which he experienced as asking him, 'What are you doing here, Elijah?' (1 Kgs 19:13).

The poet Chaim Nachman Bialik overheard this same speech in the heart of the forest, nature's holy of holies concealed behind the mantle of the great trees, which he describes in the very terms used in the Torah about the sanctuary:

> There exists a silent, wordless language, a speech of secrets,
> It has neither sound nor syllable, but shades within shades of
>   meaning,
> And magical charm, and images of splendour, and hosts of visions.
> It is in this language that God is revealed to those his spirit chooses,
> And in it the Master of the World muses his musings.[12]

But what does such a language actually convey? What of any practical bearing does God communicate to Moses? God is mentioned as speaking not once but twice in that final verse of chapter 7. The first instance is reflexive but the second is direct: 'God spoke to him.' However, it's at precisely this point that the chapter ends, so what exactly did God say? 'The primary content of revelation is revelation itself,' wrote the German theologian and philosopher Franz Rosenzweig in a famous exchange of letters in the 1920s with his contemporary Martin Buber. '"He spoke" is already the beginning of interpretation.'[13]

The entire history of religion may be summarised as the endeavour to give content to that voice. We overhear God speaking and know we are commanded. So what must we do? How do we live that in the world? That's where human responsibility begins.

BEHA'ALOTECHA (8:1–12:16)

The hidden light

'*Beha'alotecha et hanerot* – When you kindle the lamps.' God commands Aaron and his descendants to care for the seven-branched menorah in the

Tabernacle. But 'kindle' is an imprecise translation; what the Hebrew really says is, 'When you cause the lamps to ascend.' A brief midrash extends this instruction to life itself: 'Look after the lamps,' says God, because 'My lamp is in your hands and your lamp is in mine' (Devarim Rabbah 4:4).

To the mystics, every life is a temple in which the light of divinity burns, the *or haganuz*, the hidden flame that constitutes the spirit of every breathing being. The Kabbalists, the Jewish mystics, who tended to see the immanence of God in all things, would agree with Gerald Manley Hopkins that:

The world is charged with the grandeur of God.
It will flame out, like shining from shook foil.[14]

This sacred light is of sufficient strength to illumine the heart and conscience of every human being. We are all responsible for its care. How we look after that light, in ourselves, in one another and in all existence will determine the very destiny of this vital, interdependent and beautiful world that, in the words of the Midrash, is 'in our hands' and falls, often tragically, beneath our unreflecting power. We can belittle, degrade, uproot, maim and destroy; or we can nurture, respect, inspire and love. We are all, figuratively speaking, descendants of Aaron, tasked with causing the lights to ascend, with protecting and enabling the sacred flame to shine in all life. The authority is delegated to us to expand or diminish God's presence in the world. There can be no greater responsibility than this; even God, in some sense, falls within our power to hurt.

Etty Hillesum, the young Dutch woman whose writings under Nazi occupation are among the most moving documents from the Holocaust, understood this truth intuitively. When she had to leave her beloved Amsterdam, she didn't blame God for failing her but challenged herself not to fail God:

Tonight for the first time I lay in the dark with burning eyes as scene after scene of human suffering passed before me . . . [O]ne thing is becoming increasingly clear to me: that You cannot help us, that we must help You to help ourselves. And that is all we can manage these days and also all that really matters: that we safeguard that little piece of You, God, in ourselves. And perhaps in others as well . . . You cannot help us but we must help You and defend Your dwelling place inside us to the last.[15]

It was this inner light that led her to spend her time in the transit camp at Westerbork comforting and supporting everyone around her, before she too was deported east.

But it is not only God's sacred lamp that burns in our world. Fires of destruction flare out across the globe, seemingly outshining the *or haganuz*, the hidden light within. My grandfather experienced this tension at first hand. On 10 November 1938, the morning after Kristallnacht, the Night of Broken Glass, he was summoned by the Gestapo to the Hauptsynagoge in Frankfurt. Flames soared from the building; no one dared extinguish them. Yet, as he walked through the crowd of onlookers, he overheard people whispering that in the Westendsynagoge, where he'd served as rabbi for almost thirty years, the interior had been destroyed by rioting Nazis but the Eternal Light still burned. They took this as a sign from God.

My grandfather found himself caught at the intersection between two kinds of flame: the fires of destruction and the inextinguishable light of God's presence. Through the 1930s and 1940s both burnt across Europe. Devastating conflagrations engulfed synagogues throughout Germany. Their blaze crossed the Channel in the Blitzkrieg, burning whole districts of London and many British cities. They soared obscenely into the sky from the crematoria by the gas chambers. Eventually they came full circle to ravage the towns of Germany. When, after eleven years' absence, my grandfather returned to his beloved Frankfurt, he wandered through 'the unrecognisable streets and squares, while from the broken, hollow windows, horror stared'.

Yet even through those devastating years, the light of God's presence continued to burn too. It glowed in the heart of the British Consul General, Robert Smallbones, through whose interventions tens of thousands of victims of Nazism were enabled to receive transit visas to Britain, my family included. He wrote of his shame when once, overcome by exhaustion, he fell asleep at his desk and missed the opportunity to sign even more life-saving affidavits. It shone in the courage of Frank Foley, the British passport control officer in Berlin and undercover agent, whose Christian principles led him to detest Hitler and determine to help as many Jews escape Nazi Germany as he was able to help. Refusing to let the powers-that-be prevent him, he issued thousands of visas for China, because, he reputedly said, adapting an anti-slavery slogan, Jews had the right to choose their own fate and would rather die free in Shanghai than as slaves in Dachau.

It illumined the debate in Parliament, when Britain granted entry to an unlimited number of children in what became known as the *Kindertransport*.

It shone in the words of the MP for Gower, David Rhys Grenfell, who testified to the queues of despairing people outside the passport offices of Germany and Austria, waiting as if before the tribunal that would judge them for life or for death. It burned in the actions of those officials who endeavoured to process their desperate applications with courtesy. My grandparents described the British Consulate in Frankfurt as an island of humanity in a sea of violence and contempt. It flared in the hearts of Jewish leaders, Quakers, Christadelphians, good people of all faiths and none, who rescued children, taking them into their own homes.

Those same two fires burn today. The searing flames of destruction simmer in the souls of those who preach hatred of Muslims for being Muslim and of Jews for being Jewish, who torch the churches where people of colour gather, and who fan the populist fires of resurgent racism and xenophobia. They soar in the minds of those who order the bombings of civilian targets, schools and hospitals.

But God's Eternal Light also burns in the daily actions of those who create food banks and warm spaces, who shelter the homeless, who share their houses with refugees, who run drop-ins and havens for asylum-seekers, and who reach out their hands to those of different faiths, hoping they will be taken in trust and fellowship. It shines in the vision of those who care for the integrity of rivers, mountains and forests, restoring the habitats of animals, birds and insects and saving the life of whole regions of the planet. Every generous deed, every act of goodness, even the most ordinary act of in-the-street kindness, is a curling of the fingers in protection around the lamp of God's flame, whether in a friend, a frightened child or a wounded animal.

Which is more powerful: the flame of creation or the fire of destruction? I imagine asking my grandfather: 'When you stood on that November morning between those two flames, which did you think was the stronger?'

I picture him quoting that ancient midrash, '"My light is your hands," says God,' before turning to me and adding simply, 'It's up to you what you do with it; the choice is yours.'

'God, please heal her, please'

Few prayers are as heartfelt as those we say for people we love when they're ill. A father told me how, when his daughter lay sick in the crisis hours of meningitis, he sat by her bed all night repeating over and again the words of the *Shema*, clinging to them like a banister: 'God, you are one.'

The coronavirus pandemic demonstrated how fragile our health is. Many of us turned in our anxiety to prayer for critically ill relatives, for the staff caring for them and for ourselves. 'Pray for her,' is a frequent plea. In Jewish tradition one uses the matronymic when praying for the sick, to arouse God's mercy. If we don't know people's names, we assume God understands to whom we're referring. We include them among 'the sick of Israel and all nations', because prayers for a group are considered more powerful than those for one individual alone. This reminds us, too, that those who are ill must be embraced by the community and not left to suffer in isolation. We are required not just to pray but to offer practical help and companionship as well.

Moses' intercession for his sister Miriam after she's struck down with leprosy forms the basis of Jewish prayers for the sick to this day. Nothing could be more succinct and to the point: *El na refa na lah*, 'God, please heal her, please':

> No one prayed longer than Moses when he stood in supplication on Mount Sinai for forty days and forty nights, and no one prayed more briefly than Moses when he interceded for his sister in just five words.
>
> (Talmud Berachot 34a)

When a prayer is as heartfelt as this, there's no need for many words.

In the Torah and Talmud it's taken as given that sickness and health come from God. The terrifying curses in Leviticus and Deuteronomy list shocking illnesses among God's threatened punishments. But if we 'listen to God's voice and obey God's laws', we are promised that God will not inflict us with devastating plagues, 'for I am the Lord, your healer' (Exod. 15:26). The great thirteenth-century commentator Nachmanides, himself a physician, explains that if we follow God's commandments we will be healed by divine providence; however, should we fail to do so, we will be left at the mercy of the fallible skills of the medical profession. Since we're all imperfect, we all fall into the latter category.

Nevertheless, many of us turn to God as well as the doctor in times of illness. In communities across the world special prayers for those who are sick are said on *Shabbat* and at festivals; in some synagogues congregants are invited to say out loud the names of family and friends for whom they're concerned. Those who are ill are encouraged to make their troubles known 'so that the community can pray for them' and support them (Talmud: Mo'ed Katan 5a).

Prayers for the sick form part of the daily service too:

Heal us, God, and we shall be healed, save us and we shall be saved. Send complete healing for all our afflictions, for you, God, are a faithful and compassionate healer.

This wording is based on Jeremiah's plea: 'Heal me, O Lord, and I shall be healed; save me and I shall be saved' (Jer. 17:14).

But Jeremiah's words are changed into the plural: as in almost all Jewish prayers, we turn to God not just for ourselves but also on behalf of the whole community. The mystics understood us as praying for God, too, because God suffers in all our suffering and may therefore also need healing.

But for what are we actually praying? The obvious answer is that we want God to make us better. The words are not merely symbolic: as Jewish biblical scholar Marc Brettler writes, 'the non-metaphorical sense of "heal" is clearly intended'.[16] We don't want this illness to get us; we don't want to die. Even those of us who don't believe in a hands-on God capable of intervening in the course of nature are liable to suspend our disbelief at such times. The rational part of us may know that the world doesn't work like this, but that doesn't stop us from hoping. We want the treatment to work; we want those we love to get better. And who knows what can happen? Everyone has their miracle story: 'The doctors said there was no hope, but people the world over prayed for her, and here we are, three years later. Faith can achieve anything . . .'

Yet I worry whenever an anxious relative asks me, 'If I pray harder and keep the commandments, will God cure my mother?' or when I hear, 'I prayed each day, but it made no difference. Religion has failed me.' The Torah's and prayerbook's depictions of God as rewarding and punishing invite just such a theology of magical thinking. But it's liable to leave us feeling let down in the moments of our greatest vulnerability. In such circumstances, a sense of disappointment is more than understandable; loss of faith, not just in a wonder-working God but also in the purpose and meaning of life, is often a part of grief.

However, there is another way of understanding our prayers for healing. I hear it when I'm asked a different kind of question: 'How can I find the strength to support my family through this dreadful illness?' The fact that prayer may not produce cures doesn't mean that it has no value. It can enable us to reclaim our inner stillness and find the resilience to keep going. It can help us discover the grace to appreciate the care we receive and the generosity to remain grateful for the blessings life has brought us.

As Gale Warner wrote in her account of living with lymphoma, it can bring us a deep sense of companionship:

> Prayer is a call to partnership, a conscious placing of our spirits and intentions in alignment with the creative spirit. This call to partnership is always noticed. It affects the whole. It can help tilt the balance, draw forth hidden resources. So prayer – humble, undemanding, simple prayer – is always worth it.[17]

Our prayers may be for trust, hope and steadiness of heart, for the strength to help others in their troubles, or simply for God to be with us. The Talmud teaches that God's presence rests above the pillow of the sick. A beautiful night-time prayer speaks of God's light going before us, God's strength travelling beside us and God's healing following behind us. Such prayers can bring us spiritual and emotional, if not physical, healing:

> The business of prayer is not cure – that is for the physicians – but forgiving oneself, discovering acceptance, and thereby finding healing. Healing, then, is a psychospiritual state wherein we . . . realize that holiness is everywhere, perhaps even in our own infirmity.[18]

Prayers of this kind, for the insight and stamina to learn to live with our vulnerabilities yet experience life as sacred, are likely to be relevant to us all at some point in our lives.

When the end approaches, relatives often ask for prayers. But, as a daughter whose mother was dying once whispered to me, 'Not that kind of prayer; we've passed that place. Something appropriate, please.' The simplest formulation I ever heard was, 'May God be with her on her journey.' Since then, I've said those words many times.

'Because of the Kushite' – racism

Is it 'black *and*' or 'black *but*'? The letter *vav* prefixed to a Hebrew word can mean either 'and' or 'but'. So how should the verse in the Song of Songs be translated: 'I am black *and* beautiful,' or, 'I am black *but* beautiful, O daughters of Jerusalem' (Song 1:5)?

It's a shameful contradiction that faiths rooted in sacred texts proclaiming the oneness and indivisibility of God are brazenly abused to sanction racism and hatred. This is most lethal when religious zealotry is coupled with political power and weaponised to justify pogroms, rape, torture, burning at the stake, shooting and bombing in the name of the very God who is desecrated by such actions.

It is deeply dangerous when bigotry takes the form of 'merely' verbal abuse. Habitually casting people as unwanted, as a threat, as less than human, prepares the way for lynching and killing. Supposedly 'low-level', polite society prejudice is equally unacceptable. With its tacit assumptions about the inferiority of others reinforced by 'harmless' jokes, jibes and casual denigration based on the unspoken assumptions that 'everybody thinks like that' and 'we don't mean any harm, really', it forms the basis of systemic racism and sexism. Being mocked and denigrated is an all too familiar experience to many who belong, or are even thought to belong, to a different ethnicity or religion, who look different, who are black or people of colour. Antisemitism is rife.

Faiths are especially at risk of giving sanctuary to prejudice. Pulpits are powerful and dangerous places when abused to incite hatred. Like politicians, religious leaders must eschew the temptation to build identity by consciously or unconsciously creating a 'them', a hostile 'other', in order to unite and forge a coherent and strong 'us'. It's not enough to mouth rejections of such behaviours, refuting them as 'not the true' Judaism, Christianity or Islam. They must be confronted unstintingly, without exceptions or excuses.

Religions based on holy books face particular challenges. Sacred texts, including the Bible and Quran, contain not only edifying teachings but passages that appear to incite, or at the very least condone, bigotry and hatred towards nonbelievers and followers of different faiths. Even when it is understood that such texts need to be read in their historical context and must not and perhaps never were intended to be taken literally, familiarity is likely to inure us to their implications. We may simply never have thought about them from the point of view of the 'others' they explicitly or implicitly condemn. The relevant passages need to be interpreted with frankness and courage, and their assumptions made conscious and challenged.

My wife and I were visiting a cathedral when it was announced that Evensong was about to commence. Since we often find services of other faiths moving, we decided to stay. During worship, a scriptural passage was read with uncomfortable implications about Jews. 'Of course, they don't understand it like that,' I reassured myself, while thinking, 'Perhaps they do.' This troubling experience left me asking myself how my own liturgy might make others feel. A recent report on Racial Inclusivity in the Jewish

Community advises rabbis to be constantly mindful of the questions, 'Who comprises my audience?' and, 'Does my message take into account [their] sensitivities?' But this doesn't go far enough; the fact that they are not present in the pew is no excuse for denigrating others. The audience is always all humanity. Pejorative generalisations are a pernicious form of *lashon hara*, evil speech, whether said in the presence or absence of those they offend. 'Nothing about us without us,' is a salutary warning.

One of the Torah's most difficult texts is Numbers chapter 12, when Miriam and Aaron speak against Moses 'because of the *Kushite* woman he had married' (Num. 12:1). The Biblical Dictionary defines *Kushi* as the 'Land and people of the southern Nile-valley, or Upper Egypt'.[19] Hence the obvious implication that Miriam has, for some unstated reason, decided at this belated stage to object to the fact that Moses' wife, Tziporah, the daughter of Jethro the Midianite priest, is black.

Rabbinic commentaries are revealing in their tactical avoidance of the issue. The *Sifrei Bamidbar*, the ancient rabbinical midrash on Numbers, probably compiled in the third century, understands Miriam's complaint not to be aimed not at Tziporah herself, but at Moses, for refusing to be intimate with his wife. Noting that her sister-in-law doesn't wear jewellery, Miriam asks her why. Because, Tziporah answers, ever since God began to speak to him, Moses has shown no interest in such things, a clear critique of those who put religion first and family last. The *Sifrei* now turns to the significance of *Kushit*: 'This teaches that everyone who saw [Tziporah] acknowledged her beauty.'[20]

Rashi explains:

Everyone acknowledged her beauty, just as everyone agrees that a *Kushi* is black. The numerical value of '*Kushi*' equals that of *yefat mareh*, 'beautiful in appearance'.[21]

The super-commentary *Siftei Chachamim* suggests Rashi's reasons:

[Moses' wife] wasn't in fact a *Kushit*, an Ethiopian, but a Midianite. The meaning is therefore that just as a *Kushit*'s skin-colour is different, so Moses' wife stood out in form and beauty.[22]

What, though, of the second reference to *Kushit*, since, unusually given the terse style of the Torah, the word appears twice in the critical verse? Rashi offers a further explanation:

[Tziporah] is referred to as *Kushit* because of her beauty, just as a man might call his good-looking son *Kushi* so that the evil eye will have no power over him.[23]

So we shouldn't take the description literally; it doesn't in fact mean that Moses' wife was actually black. For *Kushit* is an insult, after all; Miriam calls Tziporah black to block the unwanted attentions of the envious, because black is indeed considered to be unbeautiful. It's little wonder, then, that *kushi* became a term of insult. To call someone a *kushi* in modern Hebrew is like branding them with the 'n' word; it's equally unacceptable.

Abraham ibn Ezra questions why God calls Aaron to account alongside Miriam. What did he do wrong, since it was Miriam who actually made the offensive comment? 'Miriam spoke, and Aaron either agreed or remained silent; therefore he [too] was punished.'[24]

The implication is clear: anyone who hears a racist insult and says nothing is also guilty. Aaron is held responsible because of his failure to intervene. He represents all of us who stand passively by, saying and doing nothing while racist remarks are bandied about. We, too, are to blame. Neutrality, wrote Abraham Joshua Heschel, no doubt with the Civil Rights Movement in mind, is worse than evil, because it allows evil to flourish.[25]

Following the racist murder of George Floyd on 25 May 2020, Reverend Anthony Johnson, whose grandfather founded the Southern Christian Leadership Conference together with Reverend Dr Martin Luther King, challenged the Jewish community. What we need from you, he wrote, is:

> . . . to help us put an end to the murder of innocent Blacks with the exact same fervour, dedication and commitment that you show towards preserving and defending your own families, that you show for Israel . . . We need you to understand that Blacks and Jews are in this together; white racists view you as the N-word, too. We need you to embrace Blacks as absolute equals . . . We need each other.[26]

SHELACH LECHA (13:1–15:41)

....

'We were like grasshoppers'

No one wants to feel a failure, the weakest link who lets the team down. No one wants to be identified with those on the wrong side of history, the persecutors and evildoers. We like to think of ourselves among the just and good, the bold and brave.

Moses sends twelve men to spy out the Promised Land, but when they return only two, Joshua and Caleb, bring back a positive report. The other ten take a defeatist view. In so doing, they destroy the people's morale, undermine the leadership of Moses and Aaron, frustrate God's plans and bring down on the entire people the punishment of wandering in the desert until virtually their entire generation has died out.

We would probably like to imagine that, even if we didn't have the courage to be a Joshua or Caleb and confront the hostile crowd, we wouldn't hiss them down and would at least be among the quiet supporters of their optimism and faith. We wouldn't give in to the negativity of the other ten spies. Yet our courage, too, has probably failed us, when we didn't do what we hoped we'd do, when we fell short of what we know we ought to have done.

The spies have ample cause to be afraid. They're telling the truth when they report back to Moses that they encountered giants. The text makes a point of informing us that Achiman, Sheishai and Talmai, sons of giants, were resident in the land. It's not surprising that the spies 'felt like grasshoppers in [their] own eyes', adding that 'so indeed we were in their eyes' (Num. 13:33).

The Talmud is troubled by how they could have known what they looked like to others. It creates an imaginary scenario in which, to distract the locals and enable the spies to escape safely back to Moses, God arranges for one of the leaders of the giants to die so that they're too busy with the funeral arrangements to notice the presence of aliens in their midst. Unfortunately, however, they gather for the wake exactly where the spies have positioned themselves, forcing the latter to make a hasty getaway by hiding in the canopies of a handy cluster of trees. From these uncomfortable perches they hear the giants below commenting to each other that they've 'seen a species of locust' up in the leaves (Talmud Sotah 35a).

Rebbe Menachem Mendel of Kotzk (1787–1859), always a sharp psychological observer, is more critical of the spies for 'looking like grasshoppers in their own eyes' than for surmising that this is how they appeared to others. Their sin was to let themselves be defined by what others thought of them. Aren't we created in the image of God? By what right, then, were they entitled to consider themselves worthless?

It's easy to be critical of the spies. We, too, have probably not escaped internalising other people's negative views of us, leaving us feeling worthless and helpless. I don't like thinking about them, but there have been times in my life when I lost all sense of purpose and felt a total failure. My resolve drained away. I didn't manage to do what I believed was right; at the key moment I didn't act. These wounds, self-inflicted, sit deep in my consciousness. I can't honestly say that I could never have been one of those ten spies who let their people down.

The daily morning prayers instruct us to 'acknowledge the truth always' and 'to speak truth in the heart'. It's easy to yield to the temptation, so instinctive that it sets in almost automatically, to rewrite the narrative of our lives with every mistake expunged. Perhaps we sometimes even need to, as a survival strategy. But if we're honest and have some measure of humility, we also have to admit to ourselves who we truly are. I, too, have lost my nerve and, because I felt like a grasshopper in my own eyes, have behaved like one as well.

Strikingly, it's not only the ten 'bad' spies who lack belief in themselves; an astute midrash suggests that Caleb was also short on self-confidence. Yet, because he was able to acknowledge this to himself, he managed to follow a different course. As so often, the midrash exploits a fine grammatical detail as its point of entry, noting that the text employs a plural verb to tell us that the spies 'ascended through the Negev' but then changes to the singular to indicate their arrival in Hebron. Though it's perfectly acceptable to use a singular verb to describe the actions of a group, the midrash reads into this change that only one of the spies made the choice to travel via Hebron. This was Caleb, who, well aware of the power of peer pressure, took that detour in order to pray at the graves of Abraham, Isaac and Jacob for the strength to resist what he'd already had ample opportunity to realise was the corrosive negativity of the others.

One of Hillel's most important teachings is: 'Don't believe in yourself until your dying day.'[27] Given that he also famously said, 'If I am not for myself, who am I?', it's hard to believe that he was opposed to any and every form of self-confidence.[28] Rather, his meaning is made clear by the continuation: 'Do not separate from the community,' that is, don't believe you can go it alone. It may be that only by admitting our weaknesses and acknowledging our need for support in order to do what is right are we able to find the resources to be true to our principles. We need the help of the community, not only of the living, but also of the dead, whose timeless presence in our hearts doesn't end with their departure from this world.

We all have failures; our secret autobiographies all contain moments of shame. If we can bear to face them, they can become important teachers. They may prove to be the very source of our courage in facing the unknown challenges of our future. The mistake of the spies was not primarily that they felt like insects in their own eyes, but that, feeling this way, they did nothing to try to restore their courage.

'When you eat the bread of the land'

There's little that is more delicious than freshly baked bread. After generations of slavery, the news that they would one day 'eat the bread of the land' which their children would cultivate in freedom must have brought the Children of Israel tantalising relief (Num. 15:18–19). True, they were currently provisioned with manna from heaven to make them appreciate 'that humankind lives not by bread alone, but by all that comes from the mouth of God' (Deut. 8:3). Nevertheless, the thought of their families baking their own bread in their own homes must have given them a measure of hope, especially when they'd just been punished with forty years of wandering in the desert.

Long before they reach the land, the Torah stipulates that *challah*, 'the first [dough] from your kneading bowls', must be dedicated as an offering and donated to the priests (Num. 15:20). The practice is honoured to this day when, on baking bread, we bless God who commanded us to 'separate *challah* from the dough'. But, since the Temple no longer stands and the priests no longer serve there, a small symbolic portion is burned instead. 'Taking the *challah*' serves as a threefold reminder: food is always a gift, must never be taken for granted and should be shared.

The Mishnaic tractate Challah discusses what grains qualify for making bread, what percentage of dough must be taken and, in my favourite passage, how, if shepherds bake specially for their dogs, no *challah* is given whereas, if they share their bread with them, *challah* must be separated (Challah 1:8).

The Torah describes a culture of generosity, detailed in another Mishnaic tractate, Peah, which opens with the rules governing the corners of the fields, which must be left for the poor, the fatherless and refugees. How big these corners should be is not specified, but in general less than 5 per

cent is regarded as mean and more than 20 per cent as excessively generous. Likewise, fallen stalks, *leket*, and forgotten sheaves, *shikhehah*, may not
be collected by the owners but must be left for the elderly, the destitute
and refugees to glean. In fact, Israel's national food bank is named *Leket*,
recalling the fallen ears and forgotten sheaves reserved for the poor.

Every year, the initial portion of the harvested crop, *terumah*, approximately 2 per cent, was given to the priests, following which a first tithe,
ma'aser rishon, was due to the Levites. A second tithe, *ma'aser sheni*, was
either taken to Jerusalem for a celebratory offering, or, in every third and
sixth year of the septennial cycle, given as *ma'aser oni*, a tithe for the poor.
Each seventh year was a *shemitah*, a sabbatical of 'letting go', in which
ploughing and sowing were forbidden and whatever grew naturally had to
be made available to all, local and itinerant, as well as the wild and domestic animals. In addition to these land laws, the rabbis instituted the *couppah*,
a fund distributed weekly to the local poor by a committee of three, and
the *tamchui*, a daily food collection, a prototype of the soup kitchen, for
the immediate needs of the hungry. We've never heard of any Jewish
community that has no charity fund, the great twelfth-century philosopher and halakhist Maimonides wrote, though 'charity' is a poor translation of *tzedakah*, which literally means 'righteousness' and encapsulates the
obligation to practise social justice. A favourite saying of Rabbi Elazar ben
Azariah was, 'If there's no flour, there's no Torah; but if there's no Torah,
there's no flour.'[29] If there were no Torah of social justice, there'd be no
flour for many, who would be left to starve.

In his stirring memoir of his 1930s East End childhood, Sidney Bloch
recalls how the milkman points out the letters *GF* chalked on the doorpost
of their home. Sidney's family have no idea what this means, until it's
explained to them that one of the 'knights of the road', a worthy local
tramp, must have written them there to inform other homeless people that
this house is Good for Food.

'I should think that sign costs you a fortune, sir,' the milkman observes.

'Shall I rub it off?' young Sidney asks.

'Certainly not,' my father replied very positively. 'You should consider
it an honour that our house is known for its hospitality. I would never
want to know that a hungry man had passed it by . . . That kind of
hospitality is a mark of culture.'[30]

It's a culture maintained to this day.

But sharing food is about more than the prevention of immediate hunger. Rabbi Noah Zvi Farkas, founder of the Jewish food movement *Netiya*, writes:

> Food is only the beginning; it's a deeper truth we seek, nothing less than a change in how our society is stitched together. Every morsel has a story; every baker, grower, harvester, and eater – we all have stories. For a loaf of bread is not a mere thing, it is the product of a series of choices, based on values, that tells us as much about the baker as it does about the consumer.[31]

We need to offer each other not just emergency rations to end malnutrition, but a sufficient sense of belonging and access to society's resources to prevent the gnawing anxiety of food insecurity as well. This may not always be possible. The authors of the Bible knew all too well the terrible impact of drought and war on food supplies. For anyone who's ever known it, food insecurity is liable to remain a permanent worry. For survivors of the Nazi Holocaust and other genocides, hunger is an ineradicable experience:

> The waiter was about to remove the bread. 'Leave it on the table,' said another woman. 'There is nothing more reassuring in this world than having a basket of freshly baked bread on the table in front of you.'[32]

Food isn't only about calories; it's about memory and mutuality. A friend working in The Jungle, the popular name for the huge refugee camp in Calais, told me how the chefs she took there to teach people how to make nutritious meals from basic ingredients changed more than just the process of cooking. Instead of obliging them to stand in queues for their handouts, they encouraged people to sit down together and served them in groups, like at a family meal. Food shared in this way indicates a culture of inclusion and generosity.

I'll never forget an incident from my walk along the Rhine, when I carried a symbolic flame from my grandfather's synagogue in Frankfurt back to London to kindle the Eternal Light in my community's new synagogue. I was in the hills above the river when my blood sugar ran low. Being diabetic, I urgently needed food but had forgotten to take anything with me. The only place within miles was a small castle which ran an exclusive restaurant. My heart sank as I saw the tables laid with multiple sets of crystal glasses and silver cutlery, perfectly arranged around gleaming plates. Still, I had no choice but to try my luck. When I rang the bell, a waiter duly appeared but, seeing me muddy, with a backpack and a dog, he promptly vanished. I couldn't blame him and was about to leave when he returned with a plate filled with many kinds of bread and fruit. 'No', he said firmly as I made to pay, 'it's for your pilgrimage'.

So that you remember

According to a legendary anecdote, a Hasid, a follower of the devotional path of the eighteenth-century founder of Hasidism, the Ba'al Shem Tov, was once challenged by a *mitnagged*, an 'opponent' of Hasidism, who looked down on it as cultish popularism:

'Since you claim you've so much insight, tell me what I'm thinking of right now!'
'You're thinking of the verse, "I set God before me always."'
'No, I'm not,' cried the *mitnagged* triumphantly.
'Well, then, you ought to be!' retorted the Hasid.

The language of memory and mindfulness is central in the Torah. We are commanded to remember the work of creation, how Amalek attacked the people from behind and, most of all, how we were once slaves in Egypt. But it's not only specific events that we're enjoined to recall. In a passage that forms the third part of the *Shema*, Judaism's twice daily meditation, we are exhorted to: 'Remember and do my commandments and so become holy to your God' (Num. 5:40).

Here, 'remember' carries no grammatical object; it refers neither to a specific date nor a particular event. Rather, it concerns the very nature of being itself, the awareness that we live in the presence of God.

The context is the commandment to make *tzitzit*, fringes containing a thread of blue, to be attached to each of the four corners of our garments to serve as constant reminders: 'You shall see *them* [*him*] and remember God's commandments and do them, and not turn aside after your heart and after your eyes' (Num. 15:39).

The Talmud notes an inconsistency. The object of 'see' is the fringes, which are plural, yet the Torah:

. . . doesn't say 'see them' [the threads of the fringes] but 'see him'.
This teaches that keeping the commandment of *tzitzit* is like receiving

the *Shechinah*, the presence of God. For the colour blue is like the sea, the sea is like the sky, and the sky is like the throne of glory.

(Talmud Menachot 42b)

The blue thread of the *tzitzit* takes us on a journey from this world to what lies above it or hidden within it. It reminds us to resist the temptation to follow self-interest only, the desires of our heart and eyes, but to be mindful instead of a deeper truth.

When I was a student, a man I scarcely knew turned to me as I stood on a bridge watching the slow current of the river below and said without any introduction: 'Never forget why you're here in this world. You belong to something higher which you have to serve.' He spoke with the quiet conviction of someone who knows. I never met him again.

Remembering is different from acquiring something new. Memory calls us back to what we know already, to a truth or knowledge which, though obscured by our everyday preoccupations, remains within our capacity for recall. To the mystics, this is the great challenge of living in a world of concealment. The material 'reality' in which we exist, and which appears to be all that is, hides the sacred, the life force that animates everything and which, beneath all barriers and beyond all distractions, remains present and accessible to our consciousness. The deepest gift bestowed on us, the soul's endowment, is the capacity to be aware of this inner vitality. As mystics, the Kabbalists would agree with Wordsworth that:

> Not in entire forgetfulness,
> And not in utter nakedness,
> But trailing clouds of glory do we come
> From God, who is our home.[33]

They too would understand our birth as 'but a sleep and a forgetting'.[34] A Talmudic legend describes how every child is taught the entire Torah by candlelight in its mother's womb and made to swear that it will keep its soul pure until the time comes for it to return to God. But at birth an angel strikes it on the lip, causing it to forget everything. It enters this world in sorrow for something lost yet remembered, ungraspable but known, with which it was once at home (Talmud Niddah 30b). Hence the tradition that at the gathering to welcome a newborn on the first Sabbath eve after its birth, one eats the foods of mourning out of empathy with the child's loss.

In a poem for the New Year, Nachmanides describes the soul's descent to earth:

From the first, before the origins of existence
I was present, among his hidden treasure sealed;
He fashioned me from nothing, and at the end of days
I was summoned before the King.

I am woven out of dust, yet your spirit moves within me.
You know my thoughts; on earth I am like a stranger.
How long will your journey be? When will you return?
And shall it be pleasing before the King?

The mind retains a subliminal knowledge of its true origins. This awareness is not of self but of the depths to which self belongs, from which it emerges and to which it returns, yet which is not entirely non-self either. Recollection, or reconnection, takes us beyond 'I' and 'my' to a consciousness not owned by what I call 'me' and not bounded by possession, where we dwell in the infinite space and timelessness of being itself, the sacred thing, or nothingness, of God. This awareness connects us with all existence as Arthur Green writes:

We are here to re-member, or to re-join the links of a creation that has been rent asunder. The One seeks that we become more fully conscious, that we cultivate da'at, or spiritual awareness, as fully as we are able, and spread that awareness forward among others.[35]

Mindfulness deepens our perception, so that we experience God's word not just as commandments derived from ancient text, but as emanating from life itself, from the Torah of lived experience and from the constant invisible communication of the hidden presence of God within all people and all nature, the energy and vibrancy of creation as it sings to us and within us.

The aim of such mindfulness is not mindfulness alone, but so that we 'remember and do', so that we follow the dictates of this deeper reality with its constant call to integrity and service. This balance between reflection and action, being and doing, is central to Judaism. The purpose of prayer and meditation is not withdrawal from, but deeper entry into, the life of the world so that, at least in our best moments, we come closer to the unreachable ideal of being 'holy to our God'.

KORACH (16:1–18:32)

....

Arguments for the sake of heaven

Vibrant cultures foster vibrant discourse. From parliaments to kitchen tables, from the national to the domestic, societies and communities can be known by how they handle their disagreements.

Judaism is a culture of vigorous debate. The subject matter is all-embracing, Torah and everything related to it, which means that nothing is excluded. The Torah may be the expression of God's will, but what does it actually mean? Not a sentence, a word or even a letter is too insignificant to become the object of rigorous argument.

A defining moment in the history of Jewish discourse is the disagreement between Rabbi Eliezer and Rabbi Yehoshua, leading scholars of the late first to early second century. The issue itself is abstruse: whether an oven constructed in layers is pure or impure. It's the nature of the argument that makes the scene famous. Rabbi Eliezer appeals to heaven to support his position, adducing an impressive display of miraculous proofs in his favour: a carob tree moves twenty cubits, a water channel changes course, the very walls of the house of study lean inward, all to affirm that he is correct. A voice from heaven declares categorically, 'The *Halakhah* is in accord with Rabbi Eliezer.'

Far from defeated, Rabbi Yehoshua responds with the rejoinder, 'It [that is, the Torah itself] is not in heaven!' In effect, he tells God to mind his own business: God has given the Torah to us humans, so now it's up to us to determine what it means. There's a subtle elegance to Rabbi Yehoshua's repost, since the very words, 'It's not in heaven,' are themselves a quotation from the Torah (Deut. 30:12). Thus the Torah itself delegates to them the authority under which scholars are not merely free, but enjoined and commanded to debate its meanings, unlimited by supernatural interventions. This is precisely what God wants. In a somewhat cheeky aside, the Talmud has the rabbis ask the prophet Elijah what God did on that day: 'God laughed', Elijah replies; God said, 'My children have defeated Me' (Bava Metsia 59b).

The metalanguage that frames the debates of the Talmud, the encyclopaedic foundational text of rabbinic Judaism, is a vocabulary of questioning, challenge and disagreement:

Come and hear.

Is that really so?

Didn't so-and-so say?

Hasn't it been taught elsewhere?

He attacked his proof.

He pointed out a contradiction.

There's no contradiction here.

Lest you might have thought.

That's so obvious it doesn't need saying!

In the unending dialectic of trying to fathom God's will, the debate is never over.

The contemporary scholar Rabbi Nathan Lopes Cardozo describes how he took a curious non-Jewish friend to visit the yeshivah, the college of immersive Torah study, where he was learning. Shocked at the sight of hundreds of young men engaged in fierce argument, the friend questioned whether this was 'a demonstration against the Queen of England or the British government'. No, Rabbi Cardozo replied, the students were merely discussing what precisely God had meant at Sinai three thousand years ago:

> I will never forget his response: 'You still don't know?' 'Indeed,' I said, 'we still do not know!' Just as one can have major disagreements on how to interpret Bach or Brahms . . . so it is with Jewish law. There are many possibilities, and all are legitimate! We still argue about the words of God and have therefore outlived all our enemies.[36]

It's an unforgettable conclusion: the capacity of a culture to survive depends on its ability to debate; it lives or dies by virtue of the openness and vigour with which it pursues truth.

The term for such debates is *machloket*, from the root *chalak*, 'divide'. *Machloket* stands in contrast to another kind of argument, a *brogez*. From the Hebrew *rogez*, meaning 'anger', the word subsequently entered Yiddish and became the popular term for a quarrel, a falling-out or long-standing grudge. A *brogez* may be perpetuated for generations until the family no longer even knows why it is that 'we don't talk to them'. Unlike a *machloket*, a *brogez* thrives on the refusal to communicate, on the obstinate commitment to the incontrovertible justice of one's cause and the absurdity of the claims of the other side, even if one no longer remembers what these are and would be unable to put forward a coherent case: 'What? Have a reasonable conversation? Those people don't even know what reason is! Besides, I promised my grandparents never to speak to them.'

Machloket is different, yet here too a crucial distinction has to be made, as a famous mishnah explains. It contains significant ambiguities and is hard to translate without over-simplification:

Any *machloket* which is for the sake of heaven, its end is to endure; [any *machloket*] not for the sake of heaven, its end will be not to endure. What is a *machloket* for the sake of heaven: that between Hillel and Shammai. What is a *machloket* not for the sake of heaven: that of Korach and his followers.

(Mishnah Avot 5:20)

At one level the difference is clear. Hillel and Shammai, one of the early *zugot* or 'pairs' of leading rabbis of the Mishnaic period, debated the Torah for its own sake. They were focused on seeking truth and had no personal axe to grind. The School of Hillel, in particular, was noted for its readiness to listen to the views of its opponents, and sometimes even to integrate, or cede to, them. Korach, however (in a blatant asymmetry, his partner in argument is omitted), was intent on trouble; what mattered to him was to discredit Moses (Num. 16). The key distinction, therefore, is between genuine debate with the aim of deepening our understanding, and argument motivated by the desire to triumph over our antagonist.

But what does the mishnah mean by 'its end is to endure'? The obvious explanation is that honest arguments lead to good resolutions; participants may hold widely differing views, but they share the desire to arrive at the best possible solution. In contrast, too much personal rivalry prevents issues from being settled. Such quarrels may run out of energy but are rarely brought to satisfactory conclusions.

However, a careful reading suggests that this isn't what the mishnah is saying. On the contrary, the text states that, if conducted 'for the sake of heaven', not the outcome but the argument itself will endure. This sounds counter-intuitive, but only if one assumes that the purpose of debates is to arrive at clear conclusions. Perhaps, however, the value of discussion is to perpetuate the discourse itself in the interests of a culture of open-minded, non-dogmatic pursuit of truth.

When Stephen Hawking was buried in Westminster Abbey, there was a certain irony in his being laid to rest next to Isaac Newton, whose mechanistic view of the universe Hawking, following the theories of Fermi and Einstein, had disproved. However, it was noted that what the two scientists had in common was not agreement, but a shared devotion to the quest for truth, which always eludes the theorems by which science attempts to describe its endless complexities. They had both made outstanding contributions to the search for better understanding.

What is fatal to any culture is not the pursuit of new insights but the refusal to abandon obsolete certainties and dare to think again. When that happens, dogma takes the place of truth and all too often becomes an instrument of repression.

In practice, our motives are almost always complex. Our reasons for engaging in arguments are usually neither entirely disinterested nor totally selfish; we intend to seek truth but we also relish being right. So long as the desire for personal vindication does not become overpowering, a healthy culture of debate is able to thrive. The family dinner table characterised by vigorous discussion and occasional bad temper is very different from the home in which children are too afraid of their parents to speak up, or partners so frightened of their spouses that they sit in shrunken silence. Similarly, the country that holds freedom of speech as a principle to be upheld in all but the most threatening of circumstances is radically different from the totalitarian tyranny, of state or religion, in which dissent scarcely dares to whisper. Cancel culture and no-platforming of those whose views are deemed politically incorrect and therefore undeserving of a hearing risk becoming a milestone on the road to such a sterile destination.

At an evening organised by Exiled Writers Inc, a writer who had fled President Mugabe's Zimbabwe was asked whether the country permitted freedom of speech. 'Let's put it this way,' he answered, 'there's freedom before speech.' The room filled briefly with sad laughter.

Ma'alin bakodesh – in matters of holiness we go up, not down

One day a parcel arrived from a German friend containing a disturbing gift – a series of tiny silver cups. A note enclosed with them read, 'I'm returning these to their true home.' My friend explained that her father had served in the Second World War with the Wehrmacht on the Eastern Front. Suffering from severe toothache, he'd gone to the army dentist who told him to come back with some silver so that he could melt it down and fill the cavity that was causing him the pain. Stationed in Kiev, he'd visited the black market and acquired those tiny goblets. But he'd never used them because he'd been granted leave and the dentistry had been done back at home. My friend had found the cups after her father died and, fearing they'd probably been taken from the house of one of the tens of thousands of Jews murdered at Babin Yar, determined to return them to a Jewish home.

Moved, upset and perplexed all at once, I was unsure what to do with this bewildering gift. Should I set the cups aside as a memorial? Or use them on *Shabbat*, filled with wine for the *Kiddush* blessings? Or put them in a drawer from where whatever memories they secretly carried wouldn't infiltrate my home?

I found my answer in the Torah, in a strange and seemingly distasteful instruction.

Korach and his fellow rebels are told by Moses to bring their censers filled with burning incense and stand before God for judgement. There, they meet their terrible fate: some are swallowed alive by the earth, others devoured by fire (Num. 16). But what was to be done with the debris, the metals left over from this disaster? They should surely have been buried away forever. Instead, Elazar the High Priest is commanded to pull the censers of 'those mortal sinners' out of the fire and 'beat them into a covering for the altar', where it would serve as a warning to future potential renegades (Num. 16:38–9). The Talmud notes: 'From here we learn [the principle] that in matters of holiness we raise up and do not put down' (Menachot 99a).

Formerly, the censers were only implements for serving at the altar; now they have become part of the altar itself.

The Talmud brings a further example of this principle: the twelve freshly baked loaves of bread brought weekly to the Temple were placed by the priests on a marble table. However, the previous set of loaves, left all week in the presence of God, were deposited after their removal on a table made of gold, since 'in matters of holiness we raise up and do not put down' (Talmud Menachot 99b; Mishnah Shekalim 6:4). Similarly, any object used in the synagogue for a sacred purpose, such as the mantle to clothe the Torah, or the ark where the scroll is kept, may be used for an equal or a higher purpose, but may not be refashioned into anything of lesser status.

The instruction to raise up and not put down isn't limited to objects; it's an attitude to life. The rabbis offer a poignant analogy: the broken fragments of the first tablets that Moses brought down from Mount Sinai but smashed in fury at the sight of the golden calf must be placed in the holy Ark alongside the unbroken second set on which God's writing remains intact. From this the Talmud derives: 'A scholar who forgets his learning as a result of circumstances beyond his control must be shown no disrespect' (Menachot 99a).

This inclusive approach should define our attitude towards those who suffer from dementia, from the ravages of other illnesses and from the attritions of ageing and disability. It is surely not incidental that the Talmud attributes this teaching to Rav Yosef, who was himself blind.

It's all too easy to 'put someone down' and make them feel small. The Talmud compares humiliating another person in public and making them go pale with shame, to shedding blood (Bava Metsia 58b). True humanity lies in doing the opposite, in having an attitude of generosity and understanding which makes those around us feel better about themselves. It's an art that good teachers have of intuiting and fostering the best in their pupils. It's that grace, that balance of kindness and wisdom, which one sometimes finds in the faces of older people, that glow of inner radiance which embraces us even when they reprove us. They see the best in us even when we aren't happy about ourselves; by so doing they make us feel worthwhile.

In *If This Is a Man*, Primo Levi's testament to life in the concentration camp universe, he describes how he and a French fellow prisoner, Jean, go together to collect their miserable ration of soup. Jean, the *pikolo*, so-called because he acts as 'messenger-clerk' of their unit, is wise to the opportunities this presents and takes the longest possible route to the camp kitchens to give them time to speak. It emerges that he wants to learn Italian, and Primo feels impelled to teach him from Dante's *Inferno*, specifically from the *Canto of Ulysses*. As he struggles to recall each word of the *terza rima* stanzas, he realises that what he wants to communicate is something far more than how that Greek hero cajoled his fellow sailors to accompany him on his voyage:

Think of your breed; for brutish ignorance
Your mettle was not made; you were made men,
To follow after knowledge and excellence.

As he recaptures these lines, Levi feels as if he too is hearing them for the first time: 'Like the blast of a trumpet, like the voice of God. For a moment I forget who I am and where I am.'[37]

It is a moment of raising up, of intellectual and spiritual transcendence, and of profound companionship which both Primo and Jean never forget.

A careful consideration of the Hebrew terms suggests a possible additional reading: *ma'alin bakodesh* can be understood not just as 'in matters of holiness', but also 'by means of the holy'. Through deepening our awareness of what is sacred in life, we may not only avoid putting people down but lift the spirits of both others and ourselves.

CHUKKAT (19:1–22:1)

God's unfathomable will

On the other end of the phone was a man whose wife had died a few days earlier: 'It's God's will, Rabbi,' he said calmly. I hesitated, then quietly assented, hoping my tone conveyed a concurrence I didn't fully feel.

I would never have told this grief-stricken husband that the loss of his life's partner was God's wish, and not just for reasons of tact. I don't believe God deliberately wills such things or intervenes in the natural processes of cause and effect specifically to make such sad eventualities happen. As the Talmud says, 'The world pursues its natural course' (Avodah Zarah 54b), and we should be cautious before interpreting good fortune as divine reward or sorrow and tragedy as punishment.

But it would have been inappropriate and heartless to take issue with the feelings of a man so recently bereaved. What mattered was to accept him in the manner in which he was accepting. 'Yes,' I heard myself say, 'it's God's will.' Besides, his words, softly spoken, expressed not a theological position but an attitude to life, a quiet humility, an appreciation that such is the way of the world, the reality of being mortal.

Forty years later I haven't forgotten that brief conversation. Perhaps one should add to the famous list in Ecclesiastes 3, 'To everything there is a season', that there's a time to question and a time to refrain from questioning; a time to challenge and a time to acquiesce.

Jewish thought divides religious law into two categories, *chukkim* and *mishpatim*, statutes and judgements. The latter are rational; were they not included in the Torah they could be deduced by human reason alone. From, 'You shall not murder,' and, 'You shall not steal,' to such judicial procedures as favouring neither rich nor poor in judgement and taking no bribes, they form the basis of any equitable society. 'That's obvious to plain reason,' the Talmud sometimes observes with an implied exclamation mark, although behind such rationality is the constant awareness of our responsibility before God to treat all human beings fairly because we are all created in the divine image.

However, *chukkim*, statutes, are not amenable to rational explanation. They are divine ordinances, unfathomable, sometimes even absurd from the point of view of reason. Of all such inexplicable rules, the most notorious are those concerning the red heifer, the ashes of which, mixed with water, hyssop and cedar, purify the person over whom they are sprinkled but render the priest who performs the rite impure until nightfall (Num. 19:1–10). Conscious of this irrational paradox, the rabbis put into God's mouth the words: 'I, God, have established a statute and you are not allowed to question it' (Talmud Yoma 67).

Basing himself on Midrash, Rashi takes this as an opportunity to warn against apologetic efforts to rationalise the divine commandments because sooner or later they will come up against an inexplicable injunction immune to such endeavours. Then 'the nations will try to make you abandon your religion' by taunting you with its absurdity.[38] Such attempts lead not only to failure but also to disaster. Rashi knows all too well what's at stake, confronted with the claim that the old and blind Synagogue has been divorced by God in favour of the new bride, the youthful virgin Church.

In contrast, Maimonides was opposed to the notion that God, the supreme source of all intellect, would command anything irrational. In a cultural climate in which the influence of Aristotelian thought and syllogistic logic was making its impact on Muslim theology, he was not prepared to cede that Judaism was any less intellectually compelling. In the third section of his *Guide for the Perplexed* he attempts a reasoned explanation of all the commandments, including the *chukkim*, acknowledging that some may have originated as responses to pagan practices, the details of which we no longer know.

But other thinkers, living in times more challenging to the notion that faith is rational, found meaning in the very non-rationality of *chukkim*, in the immunity of divine law to the reductionism of human reason. In the spring of 1942, Kalonymus Kalman Shapira, the Rebbe of the Warsaw Ghetto, wrote in this vein about the red heifer. He noted that there were two aspects to the process of purification: the ritual itself and the prohibition against harbouring any doubts concerning it:

Just as the waters of the *mikveh*, the ritual baths, only cleanse those who immerse themselves in them with their entire body, but if a single limb remains outside the water, they do not effect purification, so must we make ourselves as nothing and enter entirely into the domain of God. Anyone who thinks himself to be a separate entity, with independent reasoning powers, remains outside. We must nullify ourselves, for we are nothing and our knowledge is nought. But God and God's holiness are everything, and the way in which God commands us through the Torah and how God conducts his world are good, and we have no right to harbour doubts.[39]

It's clear from the time and place in which he writes that he's addressing a wider question than whether a dip in the *mikveh* is ritually valid. After two and a half years in the ghetto surrounded by every form of suffering and horror, it was impossible for the mind not to harbour questions: How could God allow this to happen? How could there even be a God? Some months later, very likely just when the great deportations to the death camp of Treblinka were commencing, during which he lost his sole remaining close family member, his daughter Rachel, he added this rare insertion in Yiddish into a discourse on the same portion about the red heifer:

> Truly, it is a wonder that the world still stands after so many and such terrible outcries . . . Innocent children, pure as angels, and adults, the holy ones of Israel, are killed and slaughtered just because they are Jews, and the entire universe is filled with their screams. But the world is not turned to water and remains as it always was, as if the matter were of no concern to God whatsoever, heaven forfend.[40]

Reason, he implies, will lead us only into despair. There are no answers to these terrible questions. We can only immerse ourselves metaphorically in the waters of acceptance that God is and knows. Thoughts that 'remain outside', questioning and doubting, serve only to separate us from God.

We surrender the faculty of reason at our peril. Unthinking conviction, coupled with unquestioning faith that we know God's will, has frequently led to merciless slaughter, supposedly in heaven's name.

Yet there are times when it is to our loss if we cannot let go of our doubting, questioning, rationalising self, when profound trust may be the only possible way to live on, accepting our destiny with courage, faith and an open heart.

Being human

Zot Ha'Torah adam – This is the Torah of being human – one who dies in the tent.

(Num. 19:14)

The question never goes away. Life's constant preoccupations may drive it from our consciousness, but it persists in returning, usually in unpredicted moments. One puts one's feet on the floor in the morning and stares at them, half awake: what does it mean to exist, to occupy this strange body, to own, or to be owned by, this incomprehensible consciousness? What is it to be human?

The sequence of three simple words, *zot*, 'this'; *Torat*, 'the Torah of'; and *adam*, 'human', occurs twice in the Bible. They form the statement: 'This is the teaching of being human.' They first appear together in the Torah's account of the ritual of decontamination after contact with a dead body. But their meaning is too powerful to be limited by their immediate context. They stand alone and apart: 'This is the teaching of what it means to be human.'

The Torah does not go on to explain exactly what that teaching is. However, its next words, 'who dies', suggest that the most salient fact about the human condition is that we are mortal. As Rebbe Simchah Bunem of Przysucha (1765–1827) comments: 'Human beings are called *adam* because they are fashioned from the dust of the earth, *"afar min ha'adamah"*. Therefore it behoves them to be humble.'[41]

It was he who famously taught that we must keep two cards in our pockets. When we're low, we should reach for the one on which is written, 'The world was created for my sake' (Mishnah Sanhedrin 4:5). When we're too full of ourselves, we should contemplate the words on the other: 'I am but dust and ashes' (Gen. 18:27).

Yet the popular saying, 'Eat, drink and be merry for tomorrow we may die,' is by no means contrary to the spirit of Judaism. After discounting almost everything it has to offer, Ecclesiastes' advice is to enjoy life because it's the gift of God. My family chose those words for my father-in-law's tombstone since he lived with a spirit of happiness and generosity. Jews are glad to raise a glass and toast *lechaim*, 'to life'.

But Judaism has never taken this to mean that we shouldn't bother ourselves about the future of the world since we'll all soon be gone. On the contrary, this 'Torah of mortals' suggests the opposite. We are vulnerable beings, subject to hunger, cold, illness, loneliness, fear and sudden death. We require shelter, food, company, comfort and community. Since these are our own needs, they must also be the needs for which we are responsible towards others. This is the message of Hillel's famous summary of the Torah on one leg, a pragmatic, unromantic reformulation of the injunction to 'love your neighbour as yourself': 'Don't do to others what you don't want them to do to you' (Talmud Shabbat 31a). We must not leave others to endure what we could not bear to suffer ourselves.

As mortals, we have limited time to act. Rebbe Shlomo of Radomsk (1803–66) takes this as the central 'Torah of being human'. He first points to an apparent contradiction:

> The sages taught that the Torah is sustained only by those who give up their lives for it (Berakhot 63b). This seems to go counter to the verse, 'You shall live by them [the commandments]' (Lev. 18:5).

He resolves the discrepancy by explaining that we 'give up' our lives through dedicating them to Torah and service. We have no time to waste:

> Consider: we should be diligent in engaging in Torah while we are still alive, experiencing this world, and 'not say, "When I have time I will study," lest [we] don't have time' (Avot 2:4). Therefore, we must cherish this day and this hour that we are in this world, for it is in our power to repair everything through devoted study. For after we die, even if we were to offer everything in the world for just one day to return to this world to fix that which we had spoiled, it would not be given us.[42]

He may also have in mind Rabbi Ya'akov's words in the Mishnah:

> One hour of repentance and good deeds in this life is better than the entire life of the world to come; but one hour of tranquillity in the world to come is worth more than one's entire life in this world.[43]

This life, here and now, is supremely precious precisely because of its brevity; the hour is always urgent. That is the essential Torah of 'man who dies'.

The same three words – 'this', 'Torah' and 'man' – appear together a second time in the Bible, when Nathan the prophet tells David about God's promise that not just he, but also his children after him, will be kings. Overwhelmed, he exclaims: 'Who am I, Sovereign God, and what is my household, that you have brought me to this estate? . . . Is this the Torah of the human being, O Sovereign God?' (2 Sam. 7:18–19).

Life may be brief and limited, but it is also an immense privilege. In the words of Solomon ibn Gavirol, one of the great Jewish poets of Muslim Spain:

> Before I ever was, your love upon me came,
> Made being out of nothing and fashioned me.
> Who is it who blew the breath of being into me? Who
> Opened the womb of the deep and brought me forth?
> Who led me from my childhood unto now,
> Who taught me understanding, filling me with wonder?[44]

We are subject to death yet endowed with a consciousness open to marvel and mystery. We are a fragment of the divine, sent down into this world to recognise what is sacred and to do what is right before we die and our spirit rejoins the undying spirit of all being. To be alive is to embody the breath of the endless vitality, to feel life's boundlessness flow through us, to be exposed to wonder and glimpse the infinite. We are mortals, traversed by the immortal. We have the capacity to know God and be transformed by the experience.

Such moments of realisation may be rare, but they change forever how we understand our lives. We lose our sense of isolated, separated selfhood and become part of a greater consciousness. We feel our breath as the breathing of an infinitely greater whole and our thoughts as a pulse of the endless. That is why each person needs to be able to say, 'For my sake the world was created.' Everyone has the capacity to recognise the sacred source of life and song, and everyone should be able to stretch out their arms and feel as if they are embracing the entire world in kinship.

'This is the Torah of being human': our mortality teaches us the urgency of compassion and our immortality the timelessness of wonder.

The deaths of Miriam and Aaron

It can't be by chance that it is specifically in the Torah portion *Chukkat* that Miriam and Aaron die and Moses is told that he too will not live to enter the Promised Land. No *chok*, no statute, is more abstruse or inexplicable than the law of the red heifer. No question is more unanswerable than the 'why me?' of mortality, no challenge more bewildering than how to mediate the mysterious boundary between this life and the unknown beyond.

The Torah tells us almost nothing about the death of Miriam. We learn only that she 'died and was buried there', at Kadesh, in the wilderness of Sin (Num. 20:1). Rashi explains that 'she, too, [like her brothers] died by a kiss, but it's not fitting for the text to say so', as if God is too coy to be thought of as kissing a woman, even with the kiss of death. We are not told that the people mourned for Miriam. Instead, we hear immediately that 'there was no water for the congregation' (Num. 20:2). Rabbinic interpretation seizes on this juxtaposition, explaining that it was because of the merit of Miriam that a miraculous well followed the Children of Israel through the desert all the way from Egypt. When she died, its waters ceased. In the vexation of their thirst, the Children of Israel vented their frustration on Moses and Aaron. Anger, which often accompanies grief as we struggle to manage the compass of our loss, displaced their sorrow. It overtook Moses, too, when he hit the rock instead of speaking to it as commanded, an action on which God hanged the blame for his and Aaron's deaths.

The rabbis try to understand God's reasons: Moses shouldn't have lost his temper, shouldn't have called the people fools, shouldn't have disobeyed instructions and used force instead of words. Looking further back into his record, he shouldn't have killed the Egyptian taskmaster he saw beating a Hebrew slave. But all these 'reasons' sound more like rationalisations. Isn't Moses' death inevitable, since he too is mortal? Isn't God's own explanation, that Moses, the long-suffering, selfless leader, failed to sanctify him in the sight of the people, also a justification, as if even God needs reasons where reason itself fails, at the border between life and death?

Aaron is the first of the brothers to go. God tells Moses to accompany him up the mountain, remove his priestly garments and place them on his son Elazar (Num. 20:23–9). It's a doubly painful task with which to entrust Moses. Rashi explains how it is to be accomplished:

'Take him' with words of comfort. Tell him, 'Happy are you, for your crown [of priestly office] is passing to your son, a [destiny] I have not merited.'[45]

Midrash offers a stirring account of how matters now unfold:

Moses said [to Aaron]: 'Your time has come to depart this world.'

When they reached the cave [on the mountain] Moses said to him: 'Aaron my brother, put on Elazar's clothes, and let him put on yours. Then you and I will enter the cave.'

This they did. When they entered, they saw a candle burning and a bed prepared.

Moses said to him: 'Aaron my brother, climb into this bed,' and he climbed in.

He said to him: 'Stretch out your arms,' and he stretched them out; 'Shut your eyes,' and he shut them; 'Close your mouth,' and thus he did. In that moment, his soul departed.

When Moses saw this, he desired such a death. The Holy One said to him: 'Upon your life "as the death of this, so is the death of that". So shall your death be too.'

(Midrash Tanhuma, Chukkat, Hosafa 2)

Nachmanides is puzzled by this description and references an alternative Midrash. Since outer clothes must always be worn on top and inner clothing underneath, Moses couldn't simply have transferred the priestly garments one by one from father to son. Rather:

God performed a greater miracle for Aaron at his death than in his life. Moses stood him upon the rock and removed [all] his priestly robes, whereupon God wrapped him in the garments of the divine presence.[46]

It's a deeply affecting image: will the 'garments of God's presence' enclothe us too when we die? Perhaps that's the true meaning of the words which I always find so moving in the traditional memorial service: 'When it shall please You to take us from earth, be Thou with us.'

Maybe this is what accounts for the deep calm one sometimes senses next to a person who has just died, the presence of something other, invisible, embracing, bringing peace. There are few thoughts more consoling than the intimation that God will clothe us in garments of love and take us like a child by the hand.

As for Moses, is he truly reconciled to the fate that will shortly overtake him? He pleads with God to let him enter the land to which he has laboured to lead the Children of Israel for so long, but to no avail. His last sight on earth will be the contours of the country whose earth his feet will never tread. Unlike his brother, he won't have the comfort of knowing that his son will inherit his mantle. In a painful vignette, travel writer and novelist Bruce Chatwin pictures him, an old man leaving the camp alone in the pre-dawn darkness, climbing the mountain for the last time to reach his 'appointment with the jackals and vultures'.[47] The Torah offers a gentler account: he dies 'by God's mouth', and none other than God sees to his burial (Deut. 34:5).

Does this allay his disappointment in his final moments? Rashi references the tradition that Moses' task is not yet over; death is not the end of his mission. God sends him off through the upper worlds to find Abraham, Isaac and Jacob in their resting places and inform them that the promise has been fulfilled: God has brought their children's children home to their land.

It's a harsh destiny that prevents the three siblings from reaching the country to which they have worked so hard to bring their people. Like them, we shall all die on the way; none of us will reach the land where all our hopes and dreams are fulfilled. What we have in life is the journey, its challenges, travails and joys.

Yet there's mercy, too, in the timing of their deaths: promised lands are never as perfect in the reality as in the imagination. Moses, Aaron and Miriam are spared the unravelling of their dreams.

BALAK (22:2–25:9)

What the donkey saw

I've always liked donkeys. Perhaps it's that meek look in their eyes with its implicit rebuke: 'Please treat me kindly.' Or maybe it's their endearing ears. So I always look forward to the story of Balaam, especially his contretemps with his ass, in which the latter gets the last word. 'I've met many talking asses,' quipped the nineteenth-century German-Jewish poet Heinrich Heine, famous for his wit, 'but all the others had only two legs.'

The poor ass gets into trouble for seeing more than his master sees, a prophet of such repute that he is hired to curse Israel by no less a figure than the King of Moab himself. Yet despite all his special powers to call on sprits and read omens, the well-attested arts of the ancient seers, he's outperformed by his donkey. Animals often perceive what we with all our sophistication are unable to detect.

One of the first Jewish prayers in the morning is a blessing to God 'who opens the eyes of the blind'. Hebrew has a choice of verbs: *petach*, meaning simply 'open', or *pekach*, the word employed here, indicating openness not just to sight but also to insight. We bless God for the gifts of physical, emotional and spiritual 'seeing'. We ask God to open our eyes and our hearts through Torah, to make us sensitive to wisdom and compassion. This is the core purpose of our time on earth, which the poet John Keats beautifully described as 'a vale of soul-making'.

In E. M. Forster's remarkable novel, *A Passage to India*, two of the most 'British' and proper of his characters, bewildered by a culture they cannot fathom, ask themselves if there existed 'worlds beyond which they could never touch, or did all that is possible enter their consciousness?'[48]

Not everything possible ever enters our minds, as those around us often know to their cost. Yet, like Balaam, we frequently act as if we have taken note of all that there is to be seen, resenting those who inconvenience us with their more astute perceptions.

Balaam's donkey sees what the famous seer can't, that the path on which he is set runs contrary to God's wishes: God does not want him to curse the Children of Israel. An angel, all too visible to the donkey but not to her master, is sent to block his path. Three times the donkey 'sees' the magisterial figure with outstretched sword in hand; three times Balaam in his blindness punishes her for saving his life. God eventually enables the donkey to speak, a miracle prepared, according to the rabbis, who were generally suspicious of such supernatural interventions, since the six days of creation. Seemingly unsurprised by the animal's sudden eloquence, Balaam enters into a furious verbal exchange with his ass, in which he is bested by the long-suffering beast.

It's at this point that God intervenes directly. The Torah employs neither of the more obvious words at its disposal but chooses instead the stronger *vayegal*. Often translated as 'God *opened* Balaam's eyes,' the verb actually means 'revealed': God *revealed* to Balaam his own eyes (Num. 22:31). Revelation often amounts to becoming more fully aware of what's right in front of us. We've all at times looked but not truly *noticed*; we can all say with 'Amazing Grace' that 'I was blind, but now I see'.[49]

Such moments of realisation may challenge us to the core, making us question, like Balaam, whether our path is headed in the wrong direction. But they can also fill us with wonder.

A gardener friend shared with me how during the handover to a new job his predecessor told him that after three months he'd begin to see kingfishers. This puzzled him: why only after the three months? But literally on the day he completed his third month he saw them, not because there'd been no kingfishers there before, but because he'd become sufficiently attuned to notice.

Deeper awareness should lead to greater compassion. Like Moses, whose life was transformed when he left Pharaoh's palace and *saw into* the sufferings of the slaves who had been labouring next door all the time, we begin to *see into* life with greater depth. A man once explained to me how, as he supported his wife through her illness, new dimensions of experience opened up before them: offers of help, organisations to turn to, people who had been through similar tribulations about which he'd never thought to ask. There were worlds right before him of which he'd not been aware. He saw into the lives of others with an empathy which, he confessed, he hadn't found in himself before. This realisation changed his priorities.

An abiding theme in the writings of Rebbe Kalonymus Kalman Shapira is how we develop our sensibilities. Comparing spiritual with physical sight, he notes that if we don't use our eyes and aren't guided to look carefully, we won't learn to notice. So too with spiritual perception: unless it is fostered it will remain latent and undeveloped within us, because:

> . . . in truth, the human being needs to be revealed. For this he needs the stimuli which will reveal him; if he is exposed to no such stimuli, then parts of his humanity will remain concealed from him.[50]

Therefore, he continues, people should not say they have no capacity for spirituality; it's only that life has not yet awakened it in them. That's why environments in which such sensitivities are valued and cultivated are essential: we need spiritual and emotional education.

Balaam has ridden his long-suffering donkey all his life. Who knows what the poor animal must have endured which Balaam failed to notice, until, with God's assistance, she finally helps him open his eyes. There are people around us like that, who bear the brunt of insensitivities of which the perpetrators never become aware. We're all sometimes guilty. It's chastening to think that those wiser than us may refrain from telling us what they perceive all too clearly, sensing that we're likely to react defensively to any attempt to make us see. Why should they suffer our aggressive response? There are people, too, who, oblivious to the end, exact from those who nonetheless remain loyal to them year after year a patient forbearance which to their dying day they fail to appreciate.

For Balaam's ass, the moment when his master finally becomes aware arrives too late. The rabbis infer from the angel's words, 'If she hadn't turned aside, it might have been you whom I killed and she whom I kept alive,' that immediately after her sorrowful remonstrations the faithful animal dies (Num. 22:33).

Perhaps that's why we are required to say prayers for God to open our eyes and our hearts every day. We constantly need to re-awaken our sensitivities, lest others suffer the hurt and injustice of what we don't even realise we're doing.

The status of animals

'Ten things were created at twilight on the sixth day,' explains the Mishnah (Avot 5:9). Among them are the well that followed the Children of Israel through the wilderness, the mouth of the earth that opened to swallow up Korach and his followers, and the mouth of the donkey who got the better of her word-merchant master, Balaam. All these ten items are 'special effects', each in its own way defying the normal laws of nature. In the case of the donkey, animals don't talk, at least not as we humans understand talking. It's precisely that capacity for speech that is often cited as *a*, if not *the*, critical difference between humans and beasts. A *medabber*, a being with the capacity for language, is considered to belong to a superior category of existence than a mere *chai*, an animal.

But what is the status of animals? It's an issue we urgently need to face before we force even more species into extinction. The Bible and the Judaeo-Christian tradition are frequently blamed for the anthropocentrism that has so often led us not only to dominate but also to decimate the rest of nature. Is that truly the position of the text: do we have an unquestionably superior right to exist?

In the Torah, animals matter. Throughout the thousand-year span of the Hebrew Bible and in all the civilisations – Egyptian, Canaanite, Babylonian, Greek and Roman, against which its literature is set – humans and animals interact on a daily basis. The Bible is intimately acquainted with animals, both domestic and wild, as well as with birds, insects and flora. Its authors were astutely sensitive to all life around them. They didn't suffer from the alienation and consequent ignorance that characterise much of modern civilisation. In their world, animals, their ways, their needs and even their rights were important. This is equally true of the world of the Mishnah.

Animals are understood as important to God. Mammals are created on the sixth day, just like humankind. The fact that they are not distinguished by being fashioned 'in the image and likeness' of their creator (Gen. 1:26) does not mean that they are of incomparably less significance. There's a beautiful, and chastening, truth in the American naturalist Henry Beston's description of the lives of animals:

> . . . the animal shall not be measured by man. In a world older and more complete than ours, they move finished and complete, gifted with the extension of the senses we have lost or never attained, living by voices we shall never hear. They are not our brethren, they are not underlings: they are other nations, caught up with ourselves in the net of life and time, fellow prisoners of the splendour and travail of the earth.[51]

Every species matters; the text repeatedly stresses that each is formed *bemino*, 'after its kind'. In contrast to the generally concise language of the Torah, the word appears three times in a single verse: 'God made wild beasts of every *kind* and cattle of every *kind*, and all *kinds* of creeping things of the earth. And God saw that this was good' (Gen. 1:25).

Noah is commanded to take two of 'each kind' into the ark (Gen. 6:19). The implication is that the extinction of even one single species is an irreparable loss, a lessening of creation.

In the book of Jonah, in which salvation comes to the prophet in the form of a fish, God chastises the unhappy prophet by reminding him that he, God, cares for the 'twelve times ten thousand people of Nineveh who cannot tell their right hand from their left, and many cattle' (Jonah 4:11). 'Cattle' is the book's last word.

If God cares, shouldn't we?

The rabbis of the Talmud rarely used the language of rights; rather, they spoke of duties. There's no doubt that they regarded animals as within the compass of our obligations. While they would probably have disputed the words 'fully' and 'equal' in contemporary philosopher Mark Rowlands' assertion that 'animals are in the moral club as fully paid up, hence equal members',[52] they would have agreed that we are commanded to treat them as subjects of our moral consideration. Since they are capable of pleasure, pain and suffering, and of acting in the interests of their own wellbeing, we are not entitled to regard them as things, mere metabolisms subject solely to our control and exploitation. We are required to pay compassionate heed not just to their needs but also to their feelings, in so far as we can understand them. In the Deuteronomic version of the Ten Commandments we are commanded to let our oxen and donkeys rest on the Sabbath along-side us; they are significant members of our household (Deut. 5:12–15). The author of Proverbs states that 'the righteous person understands the life of his animals', based on which the rabbis taught that we should not sit down to eat until their hunger has been satisfied first (Prov. 12:10).

The relevant principle in Jewish law is *tsaar baalei chaim*, 'animal suffer-ing', which we are forbidden to cause. The rabbinic consensus is that this is a Torah-enjoined law, hence of the highest legal status (Talmud Shabbat 128a). It is based on the commandments that we have to help an animal that has collapsed under its burden, even if it belongs to our enemy; that we must look after a lost animal until its owner finds it; and that it is forbidden to plough with an ox and an ass together, either because it's cruel to the ass to be partnered with so much stronger a creature, or because it's humiliating for the ox to be harnessed to a mere donkey (Deut. 22:1–4, 10). Considering the Torah's ban against removing a calf or lamb from its mother until at least seven days have passed (Lev. 22:27), and against taking the eggs or fledglings from a nest without first shooing away the mother bird (Deut. 22:6–7), Maimonides observes:

> The pain of the animals under such circumstances is very great. There is no difference in this case between the pain of man and the pain of other living beings, since the love and tenderness of the mother for her young ones is not produced by reasoning, but by imagination, and this faculty exists not only in man but in most living beings.[53]

Maimonides pre-empts by many centuries the nineteenth-century philos-opher Jeremy Bentham's much-quoted observation that 'the question is not, "Can they reason? nor, Can they talk? but, Can they suffer?"'[54] Mark Rowlands goes further: since animals lack the rational capacity to contex-tualise their pain – for example, a dog can't understand that although the sting of the needle hurts, being inoculated is ultimately for its benefit – they often suffer more than human beings.[55]

In a responsum on whether a Jew is permitted to hunt, Rabbi Ezekiel Landau of Prague (1713–93) notes that, while we may protect ourselves against danger if wild animals enter our habitations, we are not entitled to pursue them into their domains. A starving person may be forced to hunt for food, but hunting for sport is forbidden. The only hunters in the Bible are Nimrod and Esau, both seen as archetypes of cruelty. His negative answer reflects a deep respect for the place of animal, alongside human, life.

In his stirring account of life with his wolf companion Brenin, Mark Rowlands challenges the basis, and assumed justification, for human domination: 'Machination and mendacity lie at the core of our superior intelligence, like worms coiled at the core of an apple.'[56]

Being more intelligent doesn't necessarily mean being better. It may sometimes amount only to being more cunning in the pursuit of our own ends and more skilful at producing the tools required to do so. If the earth is destroyed through an ecological or nuclear disaster, it won't be the fault of the horses and cows.

In our subjugation of animals and our destruction of their homes, we forget not only their rights but also the blessings of their companionship. They bring spiritual and emotional solace, as every person who loves their dog or cat intuitively knows. They simplify us; they humble the soul. They remind us that life is ultimately one and that God's presence flows not just through us but through all beings.

PINCHAS (25:1–30:1)

Zealotry

There is only one broken letter in the entire Torah, in Numbers 25:12. The context is God's promise to Pinchas to 'give him my covenant of shalom, peace'. The vav or 'o' in the word shalom is traditionally written in two halves: in the entire Torah it is only here that the scribe must leave a small gap in the single vertical stroke of which the letter is formed. The irony is obvious: shalom means 'whole' or 'complete', but one of its letters is fractured, and incomplete peace isn't really peace at all.

Pinchas has just killed Zimri, a chief of the tribe of Shimeon, for having sex with Cosbi, a Midianite princess. The Talmud elaborates on the Torah's brief account. The Children of Israel have 'gone astray' after the daughters of Midian, worshippers of the idol Baal Pe'or. Moses has told the leaders of the tribes 'to kill, each, his men' who have sinned in this manner. In flagrant disregard of this instruction, Zimri propositions Cosbi, who initially rejects him because her father has warned her not to consort with anyone except a man of the highest rank. Zimri persuades her that he's an Israelite prince, whereupon she consents to his advances which he provocatively pursues as publicly as possible. Moses stands helplessly by and weeps. Swiftly taking in the situation, Pinchas, a grandson of Aaron, follows Zimri and Cosbi into their tent and kills them both with one stab of his spear. The Talmud adds the unsavoury detail that he caught them in the act and skewered them through their genitals. For this intervention God praises him 'for being zealous in my cause', rewards him with 'my covenant of peace' and affirms the hereditary right of his descendants to serve as priests forever (Num. 25:6–9; Talmud Sanhedrin 82a-b).

The Talmud is troubled by Pinchas' conduct. Shouldn't he have consulted Moses? Shouldn't there have been a proper legal process? By what right did he take the law into his own hands? Maybe he acted because Moses momentarily forgot the *Halakhah*, but how could such a thing have happened? The Babylonian Talmud imagines Zimri taking Cosbi by her ponytail, dragging her before Moses and saying mockingly: 'Isn't your partner a Midianite too? Aren't you married to a Midianite priest's daughter? How come she's kosher, but this woman isn't?' (Sanhedrin 82a). Moses could have answered that he married Tziporah before the Torah was given, when such a union was perfectly permissible. Instead, he's shocked into silence. Maybe he feels that, albeit unintentionally, he's set a bad example and is partly responsible for the moral disaster happening around him. Whatever the case, Pinchas rushes to fill this critical hiatus in his leadership:

> 'Pinchas saw': [What did he see?] Rav said: he saw what was going on and remembered the law. He said to Moses: 'Brother of my grandfather, didn't you teach us when you came down from Mount Sinai that when a man has intercourse with an Aramean woman, "zealots get him"?' [Moses replied:] 'Let the bearer of the letter carry out its instructions.' Shmuel [offered an alternative explanation:] 'Pinchas saw that "there can be no wisdom, no counsel and no consideration when God's reputation is at stake". When God's name is profaned, one doesn't wait for permission from one's teacher.'
>
> (Sanhedrin 82a-b)

But the Talmud isn't satisfied with these justifications and remains sharply critical. Had Pinchas not caught Zimri and Cosbi in the very act of intercourse, his action would have been considered murder. Had Zimri turned round and killed Pinchas, he would have been within his rights, since at that moment Pinchas was a *rodef* or 'pursuer' intent on his life, and one is allowed to defend oneself against such an attack. The Jerusalem Talmud is blunter: Pinchas 'acted without the approval of the sages'; what he did was unlawful.

Like many Talmudic comments, this is all obviously anachronistic. But the Talmud almost certainly has in mind not Pinchas but his spiritual descendants, the zealots of its own age, the *sicarii*, 'dagger-men', who incited the people to revolt against Rome, with disastrous results. The Talmudic rabbis saw the danger of undermining the rule of law, even in those rare situations in which the law itself permits it.

Why, then, does God reward Pinchas with a 'covenant of peace'? Rebbe Menachem Mendel of Vitebsk (*c.*1730–88) explains that there are times when awe and piety take such overwhelming possession of the God-fearing man that, seeing God's name desecrated, he acts out of instinctive devotion because he is 'sick from love'. At such moments, neither reason nor even Torah and *Halakhah* have any hold over him.[57] In an age of resurgent religious fervour, when fanatics slaughter innocent people purportedly in the name of God, such an explanation sounds like a warrant for murder.

But there may be a different way of understanding God's promise. God gives Pinchas not a reward but a challenge: God tasks him with changing his ways and upholding the cause of peace. The Talmud identifies Pinchas with Elijah, who is also, in his own words, 'exceedingly zealous for God' (1 Kgs 19:10). God responds not with thunder, fire or an earthquake but with the still small voice of a question: 'What are you doing here, Elijah?' According to popular folklore, he, alias Pinchas, is condemned, or maybe blessed, to walk the world forever in the cause of peace.

Perhaps, then, the message of the broken *vav* is that zealotry doesn't lead to true peace. A *vav* in two halves holds promise, since each part can be read as the tiny letter *yud*, and two *yuds* indicate God's name. But to do so they have to be properly aligned, next to one another rather than one above the other. Pinchas is charged with correcting this misalignment and misuse of God's name so as to bring peace, not more violence, to the world.

Leadership

There are moments in Moses' remarkable life that stand out for their exemplary selflessness, frankness and courage.

After bluntly reminding him of his small fault of hitting rather than speaking to the rock, God tells him to climb the mountain and die, without the opportunity to place one single foot on the soil of the Promised Land. Moses later acknowledges that he pleaded with God, but for now the Torah records not one word of protest. Moses' thoughts are solely for his people:

> Let the God of the spirits of all flesh set a man over the congregation who will go out before them, come in before them, lead them out and bring them in, so that the congregation of the Lord will not be like sheep that have no shepherd.
>
> (Num. 27:16–17)

Leadership, especially in roles that combine the spiritual and political, is an all but impossible task. A former archbishop is reputed to have said that his successor would need the strength of an ox and the hide of a rhinoceros. There has rarely been so concise a description of the challenges involved in being a leader as Moses offers here in Numbers. In his explanation as to why Moses employs the unusual address 'God of the spirits of all flesh', Rashi directs attention to one of the many difficulties of the role:

> He said to God: Master of the world, you know the temperaments of each and every person, how different they are from one another. Appoint a leader who will bear with each of them according to their views.[58]

There are many chiefs who know how to give orders but not how to listen. An autocrat has no interest in the sensitivities of different personalities and parties or in dissenting views, other than to crush them. Someone like that, Moses implies, is not a true leader. A diplomat told me that during peace negotiations one has to keep in mind three sets of reactions: the response across the table between the negotiating teams, the reaction along the table within the same team, and the anticipated reception from behind the table, when the people one is representing learn of the outcome. One constantly has to listen, even while speaking. Citizens' movements understand leadership as consisting precisely in the capacity to formulate policies based on careful attention to the numerous interest groups and different sectors of society. This applies no less to spiritual direction. A true sermon is not a moralising monologue, but the fruit of much listening to many concerns, subliminally processed into a thoughtful response.

The second challenge of leadership is more obvious: a leader must go out and come in before the people, and not, in Rashi's words, 'sit at home and send out the army'.[59] One can lead compellingly only if one is prepared to live by and struggle for the values one believes in. Like charity, leadership begins at home: if I say I care about compassion, am I compassionate? If I claim to represent justice, am I just? If I preach about the hardships of poverty, am I doing anything to alleviate them? If I wax eloquent about the environment, am I cutting my own carbon emissions and campaigning for biodiversity? If not, why not?

It's a matter of debate whether Gandhi actually said, 'Be the change you wish to see,' but he certainly exemplified the principle. People soon sniff out leaders who make little attempt to practise what they preach. One can't, and needn't, always succeed, but one has to try.

Moses' third claim concerns effectiveness. Leadership isn't about rushing ahead alone; leaders have not only to 'go out' themselves, but also to 'bring out' their people with them. As sixteenth-century Italian rabbi Ovadiah Sforno aptly comments, 'This refers to political management of the affairs of the people.'[60] There are many kinds of leader. Prophets, if they're not ignored entirely, are often stoned for saying what nobody wants to hear. Poets, whom Shelley calls 'the unacknowledged legislators of the world',[61] are rarely heeded by more than the eclectic few. But those who want to catalyse change through policies that can be implemented practically cannot adopt positions so out of step with the prevailing consensus that they fail to connect with the public and exert any leverage at all.

This presents major challenges to visionaries. People are liable to say, 'They've lost touch with reality; they're just another dreamer.' If leaders can't articulate their plans and objectives in clear and relatable ways and guide others towards them step by step, they almost certainly can't lead, at least not in the gritty, down-to-earth contexts in which Moses and his successors have to operate. Leadership demands pragmatism and strategic skill. Successful leaders not only inspire but also empower those around them. They don't seek power for power's sake but in order to use it to advance the values about which they care. This is usually best achieved through teamwork and the promotion of collective consensus. When Joshua advises Moses to lock up Eldad and Medad for prophesying in the camp, he replies: 'Are you jealous for me? If only all the people were prophets and the spirit of God rested on them all!' (Num. 11:29). He knows all too well the loneliness of leadership; allies are welcome – and essential.

Moses' final stipulation is that God should appoint someone who will not only lead the people out, but also 'bring them in'. Rashi takes this as a heartfelt personal plea because it's an issue Moses understands all too well: 'I ask that you should not do to him as you have done to me, for I may not bring the people into the Land.'[62] After crossing the Sea of Reeds on dry land, the people believe 'in God and in Moses, God's servant' (Exod. 14:31). But in the long wilderness years that follow, they repeatedly lose faith in him, threatening to appoint an alternative leader, to go back to Egypt and even to stone him. The final disappointment is that he's not allowed to guide his people across the Jordan into the Promised Land. Rashi is surely correct: Moses pleads with God not to burden his successors with as impossible a task as was placed upon him. 'Help them to succeed,' he begs God: 'enable them to bring the people in.' Tough as this may be, a leader has to be able to demonstrate successes; it's not enough to set ambitious goals and then prove unable to reach them. The confidence of the public will only be maintained if he or she can also 'bring them in'. God did not make this easy for Moses.

Moses encompasses all these challenges in two brief sentences. With forty years of experience behind him, he knows in his bones how tough the challenges of leadership truly are. Perhaps, despite his inimitable achievements, he harbours some nagging doubt that in certain respects he himself has failed, or that God has set him up for failure. Implicit in his words is the acknowledgement that serious leadership is an impossible task.

MATTOT (30:2-32:42)

The Torah and war

The Torah's account of the war against Midian is deeply disturbing. 'Have you left all the women alive?' Moses asks his officers after the battle (Num. 31:15). One might assume that he's checking they haven't broken the laws of war requiring the protection of non-combatants, especially women and children. But this is not the case; on the contrary, he's rebuking them for sparing the females. They should have killed them all, except the virgins, since it was the women 'who got you, on the instructions of Balaam' (Num. 31:16). The Torah refers to no such instructions, but the rabbis fill in the gaps. Balaam's parting advice to the Moabites after failing, because of God's intervention, to deliver the curses their king had hired him for, is to try sex instead and seduce the Children of Israel away from their God.[63] That's why Moses orders his victorious officers to kill 'every woman who's slept with a man' (Num. 31:17).

Today we have terms for such conduct: genocide or crimes against humanity, both initially described by Jewish lawyers in the wake of the Nazi Holocaust. For many of us, therefore, this is one of the most disturbing passages in the entire Torah. It seems inconceivable that killing women and children could ever have been construed as God's will.

In *Not in God's Name*, Rabbi Lord Jonathan Sacks writes:

> Never say, I hate, I kill, because my religion says so. Every text needs interpretation . . . Religions, especially religions of the Book, have hard texts: verses, commands, episodes, narratives, that if understood literally and applied directly would not merely offend our moral sense. They would also go against our best understanding of the religion. There are many examples in the Hebrew Bible. There is the war of revenge against the Midianites.[64]

What, then, is one to make of this ugly chapter? One approach is to see it in its historical context, in so far as this can be reconstructed: war in the ancient Middle East was bloody and merciless; the Torah is simply reflecting the brutal realities of the time. As Moses shows in his account in Deuteronomy of the conquests and reconquests that mark the region's violent history, it's commonplace for one nation to drive out another. God is the master planner, the supreme field marshal, settling different peoples in their lands according to the divine will. In the pagan world, gods regularly went into battle alongside their heroes, so there's nothing exceptional about Israel's God driving out the previous population to make a home for a favoured nation on a choice piece of land.

Even so, would the women and children have been put to the slaughter? It's been suggested that according to ancient Middle Eastern protocols of war, it was customary for the victors to claim that they'd killed off all their enemies, the more the better, but they didn't actually do so. It was merely a boast. In contrast, today many nations claim not to have harmed civilian populations while killing significant numbers of innocent people and excusing their deaths as 'collateral damage'. Reflecting on the bombing of Guernica on 26 April 1937, Nicholas Rankin writes:

> Modern war is largely directed at civilians. In the First World War only 11 per cent of casualties were civilians; in the Second, 53 per cent. In the wars of the 1970s, 1980s and 1990s, the proportions were 68 per cent, 76 per cent and 90 per cent respectively.[65]

A different approach is to read the account of the battle against Midian through the eyes of the rabbis, remembering that Judaism is not the religion of the Bible, but of the Bible as understood through the lenses of rabbinic exegesis. The Talmud relates a dispute:

> 'They fought against Midian, as God commanded Moses': This means that they surrounded Midian on all four sides. But Rabbi Natan says that they left the fourth side open, so that the Midianites could flee.
>
> (Sotah 43a)

In other words, there must be a way for non-combatants to escape, the kind of safe passage the United Nations often struggles to negotiate in the midst of bitter fighting today. In describing Joshua's conquest of the Promised Land, the rabbis go further. He had to issue a three-part warning: 'Whoever wants to leave, let them leave; whoever wants to make peace, let them make peace; whoever wants to give battle, let them give battle' (Vayikra Rabba 17:6).

An army must first allow the enemy to escape, then it has to offer terms of peace. Only if these two strategies fail may it attack.

Rabbi Brad Artson offers a contemporary summary of the direction of travel of rabbinic interpretation:

> The rabbis of the Talmud and the Midrash, as well as later authorities such as Maimonides, went out of their way to explain that this commandment [to kill the local population] was applicable only in the distant past, only within the borders of the Land of Israel, only for those Canaanite tribes which refused either to emigrate or negotiate ... Much of Jewish literature on the Conquest is an attempt to limit its scope and to prevent its recurrence.[66]

In this regard, perhaps the most significant passage in the Talmud is its insistence that none of the nations against which the Torah proclaimed war exists any longer, because the Assyrian emperor Sennacherib came and 'mixed together the nations' (Berachot 28a). After conquering much of the Middle East in the eighth century BCE he implemented a policy of mass deportation, removing entire populations, including the ten lost tribes, to unfamiliar lands, presumably to prevent rebellion. The Amalekites, Midianites, Ammonites and Moabites ceased to exist as distinct nations. Not a trace of them remained, Maimonides would subsequently declare. This is not a footnote to history, but the Talmud's way of saying that whatever the Torah's laws of war may once have been, they are now a dead letter and must on no account be applied to any future situation.

Yet the deep unease we feel at the account of the war against Midian remains. The editors of the *Etz Hayim* edition of the Torah express this well:

> Does placing the seal of approval on a military undertaking change and sanctify the battle or does it compromise the religion and contaminate it with the stain of bloodshed? When is war 'the Lord's vengeance' and when is it human vengeance to which the name of God has been attached?[67]

This leads to the wider question: does God really ever command war? Perhaps two crimes are involved, a sin against humanity for committing acts of violence, unless in genuine self-defence or in a clearly just cause, followed by the blasphemy of placing the responsibility on God.

Yet throughout history, military leaders and their followers have claimed that God is on their side. Many may genuinely have believed it. The 'knowledge' that this is God's will may serve to overcome moral scruples and justify the killing of fellow humans. It may help to conquer fear in the face of battle. It may also, especially among zealots, be an impassioned, but nonetheless misguided, response to a world experienced as unjust and corrupt.

But sometimes it is necessary to fight evil, as was the case in World War II. Judaism is not an entirely pacifist religion and does not regard genuinely defensive war, or war to protect threatened innocent people, as intrinsically and invariably wrong. The rabbis distinguished between wars of conquest, sanctioned only during Temple times and forbidden ever afterwards, and wars in self-defence against enemy attacks. Only the latter is ever considered permitted today. But even then it is always a last resort only, at best an unavoidable evil.

However, this doesn't excuse the mistreatment of non-combatants. Judaism obligates soldiers to care for civilians escaping from areas under attack and siege. Yet innocent blood is inevitably shed in the course of battle. American rabbi Irving Greenberg painfully acknowledges:

> Show me a people whose hands are not dirty and I will show you a people which has not been responsible. Show me a people which has

stopped washing its hands and admitting its guilt, and I will show you a people which is arrogant and dying morally.[68]

This is the tragedy of war.

Innocent before God and Israel

I was ten when my English teacher introduced the class to Shakespeare's *Macbeth*. I loved it, but for years afterwards I had nightmares that Banquo's body, with its 'twenty trenched gashes', lay underneath my bed. I still often think of the play, but different lines haunt me today, such as Lady Macbeth's words while she sleepwalks as she desperately tries to wash the blood of Duncan's murder from her hands and hide the evidence of her guilt:

> What need we
> Fear who knows it, when none can call our power to
> Account?[69]

This is the boast of tyrants through the ages: we have the might, so we're accountable to no one.

At least Lady Macbeth wants to remove the incriminating blood from her hands; she, at least, experiences the revenge of conscience. Too many leaders show no such remorse. Cynical and pragmatic, they operate by the principle, 'So long as we can get away with it, everything's permitted.' Selfish, brutal and false, because deeds always have consequences, it's an attitude to which no society can afford to submit. It leads only to innumerable killings, including the murder of trust.

Trust requires accountability, accountability demands integrity, and integrity is founded on the commitment to truth. At the heart of all faiths is accountability before God. 'Know what is above you,' insisted Rabbi Judah the Prince, editor of the Mishnah, 'an eye that sees, an ear which hears and all your deeds written down in a book.'[70] The Torah repeatedly enjoins us to 'fear God'; we mustn't imagine that just because there are no human witnesses, there is no God who sees our actions. God sees to the heart, understanding our intentions even when they are hidden from other human beings, even when we refuse to admit them even to ourselves.

But it's not only before God that we're held accountable. Our actions must be transparent and honest in the eyes of the human community as well. The rabbis find proof for this in Moses' warning to the tribes of Reuben, Gad and part of Manasseh before they enter the Promised Land. When they tell him that they don't intend to cross the Jordan but want to remain in the rich farmlands to the east of the river, Moses angrily challenges them: 'Are your brothers going to go to war, while you remain here?!' (Num. 32:6).

When they then promise to send all their men of military age to fight, Moses sternly warns them that they must keep their word if they are to be held 'innocent before God and Israel' (Num. 32:22). The rabbis are puzzled by why it was necessary for Moses to stipulate that they had to be 'innocent before Israel' as well. Isn't it enough to be clear in the sight of God?

Not so, the rabbis insist. Our actions must also be beyond suspicion in the eyes of the community. To emphasise the importance of transparency in all our dealings, Rabbi Yonatan brings prooftexts from all three sections of the Hebrew Bible:

> In the Torah, the Prophets and the Writings we find that one has to be innocent in the eyes of other people just as one has to be innocent in the eyes of God. From where in the Torah? From, 'You shall be blameless before God and before Israel' (Num. 32:22). From where in the Prophets? From, 'God, the Eternal, the Almighty, knows, and Israel has to know' (Josh. 22:22). From where in the Writings? From, 'Find grace and understanding in the eyes of God and humankind' (Prov. 3:4).
>
> (Jerusalem Talmud, Shekalim 3:2)

The Babylonian Talmud offers a series of small but telling examples. No bride from the family of Avtinas, who had the ancestral privilege of preparing the incense for the Temple, was ever allowed to go to her marriage canopy wearing perfume, so that no one could accuse them of using ingredients intended for the Temple for personal adornment. Similarly, the family of Garmu, who baked the shewbread placed weekly on the table before God, never ate white bread, so that nobody would suspect them of sequestering the loaves intended for the Temple to furnish their own board (Talmud Yoma 38a). The team entrusted with collecting charity monies was not allowed to swap any small change they might be given for coins of a larger denomination in their own purses. They had to exchange them through a third person to prevent anyone from thinking they were pocketing the funds (Talmud Pesachim 11a).

There has to be clarity in all spheres of human interaction. Should doubt be cast on the integrity of their actions, the suspected parties are obliged to explain their motives. Similarly, judges have to demonstrate to litigants who feel that the decision against them is unfair how they arrived at their ruling (Shulchan Aruch, Choshen Mishpat 14:4). Only a culture of honest disclosure can prevent a society from becoming permeated by currents of distrust which ultimately risk undermining not only individual relationships but also the very institutions designed to protect its moral health. Nothing, though, is as dangerous as when the rot comes from the top, when disingenuity, lying, cover-ups, suppression and intimidation become the modus operandi of the most senior offices in the land and leaders promote cultures of fake truths.

Judaism is premised not just on the belief that our deeds are known to God but also on the conviction that in our heart of hearts we wish them to be known. We want to stand before God and ourselves with a clear conscience. In the editing room of memory, when we hear ourselves say, 'It wasn't really me. So-and-So made me do it,' another voice often whispers back, 'But, you, too were responsible; you know that, don't you?' Honesty and remorse can be painful, but their sting is like the pain of a wound when it's cauterised to allow it to heal. Biblical Hebrew has no specific word for 'conscience'. But the psalmist relates how his 'kidneys chasten him at night', from which the rabbis understood that there exists *musar kelayot*, 'gut morality', a visceral inner knowledge of right and wrong (Ps. 16:7).

Ultimately, we are responsible not only for what we do, but also for what we could and should have done. We are accountable for our contribution to injustice through lacking the courage and commitment to name and combat wrong. We are answerable not just to the now of our immediate present, but also to the future. The world's children may have good cause to ask what we have done to enable them to inherit a just, viable and sustainable world.

Are we innocent before God and humanity? The present is our witness, and the future holds the verdict.

MASEI (33:1–36:13)

....

The courage to come forward

The Torah repeats three times what seems at first glance a very ordinary preposition:

> The daughters of Zelophechad drew near . . . The names of his daugh-
> ters were Machlah, Noa, Hoglah, Milkah and Tirzah. They stood
> *before* Moses, *before* Elazar the Priest, and *before* the princes and all the
> community, at the entrance to the Tent of Meeting.
>
> (Num. 27:1–2)

The Talmud debates why the text couldn't simply have said that they stood before them all. But this would miss the point. It was no simple matter for women to step forward as the daughters of Zelophechad bravely did. Since the critical moment when Moses' sister Miriam ran up to Pharaoh's daughter and offered to find a midwife for the baby she'd just rescued from the Nile, an act of courage easily underestimated by attributing it to the natural intrepidity of a child, the Torah has not recorded one single scene in which a woman, or even a group of women, has come forward to confront the powers that be.

The world of the Hebrew Bible is scarcely one of equality between the sexes. The same applies to much of the classic rabbinic canon. The almost constant assumption of the subordinate status of women, often equated with minors and slaves, sometimes reduced even further to little more than chattels, makes a significant proportion of Mishnaic and Talmudic literature painful to digest.

Arguably, a mitigating factor is that by and large the direction of travel in rabbinic writings is towards a greater recognition of women's rights. But even then, we rarely hear this from the mouths of women themselves. The place of women was either in the houses of their fathers, to whose will they were subject, or in the households of their husbands, to whose wishes they were once again almost always subordinate. Though the Bible references many remarkable women, whose achievements need to be considered in the context of the limitations they had to overcome, the exceptions nevertheless highlight the rule. The absence of women's voices in the Talmud, with very limited exceptions, has caused an irremediable impoverishment of the range and depths of sensitivity in Judaism's most formative discussions and decision-making.

Therefore, even though there were five of them, it must have taken considerable nerve for the daughters of Zelophechad to 'draw near' to the leaders of their people. Yet the sisters were brave enough to stand not only before the high priest, but in front of Moses himself, as well as before the heads of all the tribes, no doubt with the entire community keenly watching. The Torah's treble 'before' highlights their courage.

Acknowledging the justice of their claim, Moses immediately takes their case to God. 'Their case', *mishpatan,* is written with its final letter *nun,* indicating the feminine plural, enlarged to emphasise that this is *their* cause, that of a group so often marginalised and disempowered. Moses swiftly reports back that God has affirmed the validity of their position: 'The daughters of Zelophechad speak right' (Num. 36:5–7).

But this isn't the end of the matter. In the final chapter of Numbers, the sisters' uncles, together with the heads of their families – all, of course, men – bring an objection. According to the system of distribution Moses has just proposed, all lands, with a few exceptions not relevant to this case, will have to be returned every fiftieth, or jubilee, year to the tribe to which they are allocated when the Children of Israel take possession of Canaan. If Zelophechad's daughters each inherit a portion of their father's estate and then marry outside their tribe, their lands will become the property of their husbands. Then, when the jubilee arrives, they will be considered to belong to their husband's tribes and will be lost forever to the tribe of Manasseh into which the girls were born and to which those lands should therefore rightfully return.

This time Moses does not turn to God and there is no highlighted final *nun.* Fine, he says, the five daughters of Zelophechad should nevertheless inherit their father's estate and marry whomever they want. But 'whomever they want' is in the masculine, not the feminine, plural. The women's marriage options are to be constrained by what the men of their tribe demand. To protect its ancestral holdings, the girls must choose their husbands from within their own tribe. Moses expands this into a general rule that any women who inherit land must marry inside their tribe; their freedom to choose a husband, already limited, is curtailed even further. The tribe and its interests precede the rights of the individual, especially if that individual is a woman.

Zelophechad's daughters do not object; perhaps they expected as much, never imagining they would have any real choice in the matter. The penultimate verse of Numbers (36:12) records their marriages to their cousins. However, the Talmud maintains that they could have married whomever they wanted, and that the Torah merely recommends them to choose within their tribe as a form of sound marriage guidance (Bava Batra 102a). Rabbi Baruch Halevi Epstein (1860–1941) suggests that because they were important women, the Torah grants them an exclusive freedom of choice to which it does not entitle other women (Torah Temimeh, especially note 18 to Num. 36).

This seems like a case of two steps forward, one and a half steps back-wards. Rights are granted, then so severely limited that the price of obtaining them seems all but negated by the cost. Maybe, though, it's anachronistic to impose on the world of the Torah and Talmud the notion that women have genuine freedom in choosing whom to marry. Or maybe it's our modern, individualistic philosophy that is the exception, in which the claims and rights of individuals take precedence over the inter-ests of the group. Perhaps it would have been obvious to the sisters that they would have to put the demands of tribe and family first. It would have been vindication enough to know that they could at least take their father's holdings with them into their marriages.

While it is hard to know how to evaluate the outcome in its historical and cultural context, there can be no doubt about the courage Zelophechad's daughters exemplify. It is by those who have done likewise through the generations that the rights of women in Judaism have, often all too pain-fully, been advanced.

From wilderness to journey

As best-selling author Raynor Winn notes, musing on her challenging walk along the entire distance of the Salt Path on the southwest coast of England: 'If we didn't hold those memories together, would all the life they held slip from view, leaving only a faded picture behind?'[71]

Perhaps it's always only hindsight that turns wanderings into travels, which connects events and their fallout, partly foreseen, mostly unpre-dicted, into the coherence of a journey. This is what we see in the clos-ing section of Numbers when the Torah lists 'their departures and their journeyings by the mouth of God' (Num. 33:2), all the places where the Children of Israel encamped from when they left Egypt until their arrival forty years later at the border of the Promised Land. Thus the book which begins 'in the wilderness', a byword for being lost and directionless, is retrospectively turned into the account of a divinely ordained itinerary. But the events it records hardly amount to a pre-planned programme.

The opening chapters of Numbers describe in idealistic terms the perfect symmetry of the Israelite encampment and the precise order in which the tribes are commanded to decamp and travel onwards 'by the mouth of the Lord'. But reality instantly sets in. What follows reads like a constant sequence of troubles. The worst of them is the negative report brought by the spies sent out by Moses, leading to thirty-eight more years of wandering and the waste of an entire generation who die in the desert without so much as a glimpse of the much-hailed Promised Land. Next in the scale of misadventures is the revolt by Korach and his followers, followed by the outbreak of plague when the people blame Moses for their demise. Add to that the ongoing frustration with the daily menu of dry manna, when, conveniently forgetting what life there had actually been like, the people long for the fish and melons of Egypt. There's the incident with the quails, sent by a vexed God on an evil wind, supposedly to satisfy the people's demand for meat, but the flesh turns to poison in their mouths. There's thirst, too, and disaster when anger finally gets the better of Moses, who calls the Children of Israel 'fools' and hits the rock to which God has only instructed him to speak. Finally, there's the ill-fated encounter with Midianite girls, leading to sex and idolatry, whereupon God sends another plague, leaving twenty-four thousand dead. It's not just Moses who loses patience, but also God, whose anger repeatedly boils over.

All this is at odds with the picture of carefully planned progress described by the Torah at the book's close:

> These are the journeys of the Children of Israel who left the Land of Egypt according to their hosts, by the hand of Moses and Aaron. Moses wrote down their departures and their journeyings by the mouth of God.
>
> (Num. 33:1–2)

The verses read like the protestations of a map-reader who knows perfectly well that for most of the time they were lost, yet claims he'd always intended to lead his team along the route by which, late and exhausted, they do finally manage to reach their destination: it was all according to plan, all 'by the mouth of God'.

But to what do the words 'by the mouth of God' in fact refer? To the Children of Israel's journeys, explains Abraham ibn Ezra, giving the obvious answer. No, responds Nachmanides, the Torah has already told us that 'by the mouth of God they travelled and by the mouth of God they camped' (Num. 9:23). Rather, here, 'by the mouth of the Lord' refers to how Moses wrote their travels down so that future generations would appreciate the way God miraculously supported a huge army of people far from habitation throughout forty long years. It describes not what actually occurred but how it was told. Nachmanides' comment underlines the truth that it's not what happens but the narrative we create afterwards that turns events into stories, imbues them with coherence and, for better or worse, becomes the fact of the matter for future generations.

A striking midrash makes a similar point through an analogy with family life:

> To what can [listing all the places where the Children of Israel camped] be compared? It's like a king who takes his sick son to another country for treatment. On the way home his father recounts to him what happened on their journey out: 'This is where we slept. That's where we felt cold. Here's where you had headaches.' Similarly, God said to Moses: 'Tell them about all the places they upset me.'
>
> (Midrash Tanhuma Masei 3)

On the way out, all the poor child knows is that he's feeling ill and scared. It's only afterwards, on the way back, that he, and we, can properly take in what happened on the journey. What seemed like nothing but a series of troubles is framed in retrospect as part of a process of healing. Did the boy feel that way at the time? Did the Children of Israel see everything as 'by the mouth of God'? Almost certainly not.

The wilderness through which they pass is as 'a howling waste'; their travels are a gruelling test of faith which they have no choice other than to endure (Deut. 32:10). Watching from a distant hilltop, Balaam, the pagan prophet, may abandon his intention to curse and say instead:

> How good are your tents, O Jacob, your dwelling places, Israel,
> Stretched out like valleys, like gardens planted by the riverside.
>
> (Num. 24:5–6)

But nothing in the text suggests that the Children of Israel felt like well-provisioned riverside residents at the time.

The meanings we derive from our experiences are inevitably reconstructions, put together not only through remembering but also by forgetting. We work ceaselessly, consciously, unconsciously and in our dreams at editing and re-editing the narratives of our lives.

What makes all the difference is how we do this. For example, my wife and I didn't deliberately plan to hike with our children over a score of summer holidays through every town and village past which the railway winds its course through the Scottish Highlands. We couldn't have known beforehand that twenty years later, travelling on that same trainline, we would look out of the window, anxious not to miss a single mountain pass or bridge, and say to one another: 'Here's where we stayed that time when the raspberries were ripe. This is the old road along which we carried our exhausted children at the end of that long walk. That's the rickety footbridge that took us over the river.'

At the time the children moaned that the walks were too long and the midges too many. But now what remain are the good memories, the joy and the love.

The national histories of nations are no different, fashioned and refashioned in the collective memory by poets and storytellers, until setting them down in writing coalesces, and coerces, them into a final form. After that, the rest is all interpretation. What turns experience into meaning is not so much what actually happened as how we tell it afterwards. Therefore, Nachmanides and ibn Ezra are both right: 'By the mouth of God' refers to how the journeys are told, but it's precisely that telling, how they are internalised and then eternalised, recollected and related, that makes them journeys 'by the mouth of the Lord'.

It's far from insignificant that the book which begins 'in the wilderness' and describes a whole series of disasters concludes by framing those same misadventures as journeys with God. There are people who, towards the close of tough lives, look back on them as rich with blessings; there are others who recall only the difficulties. It's an issue we all have to face: how will we shape what our life comes to mean? Do we see just the troubles and vexations, or a random mixture of ups and downs, or are we able to look back on our years with enough generosity, forbearance and wisdom to turn them into a journey at the close of which we can say with gratitude, 'This is the path on which God has led me through the wilderness of my life.'?

THE BOOK OF DEUTERONOMY
דְּבָרִים

Words

Though the book is known as Deuteronomy, the repetition of the law, after the Greek, the Hebrew name *Devarim* simply means 'Words'. Chosen, as typical with biblical titles, after the first significant word in the text, it's an apt heading for Moses' final oration. Though he begins his career as 'heavy of tongue and heavy of speech' (Exod. 4:10), Moses' legacy is words, the teachings and laws he bequeaths to his people.

No clause comes more frequently than 'God spoke to Moses, saying . . .', which recurs 175 times in the Torah. Its first appearance is in Exodus 6:10, when God commands Moses to confront Pharaoh. But on an overwhelming number of occasions, it is to the Children of Israel that God tells Moses to address his words. The meaning virtually every time is that Moses should relay what he hears from God to the entire people. He is, as it were, God's public voice, God's megaphone.

As we progress through the Torah the phrase becomes so familiar that we tend to give it no thought. But its very frequency suggests that it deserves closer attention. What does *leimor*, 'saying', add, especially as it's often followed by a further instruction to 'tell the Children of Israel'?

The sentence contains two different verbs: the first, *vayedabber*, 'God spoke', is traditionally understood in rabbinic literature to signify direct 'tough talk'. Hence the thirteenth-century commentator, legalist and mystic Nachmanides' explanation that, just as God speaks to Moses 'face to face and not in riddles' (Num. 12:8), so Moses passes on God's commandments with absolute clarity.[1] In contrast, the second, *leimor*, 'saying', from the root *amar*, is often taken to imply a softer approach. The following Hasidic teaching, with its typical chain of transmission, makes much of this distinction:

> I heard from Reb Yisrael from the town of Vishgorod, who heard from Rebbe Chaim of Zhinkov, who said in the name of his father the saintly Rebbe Zusya, grandson of the Rebbe of Apt, that we know that *dibbur* indicates sternness whereas *amirah* expresses gentleness. Moses our Master had the strength to receive stern instructions from God through the medium of *dibbur* but then to sweeten and soften them before transmitting them to the Children of Israel through the

gentler mode of *amirah*. This is the meaning of 'God spoke to Moses *vayedabber*, saying, *leimor*'.

Rebbe Baruch of Medibodz (1753–1811) adds a further dimension:

> Moses' words were directed at 'all Israel', at each and every individual according to their level of understanding.[2]

In other words, Moses understood how to pass on even God's command- ments in such a way that everyone could accept them. It's a rare gift.

These Hasidic teachers were no doubt speaking about themselves and how to develop the art of conveying challenging messages in engaging ways. But their comment has an important bearing on how any of us could, and should, use language. Whereas information often becomes vaguer in the transmission, as in 'Chinese Whispers', the tone in which we relay opinions frequently becomes harsher, especially in the age of social media. One receives a tart message, responds angrily on the rebound and presses the 'send' key without taking time to reconsider. Twitter famously strips complex issues of nuance, inviting over-simplification, brash opin- ionising, verbal brutality and contempt. Far from bringing people together, it's a perfect instrument for polarisation. Verbal aggression is often more a symptom of hurt than of anger, but untempered by reflection and self- awareness it becomes part of an ever sharper exchange of insults – word rage, the linguistic equivalent of road rage.

Therefore, the art of turning tough messages into gentler and more compelling communications can scarcely be more important. The author of Proverbs understood that 'a gentle answer turns aside anger' (Prov. 15:1). The rabbis taught that 'words which come from the heart reach the heart',[3] the corollary being that words which come from the gall become even more galling. The Talmud was conscious of the geographical reach of words, even then, comparing slander to an arrow that can kill even at a considerable distance (Arachin 15b). But they couldn't have imagined the instantaneous nature of today's global communications, making the poten- tial of our words even more lethal.

A vital further dimension to the power of language as understood in the Bible is its spiritual resonance. Words are imbued with holiness, instru- ments of divine creativity; each stage of the earth's formation in Genesis 1 begins with, 'And God said . . .' To the mystics, for whom divine revela- tion is continuous and unceasing through the languages of both Torah and creation, the entire text of the Torah is replete with sacred energy;

grammatical structures and semantic meanings represent only the surface level of its fathomless significance. Ultimately, the Torah is 'white fire on black fire',[4] a communication of infinite potential between the divine and the human. Great poetry may be an articulation in language of a similar creative force which flows as a surge of energy through the artist's mind, enabling profound connections, transcending literal comprehension.

Such words retain their spiritual power as Rabbe Aharon of Karlin (1736–72) explains: 'On the far side of the Jordan, in the land of Moab, Moses began to expound, *be'er*, this Torah, saying . . .' (Deut. 1:5).

Don't read *be'er* as the verb meaning 'expound' but as the noun meaning 'wellspring', he taught: 'Moses' words are a constantly flowing well from which all Israel will drink for generations to come', and, it should be added, not only Israel. They transmit God's *kol gadol velo yasaf*, God's 'mighty voice which never ceased',[5] a voice present but latent in all things, audible to the seeker but silent to the unheeding, which we can hear in the Torah with its endless depths, in the language of the natural world and in human interaction. It is this voice to which the Torah enjoins us to listen and about which it commands us to speak 'when you walk in the way, dwell in your homes, lie down and rise up' (Deut. 6:7).

History is often cruel, and people harsh; the discourse around us generally contains more *dibbur* than *amirah*. The capacity to turn it into a medium through which we are enabled to hear the sacred and absorb it into our hearts, the ability to communicate it in a way that makes life's impact gentler yet deeper: this, at least according to Rebbe Zusya, is Moses' enduring gift.

The hinge – and the stresses of leadership

Moses is venerated in rabbinic tradition as 'Moshe Rabbenu', Moses our master, *the* teacher par excellence. Admired and beloved, he is without equal in Judaism, as the Torah says in its final verse: 'No one has arisen in Israel like Moses' (Deut. 34:12).

But the rabbis, down to earth as ever, had other names for him too, including 'the hinge' or 'the faithful hinge', an unflattering title for a hero. Yet it makes sense: a hinge is the point about which everything pivots; it's what takes the stress. Such pressure wears down even the strongest metal, let alone mere flesh and blood. It's hard being caught in the middle of an argument between friends, and worse if it's family. It's less of a problem when one doesn't care if one party storms off in anger. But if the task is to keep everybody together, then, as every mediator appreciates, one has to be skilful, subtle and, above all, endlessly patient. Being a hinge is a lonely test of endurance.

Moses survives as the 'hinge' between God and Israel for forty tough years. As he reviews his life, he admits that it has sometimes felt overwhelming: 'How can I bear on my own your troubles, burdens and quarrels?' (Deut. 1:12).

This is an echo of his earlier complaint when God suggests to him, disingenuously as it later emerges, that meat can be provided in the desert for the whole nation: 'How can I cope alone with this entire people; it's too much for me. If this is how you're treating me, I beg you, kill me first' (Num. 11:14–15).

God punishes Moses for striking the rock when he's been instructed only to speak to it. What's remarkable is not that Moses finally loses his temper after thirty-nine years, but that he has succeeded in keeping it for so long. How has he managed his impossible role as hinge?

Moses' life is marked by moments of extreme loneliness. Afloat in a reed basket on the Nile, pushed away from the riverbank by his own mother, he drifts helplessly on the water. This foretells the fate of later generations when parents had to make the heart-rending decision to send away their children with the Kindertransport in 1938–9, knowing they would almost certainly never see them again, in the hope that they might find safety in an unknown land.

Alone again after leaving the comfort of the Egyptian palace where he's been brought up, Moses witnesses the brutal maltreatment of the Hebrew slaves and comes to the realisation that from now on it is they who are his brothers. On his own once more, he stands barefoot before the flaming bush and remonstrates against the destiny he realises he cannot escape. Alone, he climbs Mount Sinai, drawing near to the thick darkness of God's presence. On his own in the final hours of his life, he stands on the mountaintop overlooking the land he will never enter, awaiting his end.

There are moments in life that can only be lived alone: birth, death and those daunting hours when, conscious of the consequences or not, we ratify internally the decisions that determine the course of our life. But what Moses experiences is something different: the loneliness of standing in the middle when the two parties with whom he has a unique and irreplaceable relationship clash, each frustrated by, yet deeply in need of, the other. On at least three occasions the Torah shows us Moses rejected by, yet still responsible for, both sides.

The first comes at the very outset of his career. As God has forewarned, Pharaoh won't listen to his plea to 'let my people go' but instead increases their burdens, refusing to provide the Children of Israel with straw while insisting on the full daily quota of bricks (Exod. 5:7–8). This provides a further pretext for the Egyptian taskmasters to beat the Hebrew officers responsible for production. Caught in the middle between the angry overseers and the resentful slaves, they complain to Pharaoh about the injustice of his demands. On leaving the palace, they encounter Moses and Aaron and turn on them in fury: 'God be the judge: you've made us stink before Pharaoh and his minions; you've put a sword in their hands to kill us' (Exod. 5:21).

Hopeless and helpless, Moses vents his frustration on God: Pharaoh hates me, the people despise me and you've let me down.

'Patience,' God replies, 'wait and see.' The Torah doesn't tell us if this makes Moses feel any better. But God at least tries to assuage his concerns; next time, God will augment them.

The golden calf brings Moses' second and hardest lonely moment. Moses has taken too long to come back down the mountain. Feeling abandoned and unnerved, the people beg for a god they can actually see and persuade Aaron to make the golden calf. Infuriated by their rejection, God turns on Moses: 'Look what *your* people have done, whom *you* brought out of Egypt.' All of a sudden, they've become Moses' responsibility, while God turns on them in fury: 'Let me be and I'll destroy them, then make you into a great nation' (Exod. 32:7–10). Meanwhile, at the base of the mountain, Aaron proclaims the calf to be the 'god who brought [the Children of Israel] up out of Egypt' (Exod. 32:4).

The people disown God, and God disowns the people. Only Moses is left in the middle, like a man holding on to ropes that have become untied from each other and are being pulled furiously in opposite directions. He refuses to let go of either end and, seizing on the opportunity half offered in God's 'let me be', steps into the breach. 'They're *your* people,' he insists, the people to whose ancestors Abraham, Isaac and Jacob you made a firm promise. You can't now break your word. And, anyway, what will the Egyptians say if you destroy them all in the desert? Even God, it appears, is susceptible to what others think. Finally, Moses puts himself on the line: *im ayin*, 'if nothing', if you can't forgive, if nothing else will persuade you, wipe me from your record. Overcome by his selfless intervention, God relents and the people also subsequently repent. It is Moses' greatest moment (Exod. 32:10–15, 32).

It is only afterwards that the immense strain of this all-or-nothing drama becomes clear. Re-ascending the mountain after destroying the golden calf, Moses begs God: 'Make known to me your ways' (Exod. 33:13). How otherwise can he understand, let alone persuade an anxious people to follow a seemingly inscrutable and unpredictable deity?

The third time Moses is caught alone in the middle comes when the spies bring back their negative report about the Promised Land. Disheartened and frightened, the people decide they've had enough of both their God and their leader: 'Let's appoint a head and go back to Egypt,' they cry (Num. 14:4). I'll kill them off with a plague and start again with you, God retorts. Moses employs the same ruse as before: Why afford the Egyptians the gratification of telling their neighbours you lacked the ability to lead your people to their land? Once again, he persuades God to hold back and the people to repent (Num. 14:11–16). His reward is thirty-eight more years of wandering with them round the desert when he's already had about as much as he can take.

But that's the challenge of leadership. It's about holding together the factions that one has been entrusted to lead. It's about turning difference and dissonance into a creative relationship. It's about keeping the balance between realism and hope.

'God,' Moses must often have felt, 'if only you knew what it's like to be human!'

'You people,' Moses must have thought every day, 'if only you had a little more vision!'

Often, the only thing leaders have to go on is an obstinate refusal to give up.

That's how Churchill must have felt as he spoke the famous words, 'I have nothing to offer but blood, toil, tears and sweat.'[6] That's the grit which kept Nelson Mandela courageous and hopeful through his long years on Robben Island. But we ordinary people have our experiences too: those lonely, frightened moments when it's hard to hold our life together; when we fight our setbacks, failures and depressions; when we refuse to let go of our future, when we determine in the core of our spirit, 'I shall not die, but live' (Ps. 118:17).

To be a faithful hinge takes courage, endurance, resourcefulness, self-lessness and faith. Mundane, even insulting, as it may sound, 'hinge' may in fact be the greatest of all Moses' titles.

This great and terrible wilderness

Deuteronomy opens with a review of the desert wanderings of the Children of Israel. It's at once a reprise of a specific itinerary and a metaphor for life's adventures through unknown territory surrounded by dangers and beset by fears. The route crosses thirst-parched lands, without water, full of snakes and scorpions. The Torah describes the journey as a trial:

> Remember the journey on which God led you for forty years through the desert, to try you and test you to know what's in your heart, whether you will keep God's commandments or not.
>
> (Deut. 8:2)

Every year millions of refugees face appalling journeys:

> My younger brother, he wanted to come too. I told him: don't go. Stay with our father. I'm tough; he's not. I made it; he wouldn't have. In the desert they give you no food; one bottle of water each day. I saw dead people. In the boat, the waves are strong. If you're alone, the others push you out. I made friends and we said, 'We'll go together.' I said, 'If I die, I die.'

As I listened to S., a teenage refugee from Somalia, I remembered the Torah's words about the wilderness 'vast and terrible' (Deut. 8:15). Physically or mentally, whether the lands and seas are literal or metaphorical, countless people traverse terrifying spaces in their lives. Few are spared entirely, though there's no equality in the challenges people face. In scattered verses, as if trying to hide the truth, the Torah reveals how harsh such journeys can be:

> From without, the sword strikes grief,
> From within, terror.
>
> (Deut. 32:25)

No one can know for certain whether and when they too will be forced to depart. There's no guarantee of peace and stability, anywhere, ever. My father came into my room one night when I was in my mid-teens and said, seemingly apropos of nothing, 'Always remember, they can take everything from you except what's in your mind.' Perhaps it was my age that brought back to him how at sixteen he was a refugee fleeing Nazi Germany for an impoverished Palestine and a decade of war, all at once the bread-winner for his parents and three sisters.

It's not only physical journeys that hold terrors. The descent to the depths of the mind can be equally full of horrors. For some, like S., or my father, who maintained his determination to study throughout the hungry years, the mind is a place of sanctuary. But for others, whose path may outwardly seem easy, it's precisely in that inner landscape that terror and desolation lie. Down we go into the darkness, the cell doors shutting behind us, unheard by anyone, leaving no hope of exit, while thought itself provides the snakes and scorpions poisoning every hope.

'Remember the route your ancestors walked, for you too shall walk it,' commented Rabbi Jacob ben Asher (c.1269–c.1343). His own family had to leave their native Germany for Castile; he'd no doubt also heard the accounts of fellow Jews similarly forced to flee their homes. Perhaps he understood too that for many the journey is internal and that the unrelenting seascape is consciousness itself. Jedaiah of Beziers compared life to crossing the ocean on a plinth stretching endlessly into the horizon, too narrow for two to walk together, with no handrail, and the violent waves all around.[7]

Are such travails sent from God to know what's in our heart? Would one tell a refugee who survived the Mediterranean in a small dinghy packed with a hundred terrified people that this is a test from above? Would one say such a thing to someone struggling with tormenting thoughts?

Clearly, that's not what Moses means. He's referring solely to the journey to the Promised Land, to which God has summoned the people 'as an eagle arouses its nest' and on which God supports them 'as a father carries his son' (Deut. 32:11; 1:31). The people receive manna every day and draw water from the well of Miriam. When they strike camp, a protective cloud surrounds them on all sides. When they decamp, it sets out ahead and prepares their way.

But where are the food, water and protective clouds on so many other journeys? Maybe kindness is the manna, as when a young man from East Africa sat penniless outside a café in Bulgaria and a waiter, who had himself been starving once and understood hunger, came out and brought him food. Maybe the protective clouds are the rescuers who help survivors out of tiny boats, greeting them with warm blankets and dry clothing. Yet, for many, such manna never comes; no magic clouds protect them from robbers and killers. Are their journeys, too, trials from God? Or is it we who are under examination, to see if we will help?

Perhaps, though, there's a different way of interpreting the Torah. If we are able to understand the journey through our personal wilderness not as a punishing test from God, but rather as a challenge through which God wills us on and tries to empower us to take the next step, we may find greater resources to continue, more strength to persist. My father's aunt Sophie learnt in early 1943 that she, her husband and her elderly mother would shortly be deported from their home in Moravia. Her final letter, dated 18 January and addressed to her siblings, eventually reached the family in Jerusalem three years later. She wrote:

> We pray to God that he will allow us to overcome successfully this trial which has been placed upon us and that we will see each other again in peace . . .

Her mother, my great-grandmother, added:

> Today I visited the grave of your beloved and good father for the last time and took my farewell; may his spirit hover over us in these difficult times.

I don't for one moment think that the terrible journeys on which they were forced to embark were in any way God's will. What I do believe is that the faith that God was with them gave them the strength to face what lay ahead.

What can one say to the millions of refugees caught by militias and smugglers, then incarcerated, raped, tortured, deprived of food and water and cut off from friends and family? The only way I can understand the Torah's words about God's tests is as a prayer:

> May you feel that God is with you, guiding you on your journey. May God inspire all those around you to support you. May God bring you to the promised land of safety.

Whose fault?

No two accounts of the same event are ever identical. This is true not only when different people describe the same incident, but even when the story is told by the same person at different times or to a different audience. Consciously or unconsciously, we reconfigure the narrative to exculpate ourselves, to inculpate others or to make it conform to how we want to understand God, the world and destiny.

This is certainly the case with the story of the twelve spies. Thirty-eight years later, recounting the disastrous sequence of events to a new generation, Moses describes them in a radically different way. As is so often the case to this very day, the issue at stake is responsibility: whose idea was it to send the spies out in the first place, opening the door to the fiasco that cost the Children of Israel almost four decades of cantankerous years of wandering in the desert?

In Numbers, where the incident is related in present time, as if as it unfolds, we are told: 'God spoke to Moses, saying, "Send men to scope out the Land of Canaan which I'm going to give to the Children of Israel"' (Num. 13:1–2).

In other words, the initiative comes from above. But when Moses recalls the events in Deuteronomy, he says: 'You approached me, all of you, and said: "Let's send men ahead of us to explore the land and report back to us which way we should go up into it and what cities we'll come against"' (Deut. 1:22).

Moses adds, 'In my view that seemed good' (Deut. 1:23). In this account, the idea comes from below: the people beg Moses to send an advance party to spy out the land.

With its customary eagerness to reconcile apparent contradictions, the Talmud notes the little word *lecha* which follows 'send' in the verse in Numbers: *Shelach lecha*, literally, 'Send out *for you*,' attributing to it a significance well beyond its negligible semantic contribution:

> Reish Lakish said: 'Send *for you*.' It was *your* idea, Moses, [says God], as it says in Deuteronomy, 'In my view this seemed good' – that is, in *your* eyes, Moses, but not in the eyes of God.
>
> (Talmud Sotah 34b)

Reish Lakish's reading lets God off the hook. It wasn't God's fault that the plan went wrong: it was ill conceived in the first place. It was never God's idea; like a parent who says, 'Well, then, if you really must!' God consented unwillingly after the decision had been made. Rephrasing Midrash, the great eleventh-century commentator Rashi has Moses consult God, who says:

> I already told them the land was good when I said, 'I will bring you up out of the misery of Egypt to a good land.' But now, [since they've

asked for an advance party to spy out the land] upon their lives if they want things to go wrong, I'll let them have the chance.[8]

As the Midrash notes elsewhere, when someone is determined to do wrong, the opportunity is provided: Satan dances before them, then taps them on the shoulder after the deed is done (Bemidbar Rabbah 20:11).

Why do the Talmud and Midrash place the blame so firmly on the people? Perhaps it's because it's always easier to fault the 'ignorant masses', the conglomerate 'them' who are the eternal troublemakers. It's an escape from the simple, short admission, 'I got it wrong.' Even God is presented as falling into the trap: God pins the blame on Moses and Moses blames the people who, of course, turn against both God and Moses.

Yet the decision to send out the spies was clearly a leadership issue. It was bound to call into question the viability of the entire plan to take the Children of Israel to the Promised Land. In the middle of the desert, there was no alternative destination. With returning to Egypt not an option and the territories of the Edomites, Moabites, Midianites and Amalekites all around them, the people had no other realistic choice than to keep on going. Why, then, did their leaders put forward, or at least agree to, a proposal that put the entire venture at risk when there was no Plan B on offer? It's not surprising that everyone preferred to blame someone else for the debacle.

They are not the last to retell their story placing the fault on others. Throughout history, leaders who take full responsibility for the consequences of their decisions are few and far between. General Eisenhower, Commander in Chief of the Allied Armies, prepared a brief note prior to D-Day to be read out in the event that the allied invasion of Nazi Europe should prove a disaster:

My decision to attack at this time and place was based upon the best information available. The troops, the air and the Navy did all that bravery and devotion to duty could do. If any blame or fault attaches to the attempt it is mine alone.[9]

Mercifully, the courageous success of the Normandy landings gave him no cause to share this communiqué. Eisenhower's courage lay not only in making the decision to proceed with the invasion but also in taking full responsibility should it fail.

Today, in what has been described as an age of shamelessness, there are senior politicians across the world who appear content to lie their way out of their own short-sightedness, self-seeking and dishonesty. Rather than integrity, their guiding principle seems to be how successful they are in appealing to the lowest common denominator of populist prejudice.

This is not the path that Moses follows. Caught once again in the middle between God and Israel, he neither denies the impact on him of popular sentiment in formulating the plan nor conceals God's disappointment in the outcome. 'It seemed good to me,' he admits as he looks back on events almost four decades later, and adds, 'God was angry with me too' (Deut. 1:23, 37). He could easily have used his final address to excuse himself and put all the blame on others. Instead, he is scrupulously honest about his own role: the people suggested the plan, I agreed, and even God appeared to consent. The responsibility for our mistakes must be borne by us all.

VA'ETCHANAN (3:23–7:11)

Listen!

'You're not listening!' Which of us has never faced that accusation from our teacher, partner or child? How many of us haven't even realised we're not listening, because the person in need of our attention has given up bothering to say, 'For goodness' sake, hear me out!' If we've never been told we're not listening, it may be because we weren't even listening to that.

Entire relationships are expended in futile attempts at communication:

Will you hear my silence,
You who failed to hear my words?[10]

wrote Rachel Bluwstein in despair, before her tragic early death.

Maybe that's how God feels. 'Listen,' commands the Torah. 'Because you didn't listen,' says Moses to the people, listing the horrors liable to befall them if they fail to hearken to God's word.

But the frustration is mutual. The Psalms are filled with complaints at the intransigent deafness of heaven. Rabbi Yishmael, martyred in the second century by the Romans, added one letter to the verse from the Song at the Sea so that it read not, 'Who is like you *ba'eilim*, among *the mighty*, O God?' but, 'God, who is like you *ba'ilmim*, among *the dumb*?' The bleak Jewish poetry of the Middle Ages, hymns of faith and desperation in the face of exile and persecution, pleads repeatedly to a seemingly unhearing God to listen and intervene. In a lament for the victims of the First Crusade, Baruch ben Shmuel of Mainz (*c.*1150–1221) turned the famous line inside out: instead of reading *Shema, Yisrael* as 'Hear, O Israel', he takes it as *Shema Yisrael!* 'Hear Israel!' Listen, you unhearing God! Do something!

Fascinated as ever by definitions and distinctions, the Talmud seeks to clarify what precisely constitutes the act of listening. We are commanded to hear, but what exactly do we have to do to fulfil that obligation? The Mishnah suggests, 'One who recites the *Shema* but does not make the words audible to his own ears has nevertheless fulfilled their duty' (Berachot 2:3).

But Rabbi Yossei disagrees, and the law follows his view. Halakhically, that is, in Jewish legal terms, 'listening' is defined in this context as hearing with our ears the words our mouth is expressing. Given how often we talk without considering what we're saying, this may not be as simple as it sounds.

What might lie behind the opinion that one doesn't even have to hear one's own words? The Talmud explains: *Shema* requires inner comprehension, not merely hearing with one's ears. The obligation is therefore to recite it in a language one understands. Doesn't Rabbi Yossei insist on this too? Yes, he does, the Talmud explains; he requires both that we hear with our ears and that we comprehend the words.

This begs a further question: what does 'understanding' mean? The Talmud gives the last word to Rabbi Meir who quotes the Torah: 'These words which I command you this day shall be upon your heart.' 'Everything depends on the attention of the heart,' he concludes (Talmud Berachot 15a).

But on what words must this attention be focused? The answer seems clear: the proposition that 'the Lord our God, the Lord is one'. This declaration has been the defining principle of Judaism throughout the ages. That's why the verses of the *Shema* are the first Hebrew words most Jewish parents teach their children and the last to pass a dying person's lips. They constitute a simple, unambiguous statement of faith.

Yet maybe the instruction to hear is addressed not merely to the proposition that God is one, but to the truth behind it. What we are commanded to hear is not just the affirmation of God's unity, but also the actuality of God's oneness. The *Shema*, then, is directed not at our thoughts, but at our experience. Were this not so, all we would have to do is repeat an inherited truism. But if what the *Shema* demands of us is rather more, then the meanings of 'hear with our own ears' and 'understand' need to be explored at a deeper level.

Judaism contains another commandment to hear – to listen to the call of the shofar, the ram's horn, on Rosh Hashanah, the Jewish New Year. The Mishnah raises the strange case of a person who blows the shofar in a pit or cistern. Those who are inside it, who hear the sound directly, fulfil their obligation, whereas those on the outside who merely catch the echo do not. The Mishnah likens this distinction to the difference between consciously focusing one's attention on listening to the shofar and happening to overhear it being blown (Mishnah Rosh Hashanah 3:7).

When we merely repeat the *Shema* we are like people playing frisbee with echoes, doing little more than throwing the words back. Only when we try to catch the original sound can we be considered to be listening. That is how the mystics understand the *Shema*, as a commandment addressed to each of us to listen for God's voice. Mercifully, God calls to us not from afar but from anywhere and everywhere. As Rabbi Israel Ba'al Shem Tov, the eighteenth-century founder of Hasidism, states: 'There is nothing in the world other than God's existence – God is one – and everything that is derives from it.'[11]

Hence, as Rebbe Yitzhak Yaakov of Biale (1766–1813) teaches:

> In whatever you hear you should hear solely and only one thing alone: 'The Lord our God, the Lord is one,' so that from everything that happens you learn to believe in God's oneness and uniqueness.[12]

There is a profound difference between hearing by report and understanding through experience; what the *Shema* asks of us is to know not just with the head but also with the heart.

Two Hasidim were once discussing the verse: 'Lift up your eyes and behold: who created these, who brought forth their hosts in all their number . . . not one lacking' (Isa. 40:26).

'Before I became a Hasid,' said one, 'I studied thirty-six interpretations of those words. None of them made sense to me or penetrated my heart until I began to study Hasidism and discovered the true meaning.'

'And what is that?' asked the other.

'The true meaning,' replied the first, 'is: Lift up your eyes and behold!'

'If that's so, why don't you write it down?'

'Because it'll become interpretation number thirty-seven!'[13]

'"One", but not one as a countable'[14]

Shema, Yisrael, 'Hear, O Israel': these are the first words most Jewish children learn, and the last a dying person proclaims. I remember how my father taught me the opening line on a winter holiday the year before my mother died, and the rest phrase by phrase, as a special treat 'if you've been good', when he came upstairs to wish my brother and me goodnight in the months following her death.

There is only one God: this has always been the great message of Judaism, virtually its only statement of creed. This, and the understanding that what is required of us above all else is to act with justice and compassion, because the one God cares about morality, and fairness and kindness matter more than sacrifice.

The *Shema* is Judaism's central meditation, the heart of every service, morning and evening, day in, day out. It's a declaration not only of faith, but also of love:

> Hear, O Israel, God is our God, God is one. You shall love your God with all your heart, with all your soul and with all your might.
>
> (Deut. 6:4–5)

It's preceded by a thanksgiving blessing for God's love towards us and followed by a blessing for salvation, expressing the hope that through faithful partnership with God the world will be redeemed. These blessings embrace the *Shema*, setting it like a jewel in a ring of gold.

But what does God's oneness actually mean? The basic answer is that this is a categorical rejection of polytheism and the idolatrous cults that characterised the religious life of the ancient world, including Zoroastrianism with its dualist separation between the lord of good and the lord of evil.

Yet for all its apparent simplicity, the statement that 'God is one' is hard to fathom. 'One' suggests something specific with boundaries that distinguish it from that which it is not. Applied to God, this would imply finitude, a notion that Maimonides is at pains to counter. God is one, not two or more than two, but one with a unity to which no other one of all the ones in the world is like; not one like a category which contains many other units; nor one like a body which can be subdivided into sections, but a unity like to which there is no other unity in the world.[15]

The mystics explore the radical implications of this proposition. If God is everywhere and present in all things, then God's oneness must be everywhere too:

'The Lord is one' [means that] there is nothing else in the world except God's existence, blessed be God. 'The Lord is one,' for God's existence is one and unified, and everything which exists flows from it.[16]

If all being flows from God, there can be nothing separate from God's presence, nothing in which God is not. The Zohar, the Book of Splendour, the foundational text of Jewish mysticism, encapsulates this in just four words: *Leit attar panui minei*, 'There is no place empty of God.' This is not intended as metaphor or hyperbole but as the literal truth: God is present in, and the core of, all existence.

Do not attribute duality to God . . . Do not say, 'That is a stone and not God,' God forbid! Rather, all existence is God, and the stone is a thing permeated by divinity.[17]

If *Ein Sof*, the Endless, God's infinite being, flows through all existence, then even a stone cannot be devoid of its presence. However, in this material world in which we interact with objects all the time, it seems harsh, if not absurd, to deny people the right to refer to things around them as stones, books or teacups. Scholar Michael Fishbane offers a mediating language, suggesting that 'if all existence is not God as such, it is also not other than God, Life of all life'.[18]

God, one might say, is the sacred energy that animates all matter; since matter is energy in potential, God is present in potential within all matter. This is not a glorified form of pantheism since, although immanent in all things, God remains transcendent. The term *panentheism* has been used to differentiate this understanding of the relationship between God and the world from a purely naturalistic view of the sacred. Many among the Kabbalists, and especially the Hasidic leadership, were panentheists, though they would never have used the term, understanding that God is within all and all is within God, yet God remains infinite and endless. The proximity of God in all things offers constant opportunity for spiritual relationship. In a remarkable testament, Rebbe Yehudah Aryeh-Leib Alter of Ger (1847–1905) wrote to his children about how the opening words of the *Shema* should be understood:

[T]he meaning of 'God is One' is not that He is the only God, negating other gods (though this too is true); the meaning is deeper than that: there is no other being than Him. [This is true] even though it seems otherwise to most people . . . Everything that exists in the world is God Himself. It is only because of the contraction that was God's will, blessed be He and His name, that holiness descended rung after rung, until actual physical things were formed out of it. These things are true without a doubt. Because of this, every person can attach himself [to God] wherever he is, through the holiness which exists in every single thing, even corporeal things.[19]

If God's oneness extends through everything, we do not have to be somewhere other than where we are to find God; we can connect with the holiness in what is immediately before us. The challenge, which Rebbe Yehudah Aryeh-Leib puts in deceptively simple terms, is that 'you have *only* to be negated in the spark of holiness': we have to get beyond our self and all our ceaseless preoccupations. It's a deeply challenging *only*, amounting to what T. S. Eliot called:

A condition of complete simplicity
(Costing not less than everything).[20]

Such an understanding of God's oneness carries moral as well as spiritual implications. No person, living being or even object is devoid of God's presence. Therefore, we may not treat anyone with cruelty or contempt. To hurt or wound anything is, in some small way, to hurt and wound the presence of God. In contrast, to cherish, value, nurture and protect any living being is to fulfil the commandment to love God.

And you shall love . . .

My community debated at length what quotations to write on the eastern wall of our new synagogue. No one can remember where the inspiration came from, but the answer eventually emerged. There are three love commandments in the Torah: we inscribed 'Love your neighbour' to the right, 'Love the stranger' to the left and 'Love your God' in the centre above the holy ark, because this embraces all other forms of love.

There is a key difference between the first two and the third of these love commandments. Love of our neighbour and of the stranger can and must be translated into action; they are meaningless unless given practical expression. But how can that be done with the love of God, which is a feeling, an orientation of the heart? Actions can be commanded, but not emotions. How can even God demand a person to feel love?

Rebbe Yehudah Aryeh-Leib of Ger offers a remarkable response to this problem. God doesn't command love; there's no need, because love of God is the heart's natural state. But it's overshadowed by our other, more selfish, emotions. The action commanded is not therefore to inject love artificially into our heart, but to remove from ourselves anger, envy and cruelty, and to peel away the callus of indifference. Then love will flow naturally from the depths of our soul, love of the God of life. His resolution indicates a profound faith not just in God but also in the fundamental goodness and purity of human nature.

According to the mystics, our soul comes from God, with whom it dwells before descending into our body at birth. The harsh realities of the material world do not entirely occlude a faint memory of this original spiritual state, to which we can draw nearer again through prayer, Torah study and especially by keeping *Shabbat*, which is both a reminder and a foretaste of the world to come. The heart understands this, because although it may temporarily forget, its capacity to be aware of God is inalienable.

Yet the heart doesn't always feel either very aware or very loving. Pain, regret, anger and frustration take root in it. It's often difficult to sense one's heart at all, as if it were shut off behind a thick, scarcely permeable membrane and one were living instead from one's guts and spleen. 'I am asleep, but my heart is awake,' says the beloved in Song of Songs 5:2. But it frequently seems like the other way round: we are awake, but our heart is asleep. Then the hope and possibility that we might somehow live differently, from the core of the self which knows and loves God, sounds like some theological phantasy with no truth in our psychological reality.

Yet this may be the very point that Rebbe Yehudah Aryeh-Leib wishes to make. The real struggle in life is to awaken the heart; once that has happened, it will do the rest. What is required is not to put something into it that isn't there, but to liberate it from the emotions that so often lay siege to it, so as to restore it to freedom and allow it to sing.

The Mishnah brings this firmly down to earth when it explains loving God 'with all your heart' to mean 'with both your good and evil inclinations', that is, with all facets of our personality (Berachot 9:1). Based on the observation that 'heart' is written with a double consonant, *levavekha*, rather than with a single letter *beit* as *libekha*, it focuses on the unromantic truth that human nature is multi-faceted and that we have negative as well as positive feelings. As the Talmud acknowledges, loving God is a struggle:

Act out of love: if you find yourself hating, know that you should love, and one who loves does not hate. Act out of reverence: if you find yourself rebelling, know that one who feels reverence does not rebel . . .

(Yerushalmi Sotah 5:5)

William Blake well understood this dual nature of the heart, writing in *Songs of Innocence*:

Mercy has a human heart
Pity a human face,

but in *Songs of Experience*:

Cruelty has a human heart,
And Jealousy a human face.[21]

Loving God is not, then, some remote, elevated ideal, but the daily challenge to manage our emotions so that the best within us shines through. This goes to the core of life's moral and spiritual struggles and concerns our most basic interactions: how I treat my partner, children, friends. For if God is present in all creation, then loving God is inseparable from loving people, animals, nature and the material world. If I hurt someone, I wound not only that individual but also the sacred presence of life within them. If I am kind to somebody, a person in the street, a bird, I express in that small way the love of God. As Coleridge's Ancient Mariner discovers in his remorse after killing the albatross:

He prayeth best who loveth best
All creatures great and small
For the dear God who loveth us,
He made and loveth all.[22]

In contrast, if we treat others cruelly, we not only fail to love God but also reinforce our capacity for giving hurt and alienate ourselves further from love. For the nature of the heart is never predetermined; just as it forms and sets the tone of all our actions, so it is reformed and, little by little, transformed by them. Moment by moment, our behaviours at once stem from and forge who we are.

To love God, then, is to deepen and follow the heart's love of life. It is the constant endeavour to respond with love, respect and understanding to all living beings. Though expressed in how we treat others, at its core it is about how we treat ourselves.

'With all your might'

I loved my grandfather, my mother's father, who had known from the age of three that he wanted to be a rabbi and went on to serve the community all his life. My grandparents lived only a few minutes' walk away, so in my teens I would often go to their house after school and ask questions. One day we discussed the meaning of the last two words in that most challenging of verses: 'You shall love the Lord your God with all your heart, with all your soul and with all your might, *uvechol me'odekha*' (Deut. 6:5). If heart and soul refer to feelings and spirit, 'with all your might' had to be about whatever was left over. 'Could it mean "with all your abilities"?' I wondered, 'or maybe "with all your opportunities"?' My father, who had so few chances in his early life, forced to flee the Nazis then to eke out a living in an impoverished, conflict-ridden Palestine, often told us never to miss a positive opportunity.

'I like that,' my grandfather said, and smiled.

I hadn't yet encountered the terse Mishnah:

'*Bechol levavekha*: with all your heart': with both your inclinations, good and bad;

'*Bechol nafshekha*: with all your life': even if God takes your life away;

'*Uvechol me'odekha*: with all your might': with all your money.

(Berachot 9:1)

Levavekha, 'heart', is understood as including all our emotions, both the *yetzer hatov*, the altruistic desire to do good, and the *yetzer hara*, the so-called 'evil inclination', better explained as the id, the drive essential to any human endeavour but dangerous if undisciplined and ungoverned. The whole self must be dedicated to the service of God.

Nafshekha is usually translated as 'soul', but 'life' is more faithful to the biblical context. It may only have been in the mediaeval period that the word's meaning migrated from the immediately physical, as in don't eat an animal's blood 'because the *nefesh*, the life force, of all flesh is its blood' (Lev. 17:14), to the more spiritual notion of 'soul'. The Talmud illustrates the raw reality of loving God with all one's life by recounting the martyrdom of Rabbi Akiva. Led out by the Romans to be burnt alive for the 'offence' of teaching Torah in public, he replies to his students who are crying out, 'Thus far?' that he's waited all his days for the opportunity to love God with all his life and doesn't intend to squander it now (Berachot 61b).

The Mishnah's explanation of *uvechol me'odekha* makes good sense at first sight: if one's entire personality and one's very life have already been included, what's left to love God with except one's money and possessions?

But the Mishnah isn't satisfied with this initial attempt; its editors evidently struggled with the significance of the phrase. *Me'od* is an adverb meaning 'very', as when God reviewed the entirety of creation 'and behold it was *very* good' (Gen. 1:31). How, then, can the word appear in the *Shema* as a noun? The Mishnah offers an alternative interpretation which, instead of explaining *me'od*, plays alliteratively on its sound:

Bechol middah umiddah she'Hu moded lekha, heveh modeh lo bime'od me'od.
Whatever measure of fortune God metes out to you, acknowledge God very, very profoundly.

If to love God with heart and soul is difficult, this may be harder still. Yet it's a challenge we will all have no choice but to face: how do we love God, how do we make the best of our portion, when our luck runs out? I admire people who counter life's misfortunes and inequities with resilience, humour or quiet good grace. I've met many people who face harsh changes of fortune with remarkable strength of spirit.

'How are you feeling?' I asked an elderly man who'd had a heart attack.

'Surprised by joy,' he replied. 'I'm not feeling down; I'm just so grateful for all life has given me.'

'I'm not afraid,' a young man told his father as they discussed whether he wanted to undergo a final round of chemotherapy or receive only palliative care.

'I'll go for it; what's the choice?!'

Such people fill me with humbling admiration.

For I've also met people who lack this capacity, who cannot overcome their resentments and who become embittered by the way life has treated them. Their reaction may be entirely justified, but it only punishes them further. When anger, which is understandable, turns to bitterness, it makes them into a double victim: they end up lonely and under-loved, because who wants to be with someone who's bitter?

These encounters leave me with the unanswerable question, 'What sort of person will I prove to be when life hits me with some terrible blow?' Which of us truly knows what we'll be like until we're confronted with those challenges that show us what lies in the depths of our personality? Is there more bile or more sweetness in the pit of our stomach?

The Mishnah isn't only concerned with times of trial but also with the totality of our experience. To 'acknowledge God most profoundly' in all circumstances means appreciating our blessings as much as making the best of our misfortunes. It may be precisely those who know how to appreciate life's gifts who prove to have the greatest resilience when the situation changes. They know not only how to count their blessings, but also how to make those blessings continue to count when harsher days come. I instinctively trust people more who sing their heart out in the happiness of the hour than those who hold back in case the kiss of fortune should suddenly turn into a slap in the face. They live in the moment, and with faith.

We can't determine our destiny, but we do have a measure of control over how we encounter it. The Talmud expresses this in the pithy saying: 'Everything is in the hands of heaven, except the fear of heaven' (Shabbat 31a). That is, God metes out the measure, but it remains up to us how we respond. Yet I sometimes wonder to what extent even this lies within our realm of choice. Victor Frankl famously wrote, based on his observations of his fellow prisoners in Auschwitz: 'Everything can be taken from a man but one last thing: the last of the human freedoms – to choose one's attitude in any given set of circumstances, to choose one's own way.'[23]

But was he entirely correct?

Maybe even here some people are more constrained than others. Perhaps they are endowed with less inner capacity, have had more to contend with emotionally or are burdened, through birth or experience, with a more complex internal chemistry and consequently have fewer resources to muster as they encounter the anguish of loneliness, old age or grief. The rabbinic dictum that 'the reward is in accord with the pain' is an opposite acknowledgement that it's harder for some than for others to bear the challenges, tribulations and sorrows life brings.[24] The demands placed on them are greater in loving God with all their might.

EKEV (7:12–11:25)

....

The bread we eat

The Promised Land, Moses assures the Children of Israel, will flow not just with milk and honey, but also with gushing streams and springs and wells in valley and mountain. It will be 'a land of wheat and barley, vines, figs and pomegranates, a land of oil from olives and honey from dates' (Deut. 8:8). So long as God is worshipped and God's laws are followed, no one will experience anything other than plenty; it will be 'a land in which you shall not eat your bread in misery . . . [a land in which] you will eat, be satisfied, and bless the Lord your God' (Deut. 8:9–10), words included to this day in the grace after meals.

Why, amid such plenty, does Moses have to stress that 'you shall not eat your bread in misery'? (Deut. 8:9). Rabbi Chaim ibn Attar (c.1696–1743) explains:

> There exist people who, although wealthy, conduct themselves as if they were poor, for two reasons. The first is fear lest their income should collapse and leave them impoverished; they therefore avoid major expenses.[25]

This is food insecurity, uncertainty about whether not just today but tomorrow and the day after there will be sufficient. Shamefully, even in affluent countries, significant sectors of the population, though not starving, have to worry each day about what they're going to feed the children. It's an exhausting and soul-destroying way to live. The recent pandemic, together with steeply rising prices, has more than doubled queues at food banks, bringing desperation and humiliation. For people who have known extreme hunger, the fear of not having enough to eat doesn't easily go away, even when times are better. Although they may have lived amid plenty for decades, many survivors of the Holocaust and other horrors continue to hoard crusts of bread to the end of their days. The dread of starvation never leaves them. Ibn Attar knew this from experience after fleeing across Morocco with his family as a child and seeing famine at first hand.

His second reason is that such people 'don't want to sate themselves, so that others won't see that they're rich'.[26] The real misery here is not the embarrassment of the person who doesn't want to be seen 'stuffing his face' when others around have far less. This is only a symptom; the true cause is the injustice of the gap between those who have and those who have not. Many of us today live in cities in which homeless people sleep in the porches of elegant shops. People with nothing watch from street level the shoes of the well-heeled walk past them, not seeing, or pretending not to see them, perhaps out of embarrassment that they should be so incomparably more fortunate. Maybe the Torah should be understood as saying that in the Promised Land, or in any land that tries to live by the 'promise' of a significant standard of social justice, there will be no embarrassment in having more than merely sufficient to eat, because the whole of society will have a share in its plenty.

Ibn Attar focuses on the awkwardness the well-off feel in exposing themselves as rich when others don't have enough to feed their families. A Hasidic anecdote suggests a different approach to differentials in wealth. A rich man came to tell his rebbe that from now on he was only going to eat bread and drink water on weekdays, out of empathy with the poor. 'On no account!' the rebbe reprimanded him. 'I order you to eat goose every day.' His students stared at him in bewilderment. As soon as the man had gone, he explained: 'If he eats only dry bread, he'll think the poor can live off stones. But if he has goose, he'll realise that the poor must at least have bread.'

There's a further kind of misery connected with food, to which ibn Attar doesn't refer. It may have been less prevalent in his day. That is the misery of those who provide it. If we could see today the conditions in which many who grow and process some of the staples that fill an average shopping basket; if, when we touched a tin of tomatoes, a jar of coffee or a cheap shirt, a ten-second video automatically showed us the impact on the land and the local community where it was produced, we might well withdraw our hands in shock. But all this remains invisible to most of us, except when some terrible disaster occurs, such as the fire that killed tens of garment workers in a high-rise workshop in Bangladesh. We don't see the poverty, the hardship, the conditions of labour or the impact on the environment that lie behind our supermarket abundance. We want things cheap and are rarely concerned about those who pay the real price.

Attacking the slave trade, the abolitionist William Fox wrote in 1791: 'If we purchase the commodity we participate in the crime . . . In every pound of sugar used . . . we may be considered as consuming two ounces of human flesh.'[27]

The slave trade has long been formally abolished, though merciless trafficking and brutal slavery persist the world over, often with the connivance of the wealthiest nations. But ruthless exploitation continues, and the commodification and monetisation of the resources of many of the world's formerly colonised and most oppressed countries goes on unabated, often with no effective regulation. That is why fair trade and ethical consumption are of such crucial importance. In a truly 'promised land', neither open nor hidden misery should be an ingredient of the bread we consume.

But until we reach such a messianic state, contrary to what the Torah says, it may be only right that we sometimes eat our bread in misery, not, hopefully, through hunger, but because of the discomfort and shame that ibn Attar describes. For, in the words of Goethe, set poignantly to music by Schumann:

Who never ate his bread in tears,
Who never through the troubled nights
Sat weeping on his bed,
Such a person knows you not, you heavenly powers!

You summon us into life,
You burden the poor with guilt
Then leave them to their wretchedness
For all guilt seeks vengeance here on earth.[28]

'Except to fear . . .'

Natan Shcharansky's most treasured possession during his years of imprisonment as a refusenik in the Soviet Union was the small Book of Psalms given to him in memory of his father, which he managed to keep despite numerous searches and repeated terms in solitary confinement. From it he taught himself Hebrew. In a letter to his mother in May 1984, he described how deeply struck he was by the psalmist's many references to fear of God, *yirat hashem*:

In the course of time, one begins to understand that fear of God is a result of an inner stirring brought about by the lofty Divine vision, by a feeling of submission and respect for God's essence . . . It is possible that fear of God is the one factor capable of conquering human fear and thus all that remains for us is to repeat the words of King Solomon, 'The fear of the Lord is the beginning of knowledge.'[29]

Fear has a bad press in much contemporary religious writing; the emphasis is almost always on love. Fear is negative, love positive; fear is a bad motive, love the best of reasons.

This is not the approach of classical Jewish literature. The Bible speaks often of the fear, not just the love, of God:

> And now, Israel, what does God ask of you, *but* to fear the Lord your God, to walk in all God's ways, and to love and serve the Lord your God with all your heart and all your soul.
>
> (Deut. 10:12)

The Talmud picks up on the word 'but', *ki im*, which literally means 'but only', as if fear were a minor matter:

> Is fear of heaven such a little thing? Yes, to Moses it was, as Rabbi Hanina said: It's like asking for a large vessel; to someone who's got it, it's a small thing. But ask for a small vessel from someone who hasn't got it, and for them it's a big thing.
>
> (Berachot 33b)

To the rabbis, especially the Kabbalists, fear of God is of central spiritual importance. They distinguish between lower and higher levels of fear. The lowest is not really fear of God but of God's punishment. The Torah appeals to this fear to remind us of our accountability: 'You must not curse the deaf or put a stumbling block before the blind, but you shall fear your God, I am the Lord' (Lev. 19:14).

Rashi explains: since the deaf can't hear and the blind cannot see, we may be tempted to think that we can get away with abusing them. The Torah therefore reminds us that the all-present God can see us and will judge us for our conduct.

This may be the lowest kind of fear, but it is nonetheless important. We don't act out of the highest motives all the time; in our weaker moments, when our better self stalls, fear of the consequences is an essential deterrent. In this age of shamelessness, when the ethos of public life often seems to be 'so long as I can get away with it', it's necessary to be reminded that there is one who knows. Whether we take this literally as God's all-seeing eye, metaphorically as our conscience, 'the God within the mind', or as other people's pain on account of the harm we've done to them, fear reminds us that our actions have consequences and, in the words of former Czech president Václav Havel, do not disappear into the black hole of time.[30]

The higher 'fear of God' is of a different order; it is awe before the unfathomable majesty and complexity of the universe. Maimonides understood such fear as co-existing with the love of God in a constant dialectic. Love inspires us to step out into the world in wonder; awe makes us step back, overwhelmed and humbled. The two emotions belong together like movements in a dance. Maimonides writes:

When one reflects on God's works, God's great and wonderful creatures, and beholds through them God's wonderful, matchless and infinite wisdom, one is at once filled with love, praise and exaltation; one is possessed of a great longing to know God's great name, as David said: 'My soul thirsts for God, the living God' [Ps. 42:2]. Pondering these matters, one is instantly taken aback and smitten with awe, realising one is a minuscule creature, humble and ignorant, standing with meagre knowledge before the all-knowing God, as David said: 'When I see your heavens, the works of your fingers, what is man that You are mindful of him?' [Ps. 8:3–4].[31]

Rebecca Elson, scientist and poet, captures Maimonides' meaning marvellously in her lines:

We astronomers . . .
Honour our responsibility to awe.[32]

Or, in the words of the Kabbalist Moses Cordovero (1522–70):

Then you wonder, astonished: Who am I? I am a mustard seed in the middle of the sphere of the moon, which itself is a mustard seed within the next sphere. So it is with that sphere and all it contains in relation to the next sphere . . . And all of these are a mustard seed within further expanses. Your awe is invigorated, the love in your soul expands.[33]

'Fear' of this kind derives from the awareness that we are an infinitesimal yet sentient part of the vast consciousness that flows through all being. The mystics described it as *yirat haromemut*, awe before the exalted nature of the divine.

The Talmud considers such fear to be the essential quality without which all other virtues, important as they may be, remain insufficient in God's eyes. It offers a series of comparisons:

To what may [those who have no fear of God] be compared? They're like the farmer who ordered his tenant to store a large quantity of grain. 'Have you added the requisite amount of preserving salts?' he asked him. 'No', replied the worker. 'Then it would have been better if you hadn't bothered.'

(Shabbat 31a)

The implication is that religion itself is liable to become rotten if awe and humility are absent. Mindless obedience is nothing if the heart and soul remain unaffected.

The Talmud goes further:

Rabba bar Rav Huna said: A person who has [knowledge of] Torah but not the fear of heaven is like a treasurer to whom they've given the keys to the inner chambers of the treasury but not those to the outer door; how is he supposed to enter?

(Shabbat 31a–b)

Fear of heaven is seen here as a necessary precondition for understanding Torah, which cannot be accessed without humility and awe. Yehudah Aryeh-Leib of Ger interprets the inner keys as symbolising the desire, implanted in our hearts since Sinai, to follow God's will. Our challenge is to find the outer keys of humility and self-discipline; once we have them, we will pass naturally through the inner gates into the depths of Torah.[34]

The Talmud now quotes Rabbi Yannai, who reverses the order of inner and outer: 'Woe to the person who has no courtyard yet makes a fence around it' (Shabbat 31a).

Awe is the courtyard, the true spiritual destination to which even Torah study is only a pathway. We can fill our mind with Torah information and carry out all the rituals, but so long as they remain just that, mere rites by which our spirit remains unmoved and unrefined, they will have little impact on our soul.

In an especially moving discourse, Kalonymus Kalman Shapira writes of *yirah shel ahavah*, fear on account of love, a concept I have encountered nowhere else.[35] He doesn't offer a definition. Perhaps his meaning can be understood by way of analogy with human relationships: when one loves someone truly, the last thing one wants to do is to cause them hurt. Love makes us acutely aware of what causes our beloved pain, and we are intuitively mindful to avoid it.

Awe is refined by love; love is purified through awe.

They too belong in the holy ark

> I took hold of the two tablets, threw them from my hands and smashed
> them before your eyes.
>
> (Deut. 9:17)

For several months I lived with an elderly couple in Jerusalem. The wife
had leukaemia and spent several periods in hospital, during which I was
alone with her husband who was suffering from increasingly severe
dementia. He was a deeply religious man, and regular attendance at synagogue mercifully remained a safe and familiar part of his routine. My main
responsibility was to look after him over *Shabbat*, accompanying him to
services on Friday evening and in the morning. He liked to attend a stie-
bel, a small community of pious worshippers twenty minutes' walk away.
Despite his failing cognition, he was always warmly welcomed. On one
occasion he was barely able to walk the last hundred metres; as I struggled
to support him, congregants came running to help. The doors of the
building were flung open before us, a seat was prepared and full respect
paid to this man whose mind had once been original and incisive.

A short Talmudic insight encapsulates the values underlying this attitude. In his instinctive horror at the sight of the golden calf, Moses smashed
the first tablets on which God had carved the Ten Commandments.
Following his successful intercession on behalf of the people, God
commands him to:

> Carve for yourself two tablets of stone like the first set . . . I shall write
> on the tablets the words which were on the first set which you broke,
> and put them in the ark.
>
> (Exod. 34:1)

The obvious meaning is that Moses should put the new tablets in the ark
God has instructed him to make. But the Talmud punctuates the verse
differently, reading it as saying 'which you broke, put in the ark:'

> . . . the [new] tablets and the broken fragments of the [first set of]
> tablets were [both] placed in the ark. From here we learn that a student
> of Torah who forgets his learning for reasons beyond his control is not
> to be treated with disrespect.
>
> (Menachot 99a)

It can be no accident that the Talmud attributes this teaching to Rav Yosef, who was blind. In contrast to the stringent bodily perfection demanded of the priests, he reads into the Torah the dignity of disability.

The Talmud is strict about learning. Of the three tears God is said to weep, one is shed for those whose life makes it all but impossible to study yet who nevertheless dedicate themselves to Torah. Another is for those who have the leisure to learn, but don't. Study of Torah is the soul of Jewish life; *bittul Torah*, neglect of Torah, is considered in many circles a serious fault. Learning knows no limit; it cannot be quantified because what matters most is the process of engagement. Failure to keep up one's learning when one has the opportunity to do so is considered just as bad as deliberately trying to forget what one has previously studied. Nevertheless, Rabbi Baruch Halevi Epstein (1860–1941) insists that 'even someone who forgot their learning due to neglect must not be treated disrespectfully in public, because of the honour due to the Torah' (Torah Temimah to Exod. 34:1). But those who can't help it, whose knowledge and mental capacity are taken from them by factors beyond their control, must be respected both in public and in private. Their stature remains undiminished, and we should honour them accordingly.

This attitude is an intrinsic part of *kevod habriyot*, the dignity that is every person's due. This sounds obvious, but it's far from easy to behave in such a manner, never patronising anyone whose conversation no longer makes sense according to our 'normative' criteria of coherence, not looking down on anyone who can no longer eat without assistance. It's not just a question of how we respond to people with dementia. It's only natural to react to other people as they appear to us now without appreciating, or troubling to find out, who they once were. Refugees are generic 'asylum seekers', not doctors, teachers or IT specialists. Somehow their situation has robbed them of all their achievements. A man in a wheelchair is 'dependent', 'incapacitated', 'old'. Unless he's wearing his medals, it might not occur to us to think that he once fought on the Normandy beaches on D-Day and that we who look down at his bent frame are profoundly in his debt.

Yet Rav Yosef's insight, long a byword in Jewish teaching about dementia, goes deeper than the recognition that what is now shattered was once whole. The fragments of the commandments belong in the ark alongside the perfect tablets not only because they too once were complete, but because they have a great deal to teach us precisely because they are broken.

This begins with the very fact of brokenness. Moses warns the people against arrogantly imagining that it's 'my strength and the power of my arm' which has brought them success (Deut. 8:17). Rather, we should be humbled by the recognition that the human condition is full of frailties; none of us knows what our own future may hold, what illness may afflict us or what accident break us. We glorify perfection at our peril. What we set before God should be the vanity neither of a perfect body nor of a perfect mind, but thankfulness for our wellbeing balanced by awareness of our vulnerability. What's fragile in us is holy too; sometimes it's our very fragility that helps recognise where holiness truly is.

It's especially hard to learn from our own brokenness, from the mistakes we make and the hurts life inflicts on us. Yet we may have more to discover from our struggles and challenges than from easy years and ready successes. What makes the broken tablets such important teachers is that they were shattered precisely because they encountered human weakness and failure. The Talmud congratulates Moses for breaking them. Playing on the sounds of the words *asher shibarta*, 'which you broke', it interpolates them as *yasher koach she'shibarta*: 'all strength to you for breaking them'. Even God is understood to approve of the smashing of the most important gift to humanity that heaven has to offer.

The Nazis destroyed hundreds of synagogues on Kristallnacht, the Night of Broken Glass, 9 November 1938, and hundreds more later in the countries they occupied. Decades after the war, during building works near the site of a ruined synagogue in the east of Holland, bulldozers unexpectedly dug up chunks of broken masonry inscribed with Hebrew writing. They belonged to the carved stone Ten Commandments which had once stood over the ark. The only words still intact were, 'You shall not murder.'

Sometimes history has most to teach us from what is broken.

There will be no rain

Maybe it's because I was born in Scotland that I love the call of mountain waterfalls and the singing of small streams. They calm the mind and cleanse the soul.

The Hebrew Bible is full of the different sounds of water: the springs and rivers for which the wild deer long, the breakers of the ocean, the fountains in the gardens of the Song of Songs and the tranquil streams of the twenty-third Psalm. In hot, dry lands no blessings are greater than rainfall and dew.

The Torah describes Israel as a land 'of rivers of water, springs and wells, flowing forth in valley and mountain'. Unlike Egypt which is 'irrigated by foot', presumably a reference to channels dug from the Nile and controlled by sluices, the Promised Land 'drinks water from the rain of heaven'; it depends on God for its fertility (Deut. 11:10–11).

Therefore, in the world of the Hebrew Bible and in the eyes of the rabbis, as in other ancient Middle Eastern cultures and beyond, rain is never considered merely a natural phenomenon. It is God's most immediate currency of reward and punishment, a gift God may grant or withhold, not capriciously but in response to the conduct of the people:

> If you listen truly to my commandments . . . I will grant the rain of your land in its season, the early and the later rains, and you will eat and be satisfied. But if you don't listen to my commandments which I command you this day, God will close up the heavens and there will be no rain.
>
> (Deut. 11:13–17)

The rabbis regarded rainfall as one of the three hidden treasures to which only God has the key, together with the mystery of birth and the secret of what happens after death. They understood that for these blessings we, and all humanity, are entirely dependent on God. 'Great is the day of the rains,' taught Rabbi Yochanan, 'as the day of the ingathering of the exiles, as it is stated: "Turn our captivity, O Lord, as the streams in the dry land" (Ps. 126:4)' (Talmud Taanit 8b).

Except in places prone to frequent flooding, this remains true today, as expressed in the Celtic prayer:

> May the blessing of the rain be on you,
> May it beat upon your Spirit and wash it fair and clean,
> And leave there a shining pool where the blue of heaven shines.[36]

Not a drop of rain, the rabbis taught, but an angel accompanies it on either side. One of the best of all reasons for reciting the blessing over good tidings, 'Blessed be God who is good and does good,' is the sound of falling raindrops in a time of need.

The rabbis of the Mishnah ruled that 'God's mighty act of *causing* the rain to fall' should be the focus of special prayers on *Shemini Atzeret*, the Eighth Day of Assembly, which closes the festival of *Sukkot*, Tabernacles, when 'the world is judged for water' (Mishnah Rosh Hashanah 1:2). Today we recite only a small portion of these magnificent prayers, for rain and dew which mark the cycle of the year. Yet even now the leader wears white robes, the ark is opened and the liturgy is chanted to melodies recalling the Days of Awe:

Remember the Twelve Tribes
Whom you brought safely through the divided waters
And for whom you turned the bitter waters sweet:
Their descendants have shed their blood like water.
Turn to us, God, for troubles surround us like water.

The Bible attests that droughts and famines were all too frequent. The Mishnah sets out a series of up to thirteen fasts of increasing severity to petition God to forgive us and send rain. At first, only pious individuals would fast, but as the drought became more severe the entire community would gather in the street to pray; even the ark was brought outside. Everyone put ashes on their forehead except the leaders of the community who had ash smeared on their heads by others. Why? the Talmud asks. Because the humiliation is so much greater (Taanit 15b–16a).

When I see the parched yellow-and-brown fields in the droughts that now afflict the southeast of England with increasing regularity, I imagine the desperate intensity of these gatherings. Nobody had to be told how much was at stake. The Talmud tells stories of the wonder-working figures whose special prayers would pierce the heavens and reach the ears of God. Most famous among them is Honi, who drew a circle round himself and refused to move from it until God had granted not just any kind of rainfall, but blessed rain to sate the fields and fill the wells and cisterns. Were you not Honi, the leading scholar Shimon ben Shetach sent to him, I would have put you under the ban for behaving in an over-familiar way with God. But you're like a member of God's family (Talmud Taanit 23a).

Prayers for rain were timed to accord with the seasons of the Middle East. Following the dispersion of the community across the Mediterranean and Central Europe through the Middle Ages, the question arose: what if rain were desperately needed at different times of the year from the Land of Israel? Our custom, Rabbi Yisrael Meir Kagan (1838–1933) strikingly noted, is to add special petitions including verses about rainfall, and, on Sabbaths and festivals, to invoke the thirteen attributes of God's mercy in prayers otherwise reserved for serious fasts and the Day of Atonement.[37]

For many decades now, we have been inclined to understand rainfall as a feature of the climate determined not by supernatural intervention but by atmospheric conditions across the globe: 'It's the weather! What can you do?' We ceased to consider that there might be any significant connection between how we behave and what happens in the skies, such a notion reflecting neither the theology nor the science in which most of us believed.

Yet, as the evidence of global warming grows ever plainer, and not just to climate scientists but also to populations across the globe who face storms, droughts and wildfires with increasing frequency, we are forced to appreciate once again that how we treat the earth and how the earth treats us back are closely interconnected. It's an awareness our ancestors took as basic. But there are crucial differences. Most significantly, those 'punished' most by climate change are generally the least responsible for bringing it about. Far from an instrument of divine justice, environmental disaster is all too often the consequence of human injustice.

Yet perhaps God, too, is part of this equation, but not as God with a hand on the valve that opens or closes a vast reservoir on high containing the 'upper waters'; not God as perpetrator but God as fellow victim. For God is present in all life, in the wonder and mystery of its growth and regeneration. If we fail to appreciate creation and refuse to treat it with the respect and restraint it requires, we damage it, ourselves, and some hidden portion of God too.

RE'EH (11:26-16:17)

Prophecy

'Think of them not as foretellers but forth-tellers,' my teacher Rabbi Louis Jacobs used to say about the biblical prophets. I little realised when I first heard his words the price that forth-tellers all too often pay.

The Torah warns severely against the allure of prophets and soothsayers; 'Don't follow them,' it insists (Deut. 13:3). 'What?' the Talmud asks rhetorically, 'You seek signs from a prophet and not from the Torah?' (Jerusalem Talmud Berachot 1:4). On the contrary, the Talmud insists, do as the Torah tells you: fear God and keep God's commandments. It elaborates:

> Is it possible to follow God's presence of which it is written that it is a devouring fire? Rather, follow in God's ways; just as God clothes the

naked, so you clothe the naked; just as God visits the sick, so should you visit the sick.

(Sotah 14a)

Look after justice and compassion, the Talmud seems to say, and the future will look after itself.

The biblical prophets rarely offer signs; what they foretell are the consequences of right- and wrongdoing. Their insight lies in foreseeing the outcomes of injustice, dishonesty and oppression. Far from preaching signs and miracles, they attack the seductive notion that God is a conjuring wonder-worker who performs sudden miracles to save us. Such a fantasy blinds us to the truth that what God responds to is the moral quality of our society. Do right: 'share your bread with the hungry, bring home the oppressed poor,' and then, and only then, will 'your righteousness shine forth like the noonday,' declares Isaiah 58:7–8. Jeremiah complains that the people say over and again, 'This is God's house, God's house, God's house,' as if that could protect them from the consequences of their folly. God cares about how you behave, not about buildings, he insists, making himself unpopular with everyone: king, priests and populace alike (Jer. 7:4).

Though the Bible refers to schools for prospective prophets to develop their skills, to the true bearers of prophecy their gift is not a choice but a terrible, sometimes even fatal, burden. 'I don't have the skills,' Jeremiah objects, trying to evade his divinely determined destiny (Jer. 1:6). But God's word proves to be a fire in his bones he cannot extinguish, forcing him time and again to cry out in protest, speaking home truths so unpalatable that the king's ministers throw him into a mud pit (Jer. 38).

'They've killed off all the others and I alone am left,' complains Elijah, before God visits him on the mountain in that still small voice with a compulsion his soul cannot resist (1 Kgs 19:10).

According to rabbinic tradition, prophecy formally ended with the last of the biblical prophets, Malachi, in the fifth century BCE. Thereafter, guidance come solely from the Torah and its interpreters, the rabbis. 'We pay no attention to voices from on high,' declared Rabbi Yehoshua during a fierce Talmudic dispute; God's teaching is 'not in heaven' any more (Bava Metsia 59a–b).

But the true legacy of the prophets of Israel remains: the moral compulsion to tell truth to power because this is what God and conscience demand. This 'truth' doesn't come out of nowhere, but from a searing sense of wrong, an inescapable awareness of cruelty and injustice and the pain of their victims. It would be more politic to keep silent. But for those whose conscience is branded by the prophetic tradition, who hear its voice ever louder in their soul, this is simply not an option. They must speak out, even at the cost of their reputation, possibly of their very life. Their ultimate choice lies between physical death and spiritual suicide.

A decade ago, when I visited Wuppertal, I was taken to the church of Karl Immer (1888–1944). Very early during Nazi rule he spoke out against the passivity of the Church, declaring that it had become a whore to the state. Summoned by the Gestapo, he told them that he was commenting on the Church, not the secular government. On the Sunday after Kristallnacht, he recited the Ten Commandments in Hebrew in his church and invited everyone who understood his meaning to meet him afterwards. He devoted the following months to helping Jews and other 'enemies' of Nazism escape the country. When war was declared, his bishop ordered him to compose a patriotic prayer. Despite having been a proud Prussian officer in World War I, he wrote simply, 'May Germany lose this war.' Incarcerated by the Nazis, he died in 1944.

In that same year Rabbi Leo Baeck (1873–1956), the official head of the Jewish community of Germany, was teaching the message of the prophets of Israel amid the horrors of Theresienstadt, his spirit uncowed by the degradation and misery he was forced to experience. At the core of his theology was the immediacy of the relationship between mystery and commandment. The very awareness that God exists and demands our response; 'I am' and 'thou shalt' are inseparable, and this gives us the courage to overcome fear.

What transformed me from a teacher living a life of contemplation into an activist, wrote Abraham Joshua Heschel (1907–72), was the legacy of the Hebrew prophets, the realisation that silence was not an option, and that 'indifference to evil is worse than evil itself':

> There is immense silent agony in the world, and the task of man is to be a voice for the plundered poor, to prevent the desecration of the soul and the violation of our dream of honesty.[38]

This led him not only to participate in the Civil Rights Movement and march alongside Reverend Martin Luther King at Selma, Alabama, but also to speak out against the Vietnam War at a time when this was not popular. Heschel died in 1972. Were he alive today, his daughter, Professor Susannah Heschel, told me in 2019, he would be horrified and tormented by the vicious racism emerging from the highest offices of the land.

Like their biblical antecedents, the future that such prophets seek to bring nearer is an age when 'justice will roll down like water' (Amos 5:24), when 'every valley shall be exalted and every hilltop and mountain brought low, and all flesh shall see it together' (Isa. 40:4–5). Theirs is a message of inalienable hope.

The heirs of the prophetic tradition today are not necessarily religious leaders. They include investigative journalists, poets and artists, politicians representing persecuted minorities and banned opposition parties, individuals and groups who refuse to be silenced by racist gangs and mafiosi, lawyers courageous enough to defend them, and everyone who speaks out in the name of human dignity against the tyranny of abusive power. What unites them is their irrepressible and outspoken commitment to truth, justice and the cause of the victimised innocent.

Keeping kosher

Mammals that do not both chew the cud and have cloven hooves; fish without fins and scales; birds of prey and rodents: these are included in the Torah's second detailed list of animals that are not kosher. It isn't the only aspect of *kashrut*, kosher, described in the Torah. From the threefold repetition of the ban against seething a kid in its mother's milk (Exod. 23:19; 34:26; Deut. 14:21), the rabbis deduced that we are permitted neither to eat, cook nor derive any benefit from meats mixed with milk, leading to the strict separation of meat and milk pots, plates and utensils that characterises the (non-vegetarian) Jewish kitchen. The absolute prohibition against the consumption of blood is stated categorically in the Torah (Gen. 9:3–4; Lev. 7:26–7; 17:10–14), indicating respect for the animal's life force or soul.

But why keep kosher at all? A simple answer is that the Torah says so; *kashrut* is a *hok*, a statute from God which cannot and, in some views, should not be explained. Yet even the most pious Jews have searched for reasons. For Maimonides, to suggest that God would command something lacking any purpose was to imply that the deity was irrational. As physician to the court of Saladin, he was deeply concerned with physical as well as spiritual wellbeing and understood keeping kosher to be good for our health:

Among all those [foods] forbidden to us, only pork and fat may be imagined not to be harmful. But this is not so, for pork is more humid

347

than is proper and contains much superfluous matter . . . You know to what extent the Law insists upon the need to remove filth out of sight.[39]

As nutritional science develops, the reasons offered may vary, but the endeavour to explain *kashrut* on health grounds itself remains healthy.

A very different interpretation is that the Torah requires us to make distinctions in many domains of life: wool and linen must not be used in the same garment; mixed seeds may not be sown in the same bed. Rather, each facet of creation should be appreciated separately for its own worth. Underlying the laws of *kashrut* is the greatest differentiation of all, between the holiness of life and the contamination of death. Whereas milk is the source of life for all mammals, eating meat entails death.

To others, the essence of *kashrut* is the avoidance of cruelty. Adam and Eve were vegetarians; only after the flood were humans allowed to eat meat, a leniency often interpreted as a concession to human weakness. But there were limits to how meat was to be consumed. The rabbis understood *ever min hachai*, the prohibition against cutting a limb off a live animal, as one of the seven universal laws incumbent on all the descendants of Noah. The strict rules of *shechitah*, slaughter, were aimed at minimising animal suffering; hunting, an activity associated with the cruelty of Nimrod and Esau, was regarded as wanton and cruel. The Talmud refers to eating meat as one of the special pleasures on festivals, indicating that it was a rare delicacy. This has little in common with the routine consumption of factory-farmed animals and dairy products today and the appalling misery this entails. Hence, to many, including the first chief rabbi of Palestine, Abraham Isaac Hacohen Kook (1865–1935), the ideal was to be vegetarian, if not vegan.

A very different but not incompatible explanation is sociological. Having to keep kosher obliges Jews to eat separately. Since meals are a key time to meet and mix, this helps prevent assimilation. As the Talmud puts it, 'the decree against non-Jews' bread and oil is because of their wine, against their wine because of their daughters, and against their daughters because of idolatry' (Avodah Zarah 36b). *What* we may eat limits *with whom* we may eat and defines us socially. This leaves a challenging question for 'veggies' like me: is breaking down barriers between people of different faiths a good thing (as, at heart, I believe), or, if the aim is to keep us apart, does eating vegetarian food together, while still complying with the formal details of *kashrut*, undermine its general purpose?

Yet despite all these reasons or rationalisations, *kashrut* remains a *hok*, a decree from God not reducible to ready explanations. *Kashrut* is connected with self-discipline and self-discipline is a part of holiness. It limits unrestrained greed and forces us to be mindful of what we put into our mouths. It constitutes a protest against wantonness and cruelty; it adds an important moral and spiritual dimension to the process of preparing and sharing food.

But if that is the goal, is keeping kosher today an adequate and effective way to achieve it? One can observe all the rules yet still be a *naval bireshut ha Torah*, a glutton with permission of the Torah, noted Nachmanides;[40] one can keep the laws but miss their moral import and continue to behave with thoughtless greed. This is all the more true in the twenty-first century: one can observe all the technicalities and still be guilty of gross exploitation of our fellow creatures, human and animal. If the aim of *kashrut* is to make consumption more ethical, the rules may need to be expanded. Across society, both Jewish and not Jewish, religious and secular, how we consume lies at the core of our ecological crisis.

Some, myself included, believe that we need to develop an eco-*kashrut*, not disregarding but adding to the traditional rules. Its key principles must include fair trade, to ensure the avoidance of *oshek,* 'oppression', through underpayment or exploitation of growers and their communities. Equally important is *bal tashchit*, 'not destroying', not polluting the earth through intentionally or ignorantly subsidising farming methods that poison the soil and cause the destruction of habitats, ruining the lives of local people and wildlife populations. A further aspect of *bal tashchit* is preventing the vast wastage that is such a deplorable part of the current food economy, as well as the damage caused by non-degradable packaging, especially plastic. It's often said that the amount of food thrown away today would be sufficient to provide for most of the world's hungry.

A third dimension to eco-*kashrut* is *tza'ar ba'alei chayim*, 'the suffering of animals' and the obligation to prevent it not only at the moment of death but also throughout their lives. This calls many of the standards of factory farming and livestock transportation into urgent question.

Last but not least is *tzedakah*, 'social justice', creating food economies in which resources are shared sufficiently fairly that the poor have affordable access to healthy food.

With the damage caused by heedless consumption foremost among our global challenges, *kashrut* should embody our values in the most comprehensive manner possible. It should help us focus on our relationship with each other, with the world of plants and animals, and with the earth itself. For 'the earth is God's' (Ps 24:1), and how we treat it with respect to our most basic needs for food and clothing is an intrinsic part of our ethical and spiritual life.

SHOFTIM (16:18–21:9)

....

Don't take bribes

Three terms can be considered as encapsulating Jewish social values: *tsedek*, 'righteousness', the practice of justice and integrity in all our dealings; *tzedakah*, which, though often translated as 'charity', expresses the responsibility to work proactively and generously for a socially just world; and *hesed*, 'faithful lovingkindness', an attitude of steadfast compassion that should permeate all our actions.

The Torah portion *Shoftim*, 'Judges', naturally focuses on the first of these terms, *tsedek*. Its famous verse 'Righteousness, righteousness shall you pursue' (Deut. 16:20), is preceded by the sharp warning: 'Do not take a bribe, because bribes blind the eyes of the wise and pervert the words of the just' (Deut. 16:19).

I had always thought that only truly corrupt people took bribes and that wherever bribery was rife it was a sign of profound systemic decay, whether in the judiciary, police, government or any institution in which it was prevalent and where others turned a blind eye. For bribes blind the eyes, not just of those who accept them but also of those who know and say nothing. Bribery creates environments of fear, distrust, bullying and abuse.

But taking bribes is not confined to accepting gifts in return for favours, and more of us may be guilty than we'd like to think. The rabbis didn't shrink from indicting the patriarch Isaac for allowing his love of hunted meat to stymy his better judgement:

'It came to pass when Isaac was old that his eyes grew dim from seeing' (Gen. 27:1). Should a man who offered his life to God and was bound on the altar be made to suffer the loss of his sight? But the Holy One wrote in the Torah, 'Do not take a bribe.' Why? 'Because a bribe blinds the eyes of the wise' (Deut. 16:19). So when Isaac received a bribe [of hunted meat] from Esau it weakened his eyes.

(Midrash Tanchuma, Toledot 8)

What parents or teachers can honestly say that they've been entirely impartial and never, even in their heart of hearts, preferred one child over another? Even God appears to be unfair, favouring Abel over Cain, Jacob over Esau and so on down the biblical generations. The pain this causes is as old as humanity itself.

In the public sphere, the need to be popular may be a subtle and seductive form of bribery when the price is compromising on what one knows to be right. 'Democracy is part of the problem,' a colleague observed in a discussion of the failure of virtually all legislatures to enact sufficiently stringent environmental legislation to curb global warming. Democracy is almost certainly the form of government least prone to corruption. But the overriding concern of the party in power to be re-elected leads almost inevitably to short-termist unwillingness to take measures requiring the public, especially its wealthier sector, to make even those sacrifices widely recognised as essential for ensuring a liveable future.

It can't have escaped the minds of politicians and executives that what's at stake is the fate not just of other people's children, but also of their own. Yet the financial power of corporations, self-interest, the fear of taking difficult steps and the desire to be popular all too frequently blind even the most fairly elected leaders from doing what is necessary. The widespread re-emergence of populism, the courting by otherwise bankrupt leaders of the lowest common denominators of collective prejudice to feed their lust for power: these are symptoms of a pervasive lack of ethical principles and moral courage in the public square.

It's not only in the political arena that the allure of popularity is hard to resist. An astute commentary connects the Hebrew for 'bribe', *shochad*, with an abbreviated form of the word for one, *chad*:

> A judge who takes a bribe becomes *at one* with the litigant who gives it . . . But the judge who refuses to take bribes is at one with neither litigant. To such a judge God says, 'Since you rejected partnership with them, I shall consider you a partner with me.'[41]

The etymology is forced but the idea is profound. The path of integrity can be lonely and hard; there's a cost to eschewing convenient untruths and following inconvenient truths. But if we want to be 'partners with God in sustaining creation', as the Talmud describes those who judge fairly, we must refuse the appeal of short-term comfort and follow the discipline of justice (Talmud Shabbat 10a).

Acutely aware of the corrosive potential of power, the Torah requires the king to write a special personal *Sefer Torah*, a copy of the Law (Deut. 17:18–19). The primary purpose is to prevent him from being corrupted by the allure of wealth, women or military might. The sovereign must keep this scroll with him always:

> When he goes to war, it must be with him; when he returns, he must bring it back with him; when he sits in judgement, it must be with him; when he reclines in bed, it must be next to him, as the Torah says, 'It shall be with him, and he shall read in it all the days of his life.'
>
> (Talmud Sanhedrin 21b)

The scroll is not simply a rule book, guiding him 'to keep all the words of this teaching and these statutes and put them into practice' (Deut. 17:19). Its primary purpose is 'so that he will learn to fear God' and pay attention not to what is seductive and popular but to the chastening voice of truth.

Whoever we are and however limited our responsibilities, it may be that this alone can engender the humility and respect, before God and each other, necessary to maintain our integrity, so that we do 'what is just and upright before God' (Deut. 21:9).

Do not destroy

The Israeli poet Zelda (1914–84) was troubled by the cutting down of trees:

> 'And the trees you're allowed to kill?'
> blurted a small boy whose eyes looked pained.
> When the snows melted,
> grim men emerged from the ruins
> to fell the ancient pines –
> powerful trees –
> that had responded to mountain winds . . .[42]

Judaism forbids the wanton destruction of fruit trees:

> When in war you lay siege to a city for a long time in order to capture it, you must not destroy its trees, wielding the axe against them. You may eat their fruit, but you must not cut them down . . . Only trees which you know do not yield food may be destroyed; you may cut them down for constructing siegeworks against the city waging war against you, until it has been laid low.
>
> (Deut. 20:19–20)

Paradoxically, this rule sadly brings to mind the skeletal remains of dead trees on the mud fields of the First World War and in parts of Ukraine today. Nature always suffers when humans resort to war.

This is not a universal ban against the removal of trees. The distinction is made between fruit-bearing trees, which must not be destroyed, and other species which may be cut down and even turned into implements of war. The determining factor appears to be their potential value to humans.

In between the words quoted (in the space marked by an ellipsis) stands a critical clause: 'Is a tree of the field a human being, to come against you in the siege?'

Rashi understands this as a rhetorical question: 'Is the tree of the field a man able to join the [forces] in the besieged city [or] suffer hunger and thirst like the inhabitants of the city? Why then destroy it?'[43]

However, the eleventh- to twelfth-century commentator and grammarian Abraham ibn Ezra reads the words as a statement: '*Man is a tree of the field*; that is, the life of man depends on the trees of the field.'[44]

The two explanations are not contradictory but rather mutually reinforcing: trees aren't people, so there's no cause to attack them. On the contrary, they should be respected because they provide essential food for human beings. It must be noted, though, that it's not because of their intrinsic value or beauty that they should be preserved, but because of their contribution to human need. Even fruit trees need to 'prove themselves' by offering sufficient benefits. The Talmud discusses how much this needs to be:

> Rav said: A palm tree producing even one *kab* of fruit may not be cut down. An objection was raised: What quantity of fruit must an olive tree produce for it not be permitted to cut it down? A quarter of a *kab*.
>
> (Bava Kamma 91b)

Not surprisingly, the Talmud concludes that the reason for this difference is because olive trees are more valuable than date palms. In another context, when discussing the law that the fruit of trees overlooked by their owners in the harvest must be left for the poor, the Mishnah notes that any olive tree with a special name or reputation can never be considered forgotten (Peah 7:1). It's touching to think that people saw their fruit trees as part of the family. People still do so to this day. We all treasure our favourite trees, especially those whose yield we've looked forward to year by year since childhood. Yet, even so, trees have to justify their survival: according to the strict letter of the law, if their value as timber exceeds that of their productive capacity, they may be cut down.

Jewish teaching derives the general principle of *Bal Tashchit*, 'do not destroy', the prohibition against needless destruction, from this case of fruit trees during war. The Talmud amplifies its application to include wantonly breaking up furniture, tearing clothing and even ruining one's own health through neglect:

> A footstool was broken up for Rabbah (to provide wood for heating when he was ill), whereupon Abbaye said: 'But you are transgressing the law of *Bal Tashchit*!' [Rabbah replied] '*Bal Tashchit* with respect to my own body is more important to me.'
>
> (Talmud Shabbat 129a)

In other words, turning even a minor piece of furniture into firewood can be justified only on the grounds that there is no other fuel available.

Maimonides codifies the principle in the following terms:

> Not only trees, but whoever breaks vessels, tears clothing, wrecks buildings, stops up fountains, or wastes food in a destructive manner, transgresses the commandment of *Bal Taschit*.[45]

But both the Talmud's analysis and Maimonides' codification leave open a key question: whether needless destruction is:

> . . . to be evaluated according to the effective use of human beings, or whether there is an inherent value which exists apart from human use, which must be balanced alongside human wants and needs.[46]

In other words, is creation to be considered solely from an anthropocentric perspective, or do trees, and by extension all living organisms, possess intrinsic worth before God, which humans are required to respect?

Trees are a potent symbol for this increasingly urgent concern. In the intertextual web of the Hebrew Bible, no tree can be disconnected from the tree at the centre of creation. Trees nourish all life, as Daniel beautifully describes in his interpretation of Nebuchadnezzar's vision:

> I saw a tree of great height in the midst of the earth;
> Its top reached heaven, and it was visible to the ends of the earth.
> Its foliage was beautiful and its fruit abundant;

There was food for all in it.
Beneath it the beasts of the field found shade,
And the birds of the sky dwelt on its branches; all creatures fed on it.

(Daniel 4:10–12)

Trees represent Torah, 'a tree of life to those who grasp it'; they symbolise the spiritual as well as the physical nourishment of humankind. To the Jewish mystics, the inverted tree with its roots in heaven and its branches stretched towards earth represents the flow of sacred energy down from its mysterious source above to nourish all life below. Trees cannot be reduced to mere function; as the earth warms and climate change becomes an ever-increasing reality, the existential importance of trees and their significance as a symbol have converged in our understanding. By absorbing carbon dioxide and giving out oxygen they perform at one and the same time the most essential and the most spiritual of roles: they breathe into us the very breath of life. Wantonly cutting them down epitomises our unheeding attitude towards the rest of creation, every part of which is precious before God and necessary to the survival of our wondrously and unfathomably interconnected world.

In the middle of the discussion of how much fruit needs to be produced by date palms and olive trees, the Talmud interposes a lament by Rav Huna: 'My son Shivchat died only because he cut down a fig tree before its time' (Bava Kamma 91b).

This painful interjection can be seen today as symbolic of the connection between tree life and human life; to hurt the former is ultimately to injure the latter. In traditional Jewish epigraphy, a broken tree indicates a young life cut short. What, then, might an entire broken forest represent? According to rabbinic tradition, when a tree falls a great cry traverses the world, yet no one hears. There is a terrible eloquence to the silence when the hedgerows, copses and woodlands are no longer there and there's nowhere left for the birds to sing.

'They shall measure – and the city nearest'

The Torah requires us to account for all shed blood: 'Innocent blood shall not be shed in your land which the Lord your God is giving you as an inheritance, placing blood [guilt] upon you' (Deut. 19:10).

Onkelos (c.35–120), whose Aramaic translation the rabbis considered authoritative, understands the last clause to mean that we have an obligation to do right by the person killed. Where blood has been shed, those responsible must be brought to justice and tried before a rabbinical court of no fewer than twenty-three members.

But in the case in question, a person has been found dead in the fields and there are no clues as to what has happened. Nevertheless, spilt blood must be accounted for. Therefore, the Torah insists that someone, or if not a specific person then society itself, must be held responsible. The process for doing so, referred to in the Talmud as the *eglah arufah*, '[the ritual of] the heifer whose neck is broken', may seem arcane. But it establishes a procedure for the collective acknowledgement of, and atonement for, the shedding of innocent blood. By the time of the Mishnah, the rite had already ceased to be practised. During the Roman wars and the subsequent persecutions there were simply too many killings for it to be possible to account for blood guilt in this manner.

The ritual proceeds as follows: the elders and judges of the local communities are summoned to measure which town lies nearest to where the corpse has been found; the Talmud specifies that the settlement must be large enough to have a court of twenty-three judges, hence capable of trying a potentially capital case. Once this has been determined, the elders of the relevant city take a heifer which has never borne a yoke and lead it down to an uncultivated valley where they break its neck. The local priests are then summoned to bear witness while the elders wash their hands over the body of the animal and declare:

> Our hands have not shed this blood and our eyes have not seen. Grant atonement to your people Israel, whom you, God, have redeemed; let there not be innocent blood in the midst of your people Israel.
>
> (Deut. 21:7–8)

It's tempting to regard this curious process as the perfect example of washing one's hands of responsibility. Perhaps this process lay somewhere in Shakespeare's mind when he created the scene in which Lady Macbeth desperately tries in her sleepwalk to wash herself clean of her victims' bloods: 'Out, out damned spot . . . All the perfumes of Arabia will not sweeten this little hand.'[47]

Yet the opposite is the case. The ritual is intended as a way of acknowledging, not denying, responsibility. The entire leadership of the local community is involved; its elders, judges and priests are all obliged to recognise that an unexplained death has occurred in their constituency and on their watch. They all have to answer for what has happened.

The Talmud puzzles over the words the elders say:

Could we really have thought they might be murderers [so that we require them to affirm that their hands did not shed this blood]? Rather, the Torah means that they have to declare: The victim did not come to us, but we dismissed him. He didn't approach us, but we left him without food. We didn't then leave him to continue his journey without anyone to accompany him [and keep him safe].

(Talmud Sotah 38b)

In other words, while not actually killing anyone, one can have eyes that 'see' other people without perceiving their needs, and hands that fail to take the actions necessary to keep them safe.

The Talmud understands the wellbeing of even a casual passer-by as everyone's concern. If a hungry person leaves town without being offered food, the whole community is at fault. If the roads are insecure, if the surrounding countryside is unsafe, the entire local population is to blame, with the responsibility resting first and foremost on its leaders. 'How should we have known?' is no excuse. There is such a thing as society, and society has to make due provision for the wellbeing not only of its own members, but also of wayfarers, strangers and even beggars who pass through. The Mishnah stipulates that every community must have at least two charitable funds: one, the *kuppah*, to keep money for weekly distribution to the local needy; and the other, the *tamchu'i*, 'the plate', on which food is collected daily and given to the travelling poor. A thousand years later, Maimonides wrote that 'we have not heard of a Jewish community which does not have such funds'.[48]

According to a famous midrash, the leaders and citizens of Sodom were condemned for enacting statutes threatening with the death penalty anyone offering food and shelter to strangers, a 'hostile environment' taken to its shocking extreme. According to the Torah and Talmud it is not sufficient merely to refrain from passing such nefarious laws. A community has to be positively proactive. As the ritual of the *eglah arufah* shows, however loudly leaders may subsequently claim that their hands were not guilty and their eyes did not see, they must be made to account both for their actions and for their failure to act. If they had indeed been corrupt or negligent, this highly public ritual would surely have shamed them into a thorough reassessment of their conduct as trustees of their city's institutions and policies. When something terrible happens to a member of one's family as a result of foreseeable and preventable occurrences, one of the most painful experiences is the failure of anyone in authority to acknowledge responsibility and, at the very least, apologise. The Torah refuses to countenance such evasions.

At the same time, the ritual can also be understood as freeing the local leadership from the taint of unwarranted suspicion. Interestingly, the custom among Sephardic Jews (whose ancestry goes back to the Iberian Peninsula or North Africa) is to recite the verse after washing one's hands upon leaving a cemetery, 'Our hands have not shed this blood and our eyes have not seen.' Unexplained or inadequately explained deaths leave a lingering sense of guilt in their wake. Only when there has been full accountability can innocent blood be laid to rest.

KI TEITSEI (21:10-25:19)

Caring for animals

I've loved animals since I was a child. Looking back, I can't understand why it took me until my twenties to stop eating meat. The Talmud tells of how God punished Rabbi Judah the Prince with seven years of toothache for saying to a calf which ran up to him for protection on its way to be slaughtered, 'Go, for it is for this that you were created' (Talmud Bava Metsia 85a). It's a lesson about cruelty: surely we would never do anything like that! Indeed, we wouldn't talk to calves in that way for the simple reason that most of us don't talk to them or even see them at all. We're blind to the suffering our habits of consumption entail; for the huge majority of us who aren't farmers and don't live in the countryside, 'meat' means a prepackaged product in the supermarket freezer.

The Torah sanctions the eating of meat but, it seems likely, only on special occasions. In a poor rural economy, meat was almost certainly a luxury; the Talmud comments that joy at festivals consisted in having meat for the celebratory feast. Those who treasured such gatherings would have understood what they were consuming; their animals lived alongside them, they knew the daily needs of their sheep and goats, calves and doves. There is a world of moral difference between eating the meat of an animal when one is closely aware of how that animal lived and buying the flesh of animals mass reared in factory farms and slaughtered in out-of-town abattoirs. Mark Rowlands describes the process with a brutal frankness we must find the courage to face:

From a stinking, muddy pen, the air rank with the stench of blood, you are corralled, or more likely electrically 'prodded' up a wooden plank. At the top a worker stuns you with an electric shock to the head. When you fall, someone grabs you, places your rear legs in a metal clamp, and you are hoisted upside-down on a conveyor belt. You are killed by a man who stabs your jugular with a knife. You bleed slowly to death . . . In any event, it is quite likely that you are not fully unconscious.[49]

Our habits of consumption are daily evidence of our failure of imagination and lack of honesty about our most basic needs and demands. We prefer not to know.

In no portion of the Torah are there more laws concerning the treatment of animals than in *Ki Teitsei*.

A lost animal must be kept safe until the owner reclaims it; a working animal that has collapsed under its burdens must be assisted (Deut. 22:1–4). The ancient rabbinic commentary *Sifrei* notes that this includes a lame or injured animal since the same word *va'asafto*, 'you shall gather it into your home' for safekeeping, is used by the prophet Micah to describe how God will 'gather in the lame' and the lost at the time of redemption (Mic. 4:6). The Torah twice employs the word *lehitaleim*, 'to hide oneself away', a form found nowhere else in it, to emphasise that *lo tuchal lehitaleim*, 'you are not allowed to pretend you haven't noticed'. It's the same verb used by Isaiah when he enjoins his people to feed the hungry, free the oppressed, clothe the naked and 'not hide yourself from your own flesh' (Isa. 58:7). How we respond to human and animal misery is an intimate part of 'our own flesh', our physical reality and moral identity.

In an extensive comment on the injunction not to take eggs or fledglings from a bird's nest without first shooing the mother bird away (Deut. 22:6–7), Nachmanides references Maimonides' description of animal sensitivity in *The Guide for the Perplexed*:

This commandment too can be explained in connection with 'you shall not kill it [a cow] and its calf on the same day'. The objective in both cases is that we should not have a cruel heart and fail to show mercy; or that we shouldn't root out an entire species. For [as Maimonides wrote] 'animals feel great anguish [when their offspring is killed in front of their eyes]. There is no difference between the anguish humans and animals feel concerning their offspring, for a mother's love and tenderness towards her child is not dependent on the powers of reason, but of the imaginative faculty.'[50]

Maimonides precedes Jeremy Bentham's widely quoted insight by seven centuries, that the question is not, "'Can [animals] *reason?*" nor "Can they *talk?*" but, "Can they *suffer?*"'[51] Mark Rowlands notes that animals may in fact suffer more intensely than humans precisely because they lack the cognitive capacity to contextualise their pain – for example, to understand that though it may hurt to have a wound treated, this is ultimately for their benefit. I shall never forget seeing a film of cattle being unloaded from lorries into tiny, tight pens prior to being slaughtered. Squeezed against the unyielding metal bars, separated from its mother, sensing the fear of all the animals around it, a calf simply weeps.

Nachmanides offers an additional explanation for the commandment to send away the mother bird before taking any eggs or fledglings: lest 'we root out an entire species'.[52] This would not be the first reference in the Torah to God's concern for the preservation of biodiversity. Before the great flood, Noah is instructed to take two of every kind into the ark, male and female, so that no entire species should be lost forever: creation's gene pool must be preserved.

A Hasid offered me an alternative interpretation of the law about the mother bird: at any other time she would fly away and we wouldn't be able to catch her, but parental instinct keeps her close to her nest. The Torah is teaching us not to exploit the vulnerabilities of parenthood. Of course, nowadays we should never take eggs from a wild bird's nest under any normal circumstances.

The Torah forbids ploughing with an ox and ass together but gives no reason for this prohibition (Deut. 22:10). One explanation is that an ox and a donkey have different strengths so that yoking them together would cause suffering to them both. Another approach focuses on the emotional dimension: an ox might take being partnered with a mere donkey as an insult, whereas a donkey would be tormented by the thought of its unequal power. The author of Proverbs notes that a just person *yode'a*, 'understands and cares about the lives of their animals' (Prov. 12:10).

Rabbi Abraham Isaac Hacohen Kook, the first chief rabbi of Palestine, was a passionate vegetarian. He understood the Torah's commandments about animal welfare as directing us away from meat-eating towards a future in which the full moral potential of both humans and animals would be realised, so that together we would form an enlightened partnership to follow God's will:

The hidden yearning to act justly toward animals will emerge at the proper time. What prepares the ground for this state is the commandments, those intended specifically for this area of concern.[53]

According to him, we must cover the blood of a slaughtered animal (Lev. 17:13) because this shows the 'acknowledgement of a shameful act [and] is the beginning of moral therapy'.[54] He finds equally compelling moral grounds for the commandment not to mix wool and linen: the former is forcibly taken from innocent sheep while the latter may be acquired by just labour, and the prohibitions against robbery and oppression extend to the animal kingdom. He even understands the commandment to visit the sick to apply to animals too.

But perhaps the most remarkable argument about the status of animals, albeit implied rather than fully spelled out, comes from the early Hasidic leader Mordechai Yosef Leiner (1801–54) known after his key work as the *Mei Hashiloach*. Posing the familiar question, with whom was God speaking when God said, 'Let us make man,' he answers that it's the animals:

> God first created all the other creatures. They then came to realise that they lacked anyone who could connect them spiritually with God, because it is through human beings with their capacity to raise every-thing up that all things are connected to God . . . When the animals saw what they lacked, they collectively roused God to create humans. Hence 'God said: "Let us make a human being."' That is, God told all the animals to pool their strengths to create human beings, in order that humans would have a portion in and of them all, so that if humans needed to speak [to God] about any matter, they would all lend their support. For what brings harm to humans brings harm to them, as in the generation of the Flood, and what brings good to humans brings good to them.[55]

A modern, though less gracious or poetic, way of saying this might be to note that we share most of our DNA with the animals. But the *Mei Hashiloach*'s main point is that we are the spokespeople for all life, a critical role to which, at this eleven-and-a-halfth hour, we must substantially increase our commitment.

Amalek

The Torah contains many passages that are morally inspiring and some that are morally offensive. Among the latter are the commandments to stone a rebellious son, to destroy utterly a city devoted to idolatry, and to 'wipe out the memory of Amalek' (Exod. 17:14; Deut. 25:19). In each case, Jewish tradition has not excised these passages from the Torah, but instead explained them in radical ways which render their literal application obsolete while deriving important lessons by interpreting them metaphorically. Still, the Talmud asks, why are they included in the Torah at all if they were never intended to be carried out? '*Drosh vekabbel sachar.* interpret them and receive a reward,' answers Rabbi Eliezer (Sanhedrin 71a).

There is nothing figurative, however, about the battle with Amalek in the Bible. The conflict takes place in three cycles. The first is when the Amalekites ambush the Children of Israel after they've crossed the Red Sea, attacking the faint and weary from behind (Exod. 17:8–13). They show no 'fear of God,' biblical shorthand for a basic universal morality according to which the lives and possessions of people of all nations should be respected (for example, Gen. 20:11; Deut. 25:18). Their behaviour is the ancient equivalent of targeting non-combatants, which the laws of war forbid. It is this conduct that leads to the declaration of God's war against Amalek from generation to generation (Exod. 17:16).

The second round comes when Israel's first king, Saul, is ordered to fulfil this commandment to wipe the Amalekites out (1 Sam. 15). It is difficult to read without deep distaste how, after the battle, Samuel punishes his reluctant monarch for failing to put to death all the women and children, and for capturing Agag, their king, alive instead of killing him.

The third and final round is described in the scroll of Esther, in the encounter in the court of the Persian king Ahasuerus between Agag's descendant Haman and Saul's great-grandson Mordechai. This results in the decree that each and every Jew in the Persian Empire should be killed off, a disaster prevented only by the astute intervention of Mordechai's niece Esther.

But by the rabbinic period, Amalek has ceased to exist as a distinct people. As Rabbi Yehoshua explains, Sennacherib, the Assyrian Emperor 'mixed up the nations' in the eighth century BCE, conquering the Middle East and enforcing his rule by means of a policy of mass deportations (Talmud Berachot 28a). Whether or not this is historically correct, it's the rabbinic way of rendering the commandment physically to destroy Amalek a dead letter. Therefore it is not legitimate to apply the law of mass destruction to any particular people, however evil we may consider them to be. It is especially important to bear this in mind as Jews have been the target of hatred in many different lands and under many powers throughout history. The temptation to brand all our enemies as Amalek can lead to dangerous generalisations and perpetuate, rather than diminish, hatred.

The biblical injunction goes beyond the literal annihilation of a nation. The commandment is to wipe out the very memory of Amalek and not forget. The contradiction seems obvious: how can one obliterate a memory and yet remember? One compelling explanation is that Amalek is not just a specific nation but also represents a principle; not the people itself, but its *zecher*, its imprint on history, its legacy, must be challenged generation after generation and repudiated over and over again. Hence the custom of saying the words *yimach shemo*, may his name and everything he stood for be wiped out, after any mention of Hitler and his ilk.

A key question in trying to root out evil is where it comes from in the first place. Is it, as Coleridge described Shakespeare's *Othello*, 'motiveless malignity', or is there, as King Lear demanded to know, 'any cause in nature that makes these hard hearts'?[56] The Talmud notes that Amalek is Esau's grandson, born to Eliphaz by his concubine Timna. On this slim foundation it constructs an account of how Timna wanted to convert to Judaism, clearly an anachronism since at that time there were neither rabbis nor a process of conversion, nor was there even such a thing as Judaism. But in the rabbinic imagination a court composed of Abraham, Isaac and Jacob rejected her on complex family grounds. Better then, she said to herself, to belong to this people even as a concubine than to become a princess in another (Talmud Sanhedrin 99b). Her son Amalek inherited her feelings of humiliation. The story is a warning to beware of rejecting people because their pain is liable to come back to haunt us.

Simpler and starker grounds for Amalek's feelings are that he is Esau's grandson. I couldn't take revenge on my brother for stealing my blessing, his grandfather tells him, so I bequeath to you the duty of vengeance. Time is not a healer of wrongs; hurts and grudges don't merely disappear. A striking midrash links Mordechai's 'great and bitter cry' when he hears of Haman's decree to kill all the Jews (Esther 4:1) to Esau's equally bitter cry when he finds that Jacob has taken their father's blessing (Gen. 27:34). What these Midrashic insights have in common is that they focus on our own part in the perpetuation of hatred. It's easy to see others as evil; we also need to consider whether there is anything we may have done to make them feel and behave that way.

Hasidic interpretation looks not at the external but at the internal sources of hate. Consciously mistranslating the dative *to you* as if it were the direct object *you*, Rebbe Shalom of Belz (1779–1855) reads the verse not as 'what Amalek *did to you*' but as 'what *did you*, i.e., made you, Amalek'?[57] His message is: don't let evil turn you into its own likeness. It's an astute observation; cruel and contemptuous treatment by others may have the effect not of making the victim more sensitive but rather cruel and contemptuous in turn.

Other Hasidic teachers understand Amalek as symbolising the dangers of heedlessness and mindlessness, leading us to forget that life is sacred and to deny any form of moral order. If all is chance, how we behave doesn't matter. Against this the Torah sets the command to remember and know.

These important insights focus on our inner Amalek. But there is also real, well-armed external evil in the world, and it has to be confronted and defeated. It does no favours to the cause of justice only to turn to the victims and ask them what they've contributed to their own victimhood. If Amalek is to be rooted out, it must be named, challenged and held to account.

Only then can we begin the task of reclaiming the energies that have somehow become misdirected and perverted into hatred.

KI TAVO (26:1–29:8)

A heart to know

The Torah commands us to know, but what is it that we must know and how should it influence our life?

The Hebrew word for knowledge, *da'at*, from the root *yada*, has a fascinating range of meanings. Sometimes *yada* simply means cognition, knowing some*thing*. But more often the word denotes *recognition* or, in the negative, non-recognition of a person, as when the new Pharaoh 'did not know Joseph' (Exod. 1:8) and subsequently declared that he 'did not know' God either (Exod. 5:2). Similarly, *yada* can imply taking, or failing to take, cognisance of the moral consequences of an action, as in Cain's rejoinder to God's enquiry about his murdered brother: 'I don't know!' by which he really means, 'I don't care' (Gen. 4:9). In the context of interpersonal relationships, *yada* may denote physical intimacy, as in 'the man knew Eve, his wife' (Gen. 4:1). Applied to God, it signifies deep concern, as when the Children of Israel cried out from their slavery, 'God saw . . . and God knew' (Exod. 2:25). The verb carries no object here; God's knowledge goes to the heart.

But what of the corollary? What can it mean for a person to 'know God'? The *Alenu* prayer, traditionally attributed to the second- and third-century teacher Rav, which concludes every Jewish service, quotes Deuteronomy: 'You shall *know* this day and lay it to your heart that the Lord is God in the heavens above and on the earth below; there is none else' (Deut. 4:39).

Jeremiah sees the knowledge of God as the ultimate goal of human striving: 'Let the wise not pride themselves in their wisdom or the strong in their strength. Rather, let those who wish to take pride, take pride in this: insight, and knowing me' (Jer. 9:23–4).

But is it possible to know God? For Maimonides the answer is a definite 'no'. The Torah states categorically, 'My face shall not be seen' (Exod. 33:23), meaning that God's true nature is unfathomable to humans. But God's 'back' can be seen; that is, we can obtain a sense of God's greatness from the study of God's works:

> When one contemplates God's wondrous deeds and magnificent crea-tion, one gains a glimpse of God's endless and inestimable wisdom, then at once one experiences a deep love and praise and a great long-ing to know God, as David said, 'My soul thirsts for you, God.' Then, when one ponders these matters, one at once steps back, overwhelmed with awe and fear, realising that one is merely a tiny, humble, uncom-prehending creature, standing weak in knowledge before God who is perfect in knowledge.[58]

Distinct from the thirst for knowledge for its own sake, and in sharp contrast to the pursuit of knowledge as power, the aim here is the deepening of our love and awe of God. According to the Christian theologian Jeremy Naydler, this was widely understood as the goal of knowledge through the Middle Ages and until the sixteenth century, when the understanding of the purpose of education and science underwent a radical change:

> The underlying reason for Bacon and Descartes' campaign against the wisdom tradition handed down to them was that they wanted to establish a new *kind* of knowledge, that not only cut out all reference to ancient authorities but above all re-established knowledge on the basis of what would be useful to human beings. They did not want a knowledge founded on contemplation and religious piety, that invested the world with religious meaning. They wanted a knowledge that would give human beings power to take control of the physical world and bend nature to the service of human ends.[59]

There can be little doubt that in this endeavour they were extremely successful. Yet for all its benefits, humanity's constantly growing and increasingly precise ability to analyse, describe, categorise, influence and control nature has also brought with it a profound and dangerous loss: precisely the attitude of wonder, reverence and humility so movingly described by Maimonides.

The Kabbalists regarded *da'at*, perhaps better translated in the mystical context not as 'knowledge' but as 'awareness', as one of the *sefirot*, the ten qualities that describe in descending order the stages of emanation of the divine vitality that fills all creation, including the human mind and spirit. From its unknowable source, this sacred energy flows into *chokhmah*, 'wisdom', bringing the first spark of inspiration, from there into *binah*, 'understanding', known as the 'well' or the 'womb' on high, because it is here that the initial intuition begins to receive form, then down into *da'at* where it becomes conscious apprehension. *Da'at* is therefore the recognition of the divine within creation, the 'knowledge' that behind the outward material form of things – tree, bird, squirrel – is their spiritual essence, their connectedness to the invisible but ever-present unity which sustains all life. These *sefirot* are at once transcendent spiritual domains and facets of the human consciousness.

According to Alon Goshen-Gottstein, *da'at* 'can be rendered as mind, understanding, and in my view is best captured as consciousness' and 'Broadening the horizons of awareness is in fact growing into the broader divine awareness and therefore a gateway into participating in divine compassion . . . From such fuller comprehension arises the identification with divine compassion and its extension to all beings'.[60]

Every weekday service contains a prayer for knowledge; it precedes all other requests, for which it is a prerequisite:

> You graciously bestow on humankind the capacity for knowledge and teach mortals understanding. Therefore, favour us with *da'at*, knowledge, understanding and insight.

For a long time, I simply read this as a request for knowledge, without troubling to think what kind of knowing was implied. But now I experience it as a petition for deeper insight into and empathy with all life, the whole vital world of which we are or should be a conscious and caring part. The term *chen*, awkwardly translated as 'grace' or 'favour', comes, like the word *da'at* itself, three times in the full text of this short prayer. *Chen* is often partnered with *hesed*, lovingkindness, indicating the deep

connection between consciousness and compassion, awareness and attentive concern. To know, in its deepest sense, is also to love.

Perhaps it is in this light that Moses' challenge to the Children of Israel
at the close of his life should be understood: 'God did not give you a heart
to know, eyes to see or ears to hear until this day' (Deut. 29:4). We never
know, see or hear as deeply as we might; we could always be more intuitively attuned, more perceptive and compassionate. Each day on which we
deepen such awareness becomes 'this day' to which Moses refers.

NITZAVIM (29:9–30:20)

'You stand this day, all of you, before the Lord your God'

Moses has reached the final part of his long admonition. He will shortly
sing his final song and invoke God's blessing on the people he has led for
forty years, before leaving them forever to climb the mountain, view the
land and die.

He sees before him the entire nation stretching into the future, the
generations yet unborn:

> You stand this day, *khulkhem*, all of you, before the Lord your God . . .
> those here with us this day and those not standing here with us
> this day.
>
> (Deut. 29:9, 14(10, 15))

The cycle of Torah readings is arranged to ensure that this portion is always
read on the *Shabbat* before the New Year, when 'all who enter the world
stand before the Lord your God'.[61]

Khulkhem, 'all of you', clearly means each one of you, without exception. Yet it can also be understood to indicate the whole of you, each of
you in the entirety of your being, including all your thoughts, words and
actions. Nothing of us, down to the depth of our consciousness, does not
come before the scrutiny of truth.

This does not imply that a judgemental God watches our every action
and follows our every thought with X-ray eyes. Rather, if God's spirit is
somehow present in each person, then how we behave towards everyone

and anyone, the impression we leave in their heart, is a measure of judgement over us. If God is here in all life, then the animals too, even the birds, also the trees, must somehow know us and bear the impact, the healing or the wounds, of how we treat them. We are inescapably known, and wherever we go and whoever and whatever we encounter carries not just the mark of our actions but also the flavour, the sweetness or bitterness, of our consciousness.

It is with this awareness that we must try to live, whether or not we believe in God and in whatever way we interpret such belief. Otherwise, we lay ourselves and our societies open to becoming people and cultures of unaccountability. We risk beginning the descent into a morally shameless world where we find ourselves among the disciples of Cain, who say, as he allegedly did to Abel before he killed him, 'There is no judge and no judgement,' and where neither right nor goodness are the ruling values so much as power and threat.

'You stand, all of you, before the Lord your God' can be read either as a warning or as an invitation. It is preferable to want to be known than to regard such knowledge as a threat. What, then, would it be like to try to live and embrace life known before God? How would this affect our speech, actions, conscience and innermost feelings? What kind of person would we seek to be, knowing of course that such an ideal is unattainable and that we are in the end 'only human'?

I would endeavour not to say anything intentionally hurtful to anyone. I would try to curb my impulse to speak reductively about others, to answer back sharply, to deliver clever retorts and shout down those who disagree. I would try not to remain silent when anyone passed a racist, misogynist or cruel remark, refusing to be intimidated by heartlessness and bullying. I would seek to deepen my intuition as to when to keep silent and listen, when to ask a quiet question to help the other person articulate their thoughts, and when, in the Bible's beautiful idiom, 'to speak upon the heart' (e.g., Isa. 40:2). I would aspire to be like the woman in Proverbs 'who has the Torah of loving kindness on her tongue' (Prov. 31:26). I would hope to be open to feedback, so that I could hear how I sound to others and learn how to heal and not to hurt. I would want to greet people like the deputy headteacher at the school where I taught before I became a rabbi, who knew how to speak to both children and staff in a way that, despite the grim Victorian building and the challenges of the day ahead, made you want to be there.

I would try never intentionally to cause pain through my actions. My father had kind and skilled hands; he could work in wood, fashion in metal and restore old furniture. I would like hands adept as his at recognising and understanding the qualities and properties of the elements of the world. I've seen the deftness of nurses' hands, carefully but quickly administering an injection or taking blood, with quietly comforting words. I would like hands that know how to give the modest, respectful touch of reassurance, the kind of hands a child would instinctively feel it was safe to hold to cross the road. I would like the hands of Moses, which remained *emunah*, faithful, steadfast, until sunset, the close of my life, though rather in the tasks of peace and planting than in battle. I would want hands that 'don't hurt or destroy in all God's holy mountain' (Isa. 11:9).

I would want a conscience not occluded by habits of self-deception, by, 'It wasn't really me,' and, 'What else could I have done?' I wouldn't want a conscience that turns a blind eye, lends a deaf ear and acquires increasing immunity to the sufferings of others. I believe in the importance of the fear of God, not as anxious trepidation but as Rashi understood it, as the awareness that even where there are no human witnesses, when one is most tempted to say, 'Who can call me to account?' there is One present who knows. I don't want always to 'get away with it' but to do what is right before God, people and all living beings.

I would want an aware and listening heart such as the psalmist prayed for: 'Create me a pure heart, God' (Ps. 51:12(10)). Then, perhaps, I might be ready to enter the covenant of God of which Moses speaks in his final address, and which is in truth a covenant with all life, to respect and care for it in good faith.

Therefore, I feel hope and aspiration, and a haunting shame.

'And the Lord your God will return your captivity'

Teshuvah is 'homecoming'. The Torah generally uses the word to describe the return of the Jewish People to its ancestral land after the punishment of exile. But in rabbinic literature the term usually refers to the personal 'return' of repentance.

There are two ways of understanding this journey. The more obvious is that *teshuvah* means repentance from sin, coming back to our better self after the misdirection of wrongdoing. It is in this sense that the word is most commonly used, as in 'doing *teshuvah*', which refers to the challenging but cleansing process of acknowledging the wrongs we've done, apologising to those we've hurt, making reparation and resolving not to do the same again.

Such *teshuvah* requires humility and involves profound inner change, as Maimonides writes in his *Laws of Repentance*:

> It pertains to the ways of penitence that the penitent cries out constantly before God with weeping and supplication; gives charity according to his capacity; distances himself greatly from the matter in which he sinned; alters his name, as if to say, 'I am not the same person who did those deeds'; changes all his deeds to do what is good and upright; and undergoes exile from his home. For exile atones for sin in that it causes a person to be submissive and engenders humility and lowliness of spirit.[62]

At its deepest level, such *teshuvah* entails not just reflection on particular wrongs, but on the whole course of our life. That's what my teacher meant, when, at the prayers after my father died, he quietly said to me, 'This is about *teshuvah*.' Those were the most helpful words spoken to me during that difficult period. This was time to ponder the big questions: Who am I? What am I doing with my days? Where's my life going? This is why the Talmud describes *teshuvah* as a process of healing, of learning from the past and turning our wrongdoings into signposts towards a more considered and generous way of life.

This leads to the second journey of *teshuvah*. Not necessarily connected with sin at all, it is the counterforce to the spiritual alienation that is an inevitable consequence of living in this material world with all its preoccupations and demands. It is the quest to rediscover our soul and reconnect with our truest self. To the mystics, this is the deepest and most complete *teshuvah*. God is *Mekor Hachaim*, the source and reservoir of all life, and our consciousness retains the knowledge, however much occluded by our experiences on earth, that it is from God that we come and with God that we belong. The Zohar describes such *teshuvah* as originating in the *sefirah* of *binah*, intuitive understanding, which it compares to a wellspring on high. It is a well, because it is from the depths that our awareness emerges, yet it is on high because it is the fountain from which our life force flows. Like water, this awareness is essential to existence; it is life-giving and life-affirming. *Teshuvah* is reconnection with this source of our, and all, life.

These two dimensions of *teshuvah* are really part of the same journey; the first belongs within the second. The desire to be free of the burden of having wronged any person, our instinctive regret if we've caused hurt or damage to any creature, is motivated ultimately not only by remorse over the offence, but also by the longing to be pure, at one with our own heart and with all being. Both journeys, too, are lifelong; they share the same road of return to the person we believe we most truly are and seek once again to become.

Nowhere in the Torah does the word *shuv* occur with greater frequency than in *Nitzavim*, the call to homecoming which is always read on the *Shabbat* before the New Year:

> When these things have come upon you, the blessing and the curse, *vehasheivotah el levavecha, you will lay it upon your heart* among all the nations where the Lord your God has driven you.
>
> (Deut. 30:1–3)

Vehasheivotah is causative, meaning 'bring back' or 'answer'; followed by 'heart', it translates as 'you will bring yourself back' or 'you will answer to your heart'. Just as collectively, so individually the process of repentance and return begins with an inner disquiet, a feeling of not inhabiting the landscape in which we truly belong, that where we are at this moment morally and spiritually is not our true home.

The Torah continues:

> *Veshavtah, and you will return* to the Lord your God and listen to God's voice . . . *Veshav*, and the Lord your God *will return et shevutekha your captivity* and have mercy on you, *veshav* and *return* and gather you from among the nations whither the Lord your God has scattered you.
>
> (Deut. 30:2–3)

In its different forms the verb *shav*, return, occurs four times in this short passage. Twice the subject is 'you', the people, and twice it is God. As a result of your heart's prompting, 'you will return', whereupon God too will 'return', both coming back to you and bringing you back. We and God return to each other.

But does God really return? The grammar is confusing: the Torah tells us that God will return, *veshav*, an intransitive verb; yet it is followed by *et shevutecha*, 'your captivity', and *et* indicates a direct object. Surely, then, the Torah should have used the causative form of the verb, *vehaishiv*? Basing himself on the Talmud, Rashi offers a moving explanation, qualifying his words with the rabbinic term *khivyakhol*, 'as if to say', in acknowledgement of the bold anthropomorphism of his comment:

> The text should have read *veheishiv*, 'God will bring back your captivity.' From this our rabbis learn that it's as if the *Shechinah*, the divine

presence, dwells with Israel amid all their troubles in all their exiles. When they are redeemed, God will return with them: God ascribes redemption to himself. Furthermore, the day of the ingathering of the exiles will be so great and so difficult, that it will be as if God himself will have to hold each and every individual person by the hand and bring them home.[63]

God suffers exile alongside the people and returns with their return. This is profoundly important for Rashi as, especially in his commentary on the Song of Songs, he responds to the accusation that God has abandoned the Jewish People forever. God is present even in our exile; God is in exile too and will, in bringing us home, come home in our homecoming. But God's *teshuvah* depends on ours. God seeks the heart, but when our heart offers God no place, then God, too, becomes a refugee. For God wants to be at home not just in the land of our ancestors, but also, and maybe even more so, in our daily lives.

Not in heaven

My grandfather served as a chaplain on the Western Front for the duration of the First World War. He often spoke warmly about how well he and his Christian colleagues got on. Once, at a ceremonial gathering at which they each had to give a brief address, he found himself pushed forward by his Catholic and Protestant companions with the words, 'The oldest religion should go first.' When I told a friend this story, he disagreed: 'Christianity is older. People think of Judaism as the religion of the Bible, but really it was created by the rabbis, mostly after the time of Jesus.' He was right: Judaism is not the religion of the Hebrew Bible alone, but of how the rabbis chose to read it. Once the Torah had been given at Sinai, it was delivered into the people's safekeeping to interpret and apply according to their best understanding, within the complex context of the ever-changing human condition:

It is not in heaven, that you should say, 'Who will go up to heaven and bring it to us so that we can hear it and can do it?' Nor is it over the seas, that you should say, 'Who will cross the ocean and bring it to us, so that we can hear it and do it?' Rather, it is very close to you, in your mouth and in your heart, to do it.

(Deut. 30:12–14)

The words *lo bashamyim hi*, 'it is not in heaven', became a byword, the basis of and justification for thorough and sometimes radical rabbinic interpretation. To say that the rabbis of the periods of the Mishnah and Talmud were bold in how they went about this process would be an understatement. The comment that the Jewish approach to revelation is, 'Thank you, God, for giving us the Torah; now let us tell you what it means,' is only partly facetious. But the rabbis' interpretative courage was never gratuitous or arrogant; it was accompanied by a profound humility, the awareness that we are subservient to God's will, and that reason and understanding are sacred gifts to be used in God's service:

> 'The matter [i.e. the Torah] is very close to you . . .' When is it 'close to you'? When 'it is in your mouth and in your heart, to do it'.
> (Talmud Eruvin 54a, quoting Deut. 30:14)

The question of who determines meaning was, and remains, central to the entire rabbinic endeavour. In a famous passage in the Talmud, Rabbi Eliezer and Rabbi Yehoshua disagree regarding the ritual status of a stove constructed out of coiled rings, *tanuro shel akhnai*, a 'serpent oven'. Convinced that he is correct, but finding himself a lone voice among his colleagues, Rabbi Eliezer adduces supernatural proofs. He asks the water in a nearby channel to change its course and it promptly does. 'One doesn't bring proofs from a stream,' his colleagues reply. He summons a carob tree in his support; it instantly uproots itself and moves one hundred cubits. He calls upon the walls of the house of study to testify to the validity of his position; they at once lean inwards, but only partly, out of respect for his opponents. But Rabbi Yehoshua and his supporters remain unmoved. Finally, Rabbi Eliezer appeals to heaven, from where a *bat kol*, 'the daughter of a voice', declares itself in full agreement with his conclusions and challenges his opponents back: 'Why are you attacking Rabbi Eliezer, when everywhere the law accords with his views?' The Talmud can come no closer to saying that even God is on his side.

One might have thought that at this point Rabbi Yehoshua would finally acknowledge defeat. Not in the least: 'We pay no attention to heavenly voices,' he retorts. 'It is not in heaven.'

The very words with which he denies God a voice in the debate are themselves from the Torah: '*It is not in heaven*, that you should say, "Who will go up to heaven for us and bring it down to us so that we can hear it and do it"' (Deut. 30:12).

'What can [Rabbi Yehoshua] mean?' the Talmud asks in apparent surprise, Rabbi Yirmeya explains:

> Since the Torah was given at Mount Sinai, we do not pay attention to divine voices, as you, God, wrote at Mount Sinai in the Torah: 'Follow after a majority.'
>
> (Bava Metzia 59b, quoting Exod. 23:2)

The interpretation of Torah is not a matter of signs and portents, of voices from on high or even from God, but of the prevailing view of the sages.

Rabbi Yehoshua is not making an impious claim. Rather, he is affirming the supreme role of human reason and sensitivity. The age of prophecy is, to all intents and purposes, over. God's will has been expressed in the Torah; in giving this Torah to Moses at Sinai, God entrusts it to human beings, despite our limited capabilities. It's not surprising that the Talmud puts into the mouths of the angels the following objection: 'This treasure which you have kept safe in heaven for nine hundred and seventy-four generations you now intend to give to mere flesh and blood!' (Shabbat 88b). Yet, as the passage makes clear, such is indeed God's will. Thereafter, the task of interpretation belongs with us, and even God cannot circumvent the process. God is silenced by God's own word.

In a fanciful sequel to the debate between Rabbi Eliezer and Rabbi Yehoshua, the Talmud relates how Rabbi Nathan asked Elijah what God did on that day: 'God laughed and said: "My children have defeated me! My children have defeated me!"'

It's a sentiment familiar to every parent, but it's spoken with pride. God, it appears, rejoices in the fine balance of faithfulness and independence shown by these rabbinic children. Though not formally closed until the early second century CE, by the first century BCE the canon of the Hebrew Scriptures, the 'Old Testament' in Christian terms, was effectively complete. New situations, novel social, legal, economic and moral challenges had to be faced not by seeking further revelations from God or fresh visions from new prophets, but by interpreting and expanding the latitude of existing revelation.

It is in this context that the rabbinic understanding of 'it is not in heaven' should be understood. It is not a curtailment, let alone a denial, of the Torah's sanctity as God's word. Rather, it is an essential precondition for the text's potentially infinite capacity to remain relevant. This is expressed in the idea that the Oral Torah, too, was given at Sinai. Some take this literally. But many believe it to mean that the giving of the Torah includes the sanction to explain and interpret it, and to extend its application to embrace new situations as they arise. The results of this process, always rigorous, demanding and hotly debated, constitute 'Torah', that is, God's will to the best of our capacity to understand it. As Moshe Halbertal notes:

> Paradoxically, the canonical text, because it has been fixed to the last detail, becomes saturated with signifiers which, in principle, contain all knowledge – divine and natural.[64]

These 'signifiers' need to be interpreted according to 'the principle of charity', to derive the best and most apposite meanings in every circumstance.

This task of interpretation is not a free-for-all. It demands profound study, humility, faithfulness to the Torah's teachings, discipleship and life-long dedication. Any new legal situation has to be considered in congruence with the past, via the complex route of rabbinic interpretation across history, down to the possibilities open in the present time.

Lamenting the impoverishment of Jewish learning in the early twentieth century, and sharply critiquing liberalist thinkers who pulled out from the Torah only those lines that supported their positions, Franz Rosenzweig observes that only a:

> ... laborious and aimless detour through knowable Judaism gives us the certainty that the ultimate leap, from that which we know to that which we need to know at any price, the leap to the teachings, leads to *Jewish* teachings.[65]

VAYELECH (31:1-30)

'I shall surely hide my face from you' – *Hester Panim* as theology of history

Throughout the generations, parents have blessed their children with the familiar words from the Torah, which we repeat in every service: 'May God's face shine upon you and give you grace; may God's face be turned towards you and give you peace' (Num. 6:25–6).

But the Torah also speaks of the opposite, the concealment of God's face and the withdrawal of God's favour: 'I will forsake [the people] and hide my face from them. They will be [like prey] to be devoured; numerous evils and troubles will befall them' (Deut. 31:17).

Hester Panim, 'the hiding of the face', is the doctrine that God may deliberately remove divine providence from us, leaving us at the mercy of the random forces of history. God will behave 'as if not seeing [our] sufferings' and 'paying no attention'.[66] God will take leave of absence from human affairs; to all intents and purposes, it will be as if God doesn't exist. We will stand alone, with no protection against the tyrants who swallow up small nations, the persecutors who imprison, torture and murder whomever they choose.

The Torah presents *Hester Panim* as God's punishment for our unfaithfulness: turn away from me, says God, and I'll turn away from you. It places the responsibility for our setbacks and defeats firmly on us. Had we not sinned, failing to fulfil God's commandments and ignoring the demands of social justice, God would not have allowed such disasters to befall us. This can read like a retrospective theological explanation for the horrors of history. The reason Judaea was conquered by Babylon and destroyed all over again by Rome is not that it was a tiny nation confronting a superpower, but because it ignored God's word. To this day we say in our festival prayers, as we recall the joys of the pilgrimage to Jerusalem in Temple times, that 'on account of our sins, we were exiled from our land'. This reads like an ancient form of blaming the victim, evidently as much in vogue millennia ago as it is today. As the Czech poet Miroslav Holub wrote, presumably referring to the Soviet invasion of his homeland in 1968:

> Just as it is the fault of towns and nations that they've stayed small.
> I blame the small nations for not having become powerful.
> So much the worse for them.[67]

Yet there are also positive aspects to the theology of *Hester Panim*. Unlike a historical-theological context in which, if your temple was destroyed your deity was defeated, it affirms the eternal existence of the God of Israel. The nation, not its God, has been vanquished; the fault lies not in God's weakness but in the sins of the people. Accepting responsibility is, in fact, a way of preserving faith. Paradoxically, the doctrine of *Hester Panim* is empowering. Had we behaved differently, God would not have turned away from us. It is our conduct that has left God with no choice:

'Alas for the father, whose house has been destroyed and whose children have gone into exile on account of their sins' (Talmud Berachot 3a).

But if the cause lies with us, so does the cure. 'Return to me,' says God, 'and I will return to you' (Mal. 3:7). The decisive factor is not God's will but our behaviour. As Samson Raphael Hirsch explains:

> Israel's national defeat is a natural consequence of its self-induced weakness . . . People seek the cause in God, not in their own conduct . . . The people abandoned God; therefore, God has abandoned them.[68]

Quoting Amos, 'Only you have I known out of all the families of the earth' (Amos 3:2), he notes that special relationships entail special responsibilities the neglect of which exacts a high price.

Hester Panim thus serves as a theological explanation for the miseries and defeats of Jewish history, while holding out the hope that however harsh the current reality may be, the future has the potential to be better. God is not dead and will not hide forever; God is not impotent or uncaring, but waiting for our return.

Yet, like any attempt to explain evil and disaster, the doctrine is highly problematic. In a disturbing but moving discussion, the Talmud notes how Jeremiah and Daniel each leave out in their prophecies one of the qualities 'great, mighty and awesome' attributed to God in the Torah (Deut. 10:17). Jeremiah omits 'awesome', because, the Talmud has him say, heathens are profaning the temple (Jer. 32:18). Daniel omits 'mighty' asking, 'where is God's might if the nations have enslaved his children?' (Dan. 9:4). However, the rabbis reinstate both adjectives and include them in the wording of the daily *Amidah* prayer as we recite it to this very day. But how can they refer to God as 'mighty' and 'awesome' when the Babylonians have destroyed Jerusalem and exiled the nation from its land? Because, the Talmud answers, God's might sometimes lies not in acting, but in patiently refraining from intervention (Yoma 69b).

This supposed restraint has had the most terrible consequences. In the disastrous interim during which God's face is hidden, the powerless are not protected from their oppressors. The victims of the Inquisition were not rescued from the *auto-da-fé*, the burning of the heretics; neither Jews, Roma, homosexuals, nor any ideological opponents of Nazism were saved from the gas chambers. So the question inevitably arises: is God only hiding the divine face? Or is the doctrine in fact hiding something else: God's impotence, God's inability to protect the innocent against the cruel? Or is it even a cover-up for God's non-existence?

The notion of a God who has the capacity to act but chooses not to is scarcely morally credible. What kind of God hears the cry of the oppressed yet opts not to respond? One much-repeated answer is that God wants people to exercise freedom of choice and is therefore obliged to refrain from interfering in human history. Were God to determine the outcome of every conflict we would be mere pawns, devoid of responsibility for the consequences of our actions. But the immeasurable horrors of the Holocaust, the World Wars and subsequent genocides have made this approach untenable. Who would want to believe in such a dispassionate, bystander God?

In a remarkable lecture delivered at Marburg, the very university where Martin Heidegger, an unrepentant supporter of Nazism, had previously occupied the chair of philosophy, Hans Jonas argued that the idea that God is all-powerful is to be found neither in the Bible nor in the rabbinical writings, but only entered Jewish thought later, with Maimonides. God, in the classic sources, encounters failures and weeps for them. God can't do everything. He quotes Etty Hillesum's diary entry on the day the Nazis forced her to leave her beloved Amsterdam: 'There is little you can do for us God. Nor do I hold you responsible.' On the contrary, she writes, it is our responsibility to preserve and protect the presence of God in ourselves and in each other.[69]

Nevertheless, there are recent thinkers for whom the concept of *Hester Panim* has remained compelling. Twentieth-century American rabbi Joseph Soloveitchik understands the re-establishment of the Jewish home-land as God's return to human affairs. God has knocked once more on the door of history with the creation of Israel:

> The sixth knock, which we must not ignore, was heard when the gates
> of the land were opened [to refugees and survivors of the Holocaust in
> 1948] . . . the era of divine self-concealment (*hester panim*) is over.[70]

In the context of the horror and the hope, as the full extent of the system-atic murder of Jews by the Nazis was revealed, while at the same time the United Nations recognised the right of the Jewish People to its ancient land, Soloveitchik's response is a profoundly moving affirmation of faith. But just as there is a price for believing in God's deliberate restraint, so there are costs to believing in God's active intervention.

This may be why twentieth-century Jewish philosopher Martin Buber preferred to stay with the pain of God's hiddenness:

The Bible knows of God's hiding His face, of times when the contact between heaven and earth seems to be interrupted. God seems to withdraw Himself utterly from the earth and no longer to participate in its existence. The space of history is then full of noise, but empty of the divine breath. For one who believes in the living God, who knows about Him, and is fated to spend his life in a time of his hiddenness, it is very difficult to live.[71]

Hester Panim in mystical theology

Life, including the life of faith, inevitably has low points, not just days of doubt but of the utter collapse of belief. Sometimes one feels hopeless: how can I believe in anything? It's not just the tragedies that befall us, both individually and collectively. It's not only the patent injustice when children can't go to school because they're hungry and have no shoes, while others in the same city throw away food that could feed a family for a week. It's not only that nature, full of beauty despite being red in tooth and claw, is constantly encroached upon and ruined by humans' mistreatment of it.

The very desire to seek God and find spiritual meaning has sputtered and gone out. The soul yearns for nothing; prayer feels futile. One wonders: is it only fools who say in their heart, 'There is no God'? (Ps. 53:1). Maybe the real fools are those who pretend there is? Where's the evidence? One stands like Matthew Arnold on life's shore and hears only the 'melancholy, long, withdrawing roar' of:

> The Sea of Faith, which once was full,
> . . . and round earth's shore
> Lay like the folds of a bright girdle furled.[72]

The Hasidic teachers understood the rocky unevenness of faith. They appreciated that everybody has periods of what they called *katnut mochin*, smallness of mind, spiritual shutdown, as well as privileged moments of *gadlut mochin*, expansiveness of consciousness and soul. The Hasidic motto, succinctly expressed by Rebbe Nachman of Breslav, is 'don't give up', *asur lehitya'esh*, it's forbidden to despair. Only someone familiar with mental struggle and the challenges of depression could have coined such a phrase.

But never for a second would the Hasidic masters have entertained the thought that God was dead, or that God had never existed in the first place

379

but was purely a fiction of the human imagination. They would never have conceded either that God was truly absent, or that, frustrated by its failures, God had taken a break from humanity. On the contrary, God couldn't be nearer. Only, God was in hiding, and God's chosen hiding place was neither distant nor remote but inside creation, within all life, even inside our own selves.

In Hasidic theology, *Hester Panim,* the hiding of God's face, is not therefore a form of punishment. It is simply where God is in relation to our world, because God is present but concealed in all things. *Olam,* 'world' in rabbinic Hebrew, derives from the root *a.l.m.,* meaning 'to hide' or 'to be hidden'. In the higher realms of creation, God's presence may be obvious, but here on earth in this *olam ha'asiah,* this physical world of doing and making, of things and objects, God is hidden behind the facade of its materiality. Our task is to see beyond the seeming, to look behind the veil and to perceive the sacred within the everyday, within every person, within every living being and in every act.

Hester Panim is thus an intrinsic part of our earthly reality. What varies is not where God is, but where we are, where our consciousness is. In moments of spiritual expansiveness we become conscious of the sacred in anything and everything; at other times we cannot penetrate beyond the outward, mundane appearance of things to perceive the divine that resides within them. The challenge is to keep seeking:

> 'I shall hide my face from them:' The Torah tells us that God hides because God wants us to yearn for him so much that we keep looking until we manage to find him, just as a small child chooses a hiding place and conceals himself there so that others go looking for him and find him.[73]

My teacher, Louis Jacobs, used to quote this saying, adding a further twist: 'Children who have been hiding for a long time cry because they're afraid their friends have abandoned looking. God weeps too, when human beings give up.' *Bakshu Panai,* 'Seek my presence,' says the psalmist (Ps. 27:8), which Rashi explains to mean that our heart speaks out on God's behalf, reminding us never to abandon the spiritual search. Moments of connection, of wonder and awe, allow us to glimpse God's hidden nearness. Sometimes, as if we were following a thread of light perceptible only to the spirit, we can even climb back up the path of emanation, down which the divine energy unceasingly flows to re-create and sustain this world.

This search for the hidden God is never merely a solipsistic pursuit for the sake of the soul's satisfaction, important as that is. The awareness of the presence of God in all life adds commitment to commandment: everything calls out, 'Care for me!' We seek God not just to gain respite from the demands of this world, but also to find the energy and inspiration to re-engage with them.

Yet there are times when we feel God is more than just hidden. We lose hope, lose any connection with the notion that there may even be anything to look for. It is to these moods, taught the Ba'al Shem Tov, that the Torah addresses itself when it employs the emphatic doubling of the verb: '*Ve'anokhi haster astir pananai bayom hahu*: I shall surely hide, hide my face on that day' (Deut. 31:18).

> [Sometimes] the hiddenness goes so deep and is itself so thoroughly concealed – hiddenness within hiddenness – that one cannot feel God's presence in the least. Then it seems as if, heaven forbid, there is no God there at all.[74]

It's not just that God's face is hidden; that very hiddenness is itself concealed. In such bleak periods one feels that there's no point even trying: this world is entirely material, governed solely by laws of natural causality. There's nothing deeper, nothing awesome, no inner life there at all. We have only the vast injustice of a world full of cruelty, mitigated by a mere modicum of altruism and compassion.

Yet even when we feel that low, the Ba'al Shem Tov taught, we must not give up, but should remember that God's name is *El Mistater*, God who hides God's self away. His disciple, Rebbe Moshe Chaim Ephraim of Sudlikov (1748–1800), added: 'Even in the deepest hiding it is possible to find God, for the very verse [about the hiddenness of God's hiding] begins *Ve'anokhi* – "and I".'[75]

Despite the bleak and impenetrable darkness, God still speaks; God is still there, saying, 'I am,' hiding within the hidden.

Evidently the mystics, too, knew times of despair. But they didn't give up.

HA'AZINU (32:1-52)

On song

Moses closes his forty years of leadership with a song and a blessing.

'This song shall answer as witness,' he warns his people, calling heaven and earth to listen (Deut. 31:21). It's strange to think of music as evidence. Presumably what Moses means is that the words of his song will testify against the Children of Israel should they turn aside from God's commandments.

But song itself is by its very nature testament of the deepest kind. All life sings and all creation bears witness, as the mystics of every faith have always understood. Song is the essence of prayer; and prayer, not petitionary or confessional but the simple prayer of breathing and being, is the soul of existence. When the mind is at one with life, then everything is bound together and all existence sings.

This is beautifully expressed in a meditation at the close of *Perek Shirah*, The Chapter of Song, a mediaeval tractate that ascribes a song based on a matching verse in the Bible to every element of creation, from the wind to the mountains, and from the wild birds to the donkeys and dogs:

> By the merit of this song which I have read, which is the song of all existence, the song of the minerals, plants and all living beings, and of the angels appointed over them by God, and of the divine presence which connects all the worlds, and of the bond which unites what is on high and what is below, may this be an hour of mercy, an hour of listening and of hearing.[76]

The songs of nature nourish and inspire the songs of humankind. Just as a folk singer listens out constantly, even when not consciously aware of so doing, for new melodies, paying attention to every local dialect and nuance of language, remembering, recording and collecting songs, so the soul listens intuitively to life, gleaning and gathering the music of existence and forming it into prayer. This is beautifully expressed by Rabbi Kalonymus Kalman Shapira:

> The essential reason for the creation of all beings is that they should sing, for in this way they reveal the greatness of God. Every single

382

created being sings, as we know from *The Chapter of Song*. Each and every being reveals a spark of the glory of the God of blessing . . . For all creation, even the angels, long to hear those songs in which God's holiness and God's glory are revealed. [A person who sings in this spirit] does not sing for the sake of others only, to share his song with those who do not know, but also for himself, for his own sake. The whole purpose of service in prayer consists in enabling the soul to reveal itself through song and in this manner fill us with the dew of inspiration to do good deeds.[77]

But singing such songs is not always easy. Our constant preoccupation with the material world can impede our ability to listen; the tyranny of irritating distractions and the backlash of angry thoughts can shut down the subconscious sensors and feelers of our spirit. We become mute, unable to sing or even to remember that the song of creation exists. Rabbi Kalonymus Kalman Shapira continues:

Sometimes external preoccupations interpose themselves, gaining in dominance until they silence our song, as the psalmist says: 'For I was left silent and mute.' I became mute because of the silence of God in my soul. But when the soul is aroused and reawakened by hearing God's songs, the awareness of the presence of God grows strong once again, and one can sing to God.[78]

More disturbing than those inevitable periods in which the soul experiences only absence and silence because the consciousness is too distracted to listen is the possibility that life's song itself may have ceased. It's just such an absence of the music of the trees and animals that Jeremiah laments as he sits alone in the mountains contemplating what he foresees as the inevitable destruction of Jerusalem. Seeking refuge from the beleaguered city, he finds little consolation in the countryside:

I weep and cry for the mountains, and lament for the pastures in the wilderness because they are desolate; there are no passers-by. The call of cattle cannot be heard; the birds of the skies and the beasts of the fields have fled and are all gone.

(Jer. 9:10)

Nature, too, is a temple, the greatest and most wonderful in which God's presence abides. The terrible fear today is that we are in danger of destroying its music forever. It's precisely such lifeless, songless desolation that Rachel Carson presages in her seminal *Silent Spring*, the book which more than any other forewarned us of the climate challenges through which we are now living.[79] That is why Moses' closing words are so disturbingly prophetic: he too utters a warning. *Ki hashcheit tashchitun*, 'You will be destructive and destroy and evil will befall you,' he predicts (Deut. 31:29), using in its most emphatic form the very word with which the Torah has commanded *lo tashchit*, that destructiveness is forbidden (Deut. 20:19).

Moses is not being hyperbolic when he calls them to witness; heaven and earth do indeed know us. They are not inarticulate entities that can never be summoned to give evidence. The song to which they testify is in truth the music of all creation, of every living being. There is no greater testament to *Chei HaChayim*, the Life of all Life, the essence and spirit of all things, than such song, whether it emerges with the dawn light from the tiny beak of the wren in the hedgerow, from the night cry of the wind across a pass in the mountains, or in the just and compassionate conduct of human beings.

The daily morning prayers affirm that God loves this music, that God, 'Sovereign of life of all the worlds,' chooses above all to be praised in melodies of song. Should they all fall silent, creation will have failed.

Remember the days of old

In the last years of my father's life, when his mobility was compromised and we could no longer work in the house or garden and simply sat together, he would often chant the verses of Moses' last song: '*Zechor yemot olam*: Remember the days of old, consider the years of generation after generation. Ask your father and he will tell you, your elders and they will say' (Deut. 32:7).

I don't believe the choice of verses was consciously didactic; I'm sure he didn't want to impose on me. I took his singing as part of a love of Torah absorbed in childhood and now returning and deepening in him in his last years. I hummed along with him and we enjoyed our quiet solidarity.

After he died, I found myself driven to research the fate of his family as they fled, or tried to flee, Nazi Europe. I read with passion, devouring footnotes and bibliographies, ordering abstruse articles, unable to stop.

'Was the process painful?' a reader of the book which eventually emerged, *My Dear Ones: One Family and the Final Solution*,[80] asked me.

The truth is that most of the time I was drawn by a strange compulsion, a need to know every discoverable detail. Had I been able to find out what, if anything, my great-grandmother ate for breakfast on the day she was finally driven from her home in Moravia, I would have gone out and tried to find that very food.

At a conference on writing and exile, Edmund de Waal, author of *The Hare with Amber Eyes*, commented that there is safety in silence: one doesn't pass on to one's children the burden of the past. In response, the novelist Elif Shafak noted that we have become a society of collective amnesia. The cause may lie in the unconscious desire to protect our offspring. Or the reason may be that refugees, robbed of home, family, friends, work, language and familiarity with how things are done which one so painfully and clumsily lacks in a strange new culture, need to look strictly ahead in order to start again. Like Lot's wife fleeing Sodom, looking back would be totally immobilising. Or it may be, as many survivors have testified, that 'other people simply don't want to know'. As a result, the narrative of our history is broken into fragments interspersed with silence. It can be forced into an artificial coherence, but only by failing to acknowledge the unspoken.

The Torah shows no reluctance about burdening the future with knowledge of the past. At the beginning of his masterly study, *Zakhor: Jewish History and Jewish Memory*, Yosef Hayim Yerushalmi notes that words from the root 'remember' occur 169 times in the Torah.[81] It's not in remembering but in forgetting that danger is seen to lie. Lest you forget what God did for you, the Torah repeatedly warns; lest you tell yourselves, 'By my own might and power have I achieved all this' (Deut. 8:17).

Knowing our history is an obligation precisely because it is, and should be, challenging. This is not intended to be because it is a heavy load to bear, but because we have to appreciate our past if we are to understand our own identity and responsibilities, the direction of our journey through life. Samson Raphael Hirsch compellingly paraphrases the Torah's instruction:

Ask your father about your history; he will make it vividly contemporary. Your elders, gifted with wisdom and insight, will tell you the meaning of your history, they will explain your origins and your historical mission.[82]

Yet history does place a burden on the future. My wife and I called our eldest child Amos Gershom; it was only many years later in conversation with him that we came to appreciate fully the meanings of these names.

Our reasons were typical and innocuous: we chose Amos because we liked it, and Gershom because it had been my late grandfather's Hebrew name. It hadn't occurred to us at the time that Amos means 'burdened' and Gershom 'stranger there'. 'Burdened outsider': to how many millions in this world today might such a name apply?

In Judaism, history is not merely an academic discipline. At the Hebrew University in Jerusalem, the Faculty of History is simply called *Hamachlakah le'Historia*. But the Department of Jewish History is *Hamachlakah le Toldot Am Yisrael*, 'the Department for the study of the Generations of the People of Israel'. It's a family matter, close to home, personal.

At the heart of Yosef Hayim Yerushalmi's argument in his remarkable book *Zakhor* (Remember!) is that the reason for the apparent paucity of specifically historiographical Jewish writings until the modern period is because memory is carried in different, more intimate ways. It is passed from generation to generation in stories and rituals; it seeps beneath the skin. Its transmission is not necessarily cognitive or even conscious; it takes place largely through osmosis. It begins in earliest childhood; awareness is absorbed in the taste of sweet *challah* and the Passover bitter herbs, in Sabbath songs and synagogue melodies. The daily prayer book is history; the daily service carries us from God's promise to Abraham to the redemption from slavery under Pharaoh. *Shabbat* itself is both recollection and repetition: an echo of the very first Sabbath on which God and all creation rested, and 'a memorial to the Exodus from Egypt' where slaves never knew a single day of freedom from labour. The *machzor*, the prayer books of the yearly cycle, and most especially the *kinot*, the collection of elegies for the fast of the Ninth of Av, the date on which we recall most of the terrible tragedies of Jewish history, are historical anthologies covering the destruction of the temples, the aftermath of the Crusades, the expulsions from France, England and Spain. In Judaism, liturgy is memory, rendering it inescapable, communicating its triumphs and its unhealed wounds.

A teacher reputedly told a group of children leaving Vienna on the Kindertransport that 'memory is a paradise from which we cannot be banished'.[83] No doubt those words were intended as a comfort to these young boys and girls who would probably never see their home or parents again: they needed to know that no one could take from them the love they carried in their hearts. The message is true, but searing. For sometimes it may simply be too painful to revisit the happiness from which one has been cut off; that memory, real or half imagined, of being enveloped in unbreachable warmth and security which is the greatest blessing of a happy childhood. So why torment oneself by revisiting it mentally, now that the world has become cruel and life dangerously uncertain?

Memory is therefore composed of silence as well as story. Generations are haunted by the unspoken: what are these unnamed feelings and who are these spirits that inhabit my home, my mind, my very body, which have never been explained to me and which I cannot therefore address? It's disturbing to feel compelled by subterraneously transmitted memories we cannot bring to consciousness to examine and understand.

In the Torah, memory is neither heaven nor hell, but commandment; we are required to engage with remembering so that it becomes a deliberate process of learning from the past. This is a lifelong task. The phrase 'consider the years', explained Rebbe Yitzhak Meir of Ger (1799–1866), refers not to the objects of memory, the recollection of what happened in times past, but to the remembering subject: 'Every year a person is granted renewed understanding; hence the name *shanah*, "year", from the meaning *shinu'i*, "change".'[84]

As we ourselves change and develop through our lives, we must allow the past and its possible meanings to grow with us. We have not only to consider, but constantly to reconsider, the significance of 'the days of old'. The import of events is not fixed and intractable; it unfolds and mutates as we grow older and change.

'A people without history is not redeemed from time,' wrote T. S. Eliot in *The Four Quartets*.[85] Judaism would phrase this differently. The aim is not to be redeemed *from* time, but to redeem time itself, to bring this world to a place of integrity and harmony. Without history and memory, without the burden as well as the blessings of absorbing what we can and must learn from the past, such an outcome is even more unlikely.

VEZOT HABERACHAH (33:1–34:12)

You too shall not go there

'Now die,' commands God.

Except for Rachel, who died in childbirth, the forefathers and fore-mothers lift their feet onto the bed, expire full of days, are gathered unto their people and are buried at Hebron, in the cave of Machpelah. The verbs that describe the end of their lives are all in the imperfect; only in the case of Moses is there an imperative: go die! It's God's final instruction to his most faithful servant.

Moses does not accept his fate with equanimity, at least not at first. 'I pleaded with God at that time, saying . . . "Let me cross over and see the good land on the other side of the Jordan"' (Deut. 3:23, 25). But it's a different border he's ordered to pass over, and God will not relent. 'For I am going to die in this land,' he is obliged to tell the people, that is, in Moab on the east side of the Jordan. Yet he has the courage and generosity to bless his successor with open hands. 'Put *a* hand on his head,' God commands him at the ceremonial appointment of Joshua; but, a detail carefully noted by the commentators, Moses places *both* his hands on Joshua's head (Num. 27:18, 23).

God softens the blow, somewhat: 'Die on the mountain . . . and be gathered to your people just as Aaron your brother died on Mount Hor and was gathered to his people' (Deut. 32:50). Rashi understands this as a consolation:

> The same kind of death as you saw and wished for. For Moses removed the outer garment from Aaron and put it on Elazar [his son]. He did similarly with the second and again with the third, so that Aaron could see his son in his glory. Then Moses said to him: 'Aaron, my brother, climb into this bed,' and he climbed. 'Rest your arms straight,' and he rested them; 'your legs,' and he stretched them out. 'Shut your eyes,' and he shut them; 'Close your mouth,' and he closed it. Then he departed. Moses said, 'Happy the person who dies such a death.'[86]

But Moses' son will not succeed him; he won't have the comfort of seeing a child of his own don the robes of his office. Nor does he know who will attend to him with the tenderness with which he attended to his brother. No one, or so it seems.

Yet Moses does not die alone: none less than God accompanies him to his final resting place and buries him. Ever since, compassionate fulfilment of the needs of the dying and the dead has been understood in Jewish teaching as an act of *imitation dei*, doing as God did for Moses.

But before Moses can fulfil God's final instruction, there is one more imperative he has to obey: 'Climb this Mount Avarim, Mount Nevo . . . and see the land' (Deut. 32:49). This could be a torment, as if God were saying: 'I shan't let you go there, but I'll tantalise you with the sight.' Or it could be a consolation: you will behold the country with your own eyes; you will die in the knowledge that your work as leader over these four impossible decades has been crowned with success. The Torah doesn't tell us.

Does Moses feel like Reverend Martin Luther King in his prophetic speech the night before his assassination?

> I've looked over, and I've seen the Promised Land. I may not get there with you. But I want you to know tonight, that we, as a people, will get to the promised land! And so I'm happy, tonight.[87]

Or does he feel like the poet Rachel, contemplating her lonely and untimely death from tuberculosis: 'Each and their Nevo in the wide, empty land.'?[88]

It's a question that awaits us all when we reach our final mountain.

The Torah refers to Moses' resting place both as *Har Nevo* and as *Har Ha'Avarim*. The second name, *Avarim*, means 'pasts', suggesting, perhaps, that scenes from our closing life pass as fleeting images through our fading consciousness. But it can also be translated as 'passes' or 'transitions', the place where we move from this world into the unknowable beyond. Or it may not refer to those who are dying, but rather to those who travel onward after we're gone: what 'crossings over', what adventures, await them which we will not share?

'See the land,' God instructs Moses, pointing out its various features: 'the Negev, the plains, the vale of Jericho, city of date palms, all the way to Tso'ar' (Deut. 34:3). Rebbe Yeshaya of Yassi (1851–1925) offers a stirring explanation of why God insists on describing it to him in such detail:

> Moses our master was commanded to draw down holiness into the land by looking at it 'with a good eye', similarly to how, on sighting the new moon, the rabbis had to 'see it and pronounce it sanctified'.[89]

To see with 'a good eye' means to regard with generosity. It requires a special graciousness to bless for others a future we know we won't share. Rebbe Yeshaya refers to the sanctification of the new month by the rabbinical court after verifying that the new moon has been sighted. Though this is a legal declaration, he interprets it spiritually as an act of blessing the future, or even time itself as symbolised by the waxing and waning of the moon. God wants Moses not just to see the land but to bless it and its future.

This is something we must all try to do before we die. The path ahead feels different when it has been blessed by those who have gone before us, especially if they are people we loved and respected. It's a benediction we in turn must try to pass on to those who come after.

The first mention of death in the Torah is connected with knowledge: 'In the day you eat of [the tree of the knowledge of good and evil] you will die' (Gen. 2:17). Among the most profound forms of knowledge is the wisdom to be gained from recognising that the day will come on which we're going to die, from the awareness that we are mortal. Can we, too, learn this wisdom deeply enough to bless the land, rivers and mountains where we won't be walking, and the generations we won't see, before we in turn are gathered to our people? Can we fill, with generosity and grace, the final commandment: to die?

Journey unending

Dead, you whispered *where is the road?*
There, through the last of the sentences, just there –
Through the last of the sentences, the road . . .

Carolyn Forche[90]

The Torah ends, but never arrives. It concludes, like Moses' life, on the far side of the Jordan. Before we cross the river, we restart the journey once again from *Bereshit*, the beginning of the beginning, without ever reaching the Promised Land. Life is always travel, always travail, never arrival. 'Life gave you the journey,' wrote Cavafy in *Ithaca*;[91] even if you get there, it's always also the road and never just the destination that is the true goal.

Even after death, Moses' mission isn't over. God has one further command for Moses, after he has ascended the final mountain: 'I have shown you the land I swore to Abraham, Isaac and Jacob, saying . . .' (Deut. 34:4). Rashi questions what the word 'saying' adds, since Moses will never again return to human company: 'God is instructing him to go and tell the forefathers in their resting places at Hebron that the promise God made to them to give the land to their descendants has now been fulfilled.[92]

Even in that 'undiscovered country from whose bourn no traveller returns',[93] Moses' work will continue. Apparently, we are still travellers and explorers in the world to come, not only in the here and now.

Just as Moses' journey never ends, neither does the cycle of reading Torah. Until when are we commanded to study? asks Maimonides, before answering, 'Until the day we die.' Life's voyage of discovery is never done.[94] Students of Torah, even if they are great scholars, are honoured with the title of *Talmidei Chakhamim*, pupils of the sages; true wisdom lies not in becoming storehouses of knowledge or in having lots of the answers, valuable as this might sometimes be, but in continuing to learn, in remaining open to not knowing and to new discoveries. Twentieth-century philosopher of Judaism Martin Buber reputedly said on his eighty-fifth birthday that old age is fine so long as one knows how to begin again. The art is never to finish, but always to return to *Bereshit*, the beginning. It's on the readiness not to know that true exploration depends.

That is why we return anew every year anew to the Torah's very first words and never cross the border and arrive. Within minutes of reciting the final verses of Deuteronomy on *Simchat Torah*, the festival of Rejoicing in the Torah, we start all over again from, 'In the beginning God created . . .' The joy of Torah lies in continuing to learn, in setting out once again from the start.

There's an expression for a people who once took their faith, or atheism, for granted but have since become open to doubt: *chozer lishe'eilah*, 'someone who returns to the questions'. The Torah invites us all to return to the big questions: Is there a God who creates? What is God's relationship with the world? Why are there tyrants who deny others liberty? What do we learn about freedom from the experience of being slaves? What does God want from us? How should we treat the poor, the sick and refugees?

These are issues that must never be allowed to disappear from our conscience. We may have ready answers in our heads; we don't and can't rethink everything all the time. But there is a mental staleness, a spiritual sterility in repeating the same familiar responses. If existential questions cease to disturb us, we become morally moribund. When they fail to provoke us into fresh exploration, they have ceased to be commandments of the living God and have instead settled inside us into weary dogmas with little power to motivate us to action.

The Torah ends with the word *Yisrael*; its final Hebrew letter is *lamed*. When the stress is put on the second syllable, *lamed* becomes an imperative, meaning, 'Teach!' The Torah begins with the word *Bereshit*, the first Hebrew letter of which is *beit*. Were it possible to complete the cycle of Torah readings not by rolling the scroll back to the start but by going straight from the end to the beginning as if the text were a loop, the final *lamed* and the opening *beit* would be adjacent to each other, spelling the word *lev*, heart. Hence the teaching that the entire Torah can be summed up in the beautiful saying from the Zohar that 'the Merciful God wants the heart'.[95]

But the long gap between the two letters is significant. The heart must never be closed but always receptive to new stories and questions. Every day and every year we need to hear life's imperatives afresh; hence the petition that concludes every prayer: *Petach libbi betoratekha*, 'Open my heart through your Torah,' *uvemitzvotekha tirdof nafshi*, and (translated freely) 'pursue me with your commandments'.

If our hearts are awake, then God, the world, and everything in it will teach us what is wanted from us and direct our actions. In the heart's wakefulness lies our awareness of God, beauty, awe, and the manifold songs, sorrows, outcry, outrage, tenderness and wonder of life. Then, in response, as Moses says in a beautiful expression of faith and hope for the future:

> God will open your heart and the hearts of your children to love the Lord your God with all your heart and all your soul, so that you shall live.
>
> (Deut. 30:6)

NOTES

Introduction

1 '(1963) Rabbi Abraham Joshua Heschel, "Religion and Race"', Blackpast, 12 August 2017, www.blackpast.org/african-american-history/1963-rabbi-abraham-joshua-heschel-religion-and-race (accessed 8 June 2023).
2 William Wordsworth (1770–1850), 'Lines Written a Few Miles Above Tintern Abbey'.
3 Rashi, commentary to Exodus 19:1.
4 Moshe Halbertal, *People of the Book: Canon, Meaning, and Authority* (Cambridge, MA: Harvard University Press, 1997).
5 Rabbi Ishmael, *Beraita deRabbi Yishmael, Introduction to Sifra*.
6 See, for example, Rashi, commentary to Genesis 3:8 and 37:2.
7 Michael Fishbane, *Sacred Attunement: A Jewish Theology* (Chicago and London: University of Chicago Press, 2008), p. 87.
8 Melila Hellner-Eshed, *A River Flows from Eden: The Language of Mystical Experience in the Zohar* (Stanford: Stanford University Press, 2009), p. 14.
9 Louis Jacobs, *God, Torah, Israel: Traditionalism without Fundamentalism* (Cincinnati: Hebrew Union College, Press, 1990), p. 33.
10 Neil Gillman, *Sacred Fragments: Recovering Theology for the Modern Jew* (Philadelphia: Jewish Publication Society, 1990), p. 16.
11 Jacobs, *God, Torah, Israel*, p. 28.

Note to readers

1 I am very grateful to Sefaria: a Living Library of Jewish Texts Online (www.sefaria.org) for making such a rich range of classical Jewish texts and commentaries so widely and readily accessible.
2 *Chumash Peninei Hahasidut* on the five books of the Torah (Jerusalem: Wato, 1985).

The book of Genesis

1 Richard Dawkins, *The God Delusion* (London: Black Swan, 2007), p. 51.
2 Zohar 1:15a, cited by Arthur Green, 'The Zohar: Jewish Mysticism in Medieval Spain', in Lawrence Fine (ed.), *Essential Papers on Kabbalah* (New York and London: New York University Press, 1995), p. 46.
3 Cited in Charlotte Peacock, *Into the Mountain: A Life of Nan Shepherd* (Cambridge: Galileo Publishers, 2018), p. 580.
4 *Perek Shirah*, chapter 1.

5 *Perek Shirah*, chapter 3.

6 *Perek Shirah*, chapter 4.

7 Adam Kirsch, 'Can humans ever understand how animals think?' *The Guardian*, 30 May 2023.

8 Cited in Shlomo Yosef Levin, *Sippurei Hasidim, Torah* (Jerusalem: Beit Klal) (author's own translation).

9 *The Brown-Driver-Briggs New Hebrew and English Lexicon* (first published Oxford, 1906), p. 921.

10 Rashi, commentary to Genesis 1:26.

11 Malcolm Ferdinand, cited in Aurore Chaillou, Louise Roblin and Malcom Ferdinand, 'Why We Need a Decolonial Ecology', *Green European Journal*, 4 June 2020, www.greeneuropeanjournal.eu/why-we-need-a-decolonial-ecology (accessed 6 June 2023).

12 Naomi Klein, *This Changes Everything* (London: Penguin Books, 2015), p. 18.

13 Thomas Berry, 'The World of Wonder', in Llewellyn Vaughan-Lee (ed.), *Spiritual Ecology: The Cry of the Earth* (California: The Golden Sufi Centre, 2013), p. 16.

14 Ellen F. Davis, *Scripture, Culture and Agriculture: An Agrarian Reading of the Bible* (Cambridge University Press, 2009), pp. 29–30.

15 Davis, *Scripture, Culture and Agriculture*, p. 30.

16 Llewellyn Vaughan-Lee, 'The Call of the Earth', in Vaughan-Lee, *Spiritual Ecology*, p. 249.

17 Tikkunei Zohar 122b.

18 Cited in Jules Cashford, 'Gaia and the Anima Mundi', in Vaughan-Lee, *Spiritual Ecology*, p. 182.

19 Basil the Great, cited in Davis, *Scripture, Culture and Agriculture*, p. 47.

20 Rebbe Avraham Mordechai of Ger, Likkutei Yehudah, cited in *Chumash Peninei Hahasidut* to Genesis 1:26.

21 Cecil Day-Lewis, 'Walking Away', Genius, genius.com/C-day-lewis-walking-away-annotated (accessed 12 June 2023).

22 Hans Jonas, 'The Concept of God after Auschwitz', in Lawrence Vogel (ed.), *Mortality and Morality* (Evanston Illinois: Northwestern university Press, 1996), pp. 135–6.

23 Erich Fromm, *The Fear of Freedom* (London, Melbourne and Henley: Ark Paperbacks, 1984), pp. 27–8.

24 Rashi, commentary to Genesis 1:26.

25 Maimonides, *The Guide for the Perplexed*, part 1, chapter 2.

26 Nachmanides, commentary to Genesis 1:24.

27 Samson Raphael Hirsch, commentary to Genesis 1:27.

28 Cited by Arthur Green, *Judaism's Ten Best Ideas: A Brief Guide for Seekers* (Woodstock: Jewish Lights Publishing, 2015), p. 12.

29 Based on Shlomo Yosef Zevin, *Sippurei Hasidim, Torah* (Jerusalem: Beit Klal), p. 13.

30 Rashi, commentary to Genesis 3:9.

31 Nikolaus Wachsmann, *KL: A History of the Nazi Concentration Camps* (Great Britain: Little Brown, 2015), p. 537.

32 Hugo Gryn with Naomi Gryn, *Chasing Shadows: Memories of a Vanished World* (Great Britain, Viking, 2000), p. 257.

33 Gryn and Gryn, *Chasing Shadows*, p. 257.

34 Mladen Vuksanovic, *From Enemy Territory: Pale Diary*, translated by Yasmine Gaspard (London: SAQI, 2004), pp. 150–51.

35 Eleanor O'Hanlon, *Eyes of the Wild: Journeys of Transformation with the Animal Powers* (Winchester, UK, and Washington, USA: Earth Books, 2012), p. 250.

36 Martin Luther King, 'I've Been to the Mountaintop', 3 April 1968, www.american-rhetoric.com/speeches/mlkivebeentothemountaintop.htm (accessed 6 June 2023).

37 Cited in Rev. Ellen Jennings, 'Sermon "Francis Too" 10.4.15', Cleveland Park Congregational UCC, cpcchurch.org/sermons/sermon-francis-too-10-4-15 (accessed 12 June 2023).

38 Avivah Gottlieb Zornberg, *The Beginning of Desire: Reflections on Genesis* (Philadelphia: Jewish Publication Society, 1995), p. 58.

39 André Neher, *Exile of the Word: From the Silence of the Bible to the Silence of Auschwitz* (Philadelphia: Jewish Publication Society, 1981), p. 101.

40 Zohar 1:69.

41 David of Lilov, Likkutei Divrei David, commentary to Genesis 12:1, cited in *Chumash Peninei Hahasidut*.

42 Shneur Zalman of Liadi, Torah Or to Genesis 12:1.

43 Elimelech of Grodzisk, *Divrei Elimelech*, commentary to Genesis 12:1, cited in *Chumash Peninei Hahasidut*.

44 Hillel, *The Chapters of the Fathers*, 1:14.

45 Maimonides, *Mishneh Torah: Laws Concerning Idolatry*, 1:3.

46 David Luria, commentary to Midrash Bereshit Rabbah 39:1.

47 Rachel Naomi Remen MD, *My Grandfather's Blessings: Stories of Strength, Refuge, and Belonging* (New York: Riverhead Books, 2001), p. 5.

48 Remen, *My Grandfather's Blessings*, p. 6.

49 Remen, *My Grandfather's Blessings*, pp. 6–7.

50 Richard Kearney, *Anatheism: Returning to God after God* (New York: Columbia University Press, 2011), p. 6.

51 'Revelation in the Jewish Tradition' in Seán Hand (ed.), *The Levinas Reader* (Oxford: Blackwell, 1989), p. 202.

52 *Ethics of the Fathers*, 5:13.

53 Abraham ibn Ezra, commentary to Genesis 18:26.

54 Nehama Leibowitz, *Studies in Bereshit: Genesis* (Jerusalem: World Zionist Organisation, 1981), pp. 185–6.

55 Cited by his daughter Professor Susannah Heschel in 'Remembering the teaching of Abraham Joshua Heschel', *Tikkun*, 4 January 2018, www.tikkun.org/susannah-heschel-remembers-her-father-abraham-joshua-heschel (accessed 6 June 2023).

56 Abraham Joshua Heschel, 'My Reasons for Involvement in the Peace Movement', in Susannah Heschel (ed.), *Moral Grandeur and Religious Audacity* (New York: The Noonday Press, 1997), p. 224.

57 Timothy Snyder, *On Tyranny: Twenty Lessons from the Twentieth Century* (London: The Bodley Head, 2017), pp. 32–3, 51.

58 Shimeon Barnfeld (ed.), *Sefer Hadema'ot*, The Book of Tears, Volume 1 (Berlin: Eshkol, 1923), p. 209 (author's own translation).

59 Rashi, commentary to Genesis 22:1.

60 Leonard Cohen, 'Hallelujah' (1984).

61 Simcha Raz, *A Tzaddik in Our Time: The Life of Rabbi Aryeh Levin* (Jerusalem, New York: Feldheim Publishers, 1977), p. 150.

62 Carolyn Custis James, *Lost Women of the Bible: The Women We Thought We Knew* (Grand Rapids: Zondervan, 2005), p. 92.

63 Rashi, commentary to Genesis 18:9.

64 Rashi, commentary to Genesis 23:2.

65 Penina Adelman, 'Home and Homeland', in Debra Orenstein and Jane Rachel Litman, *Lifecycles, Volume 2: Jewish Women on Biblical Themes in Contemporary Life* (Woodstock: Jewish Lights Publishing, 1997), p. 33.

66 Rashi, commentary to Genesis 16:13.

67 Zohar III, 69b–70a.

68 Nachmanides, commentary to Genesis 24:62.

69 Kadya Molodowsky, 'Women-Poems', in Kathryn Hellerstein (trans. and ed.), *Paper Bridges: Selected Poems of Kadya Molodwsky* (Detroit: Wayne State University Press, 1999), p. 79.

70 Tamar Meir (author's own translation). The original Hebrew poem is available at mashiv.org.il/product/%d7%92%d7%99%d7%9c%d7%99%d7%95%d7%9f-%d7%a4-%d7%9e%d7%aa%d7%97%d7%99%d7%9c%d7%99%d7%9d-%d7%9e%d7%91%d7%a8%d7%90%d7%a9%d7%99%d7%aa (accessed 12 June 2023). It is translated and quoted here with the poet's permission.

71 Rashi, commentary to Genesis 27:1.

72 John Milton, *Paradise Lost* (1667), book 3, line 25.

73 Rashi, commentary to Genesis 27:1.

74 Rashi, commentary to Genesis 28:16.

75 Moshe Chaim Ephraim, *Degel Machaneh Ephraim* on Genesis 28:16, cited in *Chumash Peninei Hahasidut*.

76 Menachem Nachum of Chernobyl, cited in Arthur Green, 'Da'at, Universalising a Hasidic Value', in Alon Goshen-Gottstein (ed.), *Religious Truth: Towards a Jewish Theology of Religion* (Liverpool: Liverpool University Press, 2020), pp. 83–107.

77 Kalonymus Kalman Shapira, *Derech Hamelech* (Jerusalem: Va'ad Hasidei Piazetzna, 1995), pp. 30–31.

78 Rashi, commentary to Genesis 30:2.

79 Molodowsky, 'Women-Poems', in Hellerstein, *Paper Bridges*, p. 79.

80 Molodowsky, 'Women-Poems', in Hellerstein, *Paper Bridges*, pp. 79–80.

81 John Keats (1795–1821), 'To Sleep'.

82 Rashi, commentary to Genesis 32:25.

83 Be'eri Tsimmerman, 'Vayeitsei', in Tania Tsion (ed.), *Sippurei Reishit* (Tel Aviv: Yediot Acharonot, 2022), p. 425 (author's own translation).

84 Jonathan Wittenberg, *My Dear Ones: One Family and The Final Solution* (London: William Collins, 2016).

85 Rashi, commentary to Genesis 33:4.

86 Thomas Mann, *Joseph and His Brothers* (London: Penguin Books, 1988), p. 320.

87 Rashi, commentary to Genesis 37:31.

88 Rabbi Shmuel Yaffe Ashkenazi (c.1520–95), *Yefeh To'ar*, commentary to Midrash Bereshit Rabbah 84:21.

89 David Grossman, *Falling Out of Time*, translated by Jessica Cohen (London: Jonathan Cape, 2015), pp. 175–6.

90 Attributed to Moses ibn Ezra (1055–1140), adapted from Islamic tradition.

91 Rashi, commentary to Genesis 37:35.

92 Rashi, commentary to Genesis 42:22.

93 William Shakespeare, *King Lear*, act 5, scene 3.

94 Rashi, commentary to Genesis 45:27.

95 Rashi, commentary to Genesis 46:29.

96 Nachmanides, commentary to Genesis 46:29.

97 Cited in Franz Kobler (ed.), *Letters of the Jews Through the Ages, Volume 1* (London: Ararat Publishing Company in association with the East and West Library, 1952), p. 227.

98 Rashi, commentary to Genesis 46:29.

99 Rebbe Yisrael of Tshortkov, *Tiferet Yisrael* to Genesis 46:29, cited in *Chumash Peninei Hahasidut*.

100 Rabbi Yonatan Neril and Rabbi Leo Dee, *Eco Bible, Volume 1: An Ecological Commentary on Genesis and Exodus* (Jerusalem: The Interfaith Center for Sustainable Development, 2020), p. 80.

101 David Goldblatt, cited in *Eco Bible, Volume 1*, p. 87.

102 Avraham Greenbaum, cited in *Eco Bible, Volume 1*, p. 87.

103 Nahum M. Sarna, *Understanding Genesis: The World of the Bible in the Light of History* (New York: Schocken Books, 1996), p. 225.

104 Rashi, commentary to Genesis 47:21.

105 Rashbam, Rabbi Samuel ben Meir, commentary to Genesis 47:21.

106 Jonathan Sacks, 'Reith Lectures 1990: The Persistence of Faith', 'Lecture 4: Paradoxes of Pluralism', 5 December 1994, downloads.bbc.co.uk/rmhttp/radio4/transcripts/1990_reith4.pdf (accessed 12 June 2023).

107 Osip Mandelstam, poem no. 341, in Clarence Brown and W. S. Merwin (trans.), *Osip Mandelstam: Selected Poems* (Oxford: Oxford University Press, 1973), p. 84.

The book of Exodus

1 Nachmanides, commentary to Exodus 1:10.

2 Nachmanides, commentary to Exodus 1:10.

3 Nachmanides, commentary to Exodus 1:10.

4 Nachmanides, commentary to Exodus 1:10.

5 Rashi, commentary to Exodus 5:6.

6 Nikolaus Wachsman, *KL: A History of the Nazi Concentration Camps* (New York: Little, Brown, 2015), p. 122.

7 Wachsman, *KL*, p. 124.

8 Wachsman, *KL*, p. 124.

9 'Adam Czerniaków', Yad Vashem Shoah Resource Centre, www.yadvashem.org/odot_pdf/microsoft%20word%20-%205934.pdf (accessed 31 May 2023).

10 Rebbe Shalom Noach Berezovsky, *Sefer Netivot Shalom, Part 2* (Jerusalem: Yeshivat Beit Avraham Slonim, 1989), on the festivals, essay on Pesach, p. 249.

11 *Sifrei* to Deuteronomy 26:7.

12 '"Break Their Lineage, Break Their Roots": China's Crimes against Humanity Targeting Uyghurs and Other Turkic Muslims', Human Rights Watch, 19 April

2021, www.hrw.org/report/2021/04/19/break-their-lineage-break-their-roots/chinas-crimes-against-humanity-targeting (accessed 31 May 2023).

13 Dr Lessie Branch, The Metropolitan College of New York.

14 Rashi, commentary to Exodus 38:8.

15 Rashi, commentary to Exodus 2:11.

16 Abraham ibn Ezra, commentary to Exodus 2:11.

17 Rashi, commentary to Exodus 2:11.

18 Rashi, commentary to Exodus 2:11.

19 Nelson Mandela, *Long Walk to Freedom* (Great Britain: Little, Brown, 1994), p. 617.

20 The Passover Haggadah.

21 The Passover Haggadah.

22 Harold S. Kushner, *When Bad Things Happen to Good People* (Great Britain: Pan Books, 1982), p. 141.

23 Kushner, *When Bad Things Happen to Good People*, p. 141.

24 Hugo Gryn with Naomi Gryn, *Chasing Shadows: Memories of a Vanished World* (Great Britain: Viking, 2000), p. 251.

25 Cited in Hans Jonas, *Mortality and Morality: A Search for the Good after Auschwitz*, edited by Lawrence Vogel (Evanston Illinois: Northwestern University Press, 1996), pp. 140–41.

26 Nachmanides, commentary to Exodus 11:3.

27 Rashi, commentary to Exodus 12:37.

28 William Shakespeare, *King Lear*, act 3, scene 6.

29 Attributed to Lord Acton.

30 Maimonides, *Mishneh Torah, Laws of Repentance*, 6:3.

31 Yehudah Aryeh-Leib of Ger, Sfat Emet to Exodus 10:23.

32 Chaim ibn Attar, *Or Hachayim*, commentary to Exodus 10:23.

33 Bertolt Brecht, 'Motto', in Carolyn Forche (ed.), *Against Forgetting, Twentieth Century Poetry of Witness* (New York, London: W. W. Norton & Company, 1993).

34 Simon Lichman, comment to the author.

35 Dmitri Sollertinsky and Ludmilla Sollertinsky, *Pages from the Life of Dmitri Shostakovich*, translated by Graham Hobbs and Charles Midgley, cited by Wikipedia, en.wikipedia.org/wiki/Leningrad_premi%C3%A8re_of_Shostakovich%27s_Symphony_No._7 (accessed 31 May 2023).

36 John R. Schlapobersky, *When They Came for Me: The Hidden Diary of an Apartheid Prisoner* (New York, Oxford: Berghahn Books, 2021), p. 71. The exact words cited are from a personal note to the author by John Schlapobersky.

37 Kalonymus Kalman Shapira, *Esh Kodesh* (Jerusalem: Vaad Hasidei Piazetsna, 1960), p. 153.

38 Abraham Isaac Kook, *The Fourfold Song: The Classics of Western Spirituality* (London: SPCK, 1979), pp. 228–9.

39 Kook, *The Fourfold Song*, p. 229.

40 Nachmanides, commentary to Exodus 14:5.

41 Nachmanides, commentary to Exodus 14:5.

42 E. Amy Buller, *Darkness Over Germany: A Warning from History* (London: Arcadia Books Ltd, 2017), p. 186.

43 Arthur Green, *Ehyeh: A Kabbalah for Tomorrow* (Woodstock: Jewish Lights Publishing, 2004), p. 1.

44 Rebbe Yehudah Aryeh-Leib of Ger, *Sefat Emet* on *Shavuot* (5631, second night).

45 Abraham Joshua Heschel, 'Ich *und Du* – I and You', in *The Ineffable Name of God*, translated by Morton Leifman (New York, London: Continuum, 2005), pp. 30–31.

46 Abraham Joshua Heschel, *God in Search of Man* (New York: Farrar, Straus and Giroux; reprint edition, 1997).

47 William Shakespeare, *King Lear*, act 3, scene 4.

48 Maimonides, *Laws of the Foundations of Torah*, chapter 5.

49 Rachel Naomi Remen MD, *My Grandfather's Blessings: Stories of Strength, Refuge, and Belonging* (New York: Riverhead Books, 2001), p. 186.

50 Rachel Clarke, *Breathtaking: Inside the NHS in a Time of Pandemic* (London: Little, Brown, 2021), p. 215.

51 Joseph Caro, *Yoreh De'ah*, 336:1.

52 Maimonides (attributed), 'Jewish Prayers: Daily Prayer of a Physician', Jewish Virtual Library, www.jewishvirtuallibrary.org/daily-prayer-of-a-physician (accessed 12 May 2023).

53 Rachel Naomi Remen MD, *Kitchen Table Wisdom: Stories That Heal* (New York: Riverhead Books, 2000), p. 65.

54 Remen, *Kitchen Table Wisdom*, p. 249.

55 Rabbi Yonathan Neril and Rabbi Leo Dee, *Eco-Bible, Volume 1* (Jerusalem: The Interfaith Centre for Sustainable Development, 2020), p. 145, note 590.

56 Neril and Dee, *Eco-Bible, Volume 1*, p. 145, note 590.

57 Nachmanides, commentary to Leviticus 19:2.

58 *Mechilta* to Exodus 15:2.

59 Kalonymus Kalman Shapira, *Derekh Hamelech on Shavuot*, p. 382.

60 Shapira, *Derekh Hamelech on Shavuot*, p. 381.

61 Shapira, *Derekh Hamelech on Shavuot*, p. 382.

62 *Encyclopedia Mikra'it* (Biblical Encyclopaedia), *Volume 2* (Jerusalem: Mosad Bialik, 1954), p. 546b.

63 Rashi, commentary to Exodus 22:20.

64 Abraham ibn Ezra, commentary to Exodus 22.20.

65 Cited in Franz Kobler (ed.), *Letters of the Jews Through the Ages, Volume 1* (Great Britain: Ararat Publishing Company, in conjunction with East and West Library, 1952), p. 227.

66 Nachmanides, commentary to Exodus 22:20.

67 Nachmanides, commentary to Exodus 22:20.

68 Samson Raphael Hirsch, commentary to Exodus 22:20.

69 Yehudah Halevi, 'Yah Ana Emtsa'echa'.

70 Chaim Nachman Bialik (1873–1934), 'The Pool', author's own translation.

71 Isabel Allende, *Paula* (London: Flamingo, 1996), p. 272.

72 Allende, *Paula*, p. 272.

73 Dorothy L. Sayers, 'The Image of God', in Jaroslav Pelikan (ed.), *The World Treasury of Modern Religious Thought* (Boston, Toronto, London: Little, Brown, 1990), p. 188.

74 Osip Mandelstam, 'Tristia', in Clarence Brown and W. S. Merwin (trans.), *Selected Poems* (London, Melbourne, Toronto: Oxford University Press, 1973), p. 23.

75 Rabbi Shlomo of Radomsk, commentary to Exodus 35:31–2 in *Chumash Peninei Hahasidut*.

76 William Shakespeare, *Othello*, act 3, scene 4.

77 Robert Weltsch, 'Wear it with Pride, the Yellow Badge', *Juedische Rundschau*, No. 27, 4 April 1933, www.yadvashem.org/odot_pdf/Microsoft%20Word%20-%20 3830.pdf (accessed 31 May 2023).
78 Rebbe Yisrael of Modzhitz, *Divrei Yisrael* to Exodus 28:8.
79 Kedushat Levi to Exodus 28:5, cited in *Chumash Peninei Hahasidut*.
80 Achad Ha'am, 'Shabbat and Zionism', in *Hashelach*, Volume 3, issue 6, 1898.
81 Rashi, commentary to Exodus 31:13.
82 Abraham Joshua Heschel, *The Sabbath: Its Meaning for Modern Man* (New York: Farrar, Straus and Giroux, 1986), pp. 28–9.
83 Rashi, commentary to Exodus 31:17.
84 Rashi, commentary to Exodus 31:17.
85 Ralph Waldo Emerson, wisdomquotes.net/ralph-waldo-emerson-quotes/?quotes_ page=4 (accessed 31 May 2023).
86 Maimonides, *Hilchot Avodat Cochavim*, 1:1-2.
87 Paul Tillich, *Dynamics of Faith* (London: Perennial Classics, 2001), p. 58.
88 Tillich, *Dynamics of Faith*, p. 61.
89 Mordechai Yosef Leiner, *Mei Hashiloach* (New York: independently published, 1973), p. 25.
90 Rebbe Avraham of Slonim, Torat Avot to Exodus 25:1.
91 Rebbe Avraham of Sokatchev, *Shem MiShemuel* to Exodus. 25:1.
92 Rashi, commentary to Exodus 25:1.
93 Rebbe Chaim Tsvi, *Atsei Chaim*, commenting on Rashi's commentary to Exodus 25, in *Chumash Peninei Hahasidut*.
94 Rebbe Yekutiel Yehudah of Sighet, *Yitav Lev*, commenting on Exodus 35:21 in *Chumash Peninei Hahasidut*.
95 Rashi, commentary to Exodus 1:12.
96 Percy Bysshe Shelley (1792–1822), 'Ozymandias'.
97 Shlomo Yehudah Leib of Lantshna, Toldot Adam, commentary to Exodus 35:1, cited in *Chumash Peninei Hahasidut*.
98 Rebbe Yehoshua Heschel of Choliov, Nachalat Yehoshua, commentary to Exodus 39:32, cited in *Chumash Peninei Hahasidut*.

The book of Leviticus

1 Be'er Moshe, commentary to Leviticus 6:2, cited in *Chumash Peninei Hahasidut*.
2 Rebbe Menachem Nachum, *Me'or Einayim*, commentary to Leviticus 6:2, cited in *Chumash Peninei Hahasidut*.
3 Yaakov Yosef of Polnoye (1710–84).
4 Nick Naydler, *For Anne Frank* (Bristol: Loxwood Stoneleigh, 1991).
5 Maimonides, *The Guide for the Perplexed*, part 3, chapter 32.
6 Maimonides, *The Guide for the Perplexed*, part 3, chapter 32.
7 Maimonides, *The Guide for the Perplexed*, part 3, chapter 32.
8 Arthur Green, *Ehyeh: A Kabbalah for Tomorrow* (Vermont: Jewish Lights, 2004), p. 158.
9 Green, *Ehyeh*, p. 158.

10 Anonymous (author's own translation).

11 Dov Baer of Mezerich, *Imrei Tsaddikim*, commentary to Leviticus 1:2, cited in *Chumash Peninei Hahasidut*.

12 Likkutei Torah, commentary to Leviticus 1:2, cited in *Chumash Peninei Hahasidut*.

13 Da'at Moshe, commentary to Leviticus 1:2, cited in *Chumash Peninei Hahasidut*.

14 Rebbe Kalonymus Kalman Shapira, *Esh Kodesh*.

15 Cited in Nehemia Polen, *The Holy Fire: The teachings of Rabbi Kalonymous Kalman Shapira, the Rebbe of the Warsaw Ghetto* (Lanham, Maryland: Rowman and Littlefield, 2004), p. 67.

16 Samuel Raphael Hirsch, commentary to Leviticus 4:22.

17 William Shakespeare, *Macbeth*, act 5, scene 1.

18 Nachmanides, commentary to 4:22.

19 Maimonides, *Laws of Repentance*, 2:4.

20 Tosafot to Berachot 35b.

21 Osip Mandelstam, *Stone*, translated by Robert Tracy (London: Collins Harvill, 1991), p. 59.

22 Joan Halifax, *Being with Dying: Cultivating Compassion and Fearlessness in the Presence of Death* (Boston: Shambala, 2009), p. 10.

23 Halifax, *Being with Dying*, p. 10.

24 Abraham Joshua Heschel, *God in Search of Man: A Philosophy of Judaism* (1955).

25 Michael Fishbane, *Sacred Attunement: A Jewish Theology* (Chicago, London: University of Chicago Press, 2008), p. 75.

26 Fishbane, *Sacred Attunement*, p. 76

27 Rebbe Shlomo of Radomsk, Tiferet Shlomo, commentary to Leviticus 13:2.

28 *Turei Zahav to Shulchan Aruch, Yoreh De'ah*, 336:1.

29 Christie Watson, *The Language of Kindness* (London: Chatto & Windus, 2018), p. 41.

30 Rabbi Pinchas Menachem Elazar of Pilin, *Siftei Tzaddik* on Leviticus 13:3.

31 Rashi, commentary to Arakhin 16b.

32 Victoria Hislop, *The Island* (London: Hodder Headline, 2005).

33 Simcha Raz, *A Tzaddik in our Time* (Jerusalem, New York: Feldheim, 1977), pp. 130–31.

34 Rachel Clarke, *Breathtaking: Inside the NHS in a Time of Pandemic* (London: Little, Brown, 2021), p. 199.

35 Rabbi Baruch Halevi Epstein, *Torah Temimah*, commentary 185 to Leviticus 13:45.

36 Halifax, *Being with Dying*, p. 72.

37 John Keats, *The Complete Poetical Works and Letters of John Keats* (Cambridge Edition: Houghton, Mifflin and Company), p. 277.

38 David Kraemer, *Responses to Suffering in Classical Rabbinic Literature* (Oxford: Oxford University Press, 1995), p. 4.

39 Cited in Halifax, *Being with Dying*, foreword, p. xii.

40 Rebbe Yehoshua of Ostrovo, Toldot Adam, commentary to Leviticus 14:2, cited in *Chumash Peninei Hahasidut*.

41 Milton Steinberg, 'To Hold with Open Arms', in Jack Rimer (ed.), *Jewish Reflections on Death* (New York: Schocken Books, 1976), p. 135.

42 William Shakespeare, *King Lear*, act 4, scene 6.

43 Adapted from the translation in *Forms of Prayer, Days of Awe* (Oxford: The Reform Synagogues of Great Britain, 1985), p. 448.

44 Paul Gallico, *The Day the Guinea Pig Talked* (London: William Heinemann, 1963).

45 Rashbam, Rabbi Samuel ben Meir, commentary to Leviticus 16:22.

46 William Shakespeare, *The Tempest*, act 5, scene 1.

47 Jacques Derrida, 'Deconstruction and the Other', in Richard Kearney (ed.), *Dialogues with Contemporary Continental Thinkers* (Manchester: Manchester University Press, 1984), cited in Laurence J. Silberstein and Robert L. Cohn (eds), *The Other in Jewish Thought and History* (New York: New York University Press, 1994), p. 6.

48 Steven Greenberg, *Wrestling with God and Men: Homosexuality in the Jewish Tradition* (Madison, Wisconsin: University of Wisconsin Press, 2005), p. 75.

49 Private communication to the author.

50 Chaim Rapoport, *Judaism and Homosexuality: An Authentic Orthodox View* (Elstree: Vallentine Mitchell, 2004), note 40 to chapter 1, p. 151.

51 Louis Jacobs, *A Jewish Theology* (New Jersey: Behrman House, 1973), p. 228.

52 Jacobs, *A Jewish Theology*, p. 230.

53 Rapoport, *Judaism and Homosexuality*, p. 8, note 42.

54 Rapoport, *Judaism and Homosexuality*, p. 10 (their comments on *TB Nedarim* 51a).

55 Maimonides, *Laws of Forbidden Unions*, 1:14.

56 Rabbi Jeremy Gordon, *Spiritual Vagabondry and the Making of a Rabbi* (London: Masorti Publications, 2015), p. 157.

57 Samson Raphael Hirsch, commentary to Leviticus 19:14.

58 'With a Little Bit of Luck', from Frederick Loewe and Alan Jay Lerner, *My Fair Lady*, 1956.

59 *Sefat Emet* to Deuteronomy (Jerusalem: Descendants of the Sefat Emet, 1971), in Hebrew, p. 120a.

60 Nachmanides, extended commentary to Leviticus 19:17.

61 Cited in Franz Kobler (ed.), *Letters of Jews Through the Ages, Volume 2* (London: Ararat Publishing Society together with East and West Library, 1952), p. 227.

62 Nachmanides, cited in Kobler, *Letters of Jews*, p. 227.

63 Nachmanides, cited in Kobler, *Letters of Jews*, p. 227.

64 Samson Raphael Hirsch, commentary to Leviticus 19:18.

65 Richard A. Cohen, 'Emmanuel Levinas', in Steven T. Katz (ed.), *Interpreters of Judaism in the Late Twentieth Century (The B'Nai B'Rith History of the Jewish People)* (Washington: Bnai Brith Books, 1993), p. 216.

66 Commentary to Leviticus 19:18, cited in *Chumash Peninei Hahasidut* (Jerusalem: Wato, 1985).

67 Olive Fraser, 'The Unwanted Child', in *The Pure Account: Poems by Olive Fraser*, edited by Helena M. Shire (Aberdeen: Aberdeen University Press, 1981).

68 Elliott Dorff, *Matters of Life and Death: A Jewish Approach to Modern Ethics* (Philadelphia: Jewish Publication Society, 1998), p. 15.

69 Samson Raphael Hirsch, commentary to Leviticus 19:18.

70 William Wordsworth (1770–1850), *The Prelude* (originally published 1850).

71 John Clare (1793–1864), 'Child Harold', in John Tibble and Anne Tibble (eds), *Selected Poems* (London, Melbourne: Dent, 1984), p. 245.

72 Yehudah Amichai, 'The Diameter of the Bomb', in Chana Bloch (trans.), *Yehuda Amichai: Poems of Jerusalem, A Bilingual Edition* (Tel Aviv: Shocken Publishing House Ltd, 1987).

73 Rashi, commentary to Leviticus 25:6.

74 Nachmanides, commentary to Leviticus 25:6.

75 Pope Francis, *Laudato Si* (2015), introduction, paragraph 16.

76 Hans Jonas, *Morality and Mortality: A Search for the Good After Auschwitz* (Evanston: Northwestern University Press, 1999), p. 202.

77 Inger Andersen, Opening speech at Biodiversity COP 15, 2022.

78 *The Brown-Driver-Briggs New Hebrew and English Lexicon* (first published Oxford, 1906), p. 145a.

79 Rashi, commentary to Leviticus 25:35.

80 Maimonides, *Laws of Gifts to the Poor*, chapter 10.

81 Julian Sinclair, *Jewish Chronicle*, 28 October 2008.

82 Rashi, commentary to Leviticus 26:21.

83 Abraham ibn Ezra, commentary to Leviticus 26:21.

84 Maimonides, *The Guide for the Perplexed*, part 3, chapter 36.

85 George Santayana, *The Life of Reason* (1905).

86 Hugo Gryn with Naomi Gryn, *Chasing Shadows: Memories of a Vanished World* (Great Britain, Viking, 2000), p. 251.

87 Gryn and Gryn, *Chasing Shadows*, p. 251.

88 Cited in Nehemia Polen, *The Holy Fire* (New Jersey, London: Jason Aronson, 1994), p. 119.

89 Raymond P. Scheindlin, *The Book of Job, Translation, Introduction, and Notes* (New York, London: W. W. Norton & Company, 1998).

The book of Numbers

1 Rashi, commentary to Numbers 1:1.

2 Rebbe Yitzhak Yaakov of Biale, *Divrei Binah*, commentary to Numbers 1:1, cited in *Chumash Peninei Hahasidut*.

3 Daniel Lavelle, 'I tried to track down all the friends I grew up with in care – here's what I found', *The Guardian*, 23 May 2018, www.theguardian.com/society/2018/may/22/track-down-friends-grew-up-with-in-care-system (accessed 27 April 2023).

4 Thank you letter from a Ukrainian family supported by World Jewish Relief.

5 Nehama Leibowitz, *Studies in Bereshit (Genesis): Translated and Adapted from the Hebrew by Aryeh Newman* (Jerusalem: The Jewish Agency, 1972), p. 185.

6 Hillel, *Ethics of the Fathers*, 2:4.

7 William Shakespeare, *Othello*, act 3, scene 4.

8 Rachel Remen, *My Grandfather's Blessings: Stories of Strength, Refuge, and Belonging* (New York: Riverhead Books, 2001), p. 5.

9 Arthur Green, *Seek My Face: A Jewish Mystical Theology* (Woodstock: Jewish Lights Publishing, 2003), p. 93.

10 Ovadiah Sforno, commentary to Numbers 7:89.

11 Kalonymus Kalman Shapira, *Derech Hamelech to Beha'alotecha*.

12 Chaim Nachman Bialik (1873–1934), 'Habreichah' (author's own translation).

13 Franz Rosenzweig to Martin Buber, 5 June 1925, in Franz Rosenzweig, *On Jewish*

Learning, edited by N. N. Glatzer (Wisconsin: University of Wisconsin Press, 1955), p. 118.

14 Gerald Manley Hopkins (1844–89), 'God's Grandeur'.

15 *Etty: The Letters and Diaries of Etty Hillesum 1941–1943* (Grand Rapids, Michigan, and Cambridge, UK: William B. Eerdmans Publishing Company, 2002), pp. 488–9, entry for 12 July 1942.

16 Cited in Rabbi Lawrence A. Hoffman (ed.), *My People's Prayer Book, Volume 2 – The Amidah* (Woodstock: Jewish Lights Publishing, 1998), p. 116.

17 Gale Warner, *Dancing at the Edge of Life: A Memoir* (Westport: Hyperion Books, 1998).

18 Lawrence Kushner and Nehemia Polen, cited in Hoffman, *My People's Prayer Book, Volume 2 – The Amidah*, pp. 118–19.

19 *The Brown-Driver-Briggs New Hebrew and English Lexicon* (first published Oxford, 1906). p. 469a.

20 *Sifrei*, Numbers 99.

21 Rashi, commentary to Numbers 12:1.

22 *Siftei Chachamim* on Rashi's commentary to Numbers 12:1.

23 Rashi, commentary to Numbers 12:1.

24 Abrahan ibn Ezra, commentary to Numbers 12:1.

25 Abraham Joshua Heschel, 'The Reasons for My Involvement in the Peace Process', in Susannah Heschel (ed.), *Moral Grandeur and Spiritual Audacity* (New York: Farrar, Straus and Giroux, 1996), p. 224.

26 Anthony Johnson, 'What we in the Black community need from Jews right now', *Forward*, 31 May 2020, forward.com/opinion/447721/what-we-in-the-black-community-need-from-jews-right-now (accessed 16 May 2023).

27 Hillel, *The Chapters of the Fathers*, 2:5.

28 Hillel, *The Chapters of the Fathers*, 1:14.

29 Rabbi Elazar ben Azariah, *The Chapters of the Fathers*, 3:21.

30 Sidney Bloch, *No Time for Tears: Childhood in a Rabbi's Family* (London: William Kimber, 1980), pp. 84–5.

31 Noah Zvi Farkas, 'Without Flour There Is No Torah', *Forward*, 8 December 2011, forward.com/food/147426/without-flour-there-is-no-torah (accessed 27 April 2023).

32 Ellen Frankel, *The Five Books of Miriam* (New York: Grosset/Putnam Books, 1996), p. 192, cited in 'No Food, No Torah; No Torah, No Food', *My Jewish Learning*, commentary on Parashat Bechukotai, Leviticus 26:3–27:34, www.myjewishlearning.com/article/no-food-no-torah-no-torah-no-food (accessed 27 April 2023).

33 William Wordsworth (1770–1850), 'Intimations of Immortality'.

34 Wordsworth, 'Intimations of Immortality'.

35 Arthur Green, *Judaism for the World: Reflections on God, Life and Love* (New Haven and London: Yale University Press, 2020), p. 84.

36 Nathan Lopes Cardozo, 'Autobiography – Lonely But Not Alone', David Cardozo Academy, www.cardozoacademy.org/thoughtstoponder/autobiography-lonely-but-not-alone-ttp-344 (accessed 16 May 2023).

37 Primo Levi, *If This Is a Man: The Truce*, translated by Stuart Woolf (Great Britain: Abacus, 1987), p. 119.

38 Bemidbar Rabbah 88:1; Rashi, commentary to Numbers 19:2.

39 Kalonymus Kalman Shapira, *Eish Kodesh* (Jerusalem: Vaad Hasidei Piazetsna, 1960), entry for Parashat Parah, 1942.

40 Kalonymus Kalman Shapira, *Eish Kodesh,* Parashat Chukkat, 1942.

41 Rebbe Simchah Bunem, Kol Simchah to Numbers 19:14, cited in *Chumash Peninei Hahasidut.*

42 Rebbe Shlomo of Radmosk, Tiferet Shlomo (quoting *Ethics of the Fathers*, 2:4), in Jonathan Slater, *Mindful Jewish Living: Compassionate Practice* (New York: Aviv Press, 2004), p. 77.

43 Rabbi Ya'akov, *Ethics of the Fathers*, 4:22.

44 Solomon ibn Gavirol (*c.*1021–*c.*1070), 'Before I Was Born' (author's own translation).

45 Rashi, commentary to Numbers 20:25.

46 Nachmanides, commentary to Numbers 20:26.

47 Bruce Chatwin, *The Songlines* (London: Pan Books, 1988), p. 209.

48 E. M. Forster, *A Passage to India* (London: Penguin Books, 1985), p. 261.

49 John Newton (1725–1807), 'Amazing Grace', verse 1.

50 Kalonymus Kalman Shapira, *Derech Hamelech* (Jerusalem: Vaad Hasidei Piazetsna, 1992), entry for *Shavuot* 5685.

51 Cited in Adam Nicolson, *The Seabird's Cry: The Lives and Loves of Puffins, Gannets and Other Ocean Voyagers* (London: William Collins, 2017), pp. 155–6.

52 Mark Rowlands, *Animals Like Us* (London and New York: Verso, 2002), p. 31.

53 Maimonides, *The Guide for the Perplexed*, part 3, chapter 48.

54 Jeremy Bentham, *An Introduction to the Principles of Morals and Legislation* (originally published 1789), chapter 17.

55 Rowlands, *Animals Like Us*, p. 15.

56 Mark Rowlands, *The Philosopher and the Wolf: Lessons from the Wild on Love, Death and Happiness* (London: Granta, 2018), p. 64.

57 Menachem Mendel of Vitebsk, *Pri Ha'aretz* (Jerusalem, Hamesora, reprinted from the first edition, Kapost,1814), entry for Pinchas.

58 Rashi, commentary to Numbers 27:16.

59 Rashi, commentary to Numbers 27:17.

60 Ovadiah Sforno, commentary to Numbers 27:17.

61 Percy Bysshe Shelley (1792–1822), *A Defence of Poetry* (1840), closing words.

62 Rashi, referencing Midrash Yalkut Shimoni on the Torah 776.

63 Talmud Sanhedrin 106a, referenced by Rashi in his commentary to Numbers 25:1.

64 Jonathan Sacks, *Not in God's Name: Confronting Religious Violence* (London: Hodder & Stoughton, 2015), p. 207.

65 Nicholas Rankin, *Telegram from Guernica: The Extraordinary Life of George Steer, War Correspondent* (London: Faber and Faber, 2003), p. 122.

66 David A. Israel (ed.), *A Jewish Consideration of War and Nuclear Conflict: A Mini-sourcebook by Bradley S. Artson*, www.rabbinicalassembly.org/sites/default/files/2021-07/War%26Conflict.pdf (accessed 28 April 2023).

67 Torah *Etz Hayim* (New York: Jewish Publication Society, 2001), pp. 943–4.

68 Irving Greenberg, 'The Ethics of Jewish Power', in *Contemporary Jewish Ethics and Morality, A Reader*, edited by Elliot Dorff and Louis E. Newman (New York: Sanhedrin Press, 1978), p. 410.

69 William Shakespeare, *Macbeth*, act 5, scene 1.

70 Rabbi Judah the Prince, *Ethics of the Fathers*, 2:1.

71 Raynor Winn, *The Wild Silence* (London: Penguin, 2021), p. 92.

The book of Deuteronomy

1 Nachmanides, commentary to Exodus 6:10.

2 Imrei Baruch to Devarim 1:1, cited in *Chumash Peninei Hahasidut*.

3 Cited by Moses ibn Ezra in his *Sefer Shirat Yisrael*, originally written in Arabic, from an Arabic source by Amir ibn Abd al-Qays.

4 Rashi, commentary to Deuteronomy 33:2, 'A fire of law'.

5 Rebbe Aharon of Karlin, Beit Aharon to Deuteronomy 1:5, cited in *Chumash Peninei Hahasidut*.

6 Winston Churchill, inaugural speech, 13 May 1940, www.parliament.uk/about/living-heritage/transformingsociety/private-lives/yourcountry/collections/churchillexhibition/churchill-the-orator/blood-toil-sweat-and-tears/#:~:text=Churchill's%20inaugural%20speech%20as%20wartime,hard%20the%20road%20may%20be (accessed 2 May 2023).

7 Cited in Jonathan Magonet, *Bible Lives* (London: SCM Press Ltd, 1992), p. 135.

8 Rashi: commentary to Numbers 14:2.

9 'General Eisenhower's drafted message: D-Day files', D-Day Overlord, www.dday-overlord.com/en/d-day/files/eisenhower-drafted-message (accessed 2 May 2023).

10 Rachel Bluwstein (1890–1931), 'Et Kuli Siparti Ad Tom', in *Shirat Rachel* (Hebrew) (Tel Aviv: Dvir, 1978), p. 132 (author's translation).

11 Ba'al Shem Tov, commentary to Deuteronomy 6:4, cited in *Chumash Peninei Hahasidut*.

12 Rebbe Yitzhak Yaakov of Biale, *Divrei Binah* to Deuteronomy 6:4, cited in *Chumash Peninei Hahasidut*.

13 Shlomo Yosef Zevin, *Sippurei Hasidim, Torah* (Jerusalem: Beit Hillel), p. 428.

14 Maimonides, *Mishneh Torah: Laws of the Foundations of Torah*, 1:7.

15 Maimonides, *Mishneh Torah: Laws of the Foundations of the Torah*, 1:7.

16 Ba'al Shem Tov, commentary to Deuteronomy 6:4, cited in *Chumash Peninei Hahasidut*.

17 Moses Cordovero, cited in Daniel Matt, *The Essential Kabbalah: The Heart of Jewish Mysticism* (New Jersey: Castle Books, 1997), p. 24.

18 Michael Fishbane, *Sacred Attunement: A Jewish Theology* (Chicago and London: University of Chicago Press, 2008), p. 34.

19 Cited in Arthur Green, *Ehyeh: A Kabbalah for Tomorrow* (Woodstock: Jewish Lights Publishing, 2004), pp. 22–3.

20 T. S. Eliot, *The Four Quartets: Little Gidding* (London: Faber and Faber, 2001), p. 43.

21 William Blake (1757–1827), *Songs of Innocence and Experience* (originally published 1789).

22 Samuel Taylor Coleridge (1772–1834), 'The Rime of the Ancient Mariner' (public domain).

23 Victor Frankl, *Man's Search for Meaning: The Classic Tribute to Hope from the Holocaust* (New York: Pocket Books, 1984), p. 86.

24 *Ethics of the Fathers*, 5:21.

25 Rabbi Chaim ibn Attar, *Or Hachayim*, commentary to Deuteronomy 8:9.

26 Rabbi Chaim ibn Attar, *Or Hachayim*, commentary to Deuteronomy 8:9.

27 Cited in David Olusoga, *Black and British: A Forgotten History* (London: Picador, 2021), p. 208.

28 Johann Wolfgang von Goethe (1749–1832) (author's own translation).

29 Martin Gilbert, *Shcharansky: Hero of Our Time* (London: Penguin Books, 1987), p. 402.

30 Václav Havel, Address to the Polish Parliament, 21 January 1990.

31 Maimonides, *Laws of the Foundations of Torah*, 2:4.

32 Rebecca Elson, *A Responsibility to Awe* (Manchester: Carcanet Classics, 2018), p. 9.

33 Cited in Matt, *The Essential Kabbalah*, p. 22.

34 Yehudah Aryeh-Leib of Ger, *Sefat Emet Part 5* (Jerusalem: Descendants of the Sefat Emet, 1971), 52b, 'Ve'attah'.

35 Kalonymus Kalman Shapira, *Derech Hamelech* (Jerusalem: Vaad Hasidei Piazetsna, 1995), p. 203.

36 From a Scottish Celtic blessing, www.faithandworship.com/Celtic_Blessings_and_Prayers.htm#gsc.tab=0 (accessed 2 June 2023).

37 Yisrael Meir Kagan, Mishnah Berurah note 9, to Shulchan Aruch, Orach Chayim 117:2.

38 Abraham Joshua Heschel, 'The Reasons for My Involvement in the Peace Movement', January 1973.

39 Maimonides, *The Guide for the Perplexed*, part 3, chapter 48, translated by Shlomo Pines (Chicago and London: Chicago University Press, 1963).

40 Nachmanides, commentary to Leviticus 19:2.

41 Likkutei Anshei Shem, commentary to Deuteronomy 16:19, cited in *Chumash Rav Peninim* (Jerusalem: Levin-Epstein).

42 Extract from Zelda, 'Ancient Pines', translated from the Hebrew by Marcia Falk, in Ari Elon, Naomi Mara Hyman, Arthur Waskow (eds), *Trees, Earth and Torah: A Tu B'shevat Anthology* (Philadelphia: Jewish Publication Society, 1999), p. 225.

43 Rashi, commentary to Deuteronomy 20:19.

44 Abraham ibn Ezra, commentary to Deuteronomy 20:19.

45 Maimonides, *Sefer Ha-mitzvot, Positive Commandments*, no. 6.

46 Eilon Schwartz, 'Is the Tree Human?', in Elon, Hyman and Waskow, *Trees, Earth and Torah*, p. 93.

47 William Shakespeare, *Macbeth*, act 5, scene 1.

48 Maimonides, *Mishneh Torah, Laws of Gifts to the Poor*, 9:3.

49 Mark Rowlands, *Animals Like Us* (London and New York: Verso, 2002), p. 114.

50 Nachmanides, commentary to Deuteronomy 22:6.

51 Jeremy Bentham (1748–1832), *An Introduction to the Principles of Morals and Legislation*, cited in 'Jeremy Bentham on the suffering of non-human animals', BLTC Research, www.utilitarianism.com/jeremybentham.html (accessed 2 June 2023).

52 Nachmanides, commentary to Deuteronomy 22:6.

53 Abraham Isaac Kook, 'Fragments of Light: A View as to the Reasons for the Commandments in Contemporary Jewish Philosophy', cited in Dan Frank, Oliver

Leaman and Charles H. Manekin (eds), *The Jewish Philosophy Reader* (London: Routledge, 2000), pp. 522–5.

54 Kook, 'Fragments of Light'.

55 Mordechai Yosef Leiner, *Mei Hashiloach to Bereshit*.

56 William Shakespeare, *King Lear*, act 3, scene 6.

57 Rebbe Shalom of Belz, Leket Imrei Kodesh to Deuteronomy 25:17.

58 Maimonides, *Laws of the Foundations of Torah*, 2:4.

59 Jeremy Naydler, 'The Perennial Philosophy and the Recovery of a Theophanic View of Nature', in Nicholas Campion (ed.), *The Harmony Debates* (Ceredigion: Sophia Centre Press, 2020), p. 196.

60 Alon Goshen-Gottstein, 'Compassion – The Teachings of Rebbe Nachman of Breslav', in Animdita Balslev and Dirk Evers (eds), *Compassion in the World's Religions – Envisaging Human Solidarity* (Germany: Lit Verlag, 2010).

61 New Year liturgy.

62 Maimonides, *Laws of Repentance*, 2:4.

63 Rashi, commentary to Deuteronomy 30:3, lightly paraphrased.

64 Moshe Halbertal, *People of the Book: Canon, Meaning, and Authority* (Cambridge, MA, and London: Harvard University Press, 1997), p. 39.

65 Franz Rosenzweig, 'The Builders, Concerning the Law', in Franz Rosenzweig, *On Jewish Learning*, edited by N. N. Glatzer (New York: Shocken Books 1955), p. 81.

66 Rashi, *Siftei Chachamim*.

67 Miroslav Holub, 'Dinner', in *On the Contrary and Other Poems*, translated by Ewald Osers (Newcastle upon Tyne: Bloodaxe Books, 1984), p. 57.

68 Samson Raphael Hirsch, commentary to Deuteronomy 31:17–18.

69 Etty Hillesum, *Etty: The Letters and Diaries of Etty Hillesum*, edited by Klaas A. D. Smelik (Grand Rapids, Michigan, and Cambridge, UK: William B. Eerdman's Publishing Company, 2002).

70 Joseph Soloveitchik, Kol Dodi Dofek, *The Voice of My Beloved Knocks*, in Steven T. Katz, Shlomo Biderman and Gershon Greenberg (eds), *Wrestling with God: Jewish Theological Responses During and After the Holocaust* (Oxford: Oxford University Press, 2007), p. 393.

71 Martin Buber, 'Dialogue between Heaven and Earth', in Katz, Biderman and Greenberg, *Wrestling with God*, p. 373.

72 Matthew Arnold (1822–88), 'Dover Beach' (public domain).

73 Rebbe Menachem Mendel of Warki, *Gedulat Hatsadikim* to Deuteronomy 31:18, cited in *Chumash Peninei Hahasidut*.

74 Ba'al Shem Tov, commentary to Deuteronomy 31:18, cited in *Chumash Peninei Hahasidut*.

75 Rebbe Moshe Chaim Ephraim, *Degel Machaneh Ephraim* (1810), on Deuteronomy 31:18, cited in *Chumash Peninei Hahasidut*.

76 *Perek Shirah*, The Symphony of Creation (Jerusalem: Feldheim Publishers, 2013), pp. 208–9.

77 Kalonymus Kalman Shapira, *Derech Hamelech on Rosh Hashanah, Ashrei Ha'am Yode'ei Teruah*.

78 Kalonymus Kalman Shapira, *Derekh Hamelekh on Rosh Hashanah, Ashrei Ha'am Yode'ei Teruah*.

79 Rachel Carson, *Silent Spring* (London: Penguin, 1962).

80 Jonathan Wittenberg, *My Dear Ones: One Family and the Final Solution* (Glasgow: William Collins, 2017).

81 Yosef Hayim Yerushalmi, *Zakhor: Jewish History and Jewish Memory* (Seattle: University of Washington Press, 1983).

82 Samson Raphael Hirsch, commentary to Deuteronomy 32:7.

83 Bea Lewkowitz, *'This is the Story of my Life': An interview with Julius Carlebach* (Centre for German-Jewish Studies at the University of Sussex, 2020), p. 6.

84 Rebbe Yitzhak Meir of Ger, *Chiddushei Harim al HaTorah* to Deuteronomy 32:7, cited in *Chumash Peninei Hahasidut*.

85 Eliot, *The Four Quartets: Little Gidding*, p. 42.

86 Rashi, commentary to Deuteronomy 32:50.

87 Martin Luther King, 'I've Been to the Mountaintop', 3 April 1968, www.american-rhetoric.com/speeches/mlkivebeentothemountaintop.htm (accessed 5 June 2023).

88 Rachel Bluwstein (1890–1931), 'Mineged' in *Shirat Rachel* (Tel Aviv: Dvir, 1978), p. 118 (author's own translation).

89 Rebbe Yeshaya of Yassi, *Kelil Tiferet* to Deuteronomy 32:49.

90 Carolyn Forche, 'Travel Papers' in *The Lateness of the World* (New York, London: W. W. Norton & Company, 1995).

91 Constantine P. Cavafy (1863–1933), 'Ithaca'.

92 Rashi, commentary to Deuteronomy 34:4.

93 William Shakespeare, *Hamlet*, act 3, scene 1.

94 Maimonides, *Mishneh Torah: Laws of the Study of Torah*, 1:6, 1:10.

95 Zohar, *Ki Teitsei* 281b

INDEX OF SUBJECTS

This is intended as a guide to readers who may want to follow a specific topic, rather than the weekly order of Torah readings. Most of the sections in the book do not fit easily under any heading so what follows is only a broad indication of subjects touched upon. Some themes such as wonder, compassion and the spiritual search run through everything, making it hard to suggest specific passages. Nevertheless, I hope what follows is of some value in locating particular topics.

noosa

THE COOKBOOK

noosa
THE COOKBOOK

Text by Madonna Duffy

Photography by Chris Chen

VERVE

Stylist: Kirsty Cassidy

Designer: Matthew Tanner

Publisher: David Oliver

VERVE, an imprint of Wordsworth Publishing,
PO Box 393, Noosa Heads, Queensland 4567, Australia

First published 1998
Reprinted 1999

National Library of Australia
cataloguing-in-publication data:

Noosa: the cookbook
includes index.

ISBN 0 646 35810 3

1. Cookery - Queensland - Noosa. I. Duffy, Madonna

641.5099432

Colour-separated and waterless printed in Australia by Fergies Image to Press, Brisbane

contents

picture captions

Note: *Not all photographs are captioned above. Those not listed feature the landscape and local scenery of Noosa.*

introduction

Part of Noosa's great appeal is its diversity. It's one of the few places where you can take a peaceful cruise on the river, a hike in the national park, or sunbathe on the beach – all in one day. And then go out for dinner.

Eating well and enjoying meals with friends is the staple of Noosa life. Whether it's breakfast at a beachside bistro, lunch on a terrace by the river, or coffee and the day's newspapers at a Hastings Street café, Noosa's social rituals

always revolve around food – especially food served al fresco.

Noosa: The Cookbook draws together the food, the lifestyle and the landscape to offer a sumptuous feast for the senses. We hope it brings memories of special holidays in the sun, that it inspires you with great food ideas and makes you long to eat, and most of all, that it reminds you of how important it is to take time out and enjoy life.

Woven through the book are recipes from Noosa's best restaurants which reflect the unique Noosa lifestyle and celebrate the fantastic local produce. Some of Noosa's well-known chefs and restaurateurs also share their thoughts on how living in this very special place has influenced them.

The philosophy of Noosa: The Cookbook, *as for life in Noosa, is 'keep it simple, keep it fresh and make it fun'. After all, you might have to rush down to the beach for a late afternoon swim, or to watch a spectacular sunset, so you don't want to spend hours in the kitchen. But you do want to serve food that looks and tastes wonderful.*

We want this book to be more than just a cookbook. We want it to be an experience.

Madonna Duffy

Noosa Heads, 1998

the river

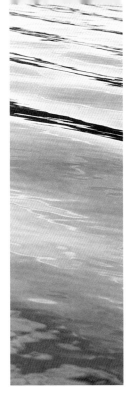

the silhouette *of a fisherman on the jetty*

pelicans skimming *the water*

houseboats *floating on the tide*

a long lunch merging into dinner

diamonds of sun reflecting *on the water*

coloured sails *at the marina*

fish and chips on the river bank

a glass of wine and a perfect sunset

eugaries (pippies) with sea vegetable pasta

40 plus	beach eugaries, cleaned overnight in fresh water
10 cloves	golden eschallots
1 packet	fine sea vegetable, soaked for 1 hour in fresh water
	freshly made pasta for 4
	olive oil

Slow roast whole eschallots at 150°C for up to an hour until they have softened slightly but are still in shape. Cool and peel.

Chop sea vegetable to manageable bite-size pieces. Set pasta cooking in a large pot. Warm good olive oil in a heavy-based pan with a lid. Drain the eugaries and slide them into the oil. Cover with lid and steam for up to 5 minutes. Check regularly and, as they open, remove eugaries onto a warmed plate.

Once all the eugaries have opened, quickly toss together the sea vegetable and eschallots into the same pan to warm and absorb flavours.

Drain pasta well, toss with other ingredients and serve.

Serves 4

Recipe: *Stephen and Lisa Cross, Saltwater*

From dawn till dusk, life on the river ebbs and flows. Sit on a jetty and watch the changing light and river traffic. Stroll along the bike path and see the fishermen waiting patiently for the day's catch. Take a boat and enjoy the gentle breezes and the tranquil setting.

Eating by the river can be as simple as locally caught and cooked fish and a chilled glass of wine. Or a late summer's afternoon picnic with delicious goodies from a local deli. Wait for the setting sun to transform the river into brilliant shades of pink and gold.

salad of warm duck breast
with beetroot and buderim ginger vinaigrette

300g	duck breast, cut in half
2	leaves spring roll wrapper (cut in 4 and lightly baked)
50g	Asian leaves (assorted mix)
pinch	salt
pinch	pepper
40ml	sweet soy sauce
20ml	honey

Beetroot vinaigrette

100g	beetroot, blanched and finely diced
60ml	good balsamic vinegar
pinch	salt
pinch	pepper
30ml	juice of pickled ginger
100ml	extra virgin olive oil
1 tbs	Dijon mustard, unseeded

Combine soy and honey with salt and pepper and marinate duck breasts for 2 hours.

Make up the vinaigrette by combining mustard, ginger juice, balsamic vinegar, salt and pepper. Finally, add beetroot and then olive oil.

Lightly chargrill duck breasts, then bake in oven for 8–10 minutes on 180°C. Allow to rest for 3–5 minutes. Slice each breast into 1cm thick pieces.

Assemble salad by placing duck slices over tossed Asian leaves, drizzle with vinaigrette and layer with pre-baked spring roll wrappers.

Note: *This recipe also works well with chicken instead of duck.*

Serves 2

Recipe: *Patrick Landelle, Soleil*

The river has always been a source of fresh fish and seafood, but more recently it has bred a thriving café culture that buzzes from morning till night. It's the ideal spot for a Sunday breakfast with the weekend's newspapers, a decadent afternoon aperitif, or a casual dinner with friends.

Noosaville's river esplanade and Noosa Wharf are now fixtures on the culinary map. Combine the food with the views and before you know it the day will be merging into evening.

king snapper fillet with black sticky rice

800g	snapper fillet (allow 200g per serve)
200g	black glutinous rice
	Curry sauce
1 stick	lemongrass
1 head	garlic
5	shallots
1	chilli, finely sliced
100g	dark palm sugar
250ml	fish sauce
900 ml	water
	Salad garnish
½ bunch	Vietnamese mint
½ bunch	fresh coriander
½ bunch	basil
200g	bean shoots
20ml	fish sauce
1	lime

Rinse black rice in a colander. Using ratio of 1½:1 water to rice, bring to rapid boil, reduce heat, cover and allow to simmer for 20 minutes.

To prepare curry sauce, slice lemongrass, garlic and shallots finely. Fry in a little oil until a light colour. Add chilli and cook a little more. Then add grated palm sugar, and cook out until caramel in colour. Deglaze with fish sauce, then add water. Bring to boil, take off stove, cool and add assorted herbs.

To prepare fish, cut into 200g square portions and slash diagonally across skin to prevent fillet curling. Heat pan with a little oil, and fry fish skin side down first, then turn and colour flesh side. Deglaze with liberal amounts of curry sauce and fish stock (or water) until almost covering. Place in a hot oven and bake for approx. 5 minutes.

Mix coriander, Vietnamese mint and bean shoots. Dress with a squeeze of lime juice and fish sauce.

To assemble, fill plastic mould with rice (rice may need to be microwaved briefly to re-heat) and cup onto plate. Place snapper fillet on top and pour over cooking sauce from fish pan. Garnish with bean sprout salad and serve.

Serves 4

Recipe: *Nathan Hall/Nicolas Romer, Riva*

*'In cooking you
are a pupil for
life. You never
stop learning.
Noosa, its people
and climate have
inspired me.'*

Phil Mitchell, chef

spicy salad of caramelised pork

with green mango and star anise

	caramelised pork (see below)
1½ cups	fine julienne of green mango
1 cup	assorted fresh herbs (basil, mint, chives, coriander), leaves only
1 cup	green shallots, julienned
1 tbs	fresh lime juice
1 tbs	fish sauce

Caramelised pork

350g	pork belly, cut into 1cm diced pieces
½ cup	Indonesian sweet soy sauce (kecap manis)
2 cloves	garlic, minced
1 tsp	ground cinnamon
1 tsp	ground star anise
½ cup	palm sugar
1 tbs	fish sauce
3 tbs	vegetable oil

Pour sweet soy sauce over pork, cover and put to one side.

Heat 3 tbs oil in a pot, add garlic and ground spices and sauté for 1 minute until fragrant. Add the palm sugar, bring to the boil and cook for 2 minutes, then stir in fish sauce and pork mixture and simmer for 20–30 minutes. Remove from heat and allow to cool.

To assemble salad, warm pork slightly, then toss together with all remaining salad ingredients. Divide onto plates and serve.

Serves 4–6

Recipe: *Richard Harris, Chilli Jam Café*

Eating out by the river is about cool white surroundings with splashes of colour. Details that add interest and capture the eye.

Sit on a café terrace and admire the view – river breezes carrying pelicans gracefully across the water, boats cruising gently past, rainbow lorikeets gathering in the gum trees.

Or choose an enticing restaurant with a deck that overlooks yachts at anchor on the Sound. Indulge in an afternoon cocktail and nibble on some tapas, and watch the spectacle of the sun setting where the river meets the sea.

zuppe di pesce (fish soup)

300g	prawn meat
300g	scallops (with roe attached)
300g	fresh fish fillet (in 3 cm chunks)
24	black Tasmanian mussels
24	clams
400g	bug tails, halved
2	cooked sand crabs, cleaned and quartered

Sauce

1	small onion, diced
1	stick celery, sliced
16	capers
10 sprigs	fresh dill, chopped
10 sprigs	fresh continental parsley, chopped
1 nip	Pernod
6 threads	saffron
800g	tinned tomatoes
800ml	good fish stock

Sauté onion and celery in a little olive oil. Add Pernod, then capers, then roughly chopped tomatoes and saffron. Simmer for about 15 minutes, add fresh herbs. Season to taste with salt and pepper. Set aside.

Heat one tablespoon olive oil in a large soup pot. Throw in mussels, clams and bug tails. Place lid on pot and allow shellfish to steam in their own juices until the mussels begin to open. Tip into a large bowl and put aside. In the same pot, heat a little more oil and sauté the prawns, scallops and fish for 2 or 3 minutes. Then add the crab, mussels, clams and bug tails. Pour in the tomato-based sauce and fish stock, bring quickly to the boil. Remove from heat and serve.

Divide the seafood amongst four large warmed soup bowls. Pour broth over the top and serve with warm crusty bread.

Note: If clams are not available, use pippies or increase the amounts of the other seafood in the dish.

Serves 4

Recipe: Brian Jackson, Lindoni's

'I wanted the Riva experience to be like sailing on a luxury yacht. To let the view take diners wherever their imaginations wanted to go. The combination of the location and the atmosphere is unique.'

Nicolas Romer, Riva

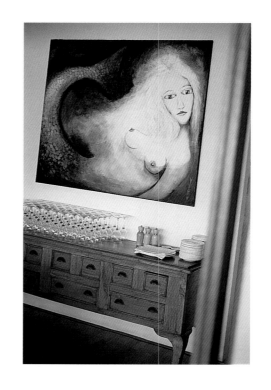

River sunsets are endlessly different.

From the rich pinks of the winter

months to the golden hues of summer.

The reflections on the water and the

colours of the sky combine to paint the

most stunning natural canvas.

The river's working day is complete and

peace descends. Locals walk their dogs

and take leisurely evening strolls. The

water becomes still, and the first stars

emerge in the sky.

13	eggs
450ml	cream
585g	caster sugar
9	lemons (juice and zest)
	cream, to serve

Pastry

400g	butter
200g	icing sugar
4	egg yolks
500g	plain flour

Note: *The pastry and lemon mix should be prepared the day before for best results.*

Bring to boil cream and zest and simmer. Whisk sugar and eggs. Then whisk in infused cream and zest mixture. Stir in lemon juice and strain. Refrigerate overnight and remove froth from top.

To make pastry, add dry ingredients to mixer. Then add butter cut in small cubes and crumb mixture. Add egg yolks. Remove from mixer and knead. Wrap in plastic and rest for half an hour.

Roll pastry on a floured bench until 3mm thick. Place in a greased 28cm tart ring. Trim edges, dock pastry with fork and chill in freezer for a few minutes. Blind bake at 150°C for 20 minutes, then refrigerate overnight, if possible, or at least until pastry is at room temperature.

When cool, add lemon mix and bake at 160°C for 40 minutes, or until the mix is just set.

To serve, dust with icing sugar and serve with a quality cream.

Serves: *This tart makes 12 portions.*

Recipe: *Nathan Hall/Nicolas Romer, Riva*

buttermilk pudding

with raspberry sauce and noosa summer berries

Buttermilk pudding

600ml	buttermilk
250ml	cream
125g	sugar
1	vanillla bean
3	gelatine leaves

Raspberry sauce

300g	raspberries
150g	sugar
½	lemon

fresh mixed berries, to serve

To make pudding, heat half the cream with the sugar and vanilla bean in a heavy-based saucepan, simmer for a few minutes, then remove from heat. Remove the vanilla bean, split it in half, scrape the seeds into the cream mixture. Discard the bean and whisk to incorporate. Add gelatine, stir until dissolved and strain the mixture through a fine sieve.

Put the buttermilk into a bowl and gradually pour in the hot cream mixture, beating constantly. Cool the mixture until tepid. Beat the remaining cream until almost in soft peaks and fold into buttermilk mixture.

Pour the mixture into small 150ml dariole moulds. Cover and refrigerate overnight or for at least 6 hours.

To make the raspberry sauce, place berries and sugar in saucepan and bring to simmer. Squeeze ½ lemon juice and strain mixture.

To serve, carefully loosen the edges of the pudding from the mould with a small knife and turn each pudding out onto a serving plate. Surround each pudding with some of the raspberry coulis and fresh berries.

Serves 6

Recipe: *Gary Skelton, Season*

tasting *the salt in the air*

a lazy *breakfast overlooking the sea*

footprints in the white sand

the cool shade *of a beach umbrella*

diving under the first breaker

a sun-warmed *beach towel*

a sandcastle being licked *by the waves*

a swimmer stroking through the surf

house-smoked salmon on toasted brioche

with ricotta and watercress

600g	smoked salmon (the best quality you can find)
400g	fresh ricotta cheese
1 bunch	watercress
1	lemon
150g	capers
1	spanish onion

Brioche dough

50g	caster sugar
50ml	milk
12g	dry yeast
10g	salt
500g	plain flour
5	eggs
250g	unsalted butter

In a mixmaster with a paddle attachment or a food processor, mix sugar, yeast, milk and salt. Add flour and mix. Add eggs, one at a time, mixing after each addition. Add butter in 50g increments, beating after each addition.

Leave in a warm place until doubled in size. Punch dough until flat again. Refrigerate overnight.

Remove from fridge, roll to form a loaf shape and leave in a warm place until doubled in size. Bake at 180°C for 30 minutes. Leave to cool.

Slice loaf and toast. Be careful as it will burn quickly. Place toast on warm plates and arrange smoked salmon and ricotta on top. Add watercress, sprinkle capers and onion over the top. Serve with a wedge of lemon.

Note: *As an alternative, you could substitute your favourite bakehouse bread for the brioche.*

Serves 6

Recipe: *Paul Leete, Sails Beach Café*

As the new day begins, start it with a stroll along the beach, or a refreshing swim, or just head straight for the cafés.

Hastings Street is the hub of café life. Choose a relaxed outdoor café where your beach towel and sandy feet will be welcomed, or opt for a stylish sidewalk spot where the coffee is strong and dark. Or perhaps what you're looking for is a beachside bistro with views to die for, where you can while away hours watching the waves.

Make breakfast healthy with a plate of tropical fruit and a dollop of your favourite yoghurt. Or treat yourself to pancakes, brioche, or bacon and eggs. Finish off with freshly roasted coffee and you're ready to hit the beach.

apple and buttermilk pancakes

with pear compote and maple syrup

Pancakes

525g	self-raising flour
225g	caster sugar
360ml	buttermilk
2	eggs
100ml	full fat milk
10ml	vanilla essence
1½	Granny Smith apples, grated

Compote

3	pears (preferably bosc)
250g	caster sugar
20ml	lemon juice

lashings of good quality maple syrup

To prepare the pancake batter, in a large bowl whisk eggs and sugar until combined. Then whisk in vanilla, buttermilk and milk. Finally, whisk in flour until smooth. Mix in grated apple.

Peel pears and dice into 2 cm pieces. Place chopped pear and sugar in a stainless steel pan and cook until soft, but not mushy. Add lemon juice and stir.

Ladle pancake batter into a buttered frying pan. Cook over medium heat until bubbles appear on surface. Flip pancakes and cook for 2 minutes longer. Remove pancakes from pan and cover with a clean cloth. Repeat process until batter is finished.

Stack 3 pancakes on each plate and top with compote. Pour over maple syrup and sprinkle with icing sugar.

Note: *The compote can be made with any fruit in season.*

Serves 6

Recipe: *Paul Leete, Sails Beach Café*

If you're not in a beach mood, take shelter in Hastings Street's shops and restaurants.

Treat yourself to the little luxuries that make a holiday memorable – a hand-painted bowl, some Provençale soap, a new swimsuit, an aromatherapy massage. Or just window-shop and watch the world go by.

When you're shopped out, restore yourself with coffee and home-made biscotti or a delicious lunch in one of the sidewalk cafés. For a sweet treat, get a Massimo's mango sorbet in a waffle cone and stroll along the beachfront boardwalk.

caesar salad with roasted scallops

320g	baby cos lettuce leaves
320g	scallops (with roe attached)
80g	shaved Parmesan cheese
120g	prosciutto shards
	garlic croutons
200ml	Caesar salad dressing (see below)
	salt and pepper

Caesar salad dressing

10	anchovy fillets
2 tbs	garlic, crushed
4	eggs
¼ cup	lemon juice
1 litre	olive oil
	salt and pepper
dash	Worcestershire sauce (to taste)

Wash and dry cos lettuce leaves. Crisp prosciutto by slow drying in a low temperature oven. Toast garlic croutons. Clean and quick sear scallops in a very hot pan.

To make the dressing, blend all ingredients, then slowly add oil until the dressing has a thick consistency. You may need to add a little warm water to bring to pouring thickness.

Mix together the Caesar dressing and baby cos leaves. Place in a serving bowl and then sprinkle with crisp pieces of prosciutto. Lay the still-warm scallops on top and finish with fresh shavings of Parmesan cheese. Top with garlic croutons before serving.

Serves 4

Recipe: *Philip Garrod, Cato's at The Sheraton*

Noosa's great charm lies in its quirky details. The vibrant colour of the Hastings Street fruit barrow, the tropical flowers blooming on the footpath, the laneways that lead you from cosmopolitan Hastings Street out onto the beach.

Life in Noosa is lived with a sense of fun and an original twist on the everyday. No matter how well you know Noosa, you will never know it completely. The food, the restaurants, the local style – Noosa life refuses to be weighed down by convention, but revels in the exotic.

crab and sweet potato ravioli *tossed with lime oil*

Pasta dough (pasta fresca all'uovo)

400g	plain flour
pinch	salt
4	large eggs

Sweet potato filling

250g	sweet potato
1 tsp	fish sauce
2	kaffir lime leaves
1/2	bird's eye chilli, seeded
1 tsp	lemon juice
	salt
50g	toasted macadamias
1	egg
1	egg yolk

Crab filling

1	medium freshly cooked crab (or 200g crab meat)
1	egg white
1 tsp	chives, chopped
1 dsp	cream
2 tsp	fresh parmesan, finely grated

Lime oil

1½	salted limes, skin and pith only
200ml	olive oil
200ml	boiling water
½ bunch	chives
2 drops	lime essential oil
20ml	lime juice
1	roma tomato, deseeded and finely chopped, for garnish

Note: *Prepare fillings before rolling pasta.*

To make pasta, put salt and flour into a bowl. Make a well in the centre. Add eggs. Work together with a fork and continue with your hands until well mixed. (A little more flour may be needed to reduce stickiness.) Knead for 10 minutes until smooth and elastic. Wrap in cling film and rest for 30 minutes. Roll on a lightly floured surface to approximately 1 mm thickness (or setting no.6 if using a domestic pasta rolling machine).

For sweet potato filling, place peeled and roughly diced sweet potato in a saucepan. Add kaffir lime leaves, chilli, salt and enough water to cover. Simmer until soft and drain. Discard kaffir lime leaves and chilli. Purée sweet potato, when cooled, with fish sauce, lemon juice and egg. Fold through chopped macadamias.

Clean crab carefully ensuring no bone or cartillage escapes your attention. In a bowl mix cream, chives and egg white. Add crab, parmesan and salt and pepper. Fold gently so as not to break up crab too much.

To assemble, use a 7.5 cm pastry cutter. Cut out lots of circles. Brush edges with egg wash. Put a dollop of sweet potato mixture onto each. Top with crab mix and fold over. Cook for 4–5 minutes in lots of boiling salted water.
To prepare lime oil, blitz all ingredients in a vitamiser until smooth.
Drain ravioli and toss in lime oil.
Garnish with chopped tomato and serve.

Note: *Fresh lasagne sheets can be used successfully, but be sure it is egg pasta.*
Salted limes can be found at most providores.

Serves 4

Recipe: *Dayle Merlo, Palmer's*

Creating the right ambience is an integral part of the Noosa lifestyle. Whether it's the aquarium and the brightly coloured cushions at Sails or the secluded nooks and crannies at Bistro C and Palmer's, Noosa restaurants have their own distinct personalities.

Clever interior ideas like the funky pastel chairs at Sierra Bar or the portholes at Saltwater make every dining experience a unique one.

And always there is the influence of the lush tropical surroundings and the ocean, as inside merges with outside.

beef and green pawpaw salad

350g	eye fillet (in 1 piece)
1 tbs	oyster sauce
4	golden shallots, finely sliced
½ cup	mint leaves
½ cup	coriander leaves
1½ cups	shredded green pawpaw
1 tsp	roasted chilli powder (see below)
1 tbs	sticky rice powder (see below)
6 tbs	lime juice
3 tbs	fish sauce
2 tbs	peanuts, roasted and crushed
1 large	red chilli, deseeded and finely julienned

Coat eye fillet with oyster sauce. Heat a small quantity of vegetable oil in a frypan and sear well all over. Transfer to a hot oven (230°C) and cook to medium-rare. This will take about 10 minutes. Remove from oven and rest in a warm place while assembling salad.

In a large bowl, combine the shredded pawpaw, golden shallots, mint, coriander, roasted chilli powder, half the roasted rice powder and julienned red chilli. Finely slice the beef, and add to the bowl with the fish sauce and lime juice. Toss thoroughly and pile onto serving plate. Sprinkle with the remaining rice powder and peanuts.

Roasted sticky rice powder

Place a quantity of sticky or glutinous rice in a shallow pan or tray and roast at 180°C until golden (about 15 minutes). Grind in spice mill or mortar and pestle.

Store in a sealed container.

Roasted chilli powder

Place a quantity of large dried chillis on a baking tray and roast in a pre-heated oven at 180°C for about 3–4 minutes. Grind in spice mill or mortar and pestle.

Store in a sealed container.

Serves 2

Recipe: *Annette Fear, The Spirit House*

'Australia is a melting pot of culinary influences, all of which are evident here. Noosa is a paradise of understated panache and culinary twists, with combinations as simple as soy and extra virgin olive oil with a touch of garlic and ginger. The result reflects the mix of culinary compatibility with sun, surf and sand.'

Garry Flynn, Artis

eye fillet with seared spinach and potato galette

800g	eye fillet (200g per serve)
1kg	desirée potatoes
500g	spinach
100g	duck fat
100ml	olive oil
200ml	beef jus (home-made or purchased from a gourmet deli; or a good quality commercially prepared beef stock)

To make the galette, peel potatoes and slice on a slicer such as a Japanese mandolin to a thickness of 2mm. Toss in a bowl with a mix of olive oil and melted duck fat. Season with Maldon salt only.

To assemble, heat some duck fat in a heavy skillet and place potato slices around pan in a lattice fashion, layering until the pan is full. Bake in a medium oven (180°C) for approx. 30 minutes. (Note: The galette can be prepared beforehand and reheated.)

To prepare the eye fillet, seal fillet in a fry pan and finish cooking in a medium oven for approx. 8 minutes. Take out and rest for 4 minutes before serving.

Wash spinach and dry. Fry in a pan with a little butter and season with salt and pepper. Squeeze out any liquid.

To serve, place eye fillet on seared spinach. Position potato galette next to the eye fillet and pour beef jus over the top.

Note: *The beef jus served at Riva takes two days to prepare. To simplify this recipe to make at home, it's possible to buy beef jus from gourmet delis, or an alternative would be a commercially prepared beef stock such as those available at supermarkets.*

Serves 4

Recipe: *Nathan Hall/Nicolas Romer, Riva*

'Living in Noosa has reinforced my philosophy that food should be fresh, simple and light.'

Paul Leete, Sails Beach Café

lime tart with mango ice cream

Lime tart

4	egg yolks
400g can	sweetened condensed milk
125ml	fresh lime juice
3	egg whites
½ cup	caster sugar
1x9-inch	pre-baked pastry tart shell

Mango ice cream

8	large egg yolks
180g	sugar
600ml	full cream milk
250ml	mango purée
200ml	cream

For the lime tart, place egg yolks in a stainless steel bowl and whisk over a pot of simmering water until thickened, being careful not to overcook. Remove from heat and whisk in the condensed milk, then whisk in lime juice.

In a separate bowl, whisk egg whites to soft peaks then slowly sprinkle in castor sugar, whisking continuously to form a meringue. Fold meringue into lime mixture, pour into tart shell and bake at 170°C for 10 minutes. Remove from oven, allow to cool thoroughly, then refrigerate until required.

To prepare the mango ice cream, whisk yolks and sugar together in a bowl until pale and fluffy. Heat milk and whisk into egg yolk mixture. Pour back into pot, return to heat and cook mixture until it coats the back of a spoon. Do not allow to boil. Strain custard into bowl and refrigerate until cold.

Stir in the mango puree and cream. Freeze in an ice cream machine according to manufacturer's instructions.

Note: *If you don't have time to make your own ice cream, a very high quality commercially prepared ice cream could be substituted.*

Serves 10

Recipe: *Richard Harris, Chilli Jam Café*

ginger ice cocktail

30ml	Midori liqueur
30ml	tequila
60ml	lemon
60ml	pineapple juice
1 tsp	fresh ginger

Fill a glass with ice. Put all ingredients in the glass. Shake and then strain into a large martini glass. Garnish with fresh tropical fruit to serve.

Recipe: *Cato's Bar at The Sheraton*

the ocean

the sun bursting from the horizon

surfers paddling out past the breaks

waves crashing on the rocks

lunch on a terrace overlooking the ocean

uninterrupted sea views

dolphins leaping in the distance

the white sails of a yacht

the night-time rhythm of breaking waves

moroccan swordfish *on date pilaf*

with citrus yoghurt and harissa

800g	fresh swordfish steaks (200g per serve)
130g	harissa (available from gourmet delis)
1/2	lime, for garnish

Pilaf

250g	long grain brown rice
700ml	chicken stock or water, brought to boil
100g	pitted dates
100g	pinenuts, lightly toasted
50ml	virgin olive oil
1	red onion, finely chopped
2	cloves garlic, peeled and smashed to a paste
2 tsp	harissa
	sea salt, to taste

Citrus yoghurt

1	orange
2	limes
1	lemon
400ml	natural yoghurt
2	pinches cumin powder

To prepare the pilaf, coat a 4-litre stainless steel pot, heat and add the rice and slightly toast. Add the onion, garlic, pinenuts, dates, harissa and some sea salt, continuously stirring to incorporate all the ingredients.

Add the hot stock to the rice, taking care, as a lot of steam is produced at this stage. Place lid on the pot, lower heat and steam for approximately 15–20 minutes.

Remove lid and all the liquid should have absorbed into the rice. If not, turn up the heat for a minute or two. Taste and correct seasoning by adding a couple of turns from the pepper mill.

To make the citrus yoghurt, zest and squeeze the citrus fruits. Pour into a pot (preferably stainless steel) and reduce by half. Remove from heat and strain.

Leave to cool and refrigerate until chilled. Place all ingredients in a blender and blend.

To serve, place a black iron pan or non-stick teflon pan on medium heat with a drizzle of olive oil. Baste the swordfish with a thin layer of the harissa and gently fry on both sides until cooked (approx. 10 minutes, depending on your preference for eating fish). Spoon the hot pilaf into a bowl, place the fish on the rice, surround with the citrus yoghurt. Garnish with half a lime and serve.

Serves 4

Recipe: Phil Mitchell

A life by the sea. A day near the ocean. The freedom, the exhilaration of open space and endless sandy beaches. The ocean inspires, recharges, excites.

Living by the sea, eating by the sea, sleeping by the sea. A seaside lifestyle is about enjoying simple pleasures and being outdoors. Building a healthy appetite, enjoying a meal with friends and then relaxing on the deck with a good book.

The cocktail of salt, sand, sea and sun is a powerful one which will always lure you back.

wok-flashed spanner crab omelette

Omelette

½ cup	oil
100g	crab meat, shredded
4	eggs, beaten as for a regular omelette
½ cup	bean sprouts

Sauce

3 tbs	fresh coriander, chopped
1 tbs	garlic, chopped
1 tbs	ginger, julienned and chopped
1 tbs	bird's eye chillis, finely sliced
250g	palm sugar, chopped
1 tbs	galangal, chopped
3	fresh kaffir lime leaves
1 cup	lemon juice, freshly squeezed (without the pips)
½ cup	fish sauce
1	cooked crab claw, for garnish

To make sauce, in a saucepan, slowly dissolve the palm sugar, stirring constantly until all is dissolved. Stir in fish sauce and lemon juice, then add all remaining sauce ingredients. Allow to reduce according to taste. (The longer it simmers, the more intense the flavour will be.) Set aside.

To prepare the omelette, heat oil in a wok to a very high temperature. (Usually when the wok starts to smoke). Carefully add beaten egg, stir through, then add crab meat, bean sprouts and the sauce.

Remove and serve in a bowl. Garnish with a crab claw and don't forget to provide a soup spoon to enjoy the sauce.

Serves 2

Recipe: *Patrick Landelle, Soleil*

Fresh fish marinated and seared on the barbeque,
a fresh summer salad, lush tropical fruit and
home-made sorbet, a chilled bottle of good wine.
After a day at the beach, a meal shouldn't take
hours to prepare. Keep the food and the setting
simple. Enjoy the company. Take in the views.

Outdoor eating is a vital ingredient of Noosa life
– whether it's on a beachside balcony, or a cool
terrace by the river. A sunny location and a
view of the water are the essential accessories for
a perfect meal, either at home or in a favourite
local restaurant.

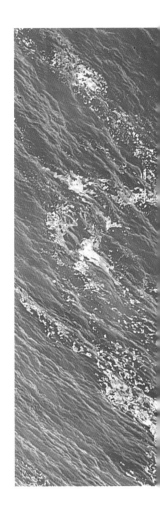

asparagi e polenta

36	asparagus spears
350g	polenta
1³/₄ – 2 litre	water
150g	butter
200g	parmesan
	cracked black pepper
	sea salt

*Bring water to boil, then simmer slowly.
Add polenta, whisk until blended.
Reduce heat to as low as possible, stir
with wooden spoon from time to time
for about 45 minutes. Stir in butter and
parmesan.*

*Place polenta mix onto a greased flat
tray with a 1½ – 2 cm lip. Smooth over
with spatula. Leave to rest until cool.
Cut into wedges, brush with olive oil
and grill on both sides.*

*Par boil asparagus and place on top
of polenta wedges. To serve, add
shaved parmesan, drizzle with olive oil
and sprinkle with cracked black pepper
and sea salt.*

Serves 6

Recipe: *Glynn Whateley, Ma' Mensa*

'Fishing one day with my young son off the rocks at Sunshine Beach, we caught tailor and squire. We walked back to the restaurant, dipped the fish fillets in tempura batter, quickly fried them and ate them with dollops of homemade mayo – wet clothes, sandy feet and all . . . '

Patrick Landelle, Soleil

goat's cheese profiteroles *with black olive vinaigrette*

100g	rocket leaves
16	profiteroles (see below)
250g	goat's cheese cream (see below)
120ml	sundried tomato and olive vinaigrette (see below)

Profiteroles

250ml	water
125g	butter
1 pinch	salt
1 tsp	sugar
125g	flour, sifted
4	eggs

Goat's cheese cream

250g	good goat's cheese
1	egg white
	salt and pepper

Vinaigrette

100g	sundried tomatoes, finely chopped
50g	pitted black olives (pre-roasted with 1 bunch fresh garlic)
200ml	balsamic vinegar
1 sprig	thyme, roughly chopped
1 sprig	rosemary, roughly chopped
160ml	olive oil (the best extra virgin)
	cracked black pepper

To make the pastry for the profiteroles, dissolve butter in water, adding salt and sugar, then stir in flour, and take off the heat. Combine eggs one at a time until the mixture is elastic. Pipe the dough onto baking sheets and bake for 50 minutes at 180°C.

Remove from oven, allow to cool and set aside. Cut in half once cold.

To prepare the goat's cheese cream, combine all ingredients in the blender until just mixed. Pipe into the base of profiterole until full, and put the other half on the top (as a lid).

To make the dressing, combine all ingredients together.

To assemble the dish, place 4 filled profiteroles on each plate, garnish with rocket leaves and drizzle vinaigrette over the top.

Serves 4

Recipe: *Patrick Landelle, Soleil*

Restaurant interiors set the mood. They frame the

food. In Noosa, strong, simple design and natural

light are used to complement the relaxed lifestyle

and climate. Large feature windows allow the

light to flood in. Interiors may be stylish or

functional, but are always comfortable. For

interest, splashes of colour echo the sun, the sea

and the spectacular scenery.

Eating out in Noosa is a complete experience.

You can be dazzled by the view, seduced by the

menu and enticed by the surroundings. And

that's before you've even ordered.

fried crab cakes *with tomato and toasted*

pumpkin seed salsa and red chilli mayonnaise

600g	fresh sand crab meat
1	egg
100g	fresh breadcrumbs
120g	crème fraîche
1 ear	corn
1 bunch	spring onion (white part only)
4	large red chillis
1	red onion
1 tbs	fresh coriander, chopped
1 tbs	fresh oregano, chopped
	cracked black pepper and salt
200g	egg mayonnaise
	mild chilli powder, to taste
500g	fresh breadcrumbs, for frying

Salsa

3	vine-ripened tomatoes
200g	unsalted pepitas (pumpkin seeds)
2 cloves	garlic
1 tbs	fresh sweet basil, chopped
50ml	extra virgin olive oil
50ml	lime juice

Roast corn in husk at 200°C until cooked (approx. 10 minutes). Roast chilli until blackened, peel and remove inside veins and seeds. Remove kernels from corn. Chop remaining ingredients and mix all ingredients together.

To make salsa, seed and dice vine-ripened tomatoes. Toast pumpkin seeds in 200°C oven for 10 minutes. Chop garlic and sweet basil. Mix all ingredients together.

Mix mayonnaise with chilli powder.

Roll crab cakes to form 3 small cakes per person. Roll all cakes to lightly coat in extra breadcrumbs. Shallow fry crab cakes in hot vegetable oil until golden on each side, turning once.

Serve hot cakes with salsa, a dollop of mayonnaise and garnish with fresh lime wedges.

Serves 6

Recipe: *Paul Leete, Sails Beach Café*

A room with a view. There is

something endlessly desirable

about a stunning view of the

ocean. The ever-changing

movement and colour of the sea

will always fascinate.

To sleep to the sound of the

surf is one of life's great

pleasures. To wake to the fresh

scent of the ocean fills you with

all the promise of the day ahead.

It is the water that defines

Noosa and its lifestyle.

antipasto plate

Roasted capsicum

6	red capsicums
2 tsp	capers
1/2 cup	lemon juice
	salt and pepper

Chargrilled zucchini

6	zucchini
1 bunch	sage
	garlic
	lemon juice
	olive oil
	salt and pepper

Marinated olives

unpitted olives, chillis, herbs, olive oil

Marinated octopus

12 pieces	octopus
1/2	carrot
1/2	onion
1 stick	celery
2	bay leaves
	peppercorns, garlic, chilli, olive oil

To make capsicum, preheat oven to 250°C. Place whole, lightly oiled capsicums in oven for 10–15 minutes until skin blisters. Remove from oven and allow to cool. Peel capsicums and cut into strips. In a stainless steel bowl place capsicums, lemon juice, capers and salt and pepper to taste.

To make chargrilled zucchini, cut the zucchinis lengthways into 1cm thick strips, salt and let rest. To make the dressing, add finely chopped sage to garlic, lemon juice, oil, salt and pepper. Chargrill zucchini whilst still warm and add dressing.

To prepare marinated olives, add some chillis, garlic and herbs to a good olive oil. Place olives in this marinade.

To make marinated octopus, bring vegetables to boil. Add octopus and boil for 8 minutes. Turn off heat, leave octopus in water for 2 hours. Remove octopus and marinate in garlic, chilli, olive oil, bay leaves, oregano and peppercorns.

Serves 2

Recipe: *Glynn Whateley, Ma' Mensa*

tropical frieze

3	eggs, separated
6 tbs	sugar
3	bananas (cavendish)
1 small tin	crushed pineapple
3	passionfruit
	juice of 2 oranges
	fresh tropical fruit, to garnish

Beat the egg yolks with 3 tablespoons of sugar until white, smooth and thick. Mash the fruit together and add the egg mix. Freeze this mixture until mushy (or half-process in ice-cream maker).

Beat egg whites with the rest of the sugar and fold through. Freeze into triangular mould or other container.

To serve, remove the mould from freezer 5–10 minutes before cutting. In the depths of summer, freeze plates for 10 minutes. Arrange fresh tropical fruit, such as papaya, melon, passionfruit, banana and mango carambola with a squeeze of lime and a chunk of coconut on a plate.

Slice through the ice with a warmed knife and serve balanced on the fruit.

Note: *The iced component of this dish is a rescued recipe from Lisa Cross' mother, Gwynneth Lee. If you have an ice-cream maker, certainly use it. However, it's not necessary, as a delicious result can be achieved in a normal freezer.*

Serves 6

Recipe: *Stephen and Lisa Cross, Saltwater*

land's edge

where the land meets the sea

majestic cliffs *rising from the ocean*

sunrise *at Hell's Gate*

the cliff path winding around the coast

lazy summer *picnics*

secluded coves fringed by trees

whales *breaking the surface*

fishing boats dotting the horizon

16	U6* tiger prawns, skewered
4	hot chillis, pounded with a little salt
	and oil
4	fennel bulbs
1	orange, segmented
	white wine vinegar
	extra virgin olive oil

Cut fennel in half lengthwise and braise in a moderate oven until just starting to soften. Remove and splash with vinegar and oil. Cover lightly and keep warm.

Brush prawns with the fresh chilli oil and sear on a griddle or over coals. Colour will indicate when they are cooked. This should take only about 1–2 minutes per side. The stripes on tiger prawns change from deep brown-red to vibrant red. If using other varieties, such as ocean king prawns, the colour goes from pale pink-cream when raw to bright red when cooked.

Toss orange segments into the warm, marinating fennel and arrange on plates. Stack the prawns over the top and serve.

***Note:** *U6 denotes 'less than 6 prawns per pound'. 4 per person should be more than generous.*

Serves 4

Recipe: *Stephen and Lisa Cross, Saltwater*

The natural beauty of Noosa's national park

area continually surprises and enthralls.

Hectares of walking tracks that allow you to get

back to nature, secluded coves for swimming

and sunbathing, and stunning uninterrupted

views of the ocean make it a unique place.

The cliff path always offers a different

perspective, whether you want to catch the most

breathtaking sunrise, or find a sheltered spot to

gaze at the ocean. Looking out to sea, there

may be dolphins leaping through the waves, or

whales on their migration north.

Just minutes from cosmopolitan Hastings

Street, the national park feels like a world away.

barbequed lamb pizza *with eggplant chips and rocket*

2	pizza bases (either homemade or commercially prepared)
100ml	Caesar dressing (see below)
60	eggplant chips (see below)
250g	rocket
4	lamb backstrap, flattened out
30g	parsley, for garnish

Caesar dressing

3	egg yolks
200ml	vegetable oil
200ml	olive oil
3 tsp	Dijon mustard
2 drops	tabasco sauce
2 drops	worcestershire sauce
25ml	red wine vinegar
10ml	lemon juice

process in blender

¼	onion
1 clove	garlic
100g	capers
50g	anchovies
¼ bunch	parsley

To make Caesar dressing, beat egg yolks and mustard and slowly add vegetable oil and olive oil. Stir in combined tabasco, worcestershire, red wine vinegar and lemon. Finally combine with processed ingredients.

To make eggplant chips, slice thin eggplant rounds and fry in hot oil until crispy. Drain on absorbent paper.

Cook pizza base at high heat (or as per instructions on packet). Remove from oven and spread with Caesar dressing. Place eggplant chips on base and pile high with rocket. Barbeque lamb on a grill plate until medium rare and place on pizza. Garnish with finely chopped parsley and serve immediately.

Serves 4

Recipe: *Gary Skelton, Season*

'I love all food, but have a particular passion for the food of Thailand, its complex flavours and total reliance on fresh ingredients. With the diverse cultural influences and wonderful range of fresh tropical produce grown locally, the Noosa area is a dream for both chefs and diners.'

Annette Fear, The Spirit House

crispy tuna nori tempura with caramelised chilli-lime dip

350g	fresh tuna loin, cut into 12 even-sized pieces
1 sheet	nori seaweed, cut in 1-x4-inch strips
1 packet	tempura batter mix
1 cup	assorted fresh herbs (basil, mint, chives, spring onions, coriander)
2 tsp	red chillis, julienned
1 tsp	lime juice
1 tsp	fish sauce
1 tsp	palm sugar
2 cups	vegetable oil, for frying

Caramelised chilli-lime dip

2	long green chillis, deseeded and sliced
3	kaffir lime leaves, julienned
½ cup	palm sugar
½ cup	tamarind water
	juice of 1 lime

Make tempura batter according to instructions on packet and set aside.

Roll each piece of tuna in a strip of seaweed and refrigerate. To make lime dressing for the salad, stir together fish sauce, lime juice, palm sugar and chilli. Set aside.

Heat oil in a wok to frying temperature. Dip each piece of tuna in batter and fry in hot oil for 30–40 seconds to cook batter and seal the outside of the fish; the middle should still be raw. Slice each piece in half.

To make the chilli-lime dip, place chilli, lime leaves and sugar into a pot. Bring to boil and simmer for 2 minutes. Add tamarind water and lime juice and simmer for 5–10 minutes. Remove from heat and cool thoroughly.

To assemble, drizzle caramelised chilli-lime dip onto a plate. Toss fresh herbs in lime dressing and arrange in a mound in the centre of the plate. Place six tuna halves around salad and serve.

Serves 4

Recipe: *Richard Harris, Chilli Jam Café*

whole crispy fish with chilli-lime sauce and thai basil

750g	whole fish, gutted, gilled and scaled (suitable fish would be snapper, coral trout, red-throated emperor, pearl perch)
	flour, to coat fish
½ cup	coriander leaves

Sauce

6 cups	vegetable oil
8 cloves	garlic
¼ cup	red and green chillis, deseeded and finely chopped
¼ cup	red or golden shallots, finely chopped
¼ cup	coriander root and stem, finely chopped
3 tbs	fish sauce
3 tbs	palm sugar
3 tbs	lime juice
¼ tsp	ground white pepper
4	kaffir lime leaves, finely shredded
¼ cup	Thai basil leaves

Heat oil in a large wok. Lightly coat the fish in flour. Carefully place fish in wok and cook for about 10 minutes, then turn over and cook for another 5 minutes. The fish should be golden brown and quite crisp. Remove from wok and drain on paper towel.

To prepare sauce, combine garlic, chilli, shallots and coriander root and stem in a food processor. Process to a paste. Heat 2 tablespoons of the oil in a saucepan and fry paste until fragrant, which should take about 5 minutes. Add fish sauce, lime juice, palm sugar and pepper and bring to the boil. Simmer for 2 minutes, add kaffir lime leaves and tear in basil. Stir until basil wilts, then remove from heat.

Serve the fish on a large plate, lined with a banana leaf. Spoon over sauce and garnish with coriander leaves.

Serves 2

Recipe: *Annette Fear, The Spirit House*

The national park reminds you to seize the

moment and celebrate nature. There are always

quiet spaces and peaceful corners to find

tranquillity. But for those who want to be active,

the landscape offers rich pickings.

There are the surfers who return daily to

catch the best waves, the morning joggers

following the curve of the cliff path to Hell's

Gate, and the hikers with picnic lunches tucked

away in their packs. For the less energetic, there

are secluded picnic spots where you can while

away a lazy afternoon.

No matter what your mood, you can get as

close to nature as you want and still be back in

town in time for an al fresco dinner.

tea-smoked salmon

with cha sui, kipfler potato salad and black bean dressing

400g	salmon fillet, skin on
1 tbs	sesame oil
200g	cha sui, thinly sliced on the diagonal
300g	kipfler potatoes, cooked and sliced on the diagonal
2 cups	frisée lettuce, picked, washed and dried

Tea-smoking mixture

4 tbs	jasmine tea
1 tbs	brown sugar
1	star anise, crushed
½ quill	cinnamon, smashed

Black-bean dressing

300ml	extra virgin olive oil
100ml	light soy sauce
1 tbs	ginger, crushed
1 clove	garlic, crushed
3 tbs	salted black bean
1 tbs	mirin

To make dressing, briefly wash black bean in running water. Crush one tablespoon of black bean and whisk into remaining ingredients.

For smoking mixture, stir all ingredients together well.

Line a tray with foil and fill with smoking mixture. Place a cake rack over tray and place salmon fillet on this. Spread one tablespoon of sesame oil over salmon.

Turn heat onto full. As soon as tea mixture begins to smoke, cover with another tray. Leave on full for 5 minutes, then turn heat to half for another 5 minutes. Remove from heat, but leave covered until cool.

Grill potato slices until coloured.

To serve, place equal amounts of ingredients on each plate, layering each ingredient alternately. Once all dishes are completed, drizzle with black bean dressing and serve.

Serves 4

Recipe: *Gary Flynn, Artis*

Pack some of your favourite gourmet treats and

find a shady nook in the park or on the edge of

the cliffs where you can gaze at the wide

summer sky and the breaking waves. If a longer

walk appeals, the more isolated beauty of

Alexandria Bay makes a stunning location for a

picnic.

Above all, choose a place with splendid views,

whether it's the ocean, the beach, the cliffs, or

the sweep of coast looking back towards Noosa.

Food always tastes better when it's enjoyed at the

land's edge.

2	sheets puff pastry (eg. Pampas butter puff pastry)
6	cavendish bananas (or similar non-floury variety)
100g	butter
200g	sugar
½	fresh coconut
50g	icing sugar
	coconut ice cream, to serve

Roll pastry in sugar and cut two circles out of each sheet. Butter non-stick paper and place puff rounds on trays. Slice bananas and arrange around centre of puff pastry. Brush tops with butter and sprinkle with leftover sugar. Bake at 180°C for 15–20 minutes or until golden and cooked through.

To make the coconut shards, remove skin and shell from coconut. Using a potato peeler, peel off shards of coconut. Dust with icing sugar and cook in a moderate oven for approx. 5 minutes or until coloured.

Place a tart in centre of each plate and top with a scoop of good quality commercial ice cream (If fortunate enough to be in Noosa, try Massimo's coconut ice cream). Sprinkle with toasted coconut shards and serve.

Serves 4

Recipe: *Gary Skelton, Season*

A late summer's afternoon. The day is cooling.

The beach empties. Picnic blankets and sandy

towels are packed away.

As the sun drops to the horizon, surfers

paddle out to catch the last waves. A lone

swimmer strokes slowly through the surf. The

first night breezes stir along the water's edge.

On an early evening stroll along the

boardwalk, thoughts turn to culinary treats

ahead. An aperitif before dinner, perhaps, and

then a delicious meal enjoyed alfresco on a

balmy night.

watermelon and star anise jelly

½	watermelon, pulp removed and juiced (keep ½ shell of watermelon aside to use as mould)
1½ cups	sugar syrup
15 sheets	gelatine
10	star anise, whole
½ cup	whipped cream
2 nips	Midori liqueur

Warm 1 cup sugar syrup in a saucepan over low heat. Add 10 sheets of gelatine, stir until dissolved. Add the watermelon juice to the saucepan. Pour saucepan contents into shell of watermelon. Put in fridge.

Mix ½ cup sugar syrup with star anise and bring to boil. Remove from stove, add 5 sheets gelatine, stir and when cooled to 'warm', add whipped cream.

When the watermelon jelly is set, pour the warm star anise mixture over the jelly to form a top layer. Refrigerate.

When set, slice into portions, place on plate and drizzle Midori liqueur around plate before serving.

Serves 4

Recipe: Patrick Landelle, Soleil

acknowledgements

Without the support of the restaurant community in Noosa, we couldn't have turned what was just an idea into this beautiful book. Thanks to all the staff, proprietors and chefs for their generosity.

We'd also like to thank the following local businesses for their help:

Alfresco, Hats for Noosa Heads, Massimo's, Menagerie Homewares, Mitre 10, Noosa Crest Apartments, Noosaville Fish Market, Riva restaurant, The Cooking Company.

Thanks to Steve and Lisa Cross for providing the location for one of our shoots.

Lizzie Brown and Noosa Enterprise Group have been hugely supportive of this book. For your assistance and enthusiasm, thank you.

To Max and Sue Colles, thank you for your vision and faith in this project.

featured restaurants

ARTIS

8 Noosa Drive, Noosa Heads

BISTRO C

'On the Beach' Arcade, Hastings Street, Noosa Heads

CATO'S AT THE SHERATON

Hastings Street, Noosa Heads

CHILLI JAM CAFE

195 Weyba Road, Noosaville

COCO'S

62 Park Road, Noosa Heads

LINDONI'S

Hastings Street, Noosa Heads

MA' MENSA

6 Hastings Street, Noosa Heads

PALMER'S

Ocean Breeze Complex, Hastings Street, Noosa Heads

RIVA

Noosa Wharf, Quamby Place, Noosa Heads

SAILS

75 Hastings Street, Noosa Heads

SALTWATER

8 Hastings Street, Noosa Heads

SEASON

30 Hastings Street, Noosa Heads

SIERRA CAFE BAR

10 Hastings Street, Noosa Heads

SOLEIL

Duke Street, Sunshine Beach

THE SPIRIT HOUSE

4 Ninderry Road, Yandina

index of recipes